TL
152
.6   Aaron
A15   Driver and traffic safety
           education

86047

DATE DUE

MAR 17	NO 24 8	
OCT 20	DE 6 '88	
OC 27 8		
MAY 4 '8	FE 7 '89	
NOV 2 '8	MY 24 '90	
APR 12 '8	AP 21 '9	
OC 25 '83	DE 18 '92	
MR 27 '84	SE 26 '95	
MY 1 '84	FE 20 '99	
DE 20 '84		
MY 1 4 '85		

SADDLEBACK COLLEGE LIBRARY
MISSION VIEJO, CALIFORNIA

DEMCO

DRIVER AND TRAFFIC SAFETY EDUCATION

DRIVER AND TRAFFIC SAFETY EDUCATION

Content, Methods, and Organization

Second Edition

James E. Aaron, Ed.D.
Coordinator, Safety Center, Southern Illinois University

Marland K. Strasser, Ed.D.
Late Professor and Coordinator, Safety and Driver Education,
San Jose State College

Macmillan Publishing Co., Inc.
New York
Collier Macmillan Publishers
London

Earlier edition copyright © 1966 by Macmillan Publishing Co., Inc. A portion of this material has been reprinted from *Driving Task Instruction: Dual-Control, Simulation, and Multiple-Car*, by James E. Aaron and Marland K. Strasser, copyright © 1974 by Macmillan Publishing Co., Inc.

Macmillan Publishing Co., Inc.
866 Third Avenue, New York, New York 10022

Collier Macmillan Canada, Ltd.

Library of Congress Cataloging in Publication Data

Aaron, James E
  Driver and traffic safety education.

  Includes bibliographies and index.
  1. Automobile driver education. 2. Traffic safety–
Study and teaching. I. Strasser, Marland Keith,
(date)   joint author. II. Title.
TL152.6.A15 1977   629.28'3'22   76-25118
ISBN 0-02-300010-4

Printing: 1 2 3 4 5 6 7 8   Year: 7 8 9 0 1 2 3

Preface

THIS BOOK has been written to serve as a textbook in college courses on the teaching of driver and traffic safety education. The purpose is to provide understanding of the elements of a comprehensive program that is consistent with the maturity that the driver and traffic safety education movement has attained. Another purpose is to provide a guide for teachers, supervisors, and administrators in the organization, administration, and planning of a driver and traffic safety education curriculum.

The organizational pattern of the text moves from the general to the specific. Part One includes discussions of the development of driver education as a field of study, school function, and citizen responsibility. There are also chapters on teacher preparation and program administration. Part Two develops the classroom phase of driver education, including organization of instruction, content, methods, and instructional aids. Part Three presents the laboratory phase of driver education, including program organization, content, methods of instruction, and instructional aids. Evaluation of classroom and laboratory programs also is considered in this section of the book. Discussed in Part Four are the Highway Safety Act of 1966, public relations, adult driver education, research, and the future of driver and traffic safety education.

The content of the book emphasizes the educational learnings from research in the behavioral, physical, and biological sciences, and is based upon current philosophy and trends in driver education. The text explains how to achieve those objectives developed at the various National Conferences on Driver Education. The concept of the driving task is basic to those lesson plans and instructional strategies presented.

Throughout the text, driver education is treated as a discipline in general education. Emphasis is given to the relationship between man and his environment and living in a traffic-oriented society.

This book should be of particular value to people professionally engaged in the preparation of driver education teachers, and it is hoped that it will serve as a useful, basic reference for all persons interested in driver and traffic safety education.

v

As this preface is finalized it is called to the attention of the readers that Dr. Marland K. Strasser passed away during the early stages of the preparation of this second edition. This is a loss to the driver education field and to me personally. For he was an intimate friend, colleague, and co-author par excellence.

James E. Aaron

Contents

INTRODUCTION TO DRIVER EDUCATION

This section contains the first six of the twenty chapters of the text. The first two chapters discuss the traffic accident problem and the historical development of the driver education movement. These chapters are followed by presentations on the function of the school, education of the traffic citizen, driver education teacher, and administration of the driver and traffic safety education program. The remaining fourteen chapters are devoted to detailed discussions of classroom and laboratory instruction in addition to ways of extending driver and traffic safety education through programs of public relations, adult driver education, the Highway Safety Act of 1966, research, and projections for the future of driver education.

Included in Part I are the following chapters:

1. The Traffic Accident Problem
2. Evolution of the Driver Education Movement
3. Driver Education as a School Function
4. Education of the Traffic Citizen
5. The Teacher of Driver Education
6. Administering the Driver and Traffic Safety Education Program

Chapter 1

The Traffic Accident Problem

OBJECTIVE: The student will be able to delineate the nation's traffic accident problem and relate it to the emergence of programs of driver and traffic safety education.

American society is a cultural complex largely oriented to the use of motor vehicles. In less than 70 years the car has become an intimate part of our life. In all probability it will not soon be replaced by any other mode of transportation that is used daily.

THE CAR AND OUR SOCIETY

Americans use about three fifths of the world's cars, trucks, and buses, and have constructed more than one third of the world's streets and highways to accommodate these vehicles. As a nation and as individuals, we are vitally dependent upon the car in our daily way of living. Dad and often mother as well use the automobile to get to work; mother uses it to shop; and the entire family relies on the automobile for many recreational and social activities. Regardless of family income, passenger automobiles account for 85.2 per cent of person trips.

The impact of highway transportation is emphasized by the significant number of Americans who are licensed to drive. Today there are approximately 125 million vehicle operators in the United States.

This number is about three fourths of the adult population. Figure 1-1 shows that there are licensed drivers in all age ranges, 15 through—and beyond—75. Approximately 12.9 million of our nation's drivers are under age 20, with another 14.4 million between the ages of 20 and 24. Thus the under-25 population constitutes about 22 per cent of all our drivers, and the use of motor vehicles by this large group of young people implies the need for a traffic safety program that will educate them at an early age to drive safely.

Age of Drivers—Total Number and Number in Accidents, 1974

Age Group	All Drivers		Drivers in Accidents					
	Number	%	Fatal		All		Per No. of Drivers	
			Number	%	Number	%	Fatal	All
Total	125,100,000	100.0%	57,800	100.0%	25,100,000	100.0%	46	20
Under 20	12,900,000	10.3	10,200	17.6	4,800,000	19.1	79	37
20-24	14,400,000	11.5	11,400	19.7	4,900,000	19.5	79	34
25-29	14,100,000	11.3	7,100	12.3	3,200,000	12.7	50	23
30-34	13,000,000	10.4	6,200	10.7	2,600,000	10.3	48	20
35-39	11,500,000	9.2	3,900	6.8	1,700,000	6.8	34	15
40-44	11,300,000	9.0	3,900	6.8	1,600,000	6.4	35	14
45-49	11,500,000	9.2	3,600	6.2	1,600,000	6.4	31	14
50-54	10,800,000	8.6	2,800	4.9	1,200,000	4.8	26	11
55-59	8,200,000	6.6	2,500	4.3	1,200,000	4.8	30	15
60-64	6,500,000	5.2	2,100	3.6	800,000	3.2	32	12
65-69	5,100,000	4.1	1,500	2.6	800,000	3.2	29	16
70-74	3,400,000	2.7	1,100	1.9	300,000	1.2	32	9
75 and over	2,400,000	1.9	1,500	2.6	400,000	1.6	63	17

Sex of Driver Involved in Accidents, 1959-1974

Year	Drivers in Fatal Accidents				Drivers in All Accidents			
	Male		Female		Male		Female	
	No.	Rate	No.	Rate	No.	Rate	No.	Rate
1959	40,400	79	5,600	29	14,400,000	282	3,600,000	189
1960	41,000	78	6,000	31	15,000,000	286	3,500,000	180
1961	40,000	75	6,000	30	14,900,000	278	3,600,000	180
1962	43,000	77	7,000	34	15,000,000	268	4,000,000	193
1963	46,200	79	7,800	36	15,700,000	267	4,300,000	198
1964	48,900	79	8,600	38	16,700,000	270	4,800,000	210
1965	50,300	78	8,900	37	18,300,000	282	5,300,000	221
1966	54,600	81	9,700	37	18,600,000	276	5,700,000	218
1967	54,600	80	9,900	35	18,500,000	272	5,800,000	205
1968	59,500	84	10,500	35	19,600,000	275	6,400,000	211
1969	59,800	80	10,900	33	20,000,000	268	6,800,000	209
1970	57,800	75	10,700	31	20,500,000	265	7,200,000	209
1971	56,700	70	11,100	30	20,900,000	256	7,400,000	199
1972	59,000	68	11,900	28	21,000,000	243	8,100,000	201
1973	55,900	63	11,400	27	20,200,000	227	7,900,000	189
1974	48,000	55	9,800	24	17,800,000	205	7,300,000	177

Figure 1-1 Age and Sex of Drivers Involved in Traffic Accidents (Courtesy National Safety Council)

Of the 125 million drivers, about 69.2 million are males and 55.9 million are females.[1] There has been a significant number of women joining the driving population within the past decade. Hence, the female population is playing a more important role in our society relative to use of the car. Moreover, women are becoming more a part of the traffic accident problem than before.

---

[1] National Safety Council, *Accident Facts* (Chicago: The Council, 1975), p. 54.

4

Motor vehicles are the major social and economic phenomenon of the first half of the twentieth century. Along with the advances that the automobile has enabled our society to make, the car is associated with the major social problem of our day—the loss of human and economic resources through traffic crashes. Air pollution and the energy shortage are among the more recent problems associated with vehicle use. The pioneers in the automotive industry could not project the negative contribution that the automobile is now making to society. But in approximately 70 years there have emerged problems involving the citizens of our nation that now demand our attention and call for the application of the most scientific knowledge in approaching the solutions of these problems. Warren, in his classic book on traffic courts, stated:[2]

> Thinking men concede that the control of traffic is today one of the nation's greatest civic problems, greater than the problem of fire, for it annually takes more lives and destroys more property; greater than crime, for it involves all humanity. The strong, the weak, the rich and the poor, the wise and the foolish, every man, woman, child or infant that walks or rides is a possible victim of traffic every minute he is upon the public roadway or street.

THE TRAFFIC PROBLEM

Since the recording of the first motor vehicle death in New York in 1899, traffic accidents have become a major social problem to the people of this nation. Since 1900 more than twice as many people have been killed in traffic accidents as were killed in all of the major wars that the United States has participated in since the Revolution. *Each* In a single year over 25 million drivers are involved in motor vehicle accidents. In 1974 a total of 46,200 persons met death upon the nation's highways. This, however, did show a decrease in the number of deaths from the high of 56,278 in 1972. Also, in 1974 approximately 1.9 million individuals sustained disabling injuries. Statistically, a person is killed on our streets and highways every 11 minutes, and someone is critically injured every 18 seconds.[3] Approximately 150,000 persons have received permanent injuries annually as a result of motor vehicle crashes. Each year an estimated 100,000 American families are affected to a major degree by traffic accidents, and our nation loses approximately 500,000 man-years of productive time.

[2] George Warren, *Traffic Courts* (Boston: Little, Brown and Company, 1942).

[3] National Safety Council, op. cit., p. 11.

Traffic Death Rates

Traffic accidents are the major cause of death for persons under 36 years of age. For all age groups traffic accidents rank fourth as a principal cause of accidental death. Motor vehicle death rates are computed by determining deaths (1) per 100 million vehicle miles of travel, (2) per 100,000 population, or (3) per 10,000 motor vehicle registrations. When computed on a mileage basis, traffic accident rates are highest among younger drivers, especially those under 24 years of age. In this particular age group traffic accidents account for approximately 40 per cent of the deaths from all causes. This indicates that persons killed and injured in traffic accidents are not in direct proportion to ages in the population. For example, the traffic death rate in a recent year for the 15- to 24-year-old age group was 40.7. The ranges for the various population age groups have varied over the years, with the exception of the younger age group, for which the death rate on a population basis has remained rather stable.

The death rate based upon 100 million vehicle miles of travel has substantially decreased over the years. For the total driving population the death rate has decreased from a high of 18.2 in 1923–27 to a low of 3.6 in a recent year. All fatal traffic accidents are reported, and therefore it is easy for one to take these data and compute a mileage death rate for the population. It is quite difficult, however, to determine exactly how many nonfatal injury accidents are incurred by the driving populace each year. Insufficient data through the lack of uniform accident-reporting procedures makes the collection of such data very difficult. However, traffic experts have determined that for each traffic fatality there are approximately 35 injury-producing accidents and 150 property damage accidents. The National Safety Council recently estimated that for approximately 34,500 fatal accidents there are 950,000 nonfatal injuries and 10,000,000 accidents of only property damage. Because some drivers are involved in more than one accident per year, it is difficult to estimate the exact number of individuals involved in traffic accidents in a given year. However, it has been said that 20 per cent of the total number of drivers in the nation are involved in some type of a traffic crash each year.

Elements of the Traffic Problem

That traffic accidents claim approximately 130 lives daily is a startling fact. The surprising fact relative to this particular statistic is that most people do not understand that throughout the past decades many elements have contributed to the mounting traffic toll. The following sections will attempt to identify and discuss briefly the various elements of the traffic problem and what each of these has contributed to the traffic crash problem confronting the American society today. Emphasis shall be placed on the dimensions of the traffic problem as it relates to the various elements to be described.

	PASSENGER CARS		MOTOR TRUCKS AND BUSES		TOTAL	
	Number	Value (000)	Number	Value (000)	Number	Value (000)
1974	7,331,256	$21,800,000	2,727,313	$10,100,000	10,058,569	$31,900,000
1973	9,657,647	26,239,996	2,979,688	9,544,112	12,637,335	35,784,108
1972	8,823,938	23,133,051	2,446,807	7,654,180	11,270,745	30,787,231
1971	8,584,592	21,409,824	2,053,146	5,963,525	10,637,738	27,373,349
1970	6,546,817	14,630,217	1,692,440	4,819,752	8,239,257	19,449,969
1969	8,223,715	18,751,176	1,923,179	4,936,683	10,146,894	23,687,859
1968	8,822,158	19,352,035	1,896,078	4,670,325	10,718,236	24,022,360
1967	7,436,764	15,653,436	1,539,462	3,592,049	8,976,226	19,245,485
1966	8,598,326	17,554,326	1,731,084	3,953,473	10,329,410	21,507,799
1965	9,305,561	18,380,036	1,751,805	3,733,664	11,057,366	22,113,700
1964	7,751,822	14,836,822	1,540,453	3,223,569	9,292,275	18,060,391
1963	7,637,728	14,427,077	1,462,708	3,090,345	9,100,436	17,517,422
1962	6,933,240	13,071,709	1,240,168	2,581,756	8,173,408	15,653,465
1961	5,542,707	10,285,917	1,133,804	2,155,753	6,676,511	12,441,530
1960	6,674,796	12,164,234	1,194,475	2,350,680	7,869,271	14,514,914
1959	5,591,243	10,534,421	1,137,386	2,338,719	6,728,629	12,873,140
1958	4,257,812	8,010,366	877,294	1,730,027	5,135,106	9,740,393
1957	6,113,344	11,198,379	1,107,176	2,082,723	7,220,520	13,281,102
1956	5,816,109	9,754,971	1,104,481	2,077,432	6,920,590	11,832,403
1955	7,920,186	12,452,871	1,249,106	2,020,973	9,169,292	14,473,844
1954	5,558,897	8,218,094	1,042,174	1,660,019	6,601,071	9,878,113
1953	6,116,948	9,002,580	1,206,266	2,089,060	7,323,214	11,091,640
1952	4,320,794	6,455,114	1,218,165	2,319,789	5,538,959	8,774,903
1951	5,338,435	7,241,275	1,426,828	2,323,859	6,765,263	9,565,134
1950	6,665,863	8,468,137	1,337,193	1,707,748	8,003,056	10,175,885
1949	5,119,466	6,650,857	1,134,185	1,394,035	6,253,651	8,044,892
1948	3,909,270	4,870,423	1,376,274	1,880,475	5,285,544	6,750,898
1947	3,558,178	3,936,017	1,239,443	1,731,713	4,797,621	5,667,730
1946	2,148,699	1,979,781	940,963	1,043,247	3,089,662	3,023,028
1945	69,532	57,255	655,683	1,181,956	725,215	1,239,210
1944	610	447	737,524	1,700,929	738,134	1,701,376
1943	139	102	699,689	1,451,794	699,828	1,451,896
1942	222,862	163,814	818,662	1,427,457	1,041,524	1,591,270

Figure 1-2. Annual Motor Vehicle Factory Sales from U.S. Plants (Courtesy Motor Vehicle Manufacturers Association of the U.S. Inc.)

VEHICLES. It is estimated that in 1900 there were approximately 8,000 motor vehicles registered in the United States. By 1915 this number had steadily grown in excess of 2 million. An average of 6,800 motor vehicle deaths per year was reported between 1913 and 1917. By 1920 the number of motor vehicle registrations in the nation had multiplied to in excess of 9 million, and this tremendous number of vehicles traveled approximately 45 billion miles during that year. Figure 1-3 identifies the growth and relationship between vehicle, travel, and traffic deaths. It is evident that by 1920 the automobile had become an essential in the life of American society. The most recent estimate given by the Motor Vehicle Manufacturers Association is that there are in excess of 130 million motor vehicle registrations in the United States today.[4] Figure 1-2 depicts the historical development of the car in America.

Although the number of automobiles manufactured multiplied at a substantial rate between 1900 and 1940, there was very little organized effort to ascertain the extent of the negative contribution that the motor vehicle was making to American life. It is quite apparent that the construction of the highways to accommodate this large number of vehicles was lagging. Moreover, programs to ascertain the safe operating condition of the vehicles lagged behind the development and manufacture of the vehicles themselves. It was inevitable

[4] Motor Vehicle Manufacturers Association, *Automobile Facts and Figures* (Detroit: The Association, 1975), p. 24.

Year	No. of Deaths	No. of Vehicles (millions)	Vehicle Miles (billions)	No. of Drivers (millions)	Death Rates Per 10,000 Motor Vehicles	Per 100,000,000 Vehicle Miles	Per 100,000 Population	Costs ($ million)
1913-17 ave...	6.800	2.9		4.0	23.80		6.8	
1918-22 ave...	12.700	9.2		14.0	13.90		11.9	
1923-27 ave...	21.800	19.7	120	29.0	11.10	18.20	18.7	
1928-32 ave...	31.050	25.7	199	38.0	12.10	15.60	25.2	1.300
1933	31.363	24.2	201	35.0	12.98	15.60	25.0	1.350
1934	36.101	25.3	216	37.0	14.29	16.75	28.6	1.550
1935	36.369	26.5	229	39.0	13.70	15.91	28.6	1.550
1936	38.089	28.5	252	42.0	13.36	15.11	29.7	1.650
1937	39.643	30.1	270	44.0	13.19	14.68	30.8	1.800
1938	32.582	29.8	271	44.0	10.93	12.02	25.1	1.500
1939	32.386	31.0	285	46.0	10.44	11.35	24.7	1.500
1940	34.501	32.5	302	48.0	10.63	11.42	26.1	1.600
1941	39.969	34.9	334	52.0	11.45	11.98	30.0	1.900
1942	28.309	33.0	268	49.0	8.58	10.55	21.1	1.600
1943	23.823	30.9	208	46.0	7.71	11.44	17.8	1.250
1944	24.282	30.5	213	45.0	7.97	11.42	18.3	1.250
1945	28.076	31.0	250	46.0	9.05	11.22	21.2	1.450
1946	33.411	34.4	341	50.0	9.72	9.80	23.9	2.200
1947	32.697	37.8	371	53.0	8.64	8.82	22.8	2.650
1948	32.259	41.1	398	55.0	7.85	8.11	22.1	2.800
1949	31.701	44.7	424	59.3	7.09	7.47	21.3	3.050
1950	34.763	49.2	458	62.2	7.07	7.59	23.0	3.100
1951	36.996	51.9	491	64.4	7.13	7.53	24.1	3.400
1952	37.794	53.3	514	66.8	7.10	7.36	24.3	3.750
1953	37.955	56.3	544	69.9	6.74	6.97	24.0	4.300
1954	35.586	58.6	562	72.2	6.07	6.33	22.1	4.400
1955	38.426	62.8	606	74.7	6.12	6.34	23.4	4.500
1956	39.628	65.2	631	77.9	6.07	6.28	23.7	5.000
1957	38.702	67.6	647	79.6	5.73	5.98	22.7	5.300
1958	36.981	68.8	665	81.5	5.37	5.56	21.3	5.600
1959	37.910	72.1	700	84.5	5.26	5.41	21.5	6.200
1960	38.137	74.5	719	87.4	5.12	5.31	21.2	6.500
1961	38.091	76.4	738	88.9	4.98	5.16	20.8	6.900
1962	40.804	79.7	767	92.0	5.12	5.32	22.0	7.300
1963	43.564	83.5	805	93.7	5.22	5.41	23.1	7.700
1964	47.700	87.3	847	95.6	5.46	5.63	25.0	8.100
1965	49.163	91.8	888	99.0	5.36	5.54	25.4	8.900
1966	53.041	95.9	930	101.0	5.53	5.70	27.1	10.000
1967	52.924	98.9	962	103.2	5.35	5.50	26.8	10.700
1968	54.862	103.1	1.016	105.4	5.32	5.40	27.5	11.300
1969	55.791	107.4	1.071	108.3	5.19	5.21	27.7	12.200
1970	54.633	111.2	1.120	111.5	4.92	4.88	26.8	13.600
1971	54.381	116.3	1.186	114.4	4.68	4.57	26.4	15.800
1972	56.278	122.3	1.268	118.4	4.60	4.43	27.0	19.400
1973	55.511	129.8	1.309	121.6	4.28	4.24	26.5	20.200
1974	46.200	135.7	1.280	125.1	3.40	3.61	21.9	19.300

Figure 1-3. Motor-Vehicle Death Rates and Costs, 1913–1974 (Courtesy National Safety Council)

that traffic congestion would become a major problem through the overloading of our highway system, thus increasing exposure of motorists to potential traffic crashes. The lack of motor vehicle inspection programs allowed unsafe vehicles to continue operating on the nation's highways. Moreover, the motor vehicles of that period had numerous design features that exaggerated traffic injuries when they occurred. Today's vehicles are much safer owing to the use of padded dashes, seat belts, recessed steering wheels, and the removal of sharp protruding instruments and control knobs, and so on.

DRIVERS. Before 1910 it was very difficult to determine the number of individuals licensed to operate a motor vehicle. In general there was a complete lack of acceptable license standards across the nation. By 1913, however, the number of drivers licensed to operate motor vehicles exceeded 4 million, and by 1920 this number had tripled to some 14 million licensed operators. Today there are in excess of 125 million licensed drivers. It is conservatively estimated that by 1990 there shall be over 150 million. Figure 1-3 depicts the increase in the number of licensed drivers since 1913.

The licensing of motor vehicle operators was principally a city function during the first two decades of the present century and was originally a revenue-producing measure. By 1920 drivers were licensed in all of the northeastern states, and by 1940 driver licensing had spread to almost all the remainder of the United States. South Dakota, the last state to initiate a driver license program, did so in 1954. Thus today all 50 states require drivers to be licensed.

The lack of adequate licensing procedures and standard license examinations has enabled countless thousands of inferior motorists to obtain driver licenses and to retain them throughout the years. It is known that many individuals operating motor vehicles on our streets and highways today were never formally examined to determine whether they could safely and efficiently operate a motor vehicle. Also, because of the significant change in the driving task, those individuals licensed several years ago would surely benefit through re-examination. The requirements for a driver in today's traffic are considerably different from those of yesteryear. The driver contributes substantially to the traffic crash problem; the driver or the human element is estimated to be responsible for approximately 85 per cent of all traffic accidents. However, most states still do not require re-examination for license renewal though the National Highway Safety Program Standard, Driver Licensing requires that states initiate re-examination programs.[5]

PEDESTRIANS. With few exceptions, each person is a pedestrian. An individual is a pedestrian twice for every occasion that he is a motorist. Prior to 1928 there are insufficient data to tabulate accurately the number of pedestrian deaths. However, between 1928 and 1932 there was an average of 12,300 pedestrian traffic fatalities. This number increased significantly to 15,500 in 1937. Since that time the number of pedestrian deaths has decreased; the number killed on our nation's streets and highways today is approximately 8,700 a year. An increased interest in pedestrian protection programs and the enactment of traffic safety legislation delimiting the responsibilities of the motorist and the pedestrian relative to highway use may have contributed to the decrease in pedestrian fatalities. The Highway Safety Act of 1966 requires that states give attention to the development of pedestrian safety programs. It would seem that this legislation has assisted in reaching and maintaining a lower pedestrian death rate. Moreover, the nation's schools have contributed through the development of educational programs that teach elementary school boys and girls to use our highways safely. The number of pedestrian fatalities appears to be rather small when it is considered that there are over 220 million people in the United States today. However, because most pedestrian fatalities are the result of carelessness or the lack of knowledge on the part of the pedestrian and the motorist alike, this number can be substantially decreased through continued efforts on the part of educators, legislators, government highway safety representatives, and local municipal governments.

[5] National Highway Traffic Safety Administration, *Highway Safety Program Manual,* 5, *Driver Licensing* (Washington, D.C.: The Administration, 1969).

9

CONGESTION. Traffic congestion is not a new development resulting from the use of the motor vehicle. It has been a problem since the days of the Roman Empire. One of Julius Caesar's first acts on seizing power was to ban wheeled traffic from the center of Rome during the day. This decision was based on the significant increase of wheeled vehicles in Rome, causing an intolerable traffic condition.

Motor vehicle congestion affects small communities as well as large metropolitan areas. Historically, cities of all sizes have been plagued by this problem regardless of the mode of transportation. Traffic congestion results when a large number of people attempt to occupy the same highway space at the same time. Inevitably they get in each other's way, whether they travel by oxcart or by automobile. Heavy pedestrian traffic in the same area further complicates the problem.

One serious result of traffic congestion is traffic crashes. The fact that traffic in a city may move at slower speeds should not lull a motorist into believing that traffic crashes are infrequent and of a minor nature. The Bureau of Public Roads and other national authoritative agencies have data indicating that speeds between 30 and 40 miles an hour are the speeds at which most of the driving populace sustain fatal or critical accidents.[6] One of the obvious solutions to the problem of congestion is the dispersal of traffic volume over a larger geographic area. This has been attempted in many communities throughout the nation, but as the number of drivers and vehicles in use continues to multiply, the problem of congestion remains an unsolved element in the causing of traffic crashes.

EDUCATION. Traffic safety education, as a formalized program in the school or as a public education endeavor, has contributed substantially in preparing elementary and secondary school students and the general public alike to live safely in a traffic environment. Such programs have experienced phenomenal growth since around 1920. It has been demonstrated that through education people can learn how to cope with and live in a society dominated by the use of the car. Evidence suggests that through the education of elementary school boys and girls the accident rate for this particular group has decreased approximately 100 per cent since the middle 1920s. Through the organization and conduct of driver and traffic safety education programs[7] in the public schools, secondary school students now have an accident record that is considerably better than that of the younger generation of two decades ago. Moreover, public traffic safety education programs have been most successful in educating adults to use motor vehicles in a safe and efficient manner. In those

---

[6] U.S. Department of Commerce, Bureau of Public Roads, *Accidents on Main Rural Highways Related to Speed, Driver, and Vehicle* (Washington, D.C.: U.S. Government Printing Office, 1964), p. 12.

[7] The terms *driver and traffic safety education* and *driver education* shall be used synonymously throughout the text. Consult *Policies and Practices for Driver and Traffic Safety Education* (1974), available from the American Driver and Traffic Safety Education Association, for current terminology.

10

states and areas where such programs have been developed on a large scale, the traffic accident experience of those states and areas tends to be better than that of similar areas where such programs have not been developed to the same degree. It is believed that educational programs contribute more to the long-range solution of the nation's traffic accident problem than do most other efforts that have been or can be put forth. However, education can be a truly effective force for traffic accident reduction only when other necessary measures of control also are used.

ENFORCEMENT. Traffic law enforcement is an integral part of a total program of traffic safety. The enforcement agencies of the nation have the legal and moral responsibility for the enforcement of those traffic laws that are enacted through the various state legislatures. The success or failure of the traffic law enforcement program is determined to the extent that the agency accepts this responsibility. Unfortunately, many police agencies, both state and local, are unprepared and unwilling to accept their full responsibility to enforce fairly and impartially traffic laws that are their charge. In some areas a police agency, through the practice of inadequate enforcement measures, contributes to the traffic crash problem rather than lends assistance to its solution. So as to make a substantial contribution to the reduction of traffic accidents, the law enforcement agency must accept its responsibility and the role it has been asked to play in the curtailing of traffic accidents. Through the use of scientific aids, intelligent planning, and organization, many police agencies are making a substantial contribution to the elimination of the nation's number-one social problem, traffic accidents. Through the leadership of organizations such as the International Association of Chiefs of Police, substantial gains are being made today in the upgrading of policy training and the improvement of police traffic services as related to vehicle accidents.

Traffic courts also play a major role in enforcement of traffic laws. The police and courts must work cooperatively if progress is to be made. The American Bar Association, through its Traffic Court Program, has helped greatly to upgrade the work of traffic courts across the nation.

ENGINEERING. Traffic engineering *is that phase of engineering which deals with the movement of motor vehicles on streets and highways and the methods, procedures, and devices used to direct them to their destination, and to maintain a space cushion between a vehicle and other movable or fixed objects, including pedestrians.* Traffic engineering, a relatively new science, emerged through the need to develop more capacity out of existing facilities. Much of our highway mileage was developed for the so-called horse-and-buggy days. With traffic engineering principles and the application of scientific facts developed from the engineering sciences, the nation's traffic problem has been reduced in a measurable degree. It should be kept in mind that without the application of these engineering principles there would be no order to the traffic stream, and we would have chaos on all of the nation's streets and highways.

Motorists are interested in safe, convenient, and economical transportation, but most of them do not realize that this has been made possible through the use of traffic engineering know-how. From an examination of the *Manual on Uniform Traffic Control Devices* (prepared by The National Joint Committee on Uniform Traffic Control Devices and The American Association of State Transportation Officials), it is evident that the traffic engineer has contributed to the decrease of traffic accidents. It is unfortunate that many states have not as yet accepted much of the content of this manual.

MOTOR VEHICLE ADMINISTRATION. An effective program of motor vehicle administration includes such motor vehicle services as registration, issuance of titles, driver licensing, driver improvement, financial responsibility, and activities relating to accident records. A single agency responsible for the administration of such a program can make a valuable contribution to a state's traffic safety program and, therefore, assist in the elimination of traffic accidents. For such a program to be successful, it must be well organized and staffed with highly competent individuals. The American Association of Motor Vehicle Administrators serves as the agency to stimulate interest in the improvement of these functions by the various states. Unless each state responds with an effective, comprehensive, and quality program of motor vehicle administration, it will not contribute as effectively as it should to the elimination of motor vehicle deaths, injuries, and property damage.

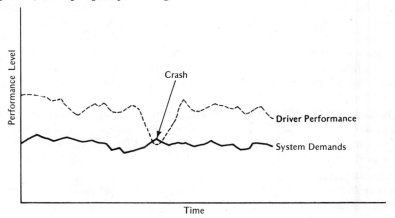

Figure 1-4. Highway Crash Event

Traffic Accident Causation Factors

The component parts of the traffic accident problem are identified as (1) *the driver*, (2) *the highway (environment)*, and (3) *the vehicle*. Each of these is closely related to theories of traffic accident causation.

THE DRIVER. Without question, the human element is the single most important factor in the cause of traffic crashes. Basically such accidents are caused by driver failure, carelessness, or violation of man-made laws or forces of nature. Estimates from several studies indicate that the human element is responsible for 80 to 85 per cent of all traffic crashes. Traffic violations, driving while intoxicated, and lack of driving courtesy are the results of human actions. The very fact that 80 per cent of all traffic accidents occur within a relatively few miles of the victim's residence suggests that he was personally unaware of the accident potential. Moreover, the fact that people commit unsafe acts while performing the driving task suggests that they lack proper knowledge, attitudes, or skills to operate a motor vehicle safely. The prudent driver conducts himself in such a manner that there is small margin for error on his part while he is behind the wheel of an automobile.

HIGHWAY. There are certain features of the nation's highway system that contribute to traffic crashes. For example, modern highway and traffic engineering principles have not been applied to older existing highways. (Unbanked curves, short curve radii, poor sight distances, and excessive crossing grades are prime illustrations.) Moreover, highway environment factors such as poor maintenance, ice, snow, rain, and improper traffic control devices are the basis for many traffic mishaps. The highway is an integral part of the driving environment and should be considered as such by the driver. However, it is estimated that about 10 per cent of all traffic accidents happen because of unsafe highway conditions.

VEHICLE. The automobile is the result of twentieth-century engineering genius. It is manufactured to meet rigid standards for safety and performance. Yet, mechanical deficiencies cause approximately 5 per cent of all traffic accidents. Recent studies suggest that the percentage of mechanical failures which cause traffic accidents is perhaps higher than that. One of the reasons for this is that there are no motor vehicle inspection laws in many states. Today approximately one half of the states require vehicles to be inspected. In those states the traffic death rate is slightly lower than those without compulsory motor vehicle inspection laws.[8] A motor vehicle must be in good mechanical condition before the motorist can operate it safely and efficiently. Although a state may not require vehicle inspection, the car owner assumes the responsibility for maintaining the sound mechanical condition of his vehicle. The National Traffic and Motor Vehicle Safety Act of 1966 requires automobile manufacturers to conform with certain motor vehicle safety standards issued by the Secretary of Transportation. As additional standards are developed and issued, the safety of all cars should be improved.

Conditions Influencing Traffic Crashes

Traffic crashes are generally the result of a combination of circumstances. Seldom is such an occurrence the product of a single identifiable factor. Behavior, environment, chance, and stress are all

[8] American Association of Motor Vehicle Administrators, and Auto Industries Highway Safety Committee, *Motor Vehicle Inspection in Perspective—Part I* (Washington, D.C.: The Committee, 1964), p. 13.

intimately related to traffic accident phenomena. The degree to which each of these enter into the accident sequence is dependent upon time, circumstances, and personality factors. The following is a brief discussion of the most frequent factors that contribute to the sequence of causes of traffic accidents. In each instance the before-mentioned conditions are related to these major contributing factors.

ALCOHOL. Driving while under the influence of alcohol is one of the most serious highway safety problems. Research studies show that a blood-alcohol concentration of 0.05 per cent (two to three drinks) impairs to some degree the driving ability of most individuals.[9] Most states have established 0.10 per cent as the blood-alcohol level for one to be considered legally "under the influence." Current recommendations are that this percentage of concentration be lowered to 0.08 per cent. Because of a lack of sufficient data, it is difficult to ascertain the exact number of people operating motor vehicles after drinking alcoholic beverages. However, most current studies support the contention that at least 50 per cent are under the influence of alcohol. The Alcohol Safety Action Projects, sponsored by the National Highway Traffic Safety Administration, are revealing more data on the drinking driver than what has been available heretofore.[10] It is evident that people who drink and drive are a menace on the highways and that alcohol is a contributing factor in numerous traffic accidents each year.

SPEED. In a recent year "speed too fast" was reported as a contributory factor in 31 per cent of all fatal traffic accidents. Certainly the severity of an accident increases greatly with increase of speed. However, by definition, speed does not always mean 70 or 80 miles an hour. At high speeds, however, capacity of the driver to adjust to hazardous conditions is always measurably reduced, and the force of impact is greatly increased. There were 46,200 recorded traffic fatalities in 1974. This was 9,600 or 17 per cent less than the 55,800 deaths in 1973. The 55 mph maximum speed limit imposed during this period of time was responsible for most of this reduction. To assure continued benefits from this lower speed limit Congress passed a maximum speed limit law in 1975. As mentioned previously, traffic accidents are the result of a combination of conditions. Speed must of necessity be related to conditions that involve differences among drivers, vehicles, highways, and environments.

NIGHT DRIVING. Death rates for night driving are considerably higher than those for day. In terms of miles of travel the nighttime death rates are twice those of daytime rates. The complexity of the night-driving task is caused by reduced visibility. Motorists should take this into consideration when driving after dark. That period of time between 10 P.M. and 4 A.M. appears to be the most dangerous period. This may be caused by fatigue, drowsiness, and a higher percentage of drivers who have been drinking being on the highways at this time.

[9] National Safety Council, op. cit., p. 52.

[10] National Highway Traffic Safety Administration, *Alcohol Safety Action Projects: Evaluation of Operations* (Washington, D.C.: The Administration, 1974).

14

Cost of Traffic Crashes

During a recent year traffic accidents cost the American public around $19.3 billion. According to the Federal Highway Administration, such occurrences cost an average of one cent for every mile driven. Such waste is a financial loss to every driver. Traffic accident costs are computed on the basis of such factors as wage losses, property damage, medical expenses, and overhead cost of insurance.

That traffic accidents have a profound effect upon the nation's economy cannot be ignored. Such happenings affect industry and the home alike. In an average year, traffic accidents kill over 20,000 males under age 25. During the 45 years between the ages of 25 and 70, these men and their families would represent $4 billion of purchasing power. This purchasing power is lost when these males are killed before age 25, and the nation's economy lowered by the reduction of potential business. Certainly, the financial impact of accidents affects the individual's family from both an economic and a social point of view.

The automobile will play an important role in the lives of almost all driver education students. The following examples show the amount of time and money spent in the use of an automobile. The estimates of time, money, speed, and so on are intentionally conservative to make the examples realistic for the majority of drivers.

Facts:

1. At least 50 driving years. Ages 16 to 66.
2. Average 10,000 miles per year.
3. Average speed, including congested traffic, 30 miles per hour.
4. Average work week: 40 hours.
5. Average work year: 50 weeks.
6. Minimum total cost per mile to operate a car including cost of car, gas, oil, repairs, insurance, taxes, etc.: 15 cents per mile.

Thus:

10,000 miles per year ÷ 30 miles per hour = 333 hours per year.

333 hours per year × 50 years = 16,650 hours of driving.

16,650 hours of driving ÷ 40 hours per week = 413.75 weeks of driving time.

413.75 weeks of driving time ÷ 50 weeks = 8.275 work years of driving time.

10,000 miles per year × $0.15 cost per mile = $1500 cost per year.

$1500 cost per year × 50 driving years = $75,000 cost per lifetime of driving.

This will mean that at least 10 cents of every dollar the average person earns in his lifetime will be spent on an automobile, and he will spend approximately 8¼ working years in driving an automobile.

Figure 1-5. Motor Vehicles Have Changed Since 1925 (Courtesy Chevrolet Division, General Motors)

Figure 1-5. *(Continued)*

THE SOLUTION—A COMPREHENSIVE
TRAFFIC SAFETY PROGRAM

The sociologist suggests that the automobile is misused because of a cultural lag. He explains it this way. We have had cars for only approximately 70 years. In view of this short period of time Americans have not adjusted their thinking to the safe use of the automobile. Moreover, engineering advancements have been more rapid than the social adjustment, just as in other aspects of technology in our society. The sociologist further indicates that the traffic problem shall be solved in some 400 years after the proper folkways and mores have developed relative to vehicle usage.

Traffic safety specialists are not willing to let this social problem remain unchecked for such an extended period of time. Therefore programs of traffic safety and driver education have been developed to solve this social dilemma.

The Three E's Concept

The three E's concept of traffic safety was originated by Julian H. Harvey while he was director of the Kansas City Safety Council, in 1923. Harvey suggested that the solution to the traffic safety problem was directly related to the development of a comprehensive program of traffic safety involving *education*, *engineering*, and *enforcement*. Thus the three E's concept emerged. Sidney Williams of the National Safety Council subsequently developed more fully the concept of the three E's. Today they still represent the essential elements of a comprehensive traffic safety program.

The Action Program

The three E's concept has served as a stimulus toward the organization of a national program of traffic safety. There were several separate efforts to establish standards and practices for traffic safety. In 1946 former President Truman called the White House Conference on Highway Safety. Approximately two thousand individuals participated, representing all sections of the nation and every possible interest and competence in the traffic safety field. Out of this vast reservoir of knowledge, experience, and talent emerged the Action Program for Highway Safety. Over a period of time, eleven specific functions in traffic safety and management were identified and defined as follows:

1. Laws and Ordinances.
2. Traffic Accident Records.
3. Education.
4. Engineering.
5. Motor Vehicle Administration.

6. Police Traffic Supervision.
7. Traffic Courts.
8. Public Information.
9. Organized Citizen Support.
10. Health and Medical Care.
11. Research.

More on the Action Program is presented in Chapter 18.

The Highway Safety Act

The Highway Safety Act was enacted in 1966 by Congress as a means of unifying and establishing a nationwide highway safety program. Eighteen Highway Safety Program Standards were subsequently approved, and a federal-state partnership distributes the program responsibility through all levels of government. Chapter 18 gives more detail on the Highway Safety Act.

TRAFFIC SAFETY IN THE SCHOOLS

"No cause, not even the highest and purest, can prosper in our day without making education its ally." These words of Horace Mann, spoken in 1857, are equally true today. Learning is the foundation of traffic accident prevention. In nurturing attitudes, knowledge, and skills, positive changes in behavior occur. Thus education becomes an indispensable part of all highway safety activities.

American educators recognize that education for safe living is an integral part of the school's responsibility to society. The challenge of driver and traffic safety education today is greater than ever. Therefore, the resources of all educational institutions are vital to the teaching of attitudes, knowledge, habits, and skills necessary for living in a motorized age. School administrators, supervisors, and driver educators view driver education as one segment of the general education program of the school. The formal driver and traffic safety education movement appeared in schools during the mid-1930s and has experienced significant growth in the number of schools involved and in the scope of the program.

Elementary Level

It has been recognized for some time that the elementary school is a very fertile place to develop attitudes, knowledge, and skills related to safe living. The accepted laws of learning suggest that what a child learns early in life has a greater possibility of establishing within him desirable patterns for safe living later. There are three basic programs of traffic safety education that our elementary schools rely on to

19

develop the elementary school child's knowledge and attitudes toward safe living in addition to molding habits and developing certain skills.

TO AND FROM SCHOOL. One of the earliest programs developed to curtail the mounting toll of traffic accidents involving elementary school children was the "to and from school" program. This is a program whereby the elementary school child becomes aware of the safest way for him to travel to and from school daily. The child is taught to recognize the traffic policemen, signals, signs, and certain highway conditions when drawing the route on a layout map of his community. The child then takes his map home, and his parent is to travel the route with him so as to verify that it is the best route. When the parent approves, he signs the map, and the child returns it to his teacher.

BICYCLES. Today there are more than 90 million bicycle riders in the nation. Most of these are under 14 years of age. Recognizing the need to educate and train these young people to ride bikes safely and efficiently, educators initiated a safety program during the early 1920s. Since then the program has met with significant success in lowering the number of bicycle traffic deaths, even though the number of bike riders has steadily increased since that day to the present high number. The typical bicycle safety program involves learning specific knowledge related to the use of the bicycle, traffic laws, and rules of safe conduct. Also, the child learns how to inspect his bicycle for mechanical deficiencies and thereby becomes aware of the need for a continuous program of bicycle maintenance. Finally, the child is given a series of tests of skill in his ability to handle a bicycle under various traffic conditions. The National Highway Traffic Safety Administration (NHTSA) reports that 48 states have some form of bicycle curriculum.[11]

SCHOOL SAFETY PATROL. The school safety patrol movement developed in the 1920s because of the need for added measures to protect the child as he traveled to and from school. The Chicago Motor Club pioneered the introduction of the program to the schools of Illinois.[12] Members of the school patrol are chosen for their ability to lead and to gain the respect of the children in all grade levels. The crossing guard patrol protects other children against traffic hazards and, at the same time, learns to identify hazards, make intelligent judgments, and determine safe practices for avoiding such hazards. Adult crossing guards are used in some schools where traffic is too heavy for a child to handle.

PEDESTRIANS. Another phase of the elementary school traffic safety education program is a major emphasis placed on pedestrian practices. Elementary school boys and girls are taught traffic patterns,

[11] National Highway Traffic Safety Administration, *Statewide Highway Safety Assessment—A National Estimate of Performance* (Washington, D.C.: The Administration, July 1975), pp. 90–91.

[12] Chicago Motor Club, *School Safety Patrol Supervisor's Manual* (Chicago: The Club), p. 1.

hazards of automobiles, where to walk, identification of traffic signs and signals, and specific traffic laws and regulations regarding pedestrian accidents. This is an excellent program and one that helps establish a basis for living in a traffic society. All states have pedestrian curriculums as reported by NHTSA.[13]

Secondary Level

The high school student needs a comprehensive program of education for safe living. However, it should not be a duplication of the program provided for the elementary school child, but must be developed on the needs and interests of the secondary school student. Recognizing a need for an education and training program in safety for secondary school students, school officials have been instrumental in developing a variety of programs calibrated to the student at this level. For example, there have emerged in recent years several co-curricular activities. Such activities include student safety councils, traffic safety courts, safety clubs, safety committees, driver education clubs, bicycle safety clubs, and school crossing guard patrols.

The most outstanding program to emerge in the secondary schools is that of high school driver education. During the latter 1920s and early 1930s, safety leaders determined that roads and automobiles alone could not be engineered to guarantee safety in traffic nor could law enforcement officers observe all traffic at all times. Because accident investigations traced the many causes of traffic accidents to driving errors, it was concluded that proper education of the driver could appreciably reduce such accidents.

HIGH SCHOOL DRIVER AND TRAFFIC SAFETY EDUCATION

The high school driver education program began in the early 1930s. Since that day this program has developed more rapidly than any other program in the school's curriculum. That a group of people under 20 years of age are involved in approximately 12 to 15 per cent of all traffic accidents is testimony to the need for such a program. The early pioneers in the driver education movement were Albert W. Whitney, Herbert J. Stack, and Amos E. Neyhart.

A complete driver and traffic safety education program is composed of a classroom phase and a laboratory phase, sometimes referred to as *practice driving* or *driver training*. Science and mathematics are used in the classroom as the student learns to apply the laws of kinetic energy, centrifugal force, and friction. He studies the highway transportation system, human characteristics, and their limitations relative to the driving task. In addition he learns traffic laws and ordinances and their enforcement by state and local police and the courts. In the laboratory phase of driver education, the individual

[13] National Highway Traffic Safety Administration, op cit., pp. 90–91.

21

is taught basic manipulative skills and how to perceive and interpret traffic hazards. He learns how to operate a car in varying conditions of traffic, highways, and weather. Essentially, the student applies classroom principles to the driving task. Driver and traffic safety education make up both an academic program and a training program. Each is designed to develop competent traffic citizens who can live efficiently in the motorized society of today.

LEARNING ACTIVITIES

1. Given the material in this chapter plus two selected resources, develop a term paper on the subject, "The Human Factor: A Cause of Traffic Crashes."
2. Develop a slide series depicting the historical development of the automobile and its impact on the American society. Be prepared to make a presentation in class as assigned by the instructor.
3. Develop a transparency series that shows the growth in the number of registered vehicles, drivers, and miles of travel. Relate all materials to the growth in traffic crashes.
4. Collect data on your local and state's traffic crash experience for the past five years. Place all clippings and data in a notebook. Submit as a class project by mid-term.
5. Organize and lead a debate with three other students on the subject, "A Major Social Problem: Traffic Crashes."

SELECTED RESOURCES

Baldwin, David. "Dimensions of the Traffic Problem," *The Annals of the American Academy of Political and Social Science* (November 1958), pp. 9–26.

Chicago Motor Club. *School Safety Patrol Supervisor's Manual*. Chicago: The Club, p. 1.

Federal Highway Administration. *Manual on Uniform Traffic Control Devices for Streets and Highways*. Washington, D.C.: The Administration, 1971.

Highway Users Federation for Safety and Mobility. *The Highway Fact Book*. Washington, D.C.: The Federation (January 1975).

Motor Vehicle Manufacturers Association. *1975 Automobile Facts & Figures*. Detroit, Mich.: The Association, published annually.

National Highway Traffic Safety Administration. *Highway Safety Program Manual, Vol. 4, Driver Education*. Washington, D.C.: The Administration, 1969.

National Highway Traffic Safety Administration. *Statewide Highway Safety Program Assessment—A National Estimate of Performance*. Washington, D.C.: The Administration (July 1975).

National Safety Council. *Accident Facts*. Chicago: The Council, published annually.

National Safety Council. *Driver Education Status Report 1972–71*. Chicago: The Council, 1974.

Robinson, Gordon H. *Accidents and Human Performance*. New York: Society of Automotive Engineers, Inc., Report No. 680555 (September 1968).

The President's Committee for Traffic Safety. *Highway Safety Action Program*. Washington, D.C.: The Committee, 1962.

Warren, George. *Traffic Courts*. Boston: Little, Brown and Company, 1942.

Chapter 2

Evolution of the Driver Education Movement

OBJECTIVE: The student will be able to relate the historical growth of driver and traffic safety education to the need for teacher preparation program standards and the influence that legislation had upon each.

Driver education has progressed rapidly to attain an important position in the secondary schools of the nation. From its beginning in the early 1930s it has grown to the point where more than 73 per cent of the eligible students in public secondary school are now enrolled in the course. There are driver education courses in the curriculum offerings of 87 per cent of the schools.[1]

Although isolated instances of the teaching of some type of driver education in the public schools dates from prior to 1920, the forces of an organized movement did not appear until the mid-1930s. Classroom instruction in driver education was given in Bergen County, New Jersey, in 1932. However, the first course called driver education was conducted at the high school in State College, Pennsylvania, in 1933. This course contained both phases of driver education, including classroom and laboratory instruction. During the late 1930s there was considerable interest generated in driver education, and a number of schools introduced courses in this subject area. The program was gaining considerable momentum prior to World War II. However, the wartime restrictions on driving and preoccupation with

---

[1] National Safety Council, *Driver Education Status Report 1972-73* (Chicago: The Council, 1974), pp. 1-3.

23

national defense efforts seriously hampered the progress of the program at that time.

Driver education has had a phenomenal growth since the end of World War II. This rapid growth brought with it many problems, including the expansion of course offerings and improvement in the quality of instruction. Standards of teacher preparation and necessary finances to provide for program growth presented additional problems. Educators, citizen organizations, public officials interested in various aspects of the control of traffic accidents, and segments of business and industry with an interest in traffic safety all contributed to a vigorous promotion of high school driver education. The legislatures of many states, recognizing the numerous problems involved, provided necessary financial assistance for expansion, particularly of the laboratory phase of the program in many states. Since the close of World War II driver education has become an important part of the total educational experience of a majority of secondary school students in the nation.

ORIGIN AND DEVELOPMENT OF DRIVER EDUCATION

Driver education has its origin in a basic social problem—traffic crashes. As the implications of this problem were studied, its solution was expressed in terms of the three E's of traffic safety: enforcement, education, and engineering. It was recognized that one of the basic solutions might lie in the process of educating young drivers as they approached legal driving age. However, before driver education could assume its function of accident prevention, it was necessary to develop and organize an instructional program that would achieve the objectives of reducing highway accidents and producing good traffic citizens. Then came the tasks of obtaining and preparing adequate numbers of teachers to provide the educational experiences to potential new drivers and developing adequate instructional materials to make the driver education program most effective. As these steps were being taken, it was also necessary to conduct a vigorous promotional campaign if driver education instruction was to be provided to more than a million students in a reasonable period of time.

As driver education was introduced into the schools, many persons became interested in the effectiveness of this program in terms of reducing crashes and serious traffic violations involving young drivers. The result was a number of studies conducted in various cities and states throughout the United States to determine the effectiveness of this instruction.[2] The studies indicated that driver education was an effective deterrent to traffic violations and crashes on the part of young drivers.

As teachers became involved in this new type of educational endeavor, they realized the need for professional growth that would lead

[2] Edward Lane-Reticker, *Driver Education in High Schools—An Inquiry into Costs, Results, and Related Factors* (Chapel Hill: Institute of Government, University of North Carolina, n.d.).

to the improvement of instruction and the solid expansion of the program. The result was the organization of professional driver education teacher associations in various states throughout the United States and finally a national organization of driver education teachers. All of these factors have been of extreme importance in the growth and development of driver education in the United States.

RECOGNIZING THE NEED

Following World War I the automobile played an important role in the social and economic growth of the country. But this growth brought with it an enormous social problem. By 1925 there were over 20,000 persons killed in automobile accidents in the United States annually. The increase in traffic fatalities was rapid. By 1929, more than 30,000 persons were killed, and in 1941, there were 39,969 fatalities. Traffic injuries rose to more than 1 million per year.[3]

The constant increase in traffic fatalities and injuries brought with it a demand for many types of controls. These included increased emphasis on traffic law enforcement, improved highway design and traffic engineering, uniform traffic laws, improved motor vehicle administration, and a great deal of public education. Studies of the traffic problem revealed the fact that basic accident causes usually resulted from human failures, such as lack of knowledge, skill, or understanding of the social responsibility involved in operating the motor vehicle in our society. Research also revealed the fact that young drivers were responsible for a disproportionate number of accidents and traffic fatalities in relation to the number of miles that they were driving.[4] This suggested the need for an adequate education program for a very large percentage of the potential young drivers reaching legal driving age who were enrolled in the high schools of the country. There were trained teachers available within the school systems who could give the driver education instruction with special in-service training in the area. It became an obvious fact that one of the major sources of control of traffic accidents would be a sound program of driver education given to all high school students.

Although this was an educational problem, it was not the educators who first recognized the need for driver education. It was, rather, police officials and driver license administrators who daily came into contact with young people who were involved in traffic accidents. Insurance companies also felt a need to help young drivers because of the many costly claims that were being filed as a result of accidents by this age group. These public officials and business interests brought to the attention of school administrators and teachers the nature and scope of the young driver problem and urged them to develop an educational program that would aid in its solution. "That

[3] National Safety Council, *Accident Facts* (Chicago: The Council, 1975), p. 58.

[4] Mary K. Moran, "The Accident Rate of High-School Drivers," *Safety Education Digest* (Fall 1951), pp. 62–67.

public opinion has raced ahead of the educators in acceptance of driver education is shown by the fact that every pronounced upswing in the number of high schools offering driver education has followed a major national conference on the seriousness of the traffic accident problem."[5]

Figure 2-1. Dr. Herbert J. Stack, Pioneer Driver Educator (Courtesy Dr. Herbert J. Stack)

Development of an Instructional Program

In 1932, Dr. Herbert J. Stack, at that time educational director of the Accident Prevention Department of the Association of Casualty and Surety Executives, introduced an organized program of classroom instruction in driver education that he taught in high schools in Bergen County, New Jersey. This was conducted as a unit of instruction in classes in science, health education, or subject areas already within the school program.

In 1933, Professor Amos E. Neyhart of Pennsylvania State College introduced the first complete program of driver education, including both classroom and laboratory instruction, into the high school at

[5] Leon Brody and Herbert J. Stack, *Highway Safety and Driver Education* (Englewood Cliffs, N.J.: Prentice-Hall, Inc., 1954), p. 382.

26

State College, Pennsylvania. These classes placed emphasis on physical, mental, and emotional limitations of drivers, the physical limitations of the vehicle and the road surfaces on which it operated, traffic laws and regulations, and sound driving habits and skills. They also emphasized a positive attitude toward the responsibilities assumed in the operation of a motor vehicle in the increasingly complex traffic pattern on the streets and highways of the nation. The program developed by Professor Neyhart organized an instructional sequence for the development of actual driving skills on the part of the potential new driver. With the introduction of these educationally sound, well-organized programs of instruction, driver education was ready to take its place in the educational program of high school youth of the nation.

Figure 2-2. Professor Amos E. Neyhart, Pioneer Driver Educator (By Permission of Amos E. Neyhart)

Promotion

The promotion of high school driver education was led by two national organizations—the Association of Casualty and Surety Companies and the American Automobile Association. Promotional activities were carried out also by the National Safety Council, many citizen groups, insurance companies, state police organizations, driver licensing departments, and state departments of education throughout the United States.

THE ASSOCIATION OF CASUALTY AND SURETY EXECUTIVES. This Association, later to be known as the Association of Casualty and Surety Companies, was composed of a large number of the major stock casualty insurance companies in the United States. The educational program of its accident prevention department, at that time called the National Conservation Bureau, was under the guidance of Dr. Albert W. Whitney, a long-time recognized leader in the safety movement. The driver education activities were under the direction of Dr. Herbert J. Stack, the educational director. Dr. Stack toured the country, meeting with leading educators, traffic administrators, and citizen groups who were interested in driver education as a means of control of the traffic accident problem. Dr. Stack also conducted classes for potential driver education teachers. The Association published a great deal of literature dealing with phases of the driver education program, including the driver education textbook *Man and the Motor Car*, which was edited by Dr. Whitney. In 1938 the Association made a grant to New York University for the establishment of the Center for Safety Education, and Dr. Stack became its first director.[6]

The Center for Safety Education became the first group in a major university to provide a specific training program for traffic safety educators. The Center was devoted to the purposes of leadership training, research, publications, and field services. Through the program conducted at the University, a large number of potential teachers and leaders of the driver education movement were prepared to assume these responsibilities. Research conducted at the University provided some of the early needed knowledge with regard to the various aspects of traffic safety education. Field services of the Center, in cooperation with the staff of the Association of Casualty and Surety Companies, provided assistance to state and local departments of education in the preparation of courses of study guides and the materials necessary for the conduct of driver education courses. They also provided training for thousands of driver education teachers who were to conduct the program throughout the country.

AMERICAN AUTOMOBILE ASSOCIATION. This national organization had a long-time interest in all aspects of the problems of drivers. It was only natural that they would have a dominant interest in the education of young drivers. The American Automobile Association retained the services of Professor Amos Neyhart of Pennsylvania State College as educational consultant. He has related to their educational program for many years in one capacity or another.

The Association developed a staff of professional consultants who provided guidance to state and local departments of education and other traffic safety officials interested in driver education. They also developed both promotional and instructional materials in the field of driver education, including the textbook *Sportsmanlike Driving*. Under the direction of the American Automobile Association and their staff consultants numerous college teacher preparation programs

[6] Center for Safety Education, *The Center for Safety Education—Program and Services* (New York: The Center, n.d.), p. 3.

for driver education teachers were conducted throughout the United States. The Association also developed numerous teaching aids, such as psychophysical testing devices, to be used by driver education teachers and assisted in making cars available for laboratory instruction. Affiliated local automobile clubs have been very helpful in the promotion and growth of high school driver education in the various communities of the country.

OTHER GROUPS. There were many other groups that contributed to the early promotional efforts of the driver education programs. They prepared materials, encouraged local school boards to start classes, provided cars and other teaching devices, sponsored teenage traffic safety conferences, and acted as resource persons in driver education classes. Dr. Leon Brody stated, "Organizations of every description are anxious to 'assist' educational institutions which are teaching safety in any form; they are particularly interested in driver education programs."[7] These groups included, among others, the National Safety Council, the Auto-Industries Highway Safety Committee, parent-teacher organizations, insurance companies, automobile dealers, public officials, service groups, fraternal organizations, and local safety councils.

Obtaining Teachers

One of the great needs for the rapidly expanding program of driver education was properly prepared teachers. Since new programs were being introduced very rapidly in various high schools in the nation, it was impossible to prepare driver education teachers through the long-range program of preservice preparation. To meet this immediate need the staff representatives of the American Automobile Association, the Association of Casualty and Surety Companies, and the Center for Safety Education conducted numerous short courses, usually of one-week duration, to provide the background and fundamentals involved in driver education to in-service teachers in the various states.

Many teachers taught classroom driver education as a unit of already existing courses. As a result, they were recruited from several areas of instruction, such as industrial arts, social sciences, physical education, health education, and English. The large majority of the early teachers taught driver education, either classroom, laboratory, or both, as only a part of their regular teaching assignment. Although this program of teacher preparation began in the late 1930s, it was not until the mid-1940s that the program was in its full operation. During the 1940s there were thousands of teachers throughout the United States who were introduced to driver education instruction through the short-course program. Gradually the colleges began to offer credit courses in driver and safety education, and at the present time there are many institutions preparing teachers for careers in driver education just as in other subject areas.

[7] Brody and Stack, op, cit., p. 317.

Developing Materials

To conduct driver education programs, it was necessary to have instructional materials, including textbooks and supplementary materials, as in other areas of instruction. The Association of Casualty and Surety Companies and the American Automobile Association took the leadership in the development of these materials. They published the two textbooks previously mentioned and supplementary workbooks, teacher's guides, and other materials necessary to the conduct of the program. As interest in driver education developed, there were other publishers that made available text materials in this field. However, the two texts developed by these private agencies were subsidized to the extent that they became the primary textbooks of the early era of the development of driver education. There are no other driver education textbooks published prior to 1945 that are still in general use in the high schools today. It was not until the late 1940s that new textbooks in high school driver education began to appear from the presses of private publishers.

Studies of Effectiveness

As driver education was introduced into the high schools of the nation, educators, motor vehicle administrators, and citizen organizations developed an interest in determining the effectiveness of this instruction as it related to the reduction of accidents among young drivers. As a result, there were within a period of about ten years, from the late 1940s to the mid-1950s, studies conducted in numerous states and cities throughout the United States that attempted to evaluate these instructional programs.[8]

In general, virtually all of these studies indicate that the trained high school student was involved in fewer crashes; he had fewer traffic citations, and the crashes in which he was involved tended to be of a less serious nature. A general conclusion from these numerous studies was that high school driver education reduced accidents by about one half. These studies were valuable in terms of gaining acceptance for high school driver education because they displayed to school administrators, and the general public as well, the values inherent in a driver education program for high school youth. A critical evaluation of most of these studies reveals the extreme difficulty in developing accurate research data to establish the value of a program of this nature on such a broad basis. Numerous questions were raised with regard to the validity of the studies conducted. These questions included such points as:

1. The matching of the compared groups to determine whether the improved driving experiences could be attributed to factors other than driver education.

---

[8] Research Division in collaboration with the National Commission on Safety Education, *A Critical Analysis of Driver Education Research* (Washington, D.C.: National Education Association, 1957).

30

2. The exposure to traffic situations by the various groups compared.
3. The absence of a standard of instruction given to the various students in the driver education program. Some of them received very short courses in both classroom and laboratory instruction, whereas others had received a course of adequate time in both areas but conducted by teachers who were not properly prepared to do their job.

These questions notwithstanding, the numerous studies that were conducted with regard to high school driver education during the early period of its development were a significant factor in the promotion of driver education in the United States. More recent studies have tended to verify the findings revealed in earlier research relating to the effectiveness of driver education, but to fully establish program validity the quality of research needs to be improved.

Professional Organization

As larger numbers of teachers were involved in the teaching of driver education, they became aware of the need for an organization that would provide them professional growth opportunities for their individual members and enable them to strengthen the instructional program in high school driver education. The first of these organizations was the Iowa High School Driver Education Association organized in 1949. There are now over 47 states that have professional organizations of high school driver education teachers.

In 1956 a number of the leaders of these high school driver education teacher organizations met in Washington, D.C., to discuss their mutual problems. One of the results of this conference was the organization of the American Driver and Safety Education Association, now known as the American Driver and Traffic Safety Education Association. The secretariat of this association was the National Commission on Safety Education of the National Education Association.

In addition to the professional organizations of driver education teachers, the School and College Division of the National Safety Council organized a driver education section in 1954. The Driver Education Section has been very active in the promotion of high school driver education throughout the United States. The Section makes available many types of promotional materials to teachers, school administrators, state departments of public instruction, and, particularly, citizen organization groups interested in the development of high school driver education. They also provide staff services to these groups and organizations for the purposes of growth and improvement of driver education programs.

GROWTH OF DRIVER EDUCATION

Driver education has grown more rapidly in the brief period of its history than any other course of instruction introduced into the high school curriculum in the United States. This rapid growth has reflected a need based on a serious social problem and the meeting of this need for high school students. Driver education has become one of the most popular subjects in the curriculum with high school students in the United States today.

Early Growth

It is difficult to record the year-by-year growth of driver education in the early years of its development, beginning with the mid-1930s and going through to 1946. However, in 1947 the establishment of the High School Driver Education Award Program gives us an indication that about 200,000 students were receiving some type of instruction in either classroom, laboratory instruction, or both by that time.[9] Many of these courses were inadequate in terms of time allocated for both classroom and laboratory instruction, the type of facilities and equipment used, and the preparation of teachers who were giving the instruction. However, driver education was growing rapidly at the time of the entrance of the United States into World War II. Because of wartime restrictions on the use of vehicles, laboratory instruction was almost nonexistent at this time. In addition to this factor, many of the teachers who had been trained were entering the armed services, so teachers were not available for this type of instruction.

Because World War II was a mobile type of warfare, involving the use of large numbers of motorized units, and because the United States was supposedly a nation of drivers, it was assumed that the young people going into the armed forces would be able to do a good job in handling this motorized equipment. This, however, proved to be something short of the fact. The Quartermaster General of the Army was compelled to call upon the State Superintendents of Public Instruction to conduct preinduction driver-training programs to provide as much background knowledge as necessary or possible for these young people to assume their responsibilities in handling motorized equipment. Twenty-three of the Chief State School Officers cooperated with this program, and in those 23 states there were conducted preinduction driver-training programs in many of the schools. The armed services developed an instructor's manual for preinduction driver education in schools and colleges to assist teachers to provide potential young drivers with certain information they felt would be helpful.[10] This suggested 45-period course of instruction followed very closely the high school driver education program, but it also placed a great deal of emphasis upon particular problems to be involved in the operation of military equipment.

[9] Insurance Institute for Highway Safety, *Annual National High School Driver Education Achievement Program, p. 7.*

[10] Office of the Quartermaster General, Military Training Division, *Pre-Induction Driver Education in Schools and Colleges—Instructor's Manual* (Washington, D.C.: The Office, 1943), p. 1.

Although the program was not instituted on a nationwide basis, the students receiving instruction proved to be very helpful to the armed forces.

The Growth Since 1946

One of the recommendations of the President's Highway Safety Conference of 1946, which will be discussed in greater detail in Chapter 18, was that high school driver education should be provided "as an integral part of the curriculum for students approaching legal driving age."[11]

As a means of implementing the recommendation of the President's Conference, the Association of Casualty and Surety Companies inaugurated, in 1946, the High School Driver Education Award Program. This program, now called the Driver Education Status Report, and conducted by the National Safety Council, gathers annual statistics regarding all aspects of high school driver education programs within the various states. As a result, a very good picture of program growth from 1946 to the present time is available. Figure 2-3 shows this growth during the past several years. During the school year 1961-62,

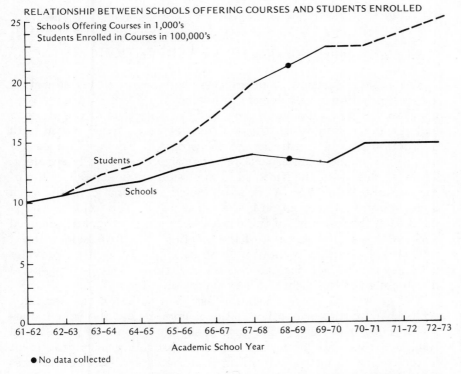

Figure 2-3. Enrollment Trends in Driver Education (Courtesy National Safety Council)

[11] The President's Highway Safety Conference, *Action Program: The President's Highway Safety Conference* (Washington, D.C.: The Conference, 1946), p. 6.

33

there were 12,612 schools of an approximate 19,100 giving driver education courses. Of the 2,962,455 eligible students, instruction in high school driver education was given to 1,649,837 students in 1963-64. Today approximately 87 per cent of the eligible students enrolled in high schools throughout the United States are receiving some instruction in driver education. However, it must be pointed out that only 2,621,684, or 73 per cent, of these students are receiving courses of instruction that provide a minimum of 30 hours of classroom instruction and 6 hours of laboratory instruction, which meet the nationally recommended minimum standards for driver education.[12] Many courses are now conducted for a full semester.

One of the factors involved in the growth of instruction, in the laboratory phase of the program particularly, was the introduction in 1947 of a driver simulator. The use of simulators permits schools to provide greater amounts of instruction at a reduced cost. Through the use of simulators a teacher can train from 8 to 25 students at one time. In this way he is able to provide a considerably greater amount of instruction than is possible in a car where the instruction is limited to one student at a time at the wheel. State reimbursement to local districts for driver education has also been a strong factor in program expansion.

NATIONAL CONFERENCES ON
HIGH SCHOOL DRIVER EDUCATION

The rapid expansion in offerings in high school driver education across the nation in the decade following World War II brought with it a great deal of confusion in the variety of objectives of the program and the manner in which those objectives were carried out in both instruction and administration of the program. The need for greater uniformity in the main aspects of the program was readily apparent. To meet this need, the National Commission on Safety Education of the National Education Association called a national conference on high school driver education in the fall of 1949. The following statement from the foreword of this conference report recognizes the need and states well the purpose of the meeting: "A profession without policies is like a ship without a compass. . . . This bulletin provides a framework of policies and recommendations to guide the sound development of high school driver education programs."[13]

The growth of driver education has been based on the standards established at this and other national conferences sponsored since 1949. They have given the movement direction and established standards that have been responsible for providing an improvement in the quality of instruction throughout the nation. The conferences

[12] National Safety Council, *Driver Education Status Report 1972-73.* (Chicago: The Council, 1974), pp. 2-3.

[13] National Commission on Safety Education, *High-School Driver Education—Policies and Practices* (Washington, D.C.: National Education Association, 1950), p. 7.

34

are usually composed of about two hundred invited delegates. The delegates include educators from each of the states representing all levels of administration, supervision, and high school and college instruction and about 25 official and nonofficial agencies with an interest in high school driver education. The five national conferences on high school driver education have been held as follows:

1. 1949   Jackson's Mill, West Virginia
2. 1953   East Lansing, Michigan
           Michigan State University
3. 1958   Lafayette, Indiana
           Purdue University
4. 1963   Washington, D.C.
           National Education Association
5. 1973   Warrensburg, Missouri
           Central Missouri State University

The basic principles and policies were established at the first conference. Subsequent conferences have revised and expanded the original recommendations in view of past experiences and existing developments as they have appeared. There has been a gradual maturity and upgrading of standards forthcoming from these five conferences, which have been conducted over 25 years. The following discussion of conference policies and recommendations is based primarily on the report of the fifth conference.[14] The discussion will be divided into the following sections: definition of terms, objectives, standards of instruction, standards of administration, teacher qualification and certification, role of state departments of education, role of colleges and universities, and research and evaluation.

Definition of Terms

There was a general lack of uniformity in the use of terms prior to 1949, which led to considerable confusion in the literature and was a deterrent to the development of desirable program standards. The most common term at the time for the classroom work was *driver education*, and *driver training* referred to the behind-the-wheel phase of the program. The conference altered this to make *driver education* refer to the total program, *classroom instruction* refer to all experiences not in the car, and *practice driving* refer to all work in the car. Over the years there has been some change in these terms, and the concepts of driver education have broadened to include traffic safety education. The following definitions were developed by the fifth national conference:

Driver education—classroom and laboratory student learning experiences designed to enable motor vehicle operators to become safer

[14] American Driver and Traffic Safety Education Association, *Policies and Guidelines for Driver and Traffic Safety Education* (Washington, D.C.: The Association, 1974).

and more efficient highway users and to acquire knowledge about the highway transportation system so that they may contribute to its improvement.

Classroom phase—that portion of a driver education course, based in a classroom environment, which is characterized by student learning under the management of a teacher or teachers.

Regular classroom mode—group or individualized student learning experiences which take place in a teacher-managed classroom environment without utilization of an electronic or mechanical student response system.

Multimedia classroom mode—group student learning experiences which take place in a teacher-managed classroom environment utilizing audiovisuals and featuring student response to multiple-choice test items depicted on a screen.

Laboratory phase—that portion of a driver education course that covers motor vehicle operation under real or simulated conditions and is characterized by student learning experiences arising from use of electronic driving simulation equipment, and off-street multiple-car driving range, and/or on-street driving practice in a dual-controlled car under the direction of a teacher.

Electronic simulator mode—group student learning experiences which permit individuals to operate vehicular controls in response to audio-visual depictions of traffic environments and driving emergencies. The electromechanical equipment provides for evaluation (by a teacher) of perceptual, judgmental, and decision-making performance of individuals and groups.

Off-street multiple-car driving range mode—student learning experiences which take place on an off-street area on which a number of cars are used simultaneously under the direct supervision of one or more teachers for the purpose of improving perceptual judgment, decision-making, and psychomotor skills.

On-street mode—student learning experiences which are supervised by a teacher and take place in a dual-controlled motor vehicle while operating on streets and highways.

Objectives

It is essential to have stated objectives or purposes toward which any course is directed if it is to attain the position of a desirable educational experience for youth. Basic objectives for driver education were developed at the Jackson's Mill conference in 1949. Over the years those stated objectives have remained basically the same but have changed somewhat as the concepts of the program have broadened. The purposes of the course as developed by the fourth national conference are as follows:

The specific objectives are to assist all students in:
1. Learning the appropriate knowledge for increasing their efficiency of living in the total traffic environment . . . physical, social, psychological, moral, and legal.

36

2. Learning fundamental driving skills and establishing basic and correct skill habits.
3. Achieving a desirable pattern for behavior in our traffic society.
4. Developing the ability to recognize, analyze, and respond to traffic situations in a manner that demonstrates proficiency in the driving task.
5. Developing understanding of both driver and pedestrian limitations, obligations, and responsibilities, from legal and social viewpoints.
6. Understanding how society may attain maximum efficiency in the operation of its motor vehicle transportation system.

The fifth conference stated that the purpose of high school driver education is to develop safer and more efficient highway users who understand the essential components of the highway transportation system and highway safety programs and who will participate in the system in a manner that will enhance the effectiveness of such components.

Standards of Instruction

The conferences have emphasized the need for providing a quality program that is developed to meet the needs of the students. The driver education teacher should use care in the selection of proper text, supplementary, and audio-visual materials to ensure that they will be a direct help to him in achieving the objectives of the course. Learning experiences should be selected thoughtfully and upon the basis of well-developed criteria.

The complete driver education course, including classroom and laboratory instruction, should be based upon the concepts of (1) the driving task, (2) human functions, (3) factors influencing driver performance, and (4) operator/non-operator functions and highway transportation system interaction. Curriculum specifications should be based upon the following units of instruction:

1. Nature of the driving task.
2. Basic knowledge and skills for vehicle operation.
3. Vehicle performance and control capabilities.
4. Habits and skills for vehicle operations and maneuvers.
5. Driving strategies and tactics.
6. Judgment of system events.
7. Decision making for a plan of action.
8. Highway user responsibilities.
9. Alcohol and other drugs.
10. Obedience to and enforcement of traffic laws.
11. Post-crash procedures and responsibilities.
12. Selection, inspection, and maintenance of safe vehicles.

Administrative Standards

Each of the national conferences has developed standards relating to the many administrative aspects of the total driver education program. For a complete résumé of these standards the student should refer to the policies and practices established by the fourth conference. However, there are several parts of the recommendations that should be mentioned here.

In general, the driver education program should be administered in the same way as any other instructional program in the school. The course should be a regular part of the high school curriculum and carry credit toward graduation. Instruction should be given when the student approaches or attains the minimum legal driving age; adequate materials and equipment should be provided for instruction; only fully qualified teachers should be employed for instruction; proper records and reports should be maintained; and a quality program should be maintained to develop solid support in the community.

The time standards established for the program have been an important aspect of the conference recommendations. The first conference recommended a *minimum* time standard of 30 clock hours of instruction in the classroom and 6 clock hours of instruction in practice driving. These standards have remained constant, but the conference in 1973 made this further recommendation: "Driver education courses provided within school districts for youthful beginners should consist of 90 hours of structured learning experiences, scheduled over a full term or more, including laboratory instruction with in-car driving experience for each student."

Teacher Qualification and Certification

The driver education teacher should have the same high qualifications as teachers of other areas and in addition should possess those special qualifications demanded in this special area. He should be in good health, intelligent, personable, skillful in teaching, and have a knowledge and understanding of adolescents. He should also have enthusiasm, maturity, even temperament, and an above-average driving record and ability.

The preservice preparation of teachers should include a teaching minor in the subject of driver and traffic safety education. Certification standards should be sufficient to assure that teachers in this area be well prepared in the subject field. For a complete discussion of teacher qualification and certification standards refer to Chapter 5.

The Role of State Departments of Education

The state departments of education have a unique role of leadership to provide in the field of driver and traffic safety education. They must establish program standards, develop certification requirements, encourage excellence in instruction, and provide for appropriate records and reports to maintain a current record of program accomplishments. The state departments must also provide leadership in the development of proper legislation for driver education, stimulate professional organizations, initiate in-service instruction, and coordinate the activities of agency and educational groups. One of their most important functions is to act in an advisory capacity to schools and colleges in the development of their program.

The Role of Colleges and Universities

Colleges and universities must provide leadership in driver and traffic safety education in many ways. They must employ qualified persons to develop substantial programs of teacher preparation from the undergraduate through graduate levels. It is also their responsibility to direct and encourage research in the traffic safety field, conduct seminars, provide conference leadership, develop publications, and consult with schools in initiating or upgrading their high school courses. A strong program in the colleges and universities can be the focal point in the development of a strong program of driver and traffic safety education within the state.

Evaluation and Research

Several national conferences have given recognition to the importance of evaluation and research in the growth of driver and traffic safety education as an important part of the total school program. They have developed guidelines for proper evaluation procedures and pointed up research needs in this area. The recommendations have included emphasis on the need to stimulate research activities and to improve the quality of research that is being conducted. Today, more than ever, evaluation of program effectiveness must be a planned part of each driver education curriculum.

TEACHER PREPARATION

The quality of instruction in any area is dependent upon the ability and dedication of the teacher who is conducting the course. A major factor in the teacher's ability to conduct a successful class is the preparation he has had in the particular discipline.

In 1946 there were few states that had specific requirements for driver education teachers and few colleges and universities that offered courses in this field. As a result, it was necessary to institute a short-course program for the preparation of in-service teachers to meet the demands of the rapidly expanding program.

Over the years teaching requirements have become more realistic. Colleges and universities in many states have developed programs that provide for the equivalent of a teaching minor or major in safety and driver education. Some institutions offer advanced degree programs leading to the Master's or Doctor's degree. Institutions with an advanced degree program include Southern Illinois University at Carbondale, Michigan State University, Texas A & M, and Central Missouri State University. Many local school districts and some state departments of education have developed in-service professional growth programs for teachers in this area. The preparation of personnel for college- and university-level instruction, although somewhat improved, is still a generally unsolved problem in driver and traffic safety education. The national conference on safety education in 1973 included upgrading of teacher preparation and certification in driver education, and established much higher standards for college programs than existed previously.[15]

The Short-Course Program

The first course for driver education teachers was conducted at Pennsylvania State College in the summer of 1936. This was followed by a short-course program beginning in 1937 that was to bring, over a period of years, a series of one-week and sometimes two-week intensive workshops to nearly every state in the nation. Most of these classes were conducted by staff representatives of the Center for Safety Education, the American Automobile Association, and the Association of Casualty and Surety Companies acting as visiting instructors on college and university campuses throughout the country.

These classes were concentrated, basic courses in driver education, usually ranging from 32 to 40 hours. The courses were designed to give the potential driver education teacher an overview of the program and as much background in each of the areas of instruction as the limited time allowed. An obvious weakness of this procedure in teacher preparation was the lack of depth achievable in so short a period of time. Most of these new teachers received very little and sometimes no instruction at all in actual behind-the-wheel teaching using dual-control cars. Very few of them taught a nondriver the fundamental skills of driving, as is now required in most college courses. Simulators and range programs were not in operation during the early stages of the development of these short courses. Most short courses included instruction in the use of psychophysical testing devices and the significance of physical and psychological characteristics of drivers among other facets of the course. They also emphasized the value of bringing resource persons, such as police officers and insurance specialists, into the classroom to supplement the instructional program.

These short courses were necessary to meet a demand that colleges were not prepared to meet. The work of short-course instructors was

[15] American Driver and Traffic Safety Education Association, *Policies and Guidelines for Preparation and Certification of School Safety Personnel* (Washington, D.C.: The Association, 1974).

40

aided by the fact that they were working primarily with teachers who had credentials in other subject areas and a knowledge of organizing and presenting instructional materials in a teaching situation. However, several states developed special credentials that permitted school bus drivers, police personnel, and other persons without a teaching background to become eligible to teach driver education. This procedure was predicated on the assumption that a person who had driven satisfactorily could also teach driver education. No state permits such credentialing practices today.

There were approximately 20,000 teachers in the United States who received their background in driver education through this type of instructional program. Many of these persons never taught high school driver education, and still others left the field after a short time. Most of those who are still teaching have received additional instruction in college classes or in-service training programs. Many of them became excellent teachers and have contributed materially to the growth and development of driver education. Through this short, intensive program it was possible to develop a great enthusiasm and a crusading zeal that very likely does not exist to the same degree in the more traditional methods of preparing teachers today. However, it was generally recognized that this was an emergency procedure and that, if driver education was to establish itself as a respected member of the secondary school curriculum, it must give way as readily as possible to well-planned programs for driver education teachers conducted in the teacher preparation institutions.

In-Service Professional Growth

It is an accepted practice in the education field to provide for in-service professional growth activities for teachers. The types of programs differ greatly, from the highly structured credit course offerings of colleges and universities to the more informal nature of activities in counties and smaller districts throughout the nation. State or regional teacher conventions are held in most states providing opportunities for special driver education meetings. Regardless of the types of programs, they are all designed for the purpose of professional betterment of teachers actively engaged in the profession.

In-service programs for driver education follow the pattern of diversity to be found in the profession as a whole. Effective programs of an in-service nature are particularly needed in the field of driver education because, first, so many teachers have a limited academic background in the subject, and second, the field is changing so rapidly that a formal contact with the profession is necessary for the teacher to keep up to date on new developments. This need is met in several ways, as follows:

1. In-service institutes or workshops set up by local school districts.
2. State or regional workshops sponsored by the state department of education or county departments.

3. Section meetings held in conjunction with state teacher association meetings.
4. Workshops and conventions sponsored by professional driver education associations at local, state, and national levels.
5. Special meetings and workshops organized by colleges and universities.
6. Special meetings and workshops sponsored by private sector agencies interested in improving the competencies of teachers.

Preparing College Instructors

Prior to 1937 there were few courses in driver education in the high school, so no need existed for classes on the college level. Some classes in safety education for teachers were taught at the college level, usually by a teacher in another field, such as health education or industrial arts, but with an interest in safety. He would gather materials from many sources because there were no college textbooks in the field, and it was almost certain that he had taken no courses. With the new demand for driver education teachers, college-level courses were not generally available for high school teachers, and there were no institutions with programs to meet the special needs of highly trained persons for colleges and universities. Many college programs were started by college teachers who had taken the short course for high school teachers or a special short course designed for college instructors who were interested in establishing a college program.

Recognizing the need for leadership training in safety and driver education, the Association of Casualty and Surety Companies provided a grant to New York University for the establishment of the Center for Safety Education at New York University in 1938. The Center provided the first doctoral-level program in the safety and driver education field. Many college and university safety educators today have received at least part of their academic training at the Center, and a large percentage of the doctoral-level studies have been conducted there.

THE INFLUENCE OF LEGISLATION

State legislation to provide reimbursement for the extra costs involved in providing driver education instruction has provided a stimulus to the growth of the program in many parts of the country. Although most states reimburse only the costs of the laboratory phase of the program, some provide for classroom instruction as well. The school districts are reimbursed from $10 to $85 per pupil trained according to the specific state law.

The first state to enact driver education legislation was Delaware, in 1947. By 1965 there were 31 additional states with similar laws. Some of the new laws provided that a young driver could obtain a license one or two years earlier if he had successfully completed a high school driver education course. With the passage of the Highway Safety Act of 1966, it is assumed that all states have some form of legislation, rule, or regulation that supports driver education.

The funds to pay for the program are taken from several different sources within the various states. The recommended practice of taking the funds from the state general funds, just as other funds for educational purposes, is followed in some states. Penalty assessments on fines for moving violations, an addition to the registration fee, or an addition to the driver license fee are some of the most frequent means of obtaining the necessary revenue to support the program.[16]

LEARNING ACTIVITIES

1. With the use of this chapter's selected resources and content, identify the ten most significant events in the evolution of the driver education movement. What was the importance of each?
2. Develop a paper, using appropriate research evidence, to justify the placement of driver education in the secondary school curriculum.
3. Compare and contrast *standards* for driver education as depicted in the text with those standards that exist in your state. Discuss your findings with the class.
4. Identify the type of driver education financial aid provided the local school districts in your state. Suggest ways of improving the state laws establishing such aid.
5. Organize a class discussion around the subject, "The Value of a Professional Organization of Teachers as a Means of Improving the Quality of Instruction in Driver Education."

SELECTED RESOURCES

Aaron, James E., and Marland K. Strasser. *Driving Task Instruction—Dual-Control, Simulation, and Multiple-Car.* New York: Macmillan Publishing Co., Inc., 1974.

Brody, Leon, and Herbert J. Stack. *Highway Safety and Driver Education.* Englewood Cliffs, N.J.: Prentice-Hall, Inc., 1954, pp. 317-27, 381-89.

Key, Norman. *Status of Driver Education in the United States.* Washington, D.C.: National Education Association, 1960.

Lane-Reticker, Edward. *Driver Education in High Schools—An Inquiry into Costs, Results, and Related Factors.* Chapel Hill: University of North Carolina, n.d.

McKnight, A. James, and Bert B. Adams. *Driver Education Task Analysis, Volume III: Instructional Objectives.* Department of Transportation. PB202-247, Hum RRO Report 71-9 (March 1971).

Moran, Mary K. "The Accident Rate of High-School Drivers," *Safety Education Digest* (Fall 1951), pp. 62-67.

National Commission on Safety Education. *Policies and Guidelines for Teacher Preparation and Certification in Driver and Traffic Safety Education.* Washington, D.C.: National Education Association, 1965.

[16] National Safety Council, *Driver Education Status Report, 1972-73.* (Chicago: The Council, 1974), p. 34.

————. *Policies and Practices for Driver Education.* Washington, D.C.: National Education Association, 1954.

————. *Policies and Practices for Driver Education.* Washington, D.C.: National Education Association, 1960.

————. *Policies and Practices for Driver and Traffic Safety Education.* Washington, D.C.: National Education Association, 1964.

————. *Special State Financial Support for Driver Education.* Washington, D.C.: National Education Association, 1963.

National Safety Council. *Accident Facts.* Chicago: The Council, published annually.

Office of the Quartermaster General, Military Training Division. *Pre-Induction Driver Education in Schools and Colleges.* Washington, D.C.: The Office, 1943.

Research Division in collaboration with National Commission on Safety Education. *A Critical Analysis of Driver Education Research.* Washington, D.C.: National Education Association, 1957.

The President's Highway Safety Conference. *Action Program.* Washington, D.C.: The Conference, 1946.

Chapter 3

Driver Education as a School Function

OBJECTIVE: The student will be able to define the role of the schools in society and understand and apply the objectives of driver and traffic safety education.

"The goals of traffic safety education—the building of responsible citizens and the conservation of human life—have unprecedented significance today and for the years ahead." Thus begins the Education Section of the Action Program for Highway Safety report of the President's Committee for Traffic Safety.[1]

In order to accomplish these goals, the secondary schools of the nation must play a prominent role. Indeed, the nation's schools have always occupied an important position in the resolution of social problems that have plagued the nation. It was but a natural approach when the schools in the 1930s accepted the challenging responsibility of developing competent traffic citizens through the organization of driver and traffic safety education curricula. The rapid growth of traffic safety and driver education is a dynamic example of the acceptance of the role of schools in the education of traffic citizens. In a free society such as ours, the schools have traditionally recognized that their roles go considerably beyond that of preparing the youthful citizen to simply read, write, and interpret history. Thus the high school curriculum of the past two decades has made a concerted

[1] President's Committee for Traffic Safety, "Education Section," *Highway Safety Action Program* (Washington, D.C.: The Committee, 1962), p. 3.

45

effort to harmonize the so-called traditional subjects and the subjects that are designed to teach individuals how to apply their intelligence and how to live successfully. The high school curriculum that is emerging in the 1970s is designed to educate the student along traditional lines but at the same time has as one of its major roles educating people toward social responsibility in a free society.

THE ROLE OF SCHOOLS IN SOCIETY

It has always seemed reasonable to look upon the school as the fundamental instrument for shaping the citizen. The school is the most nearly universal of all social institutions. It is in effect the lone social institution that seeks contact with all young persons. In addition, it reaches them during that period of their lives when they are most susceptible to influence. In the final analysis, the school's very purpose is to help young people develop. Rodgers and Cutter raise the question: "Is not the total job of our educational system to teach students both how to learn and how to live? Can we defend any system of education in this modern world which strives for the development of the mind and ignores the welfare of the body in which the mind functions?"[2]

The school aims to produce in students the ability to think about and to assume social obligations. The elementary school generally provides the child's first extended experience with society outside the home. For the elementary child the school is society. Specifically, the school provides a secure environment for learning and practicing the skills of social interaction. With the coming of adolescence, the intellectual and social abilities and the needs of young people increase in depth and scope. The task of promoting intellectual growth and social responsibility is therefore of a different nature at the secondary level.

Understanding social organization is basically a rational process involving factual knowledge, discovery of the relationship of things, and sensitivity to philosophical assumptions. The behavioral sciences in general provide understanding of the value structures that give coherence and distinctiveness to our social system. Thus the secondary school's driver and traffic safety education curriculum assumes an enhanced position of importance in the general education of the secondary school student. Fundamentally the philosophical basis and objectives of each program complement the other.

Search for a Philosophy

Throughout the years attempts have been made to give direction to the educative process by means of systems of values or philosophies.

[2] Virgil Rodgers and Walter Cutter, "Driver Education: The Case for Life," *The American School Board Journal* (October 1958).

46

Traditionally the major philosophies that have had important bearings upon educational theory and practice are idealism, realism, and pragmatism or instrumentalism. These philosophies deal with such concepts as metaphysics (nature of the universe), epistemology (theory of knowledge and the relationship of the human mind to the universe), and ethics (the principles for the guidance of individual and social action). These have influenced in large measure the foundation of the nation's educational system. However, many efforts have been made to refine, expand, or delimit the emphasis or philosophical principles on which each of these systems is based. This is as it should be, for there should be a continuing search for a philosophy of education that better interprets the educational goals of the nation's schools.

In a democratic society educational goals are quite different from those of a totalitarian society. Alberty and Alberty state that democracy may be interpreted to embrace three interrelated ideals:[3]

1. It is a form of social organization that holds that the optimal development of the individual—of all individuals—is the highest good.
2. Man can achieve his highest possible development only through acting in concert with his fellows, each individual being sensitive to the effects of his acts upon others.
3. That optimal development of all can be realized only to the extent that people have faith in intelligence as a method of solving individual and group problems.

As these ideals are interpreted in the light of educational goals, it is obvious that the secondary school curriculum should do the following:[4]

1. Provide for all America's youth.
2. Be based upon the common and specialized needs, interests, and problems of the student.
3. Use modes of behavior that are characteristic of democratic living at its best as guides to the development of youth.

The driver education curriculum is uniquely fitted to assist in the achievement of the ideals. Therefore it is a basic part of the general education program of the school and should be available to all American youth. Figure 3-1, a statement from the Michigan Department of Public Instruction, clearly identifies the contribution of driver education to the secondary curriculum.[5]

It is evident that the driver education curriculum is an integral part of the prevailing philosophies of education and makes a substantial

[3] Harold B. and Elsie J. Alberty, *Reorganizing the High School Curriculum* (3rd ed.; New York: Macmillan Publishing Co., Inc., 1962), p. 53.

[4] Ibid, pp. 66–70.

[5] Michigan Department of Education. *Driver Education Contribution to the Secondary Curriculum* (Lansing, Mich.: The Department).

MICHIGAN DEPARTMENT OF PUBLIC INSTRUCTION
Lansing 2, Michigan

DRIVER EDUCATION CONTRIBUTIONS TO THE SECONDARY CURRICULUM*

Driver Education Helps to Meet the Needs of Youth

1. It can contribute to the occupational life of all youth. Good driving skills are part of everyone's occupational skills.

2. It can contribute to the mental health of youth by improving their driving skills and attitudes toward other drivers.

3. It can contribute to the concepts of democracy as a way of life held by youth through their situational experiences of driving safely, efficiently, and courteously. Youth learn to understand the rights and duties of the democratic citizen driver, and to be diligent and competent in the performance of their obligations as democratic citizen drivers.

4. It can contribute to the wise purchase and intelligent use of automotive power—a major financial investment over the course of one's lifetime.

5. It can contribute to the good use of leisure time wisely budgeted. Youth learn to appreciate the proper role of the automobile in their leisure time activities. Such appreciations find no value in using cars for playing "chicken" or drag racing on our streets and highways. .

6. It can contribute to the understanding of the influence of science on human life through a study of automotive power and the socio-economic effects of the automobile on 20th century living.

7. It can contribute to the development of respect for other persons since other persons are also fellow drivers and highway users. In this respect, it can aid youth to grow in their insight into ethical values and principles, to be able to cooperate with other highway users. We drive as we live.

8. It can contribute to the ability to think rationally since rational thought guides the actions of the good driver behind the wheel.

Driver Education Helps to Meet the Needs of Society

As driver education helps people to become safe, efficient, socially responsible, citizen drivers, it becomes a dynamic force for:

1. Reaching our goal of a smooth, safe, efficient flow of traffic. Our free economic system must supply the basic needs of people without loss or interruption.

2. Helping people to understand democratic principles and to live these principles on our highways.

3. Saving our natural and human resources. Our society cannot afford to expend the lives of 40,000 people each year who die needlessly in traffic accidents.

4. Preserving happy families. Traffic accident results have "wrecked" too many families.

5. Preserving fundamental social, moral, and spiritual values.

---

* Contributions are derived from the imperative needs of youth and society as defined in: Planning for American Youth, Revised Edition; National Association of Secondary School Principles (1201 Sixteenth Street N.W., Washington 6, D.C. 1951) pp. 8, 9.

Figure 3-1. Driver Education Contributions to the Secondary Curriculum (Courtesy Michigan Department of Public Instruction)

contribution to the achievement of the goals of a democratic society. As secondary school curricula are reviewed and evaluated, they should include a comprehensive program of driver and traffic safety education. Moreover, a concerted effort should be made to improve substandard curricula.

Extension of Values

By 1980 there shall be an estimated 4.2 million young people who will become eligible for driver licenses yearly. Obtaining such a license should be but one of the outcomes of offering a quality driver education course. The values to be derived go far beyond teaching students to be proficient drivers. Mr. Byron W. Hansford, Commissioner of Education, State of Colorado, states that a quality course in driver education contributes directly to the goals of education. Specifically he states the following as goals of education, where driver and traffic safety education can make a major contribution:[6]

1. Command of the knowledge, skills, habits, and attitudes essential for effective learning throughout life.
2. Understanding of man and society, and the determination to strive for the welfare of all people.
3. Knowledge of self, understanding of one's own characteristics and motivations, and appropriate development of individual abilities and interests.
4. Proficiency in recognizing and defining problems, thinking critically, objectively, and creatively about them, and acting constructively toward the solution.
5. Confidence in one's own abilities, courage, and initiative in the face of difficulties, and creativity and leadership in resolving them.
6. Skills, attitudes, and understandings necessary for effective group action and satisfying human relationships.
7. A philosophy based upon values conducive to sound character, ethical and moral behavior, and democratic action.
8. Knowledge, attitudes, and self-understanding basic to the achievement and maintenance of physical and mental health.

In addition, the driver education curriculum makes other major contributions to the total school program. Some of these are discussed in the last section of this chapter.

CARDINAL PRINCIPLES OF EDUCATION

The human organism continuously absorbs, transforms, and expends energy to accomplish its goals. Basically, learning is a matter of both analysis and synthesis. Therefore, if the learner and learning

---

[6] Byron W. Hansford, *Elements of a Good Driver Education Program.* Report of the Regional Driver Education Workshop, The President's Committee for Traffic Safety (February 1964), p. 15.

are to be regarded, then the curriculum maker must study the adolescent in his environment in order to determine his needs, interests, and problems.

The seven Cardinal Principles of Education relate specifically to safety education. Within this framework the goals of the driver and traffic safety education curricula must be determined. Indeed, the goals of education emerge from such a philosophical foundation. The statement of the Commission on the Reorganization of Secondary Education sets forth best the philosophy and goals of education in a free society. These are summarized and known as the classic Cardinal Principles of Secondary Education. The principles are (1) health, (2) command of fundamental processes, (3) worthy home membership, (4) vocation, (5) citizenship, (6) worthy use of leisure, and (7) ethical character.[7]

Health

To use properly the nation's streets and highways, good physical, emotional, and mental health are essential. Good traffic citizens are better able to make correct judgments, anticipate environmental hazards, and apply acquired knowledge when the human organism functions at peak proficiency.

Command of Fundamental Processes

The efficient utilization of basic intelligence and of concepts learned through the educative process is enhanced in a good driver and traffic safety education class. Students are required to read and interpret data, and to learn and apply natural and man-made laws, in addition to gaining a more complete knowledge of human behavior.

Worthy Home Membership

Since American families rely on the car for a variety of daily occupational, recreational, and general use, personal responsibility is vital to the safety of the family unit. The family member must accept responsibility for the safety of others and himself if he is to be a worthy family member.

Vocation

Job opportunities abound that are directly or indirectly related to the use of motor vehicles. In the United States approximately one in

[7] Commission on the Reorganization of Secondary Education, *Cardinal Principles of Secondary Education* (Washington, D.C.: U.S. Office of Education, Bulletin No. 35, 1918).

seven persons are thus employed. Next to agriculture, the field of transportation employs the largest work force in the nation. Therefore, training is needed to fulfill these needs in industry and in the military.

Citizenship

The principles of citizenship related to the proper use of streets and highways are similar to the fundamental objectives of national citizenship. There are many similarities between being a good national citizen and being a good traffic citizen.

Worthy Use of Leisure

With the reduction of the number of hours required to earn a living, the average family has more time to spend in leisure-time activities. Many such endeavors require the use of the family automobile. The towing of trailers and boats, for example, exposes the family to new traffic hazards. Therefore, the safe and proper use of the family car becomes more imperative than ever before.

Ethical Character

One of the major purposes of the driver and traffic safety education program is the development of personal character. Individual responsibility, respect for the law, and a genuine concern for others are the results of a high-caliber course. The reality of self-enforcement is the ultimate in the practice of ethical principles.

Thus there is a close relationship between the Cardinal Principles of Education and the driver education curriculum. School districts should be aware of these similarities and develop them to the fullest measure possible.

GENERAL EDUCATION IN SECONDARY SCHOOLS

The discipline of driver and traffic safety education derives its content from the physical, biological, and behavioral sciences. Therefore, in the curriculum design of the typical secondary school, the driver education program is assigned to that area designated as general education.

By definition, *general education is that phase of the school's curriculum required of all students at a given level and considered necessary to the development of the common values, attitudes, understandings, and skills needed for citizenship in a democratic society*. Today there is almost universal agreement among educators that a large part of the high school program should be devoted to the development of these learnings. It is evident that the driver education curriculum can assist to a great extent in accomplishing the objectives of a general education program. Figure 3-2 depicts the essence of the driver education curriculum. It is apparent that such a course of study would provide an excellent general as well as specific education for all American youth.

BEHAVIORAL SCIENCES

Guidance
Psychology
Sociology
Behavior of People
  Alcohol and drugs
  Civics
  Economics

BIOLOGICAL SCIENCE

Concepts of reaction time
Fatigue
Perception
Physical weakness
Physiological aspects of emotion
Physical effects of alcohol and drugs

PHYSICAL SCIENCES

Friction
Inertia
Momentum
Force of impact
Kinetic energy
Optics
Acceleration
Gravity
Centrifugal force
Power transmission

Figure 3.2   Foundation of Driver Education Curriculum

Local Boards of Education

Local boards of education should recognize the values to be derived from a quality program of driver and traffic safety education, and this course should be assigned a specific place in the school's general education curriculum. A specific department of driver and safety education should be available to assume responsibility for the organizing, managing, and teaching of this course. However, if such a department is not yet realized, then the course should be assigned division status in an existing department.

State Department of Education

The responsibility of recommending that the driver education curriculum be an integral part of the general education program of the local school district lies in the hands of the respective state department of education. Because leadership for all educational programs emanates from the chief school officer of the state, he should advise schools of the proper assignment for all curriculum areas. Thus the state department of education can do much to place the driver and traffic safety curriculum in the proper perspective at the local school district level. State departments also develop state curriculum guides and set teacher certification standards.

OBJECTIVES OF DRIVER AND TRAFFIC SAFETY EDUCATION

The need for driver and traffic safety education is obvious to all who observe human behavior on the nation's streets and highways. Therefore, in a society that utilizes motor vehicles as extensively as ours, it is not surprising to find that in a relatively short period of time, the program has become an integral part of the secondary school curriculum.

In the planning and organizing of learning experience for students, the administrator, supervisor, and teacher should consider the objectives of the driver education program. Without such consideration, the foundation and direction of the curriculum would be haphazard at best.

General Objectives

The national conferences on driver education have given serious thought to the ultimate objectives of the driver and traffic safety education curriculum. The most recent conference states that upon completion of a high school driver education course, students will be able to do the following:[8]

1. Describe or, under simulated conditions, demonstrate techniques for coping with critical driving situations.
2. Formulate a set of guidelines to avoid harmful highway consequences resulting from misuse of alcohol or other drugs.
3. List the primary components of a comprehensive highway safety program and identify the general purpose of each component.

Classroom Objectives

Although the classroom phase of the driver education program seeks to fulfill the general objectives, it is best that objectives be identified that can best be achieved in the classroom setting. The basic objectives of the classroom program enable students to do the following:[9]

1. Develop a set of strategies for preventing various psychological, physiological, social, or other factors from having an adverse effect on one's ability to perform the driving task.
2. Define the legal and moral responsibilities of highway users.

[8] American Driver and Traffic Safety Education Association, *Policies and Guidelines for Driver and Traffic Safety Education* (Washington, D.C.: National Education Association, 1974), p. 14.

[9] Ibid., p. 14.

Laboratory Objectives

Through the laboratory phase of the driver education program, other specific objectives are accomplished. Such objectives may be observed in the classroom program but can be best identified as separate purposes of the practice driving phase of the total curriculum. The objectives of the laboratory course enable students to do the following:[10]

1. Be prepared with minimum performance capabilities for entry into the highway transportation system as vehicle operators.
2. Develop visual and perceptual skills to a minimum level of proficiency in the safe operation of a vehicle.
3. Learn and apply basic maneuvers necessary to operate a vehicle safely.
4. Learn and apply basic evasive action maneuvers necessary to avoid critical path crash situations.
5. Apply learning to a variety of traffic environments (including night driving) with skill and proficiency to a minimum level of safe performance.
6. Acquire the insights and motivations needed to become functioning operators and responsible members of the highway transportation system.

DUAL-CONTROL OBJECTIVES. To enable students to do the following:[11]

1. Demonstrate a level of proficiency in the human functions (identification, prediction, decision, and execution) suffcient to perform legally and safely as they interact with other highway users in routine and difficult system environments.
2. In the driver education car, demonstrate the ability to deal with oncoming vehicles by choice of traffic lane, position within the lane, and speed adjustment to avoid collisions.

SIMULATOR OBJECTIVES. To enable students to do the following:[12]

1. Perceive common and unusual traffic hazards.
2. Respond correctly to selected driving emergencies.

MULTIPLE-CAR OBJECTIVES. To enable students to do the following:[13]

1. Apply those skills involved with basic vehicle control (manipulation).
2. Apply those techniques involved with decision making for conflict avoidance.

[10] James E. Aaron and Marland K. Strasser, *Driving Task Instruction—Dual-Control, Simulation, and Multiple-Car* (New York: Macmillan Publishing Co., Inc., 1974), p. 51.
[11] ADTSEA, op. cit., pp. 14–15.
[12] Ibid., p. 14.
[13] Ibid., p. 14.

To achieve the classroom and laboratory objectives, it is necessary for the driver and traffic safety education program to be organized on the same basis as all other courses in the total school curriculum. Moreover, the program must be developed on a comprehensive and continuous basis.

TOTAL SCHOOL CURRICULUM

In addition to the contributions previously mentioned, driver and traffic safety education is uniquely constituted to make other contributions to the total school curriculum. As Rodgers and Cutter state, "Any well-founded discipline utilizing an established and substantial body of teaching material which results in the safe enjoyment of our vehicles plus the conservation of incalculably valuable human resources, merits a worthy place within the whole discipline of learning."[14] Driver education is an academically oriented secondary school discipline. The following is a general discussion of the discipline nature of driver and traffic safety education and the contributions this course can make to other important aspects of the total school curriculum.

A Discipline

Because the curriculum of driver and traffic safety education meets the requirements of an academic discipline, it is classified as such. The questions may be asked, "What are the characteristics of a discipline, and does driver education meet them?" The answer to the latter question is yes, based on the knowledge that the area being discussed meets the following requirements of an academic discipline. Shermis states that a discipline is characterized by:[15]

1. A rather impressive body of time-tested works.
2. A technique suitable for dealing with their concepts.
3. A defensible claim to being an intimate link with basic human activities and aspirations.
4. A tradition that both links the present with the past and provides inspiration and sustenance for the future.
5. A considerable achievement in eminent men and significant ideas.

De Nike reports, "The materials of instruction, teaching methods, testing, and evaluation procedures of a good course in driver education compare very favorably with any of the so-called academic subjects."[16] In the well-organized and -taught course, the subject matter can be as academic as the instructor desires. The content of driver education is derived from the behavioral, physical, and biological sciences, giving the course an interdisciplinary basis.

[14] Rodgers and Cutter, op. cit., p. 24.
[15] S. Sherwin Shermis, "On Becoming an Intellectual Discipline," *Phi Delta Kappan* (November 1962), p. 84.
[16] Howard R. De Nike, "Why Driver Education?" *Safety Education* (November 1962), p. 24.

Figure 3-3. Modern Instructional Approaches (Courtesy Photos by Paul Lambert, Eastern Kentucky University, Public Information)

In addition, the driver and traffic safety education curriculum may serve as the stimulus for the development of a comprehensive traffic safety program throughout the entire school system. However, one course does not constitute a total traffic safety program effort. Consideration should be given to those activities and projects that are beyond the formal course of instruction, and attempts should be made to identify other disciplines in which highway safety could be an integrated phase contributing to that subject. Because there is a recognized body of organized content, many colleges offer teaching minors and majors in traffic and safety education. This background is imperative to the proper teaching of this subject.

Guidance Concept

In Chapter 4 the relationship between the school's guidance and driver education programs is explored. Benefits other than those mentioned in this chapter may be derived from a close working partnership of these two departments.

These departments can work very closely in the elimination of many school dropouts. The driver and traffic safety program may serve as a motivation to the borderline student who desires to leave school because he is not interested in education. Many such students can be properly motivated and salvaged through a quality program of driver and traffic safety education. This is one of the reasons for insisting that the teacher of this subject have a substantial background in guidance, counseling, and psychology in addition to traffic and safety education. The driver education program could also serve as a deterrent to the prospective juvenile delinquent. The objectives of the driver education curriculum are such that the typical secondary school student should emerge as a responsible citizen of society. If the delinquent student is enrolled and handled properly, he too might be molded into a responsible individual with respect for the dictates of society and the willingness to cooperate with others. Of the youths under 25 years of age convicted of major crime, approximately 90 per cent are convicted of crimes involving the auto in one way or another. A driver education course that properly inculcates the concept of the socially acceptable use of automobiles could be one of the greatest possible deterrents to juvenile delinquency.

Special Education

Today there are many physically and mentally handicapped students enrolled in the secondary schools of the nation. Such students have mental, orthopedic, or sensory impairments. Many of these students are capable of learning how to operate motor vehicles safely and efficiently. However, close cooperation between the special education teachers and the driver education instructor is necessary. Moreover, each of them must mutually understand the conceptual structure of safety education for the handicapped so as to determine which students are capable of receiving instruction. These students need special equipment, such as hand brakes, accelerators, and other special control mechanisms, and they learn better through the use of the driving simulation method.[17] It would appear that programs for handicapped students are to be in more demand in the future. Therefore, the driver and traffic safety education curriculum should be designed to accommodate these students when called upon to do so. Gutshall states, "Driver education for disabled students presents some unique problems, of which lack of confidence is the most difficult. The disabled student often feels extremely insecure in the car learning situation, and needs much assurance that he is succeeding and is progressing satisfactorily."[18] The ability to drive an automobile is one of the greatest factors in making these people feel that they have adjusted to society. It increases their employment potential and goes a long way toward making them useful and productive citizens. Particular curricular recognition should be given to this great educational need.

LEARNING ACTIVITIES

1. Given the materials in this chapter and the selected resources at the end of this chapter, develop a brief paper on the subject, "The Objectives of Driver and Traffic Safety Education."
2. Identify a secondary school and obtain a copy of the written objectives of its functioning driver education laboratory program. Compare and contrast those objectives with the laboratory objectives presented in this chapter. Write a summary of your findings and give them to your instructor.
3. Conduct a study (survey questionnaire) to determine the attitude of students on your campus regarding the role of driver education in the school's curriculum. Be prepared to present your results in class.
4. Interview a member of the special education faculty on your campus to determine what competencies a driver education teacher needs to teach handicapped students how to drive.
5. Describe in a term paper how the Cardinal Principles of Education relate to the development of a driver education program.

SELECTED RESOURCES

Aaron, James E., and Marland K. Strasser. *Driving Task Instruction—Dual-Control, Simulation, and Multiple-Car.* New York: Macmillan Publishing Co., Inc., 1974.

American Driver and Traffic Safety Education Association. *Policies and Guidelines for Driver and Traffic Safety Education.* Washington, D.C.: The Association, 1974.

Bloom, Benjamin S. *Taxonomy of Educational Objectives, Handbook I—Cognitive Domain.* New York: David McKay Co., Inc., 1956.

[17] *Drivotrainer Digest,* "*Slow Learners Score High with Drivotrainer.*" III (October 1959), p. 9.

[18] Robert Gutshall, "The Handicapped Student and the Automobile," *Traffic Safety* (January 1962), p. 15.

Commission on the Reorganization of Secondary Education. *Cardinal Principles of Secondary Education.* Washington, D.C.: U.S. Office of Education, Bulletin No. 35, 1918.

De Nike, Howard R. "Why Driver Education?" *Safety Education* (November 1962), p. 24.

Drivotrainer Digest, "Slow Learners Score High with Drivotrainer," III (October 1959), p. 9.

Gutshall, R. "Handicapped Student and the Automobile," *Traffic Safety* (January 1962), p. 15.

Gwynn, J. Minor. *Curriculum Principles and Social Trends*, 3rd ed. New York: Macmillan Publishing Co., Inc., 1960.

Hansford, Byron W. *Elements of a Good Driver Education Program.* Report of the Regional Driver Education Workshop, The President's Committee for Traffic Safety (February 1964), p. 15.

Krathwohl, David R. *Taxonomy of Educational Objectives, Handbook II— Affective Domain.* New York: David McKay Co., Inc., 1956.

Michigan Department of Education. *Driver Education Contributions to the Secondary Curriculum.* Lansing: The Department.

National Education Association. *Schools for the 60's.* Washington, D.C.: The Association, 1963.

President's Committee for Traffic Safety, Education Section. *Highway Safety Action Program.* Washington, D.C.: The Committee, 1962, p. 3.

Rodgers, V., and Walter Cutter. "Driver Education: The Case for Life," *The American School Board Journal* (October 1958).

Shermis, S. Sherwin. "On Becoming an Intellectual Discipline," *Phi Delta Kappan*, Bloomington, Ind. (November 1962), p. 84.

Chapter 4

Education of the Traffic Citizen

OBJECTIVE: The student will be able to identify, discuss, and apply learning theories to the development of sound driver education curriculum and to apply the concepts of skill development, knowledge, and behavior modification to planned learning experiences in driver education.

The wide use of motor vehicles is one of the outstanding characteristics of modern life in the United States. And one of modern life's critical demands is that of learning to survive in a traffic environment. Society prior to the advent of the automobile was more simple than now. Today the citizen must learn to live and drive in an environment that makes heavy demands on the transportation of people and goods. To become an accomplished motor vehicle operator, the individual must possess the knowledge, attitudes, and skills needed for safety and efficiency in today's traffic. Besides driving skill, in an auto-dominated society, the complexity of laws, rules and regulations, and moral responsibilities ask much of the driver. In a very real sense, driving is a social interaction between people rather than an interaction between vehicles. The mark of the educated man is the capacity for perceiving relationships and meanings. This characteristic is a basic requirement for the driver and citizen today.

WHAT IS THE GOOD TRAFFIC CITIZEN?

There are several basic characteristics of the good traffic citizen. The Constitution of the United States contains those citizen rights and responsibilities that traffic citizens should strive to develop to the fullest. The very social and economic basis of our civilization is the mobility provided by cars. Individual responsibility is essential to the safe and efficient operation of our transportation system. The driver must realize that there are countless thousands of persons using highway space and that each driver must be responsible for the safety of himself, his passengers, other motorists, and other users of the streets and highways. The responsible traffic citizen makes every effort to apply his knowledge and skill to the safe operation of his car at all times.

Cooperation is another fundamental trait of the good traffic citizen. The driver must cooperate with other drivers, traffic law enforcement officers, the traffic courts, driver-licensing personnel, and others interested in traffic safety. The individual driver is an intimate part of a total scheme for the safe and efficient movement of vehicles and persons within the highway transportation system of the nation. Therefore, he must cooperate by accepting his role as seen by those concerned with his safety. The driver should be willing to cooperate for the common welfare of all persons using the highways.

Adequate knowledge is a prerequisite to the safe and efficient performance of the driving task. A person must possess a degree of the knowledge necessary to enable him to drive in all types of traffic environments in city and country, and from state to state, without becoming involved in traffic accidents or violating the intricate and often conflicting traffic laws. It is essential that the driver have knowledge relating to traffic laws, driver limitations, the vehicle, the highway, the role of traffic law enforcement, and many other concepts basic to safe motor vehicle operation.

Adequate knowledge and a high degree of skill are not enough to keep the driver accident-free in the complex traffic patterns of today. He also must utilize good judgment and a proper attitude in the application of these to the highway scene. Driver attitude is the single most important characteristic of the driver. A good traffic citizen must possess a positive attitude of responsible behavior behind the wheel of an automobile. He does this by showing courtesy, sportsmanship, and concern for others.

To develop a good traffic citizen today, the driver educator must use methods and techniques derived from twentieth-century instructional technology. Also, the driver education course must be organized and based on modern learning theories so as to inspire the student to learn and apply the habits, knowledge, skills, and attitudes essential to safe driving.

MODERN LEARNING THEORIES

Learning is a change in the individual as a result of the interaction of that individual and his environment that fills a need and makes him more capable of dealing adequately with his environment. An attempt to summarize principles of learning that underlie desirable teaching situations is always complicated, because there are several learning theories in practice. Hilgard[1] recently classified the many learning theories into two basic categories: (1) *stimulus-response* (connectionism, conditioning, and behaviorism), and (2) *cognitive* (Gestalt, organismic, and sign-significate). These learning theories apply to the teaching-learning situation in driver education. The education of the beginner driver requires much more than the teaching of the four basic components of driving—starting, stopping, turning, and backing. The driver education program content is related to the behavioral, physical, and biological sciences. Therefore the application of modern learning theories is necessary and desirable in the education of the traffic citizen.

In the development of the driver education program, it is essential that modern principles of learning be applied, based upon what is currently known about the learning process. The following seem to be solid psychological propositions concerned with learning.

The Learning Process

During the past two decades much has been discovered about how people learn. It is imperative that the driver educator be familiar with such concepts if he is to be an effective teacher. Deese states, "It is impossible to understand the behavior of human beings and that of most animals without knowing something about the basic principles of learning."[2]

The best-planned teaching provides a continuous cumulative sequence of successful experiences. A fundamental law of learning is related to the producing of successful or satisfying experiences for the student. Such experiences are the result of positive instruction. Practice or rote drill is not enough for effective learning. Repetition without indications of advancement is not an act of learning.

Individual readiness for any new learning is a complex product of interaction between such factors as physical maturity, the importance of learning to the learner, and freedom from threat. Stimulating new insights have been found effective for the learning efforts of human beings. Thus opportunity for fresh and stimulating experiences should be provided if effective learning is to result.

Students progress in the area of learning insofar as it is necessary to accomplish their specific purposes. Many times the learner will do only well enough to get by and pass a course. In this instance, the learner needs increased motivation in order to advance further and improve his learning. Another very basic fact about learning is related to the amount of frustration that the individual experiences. When the student experiences too much frustration, his behavior

[1] Ernest R. Hilgard, *Theories of Learning* (2d ed.; New York: Appleton-Century-Crofts, 1956).

[2] James Deese, *The Psychology of Learning* (New York: McGraw-Hill Book Company, 1958).

ceases to be integrated, rational, and purposeful. Therefore the student who has experienced continuous failure will have to be dealt with differently from those who have experienced varying degrees of success. In view of the fact that undesirable behavior traits are characteristic of many chronic traffic offenders, the driver educator should be aware that the student may turn his failure into anger and lose respect for society.

The process of thinking involves the designing and evaluating of solutions for a problem as understood by the thinker. Students think when they encounter a difficulty, obstacle, or intellectual challenge that interests them. The individual must feel the need to advance and be eager to remove any hurdle in order for learning to take place. Individuals remember better new information that supports their previous attitudes than they remember new material that runs counter to their previous attitudes.

Studies have demonstrated that the best time to learn is when the learning can be useful. At this time motivation is strongest and retention greatest. Learned material is more likely to be retained if it is learned in a situation much like that in which it is to be used, and immediately preceding the time when it is to be used. If there is a discrepancy between the real course objectives and the instruments used to measure accomplishment, the latter generally becomes the main influence upon the choice of method and subject matter. Therefore curriculum and teaching geared to standardized tests and programed learning are likely to concentrate solely on learnings that can be easily stored and graded.

Ability to learn increases with age up to the adult years. Generally learning declines in the adult years due to lack of motivation. But those who *wish* to continue, even past 70 years of age, may indeed continue to master new ideas, ways of solving problems, and also languages. The driver education program is appropriate for secondary school students and adults alike.

These principles, regarding what is currently known about learning, emphasize the dimension and excellence of the learning process. Therefore the driver education teacher must be thoroughly acquainted with these processes and be able to apply them to the driver education program. The several references relating to aspects of the learning process at the end of the chapter provide an opportunity for the driver education teacher's development of greater understanding.

General Principles of Learning

The overall purposes of learning are relative to the social order within which they operate. In the application of the concept previously discussed, the driver educator must understand those general principles of learning that are identified by leading psychologists and educators as pertinent to the learning task. The following is a list of such principles that can be related directly to the driver education program. The driver education instructor must use these principles as a guide if the objectives of the driver education program are to be realized:[3]

1. The learning process is experiencing, doing, undergoing, and reacting.
2. The learning situation is dominated by a purpose or goal set by the learner or accepted by him and should lead to socially desirable results.
3. The learning situation, to be of maximum benefit, must be meaningful and realistic to the learner, and take place in a rich and satisfying environment.
4. Responses during the learning process are modified by their consequences.
5. The learner will persist through unpleasant situations, obstacles, and difficulties to the extent that he deems the objective worthwhile.
6. The learning process occurs through a wide variety of subject matters and experiences that are unified around a core of purpose.
7. The learning process and the accomplishment of results are intimately related to individual differences among the learners.
8. The learning process and achievement are affected by the level of aspiration set by the learner.
9. The learning process proceeds best when the individual can see results as knowledge of his progress and status when he achieves insight and understanding.
10. The background and history of the learner may enhance or hamper his ability to learn from a given teacher.
11. The learning proceeds most effectively when materials, experiences, and desired results are carefully adapted to the maturity and background of experience of the learner.
12. Distributive or spaced recalls are advantageous in fixing material that is to be long retained.
13. There is no substitute for repetitive practice in the learning of skills or in the memorization of unrelated facts that must be automatized.
14. Learning products when properly achieved and integrated are adaptable and complex, not static and simple.
15. The learning products are useful patterns of actions, values, meanings, attitudes, abilities, skills, and appreciations. The products are interrelated functionally.
16. The learning products are incorporated into the learner's personality slowly and gradually in some incidences, and with rapidity in others.
17. Transfer to new tasks will be more effective if, in learning, the learner can discover relationships for himself, and if he has experienced during learning the application of principles within a variety of tasks.

[3] William H. Burton, "Basic Principles in a Good Teaching-Learning Situation," *Phi Delta Kappan* (March 1958), pp. 242-44.

64

MOTIVATION OF LEARNING. The individual learns more readily if he is properly motivated. The teacher of driver education should be concerned about how the student might best be motivated to become a good traffic citizen. Greater opportunities to establish within a student acceptable patterns for safe living are enhanced through proper motivation. The following are guides that the instructor should use in his effort to motivate the student enrolled in the driver education program:

1. An individual who is motivated learns more readily than one who is not motivated. Motives may be either extrinsic or intrinsic, or specific or general.
2. Motivations that are too intense may be accompanied by distracting emotional conditions and by undesirable learning products.
3. Excessive motivation may be less effective than moderate motivation, especially for certain kinds of tasks.
4. Learning under intrinsic motivation is generally more productive than learning under extrinsic motivation.
5. Goals and purposes that are clear to the learner, that meet a need, and that restore the natural equilibrium of the learner are effective.
6. Motivation by success is preferable to motivation by failure.
7. Goals and purposes should be geared to the interests, activities, and maturities of the learners.
8. The more clearly the learner sees the realistic aspect of the learning situation, the better the learning that results.
9. Learning without purpose and learning to do difficult, distasteful, and unpleasant tasks under compulsion do not train the person to persist with unpleasant learnings in real life.
10. The maintenance of motivation is important to sustained learning situations.

The teacher of driver education has opportunities daily to utilize the principles of motivation listed here. In general, students are enthusiastic when they enroll in the driver education course. The principal responsibility of the teacher is to sustain this interest and make efforts to motivate the students that have a low level of aspiration for progress.

PLANNING LEARNING EXPERIENCES

The teacher of driver education has the responsibility for selecting learning experiences for his students. These experiences should be based upon what is currently known about the learning process and specific principles of learning as they are applied to the education of the traffic citizen. Further, learning experiences provided in driver education should be based upon a modern curriculum guide that has been designed around a driving task analysis approach. It is essential that the driver and traffic safety education program be developed as comprehensively as possible. The experiences chosen should assist in achieving the objectives of both the classroom and laboratory phases of the driver education program. Driver education is a total concept of education and must include both phases of the program so that students may learn sufficiently about the driving task.

Knowledge

Sufficient knowledge is important if the individual is to remain accident-free. Studies have determined that lack of knowledge does play a role in the causing of traffic accidents, but is not a major consideration. In a comprehensive driver and traffic safety education program, an opportunity should be provided for the student to acquire as much knowledge as possible that will assist him in becoming a safe and efficient motor vehicle operator. There are several high school driver education textbooks that contain material which can be developed by the teacher in assuring that the student has adequate knowledge for safe motoring. The typical high school text has topics such as the following: the traffic problem, the driving task, driver characteristics, forces of nature, traffic laws and enforcement, development of operational skills, development of judgment, motor vehicle administration, and vehicle use. These suggested topics give evidence that many knowledge concepts are involved in the development of a well-educated traffic citizen.

Many of the knowledge concepts of a quality driver education program are based upon those that are a part of other disciplines. For example, from the behavioral sciences come such concepts as the psychology of driver behavior, guidance and accident prevention, societal influences and accidents, human behavior in relation to the use of alcohol and drugs, and economic and civic responsibility. From the physical sciences, the following concepts play a most important role in the conduct of a driver and traffic education program: concepts of friction, momentum, inertia, force of impact, kinetic energy, optics, acceleration, gravity, centrifugal force, and power transmission. Finally, there are several concepts related to biological sciences that can play a most important role in developing knowledge necessary for safe motor vehicle operation. These concepts are reaction time, fatigue, perception, physical weakness, physiological aspects of emotion, and physical effects of alcohol and drugs.

Attitudes, Characteristics, and Role

Most traffic specialists agree that driver attitude is the most important single factor in traffic safety. A driver may have considerable knowledge and unusual skill in operating a motor vehicle, but if his behavior with respect to his driving responsibilities is misdirected, then in all probability he will be a dangerous risk in control of a car.

Most studies indicate that probably 85 per cent of all traffic accidents are caused by human failure. Most often human failure is described as improper driver attitude or behavior.

To be a competent educator of drivers it is necessary for the teacher to have a thorough understanding of the concept of attitude. The teacher must be capable of applying this concept to the development of safe and efficient motor vehicle operators among the secondary school students enrolled in his class. The purpose of this section shall be to clarify attitude so the teacher will better understand the significance of the development of attitude in the driver education program.

Several definitions of attitude are suggested in various literature. However, many of these are insufficient, because they appear to be incomplete or abstract. Krech and Crutchfield have defined an attitude as an *"enduring organization of emotional, perceptual, motivational, and cognitive processes with respect to an individual's world."*[4] This definition has received general acceptance by researchers and specialists in the traffic safety field. Therefore this is the definition of attitude that will be used in this book. This definition may appear to be quite abstract and vague. However, it simply defines an attitude as a structural part of personality that predisposes an individual to behave in certain ways.

CHARACTERISTICS OF ATTITUDES. The driver education instructor needs to understand the various characteristics of attitudes in order to plan his program of instruction. From the Krech and Crutchfield definition, certain inferences about the nature and characteristics of attitudes become apparent. They are as follows:

1. Attitudes color an individual's perception of his world.
2. Attitudes color an individual's understanding of his world.
3. Attitudes are learned or acquired from his environment.
4. Attitudes do not develop from a single experience.
5. Attitudes are immediate determinants of behavior when considered in relation to such basic personality traits as factors of adjustment.
6. Beliefs are part of the psychological foundation of attitudes.
7. Attitudes are positively related to adjustment. The nature of adjustment will determine the nature of attitudes to a large extent.
8. Attitudes are preservative of nature. They are durable and tend to resist change.

FUNCTIONS OF ATTITUDES. In addition to the characteristics listed, attitudes perform certain functions for personality. These, too, are important to the driver educator as he attempts to mold the attitude of his students.

Attitudes give continuity to personality. Experiences are assimilated into patterns, thereby rendering seemingly isolated experiences as related, associated incidents guiding future behavior. They give

[4] D. Krech and R. S. Crutchfield, *Theory and Problems of Social Psychology* (New York: McGraw-Hill Book Company, 1948).

meaning to varied perceptions and activities by relating them to one another. Attitudes satisfy personal needs, especially those of a social nature. Possession of certain attitudes facilitates acceptance in social groups where acceptance seems desirable. Also, attitudes simplify the daily business of perceiving our world. A person is not forced to react separately to each individual experience but rather is governed by attitudes already formed toward that type of experience.

It is quite obvious that the student enrolled in the high school driver education program is not void of attitudes based upon prior experiences. Rather, his attitudes and behavior have been developed by an extensive and complex series of former experiences. Mann suggests that attitudes are determined by the following:[5]

1. The feelings of emotional security, or insecurity, that have developed in his early life.
2. The type of his reactions to problem solving and frustrations.
3. His concept of himself in personal adequacy, self-respect, and feelings of acceptance.
4. His perception of the attitudes of others toward him. (Is he accepted and admired or rejected and belitted?)
5. Attitudes of parents and friends that are copied by the youngsters.
6. Attitudes of his peer group and the degree of compliance demanded by the group.
7. The mores of the community in which he lives, including attitudes toward traffic regulations and toward the police.
8. His image of the driver education teacher as a person interested in his welfare or as a critical individual who responds to his own feelings of inadequacy by ridiculing or punishing his students.
9. His image of the driver education teacher as an expert in traffic safety, who knows the broad problems and participates in many aspects of the development of traffic safety.
10. His comprehension of the total problem and his knowledge of the correct way to enjoy efficient driving with minimum hazard.

CHANGING ATTITUDES. One of the major tasks of the driver educator is that of shaping driver behavior. Attitudes are self-preservative in nature. Some of the factors responsible for this tendency are (1) social support of attitudes (2) ego involvement, and (3) withdrawal behavior. For the student, the changing of behavior may mean the loss of social acceptance and support. Ego-involved attitudes are closely related to one's concept of oneself and are far less easily changed than nonego-involved attitudes. A person tends to withdraw from situations that threaten his attitudes or that do not fit in with them.

Changing behavior is not an easy task. However, despite the important effects of cultural and social factors, and despite tendencies toward self-preservation, attitudes can be changed. Many studies in social psychology have demonstrated this fact. Generally speaking, at least three things must be ascertained about a person's attitude before attempts are made to alter it.

[5] William A. Mann, "Building Attitudes for Safety," *Transactions—National Safety Congress*, The National Safety Council, 1960, **23**, pp. 138-39.

First, what is the nature of the attitude, and what is its content? Care must be exercised not to assume that the beliefs upon which the attitude is based, and the emotional overtones that have become attached to the attitude, remain constant. Although an attitude is an enduring structure, its content may change as the individual matures or acquires more knowledge and more beliefs.

One must also be careful to determine just what position in the general personality structure of the individual is occupied by the attitude being investigated. What role does it play in the total personality structure? What areas of behavior does it govern?

Second, what needs of the individual are satisfied by the attitude? Certain errors that seem to populate investigations of the needs satisfied by an attitude are (1) failing to realize the functional significance of an attitude to the individual; (2) trying to generalize from person to person in asserting the need being fulfilled; and (3) ascribing needs that in the past were fulfilled by the attitude but are being fulfilled by it no longer.

Third, what is the nature of the social support of the attitude? Specifically what are the consequences for the individual if he should change the attitude? Will he gain or lose social support; will he be rejected by his social groups?

Knowing these things, it is possible to institute an effective and integrated program of action. This program must be designed to manipulate the individual's environment in such a way as to alter and control (1) the perceptions involved, (2) the needs and emotions involved, and (3) the motivational factors involved. Buck states, "These intangibles of behavior attitudes emphasize the problem of developing a method for determining not how well one CAN drive but how well one WILL drive."[6]

APPLICATIONS TO DRIVER EDUCATION. In the driver education classroom, the teacher's task is primarily one of developing or remolding attitudes. When change is needed, these same principles can be employed, whether on an individual basis or on a group basis. When the teacher's problem is one of expanding existing attitudes, the task of expansion is one of relating existing attitudes to the driving situation. This effort might center about the social and asocial aspects and about the realities of the driving situation. It should be enacted in terms of both the student's personal welfare and the welfare of his passengers and of others on the road.

The teacher should not try to preach attitudes. Platitudes about social responsibility, courtesy, and so on, and other directive techniques serve only to set up resistance in the pupils. The program should be an application of Dewey's philosophy, one of creating situations and drawing implications from them in a nondirective nonauthoritarian fashion. In this way, by participating in the learning situation, the pupil has the feeling that *he* has seen and learned the significant elements of the task of driving and the driving situa-

---

[6] Donald S. Buck, "Attitude—Key to Accidents," *Highway Research Abstracts* (Washington, D.C.: Highway Research Board, January 1952), p. 17.

tion; the pupil does not feel things are being forced upon him. Consequently, the natural and characteristic resistance of the adolescent to directive or authoritarian measures is not engendered or irritated. The responsibility of the teacher is to provide types of learning experiences that will permit the student to develop sound, socially acceptable attitudes of his own.

Further, the teacher should evaluate the pupils in a way that emphasizes these aspects of driving that are considerably less tangible evidence of one's potentiality for safe driving, but at the same time are considerably more significant than the manipulative skills alone. Admittedly such evaluations are more demanding on the teacher and involve more effort and work, but recognizing that skills are far less significant in causing accidents than such psychological factors as attitudes should provide a definite challenge.

Because attitudes result from a complexity of factors, what can the driver education teacher do to promote the development of wholesome driver attitudes? Mann suggests the following:[7]

1. The driver education teacher, as a person, must be a well-adjusted individual with genuine liking and concern for his students.
2. The driver education teacher must be broadly educated in traffic safety. He should have informed opinion of everything from selective enforcement to the advantages of one-way streets.
3. The driver education teacher should be well versed in the dynamics of human behavior, so that he can understand why individual students behave as they do and can help them to gain insights into their feelings and actions.
4. The curriculum should include a unit on attitudes and effects of personality that goes much deeper than treatment of the subject by our present textbooks.
5. Attitudes and personal responsibility should be woven throughout the course as opportunity presents itself.
6. In the car, courtesy to other drivers and pedestrians should be stressed and errors of other drivers, which result from faulty attitudes, should be pointed out.
7. Class projects, such as a community survey of driving irritations, should be assigned to bring the importance of attitudes to the students in an effective manner as well as giving them a feeling of realism in their studies.
8. Orientation should be given to the entire school faculty of the breadth and depth of driver education, so that unprofessional remarks of colleagues will not inhibit the growth of the student.
9. The class should make field trips to traffic courts, the traffic division of the police department, and the city traffic engineer, so that the student can better understand the functions of these agencies.
10. Talks should be given by traffic judges and police officers on policies and problems to help the student in his understanding of the errant driver and the difficulties enforcement agencies face.
11. Projects should be assigned or discussions held of the physiological and psychological effects of alcohol and drugs. We have tended in the past to omit or handle poorly such psychological effects, and have thus left doubts in the minds of our students.

[7]W. A. Mann, op. cit., p. 138.

12. A cooperative effort should be made with the school counselors and other teachers in helping individuals who exhibit symptoms of maladjustment and anxiety.
13. Students should be shown that personal behavior in accepting the responsibility necessary in driving is an integral part of the course. Students whose attitudes cause the teacher to feel that they will be unsafe drivers should be failed.
14. Parents should be informed of the goals of driver education, its limitations, and any individual weaknesses of their youngsters.
15. An adult education program should be conducted, including violator schools, releases to newspapers, radio and television, and talks to community organizations.
16. The driver education teacher must practice what he preaches and should encourage other teachers to follow acceptable driving behavior.

GUIDANCE CONCEPT. There is a very close relationship between the objectives of a driver education program and those of the school guidance and counseling program. In each case individuals are concerned with the problems of students and how they influence behavior. In addition to making a concerted effort to develop good citizenship on the part of the entire student body with the development of wholesome driver attitudes, many of the techniques that are used by guidance personnel are appropriate for use by the driver educator. The section on changing attitudes suggests that many techniques and methodologies from the behavioral sciences might well be used in the development of good traffic citizens. The teacher should contact the guidance counselor of his school to determine the extent to which cooperation may be developed in the conduct of the driver education program. The use of student personnel files can be helpful in modifying improper behavior of problem students.

Figure 4-1. Drivers Must Relate to Complex Traffic Environments (Courtesy Marshall University)

Skill Development

To be a proficient motor vehicle operator, the individual must possess adequate skill in the operation of a car. Most individuals can develop a minimum level of operational skill. However, to develop skills to the degree necessary for safe motoring in a traffic environment, it is necessary for the individual to learn correctly the fundamental procedures of driving and how to apply these in the various traffic environments. This is achieved through an education and training program designed to develop driving skills.

The driver educator must consider what conditions make possible the efficient learning and retention of motor skills. The following are suggested as basic considerations in the organizing and developing of a sound laboratory program in which the development of motor skills is one of the basic objectives.

PRACTICE. There is no condition of greater importance in the development of motor skills than practice—that is, repetition of the desired response sequence until it becomes a correct habit or automatic response. Current evidence suggests that improvement in motor skills usually continues over an extended period of time. To develop sufficient skills in the typical course, it is common practice for students to drive under the supervision of parents in addition to the driving time in class. The use of practice in the learning of motor skills increases the accuracy and the speed of performance.

FEEDBACK. Feedback refers to the teacher correction of student errors. In some instances errors are immediately obvious to the student; however, in others it is necessary for the instructor to identify the results and call them to the attention of the student driver. In the typical laboratory program, the teacher is the key to providing sufficient feedback to the student. However, with the simulator equipment developed in recent years an error identification panel provides instant feedback to the student when he commits a driving error. Such feedback strengthens the learning of motor skills by the beginning driver.

DRIVER STIMULI. Another basic consideration in the learning of motor skills is the awareness that most motor skills are to some degree externally controlled. Gagne states that "inputs to the behavior system may be described in terms of energy from the environment called *stimuli* which are detected by organs called receptors."[8] The driver is constantly receiving visual or auditory stimuli that influence his behavior behind the wheel. Many times the response made is an incorrect response, because of the injection of an incorrect stimulus that motivates the driver to react in a particular way. It is best to place the beginning driver in an environment in which correct stimuli are provided. Thus the guidance of initial learning of a skill may be accomplished through the proper selection of routes by the instructor, by the use of specialized practice driving areas, or by the use of

[8] Robert M. Gagne and E. A. Fleishman, *Psychology and Human Performance* (New York: Holt, Rinehart and Winston, Publishers, 1959), p. 13.

simulator equipment with which all of the films used are free of false response stimuli. The selection of correct stimuli is in part a function of perception. Therefore this shall be considered in a following section when perception is discussed.

PRACTICE DRIVING SCHEDULE. The way in which practice driving sessions are scheduled has a direct influence upon the learning of motor skills. Two primary factors to be considered that influence performance measured during the learning of motor skills are the amount of time in continuous practice and the interval between practice sessions.

Psychologists have determined that shorter practice periods lead to better performance. In addition, it has been ascertained that when such practice sessions are accompanied by a period or interval between trials, performance is improved much more readily than when practice is done on a mass or concentrated basis. Perhaps the most significant reasons presented in the support of spaced practice sessions are the changes in motivation experienced by the individual and the effects of fatigue when one is required to respond on a continuous basis in an effort to improve skill performance. Therefore it would appear to be desirable that a laboratory program be organized to extend over a period of time whereby the individual has sufficient opportunity to develop a high degree of skill. The National Conference on Safety Education recommends 90 hours as the minimum time allotted for a driver education course.[9] This includes laboratory instruction with in-car driving experience for each student. Through structured learning experiences students can be motivated and their performances enhanced.

PERCEPTION. In the laboratory phase of the driver and traffic safety education program the development of operational tasks is a fundamental objective. However, the development of perceptual processes is a far more significant objective to achieve. The driving task places many requirements upon the driver. The driving task model in Figure 4–2 points out those processes related to perception as the most important elements of the driving task.

By definition, *perception* relates to seeing and understanding. Therefore, it is necessary for the individual to identify the various stimuli in the driving environment and then proceed to interpret such stimuli. In view of the fact that approximately 90 per cent of human discriminations are based on what is seen, it is especially significant that these incoming data be interpreted properly by one's perceptual processes.

A human being perceives the world as composed of forms, motions, locations in space, color, and objects with recognizable features. It is the function of perception to harmonize these elements into an organized nature of behavior. In order for the teacher of driver education to give attention to the development of perception in his laboratory program, he should be aware of three essential factors that

[9] American Driver and Traffic Safety Education Association, *Policies and Guidelines for Driver and Traffic Safety Education* (Washington, D.C.: The Association, 1974), p. 15.

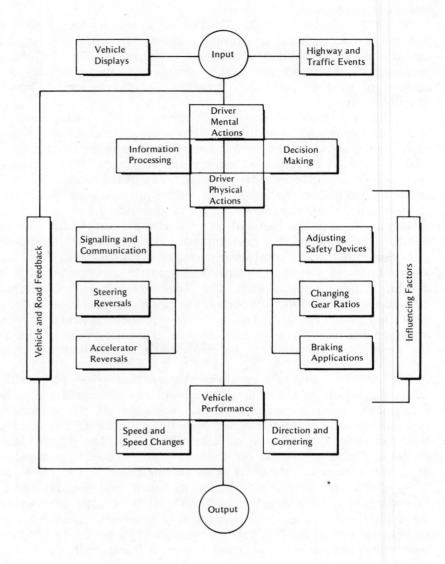

Figure 4-2. Driving Task Model (Courtesy State Board of Education—Illinois Office of Education)

have implications toward the development of the perceptual ability of the beginning driver. These factors are as follows:

1. Discriminating or sensory experiences.
2. Identifying incoming stimuli.
3. Organizing an identification response or pattern of behavior.

DISCRIMINATING OR SENSORY EXPERIENCES. One of the first prerequisites for visual perception is correct data or stimuli from the driving environment. Correct data aid in making proper responses and the development of correct habits. Individuals vary in their ability to see and interpret the visual stimuli that are received on a continuous basis while operating a motor vehicle. Platt[10] has determined there are approximately 200 events per mile that the driver sees and judges relative to the driving task. Each event must be seen properly for a correct judgment to be made. The ability to make proper judgments is based in part upon such visual skills as acuity, distance perception, depth perception, peripheral vision, glare recovery, night vision, and fixation changes.

IDENTIFYING INCOMING STIMULI. The vision faculties possessed by the average motorist serve to see or select visual stimuli that are constantly being received by the eye. The selection of the correct objects to see is important to driving; that is, information signs, pedestrians, and driver errors. Therefore the identifying of incoming visual stimuli is imperative to the safe operation of a motor vehicle.

ORGANIZING IDENTIFICATION RESPONSES OR PATTERNS OF BEHAVIOR. Psychologists inform us that as correct stimuli are received and correct responses made, the human mechanisms build what is called scales or models. These provide functional connections between sensory, neural impulses and the identification responses that the individual uses. In other words, the stimuli received undergo a process of internal organization. As additional stimuli are received the identification responses are refined and strengthened. The individual continues to utilize specific patterns formed as long as the environment provides the necessary stimuli and reinforcement for such learning to occur. Patterns of behavior must be the result of selecting correct stimuli from the environment and discarding those that are incorrect.

IMPLICATIONS FOR LABORATORY INSTRUCTION. The teacher of driver education should be able to apply these concepts of perceptual development in the conduct of the laboratory program. The following suggestions are made relative to the development of perceptual abilities on the part of the beginning driver:[11]

[10] Fletcher Platt, *Traffic Factors and the Driver* (Dearborn, Mich.: Ford Motor Company), p. 2.

[11] Warren P. Quensel, "Teaching Visual Perception in Driver Education," *ADEA News and Views*, American Driver Education Association, 3, No. 2 (May 1963), pp. 9-10.

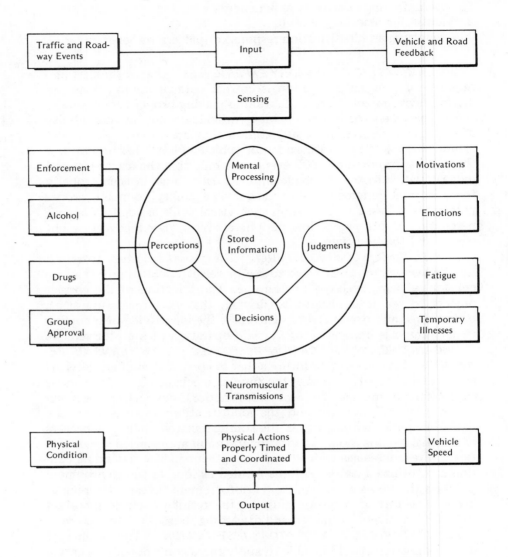

Figure 4-3. Human Functions Required for Driving Task (Courtesy State Board of Education—Illinois Office of Education)

76

1. Have the student master the basic motor skills of car operation before beginning intensive training in reading the traffic picture. Undue attention to motor skills will tend to interfere with training for visual perception, except that which is needed to learn such skills. When these operational tasks become semiautomatic so that drivers no longer have to formulate the acts in the mind, then attention is freed for perception of the overall traffic picture.

2. Demonstrate and guide student practice in real traffic situations as soon as the student is ready operationally. A student perceives something best when he has direct contact with real situations or events. By explanation, tell how and what to do, and what to look for, so that perceptual trends can be developed. Use key words that stand for certain conditions and actions, such as *margin of safety*, *space cushion*, *defensive tactic*, or *evasive action*. Try to limit guidance, so that the student will perform on his own as much as possible.

3. Choose routes with as many varied experiences as practical. Work for general patterns, so that transfer to similar situations will take place in the future. Judgment and organization of perception depend to a great extent on previous experiences.

4. Encourage and assist students to search for hazards. Try to give attention to hazardous elements that may be common to many situations. This means that an analysis of many local hazardous situations will be conducted to find out what these common elements are. Develop awareness of other drivers' errors. Strive for selection and reduction of cues.

5. Set up some situations as problems for students to solve. Make sure each problem has to do with the immediate traffic situation so that it does not become distractive to the student's immediate task.

6. Encourage the student to read the traffic picture well ahead, because perceptions take time, and reaction time can be crucial.

7. Have the student keep eyes moving so that the central vision will not become fixed. Make effective use of central vision (identification) and peripheral (detection) vision. The student should make this visual skill habitual. Explain how this skill prevents fatigue, resists distracting influences, and allows for more comfortable and pleasant driving.

8. Help the student adopt and strive for the goal of learning how to drive so as to reduce to the absolute minimum the possibility of accident.

9. Develop and have student observers (in back seat) use checklists that will assist in rating the performance of the student driver. This will also assist student observers to train their perceptual functions when not driving.

10. Demonstrate the commentary driving technique, and have students use the technique periodically. In using this technique, the student driver verbalizes what he sees. The comments must take place before the fact, not after. We are literally "picking" the driver's mind. This technique is not only useful for students in developing accurate perceptions, but it also gives the instructor a chance to evaluate the progress of the learning and teaching experiences and to plan for remedial instruction.

LEARNING ACTIVITIES

1. Given the selected resources at the end of this chapter, develop a research project on the subject, "Perception and How It Affects the Driving Task." Submit your report to your instructor.
2. Study the driving task model on page 74. Be prepared to lead a class discussion on your interpretation of the model.
3. Through the use of six selected resources, construct a definition of driver behavior. Compare your definition with those of other class members.
4. Visit a local high school driver education program. Discuss with the teacher the methods he uses to influence the driving behavior of a beginner driver.
5. Develop a classroom teaching aid that would assist in clarifying the principles of learning used in teaching driver education.

SELECTED RESOURCES

Aaron, James E., and Marland K. Strasser. *Driving Task Instruction—Dual-Control, Simulation, and Multiple-Car.* New York: Macmillan Publishing Co., Inc., 1974.

Automotive Safety Foundation. *A Resource Curriculum in Driver and Traffic Safety Education.* Washington, D.C.: The Foundation (January 1970).

Bloom, Benjamin S. *Taxonomy of Educational Objectives, Handbook I—Cognitive Domain.* New York: David McKay Co., Inc., 1956.

Buck, Donald S. "Attitude—Key to Accidents," *Highway Research Abstracts.* Washington, D.C.: Highway Research Board (January 1952), p. 17.

Gagne, Robert. "Modern Learning Principles and Driver Education," *Concepts.* Hartford, Conn.: Aetna Life & Casualty, Vol. 4, No. 2 (Spring-Summer 1971).

Gagne, Robert M., et al. *Psychological Principles in System Development.* New York: Holt, Rinehart and Winston, Publishers, 1962.

Gronlund, Norman E. *Stating Behavioral Objectives for Classroom Instruction.* New York: Macmillan Publishing Co., Inc., 1970.

Hilgard, Ernest R. *Theories of Learning,* 2nd ed. New York: Appleton-Century-Crofts, 1956.

Krathwohl, David R. *Taxonomy of Educational Objectives, Handbook II—Affective Domain.* New York: David McKay Co., Inc., 1956.

Krech, D., R. S. Crutchfield, and E. L. Ballachey. *Individual in Society.* New York: McGraw-Hill Book Company, 1962.

Mann, William A. "Building Attitudes for Safety," *Transactions —National Safety Congress,* The National Safety Council, 23 (1960), pp. 138–39.

Mourant, Ronald R., and Thomas H. Rockwell. "Strategies of Visual Search by Novice and Experienced Drivers," *Human Factors.* (August 1972), Vol. 14, No. 4, p. 325.

Platt, Fletcher. *Traffic Factors and the Driver.* Dearborn, Mich.: Ford Motor Company, p. 2.

Quensel, Warren P. "Teaching Visual Perception in Driver Education," *ADEA News and Views,* American Driver Education Association, 3, No. 2 (May 1963), pp. 9–10.

Chapter 5

The Teacher of Driver Education

OBJECTIVE: The student will be able to identify those qualifications necessary for one to become an effective teacher and to learn of those professional organizations, activities, and resources that enhance teacher competencies.

The teacher of driver and traffic safety education should have background preparation in his field comparable to that of teachers of the other disciplines in the secondary school curriculum. Success in accomplishing the objectives of the driver and traffic safety education program is in a large measure related to the competence of the teacher. Therefore, all teachers in the classroom and the laboratory phase should be required to meet the highest of standards.

During the past 25 years, teacher certification standards have advanced for all teachers of secondary school subjects. Certification requirements for the teacher of driver education have also advanced but not to the same level as for teachers of other disciplines.

HISTORICAL BACKGROUND

First evidences in requiring teachers of driver education to be certified are isolated instances among the various states. It was not until the latter 1940s that specific teacher education certification requirements began to emerge.

The first effort that attempted to give guidance to the various state certification boards and state departments of education developed as

79

a result of the first National Conference on High School Driver Education conducted by the National Commission on Safety Education in 1949. Efforts were made at this conference to recommend a minimum level of preservice education requirements for all prospective teachers of driver education. Certification standards recommended were within the reach of all states. It was further recommended that those states already meeting the certification standards make further efforts to expand their requirements and begin to strive for a teacher education program comparable to similar programs in other teaching fields. Specific recommendations from the first conference were a course of two or three semester hours of credit in driver education, including supervised teaching experience for the classroom and laboratory phases, and a course of two or three semester hours of credit in general safety education.[1]

In subsequent conferences efforts have been made to continue the upgrading of preservice teacher education requirements for those desiring to teach in the field of driver and traffic safety education.

TEACHER QUALIFICATIONS AND CERTIFICATION

The teacher of driver education should comply with certification requirements that are equal to those required for other school subjects. Teacher preparation curricula should be based on enlightened knowledge gained during the past decade. The fund of knowledge in the world has increased significantly in the past 20 years. Without question, much of this knowledge about man and his environment relates specifically to living in a traffic-oriented society. Therefore, modern curricula designed for the preparation of driver and traffic safety education instructors should take into consideration the newer ideas that have resulted from vast experimentation in the fields of the behavioral, physical, and biological sciences especially.

Teacher Competencies

In order to accomplish the objectives of the driver and traffic safety education program and to meet the challenge of preparing competent traffic citizens, teachers should have many competencies based upon modern concepts of principles of learning, course organization, and instructional technology. Some of these competencies are shown by the following actions. The teacher:[2]

1. Adapts safety curricula provided by state or local boards of education to his or her school's program in accordance with local needs and resources.

[1] National Commission on Safety Education, *High School Driver Education Policies and Recommendations* (Washington, D.C.: National Education Association, 1950), p. 49.

[2] American Driver and Traffic Safety Education Association, *Policies and Guidelines for Preparation and Certification of School Safety Personnel* (Washington, D.C.: The Association, 1974), p. 8.

80

2. Demonstrates ability to identify key elements in complex situations, predict risk involvement, and execute safe decisions.
3. Provides students with learning experiences in the cognitive, psychomotor, and affective domains which will help them to perform safely within the highway transportation system and other technological environments.
4. Selects and conducts learning activities, from simple to complex, which correspond with the learners' mental, physical, and emotional performance capabilities.
5. Selects routes for on-street and on-site lessons to facilitate learning experiences in a systematic manner.
6. Enlists and utilizes community safety resources which enhance the instructional program (such as police, courts, auto dealers and clubs, safety councils, driver licensing, and insurance agencies).
7. Selects or develops evaluation devices which measure the behavior sought in specified objectives.
8. Interprets the school safety program to the public.
9. Participates in activities leading to professional growth, such as graduate study, workshops, and activities of professional associations.

Figure 5-1. Professional Teachers Plan Instructional Activities (Courtesy Mesa Public Schools)

Preservice Education

The upgrading of preservice education programs has been developing on a continuing basis since the recommendations of the First National Conference on High School Driver Education. In recent years the basic recommendation has been that the teacher be required to possess a minor or major in traffic and safety education in order to be certified by the state department of education as a teacher of driver and traffic safety education. A minor in this particular field is a necessity if the teacher is to acquire the background that will prepare him to deal effectively with curriculum development activities, instructional problems, and evaluation methods.

GENERAL QUALIFICATIONS. Apart from specific course curricular requirements, it is desirable for the teacher of driver and traffic safety education to possess the following general qualifications:[3]

1. Desirable physical and mental capabilities for teaching driver education as determined by screening examinations and other evaluative tools.
2. A bachelor's degree or its equivalent from an accredited institution of higher education.
3. A valid state driver license with a satisfactory driving record as defined by the state department of education. (In determining what is satisfactory, the driving record should be checked at least annually.)
4. At least a teaching minor (or equivalent) of 18 to 22 semester units in driver or safety education.
5. Competencies essential to successful performance as a driver education teacher.
6. Preservice preparation and direct experience or supervised student teaching with experiences in both classroom and laboratory phases of instruction.
7. Specific knowledge of the dual-controlled car plan, electronic simulation systems, off-street multiple-car driving ranges, multimedia response systems, and related literature.

These general qualifications are important to the success of the school's driver education program. Therefore it is recommended that the school administrator check each of these general qualifications before he employs a teacher to fill a driver education position. This may be accomplished by a routine check through the proper state certification agency and the state agency responsible for the issuance of driver licenses.

PERSONAL QUALIFICATIONS. The teacher of driver education should also possess the personal qualifications of a well-prepared teacher. Among these qualifications are (1) a positive attitude toward driver education as a solution to the traffic accident problem; (2) an enthusiasm and desire to be a driver educator; (3) a willingness to discipline himself to make his own driving a positive example at all times; (4) a look upon attitudes, legislation, enforcement, and engineering as necessary in a traffic-oriented society; (5) a sufficient maturity to command respect of students; (6) an above-average driving ability; (7) an interest in traffic safety programs at the local, state, and national levels; and (8) an association with professional driver education associations at the state and national levels.

[3] American Driver and Traffic Safety Education Association, *Policies and Guidelines for Driver and Traffic Safety Education* (Washington, D.C.: The Association, 1974), pp. 22–23.

Driver and Traffic Safety Education Minor

The Fourth National Conference on Driver Education conducted in 1963 gave considerable attention to the background preparation necessary for the teacher of driver and traffic safety education. The conference subsequently approved a core of courses to be included in the teaching minor as the minimum requirements for preservice preparation of teachers of driver education. For the most part the core of courses recommended is in the areas of traffic and safety education, behavioral sciences, with additional electives in traffic safety and the behavioral sciences. The recommended courses from the behavioral sciences are beyond those of an introductory nature, included in the curriculum of most college general education requirements. The following is an outline developed by the participants of the Fourth National Conference on Driver Education that should be used as a guide in the development of the undergraduate teacher education program for instructors of driver and traffic safety education.

It is recommended that there be a teaching minor in driver and traffic safety education with the following minimum requirements:[4]

Minor: Traffic Safety Education

A. Required core courses totaling   12 semester hours
    Introduction to Safety   3 semester hours
    Driver and Traffic Safety Education   9 semester hours

B. Electives in the Behavioral Sciences*   3–6 semester hours
    Sociology, social psychology, and cultural anthropology courses dealing with culture and personality, behavior of youth, and attitude development.
    Abnormal psychology and those courses dealing with theory of personality.

C. Electives in Traffic Safety   3–6 semester hours
    Courses, seminars, or individual problems dealing with enforcement, engineering, legislation and licensing, state and local administration, traffic management, and community support.

    Courses in power and/or transportation.

---

*These courses are beyond those of an introductory nature and as such are not included in the college general education requirements.

Examples of outstanding teacher education programs in this field are offered by Central Missouri State University, Michigan State University, Southern Illinois University, and Texas A & M. These institutions of higher learning are among the leaders in the preparation of qualified teachers of driver education.

GRADUATE PROGRAM. There are graduate programs in traffic safety education for the teacher desiring to improve his background in this field. A few graduate programs are available that culminate in

[4] National Commission on Safety Education, *Policies and Practices for Driver and Traffic Safety Education*, pp. 12-13.

83

a doctorate degree. Such programs prepare university instructors, safety center administrators, and researchers. However, at the present time there is a need for more graduate programs that lead to an advanced degree in driver and traffic safety education. The following is a listing of courses that should be considered as core courses for a graduate program:

1. Organization, administration, and supervision of safety education.
2. Psychology of accident prevention.
3. Problems and research in traffic and safety education.
4. Traffic law enforcement.
5. Traffic engineering.
6. Organization for community traffic safety.
7. Traffic safety management.
8. Curriculum development in traffic and safety education.
9. Alcohol and other drugs as related to highway safety.
10. Research statistics methods, and independent research in traffic and safety education.
11. Thesis/Dissertation project.

The individual institution should alter the requirements based upon undergraduate offerings and the staff available. It is evident that most of the offerings should come from a college of education or a safety center. Because the graduate program is necessarily interdisciplinary in nature, it would be well to develop these graduate courses on a cooperative basis with the department or departments involved.

Figure 5-2. Qualified Instructor Instructing Student (Courtesy Richard Carpenter)

SIMULATION. Recognizing that numerous schools across the nation are now utilizing the simulation method in their driver education programs, it is necessary that the individual teacher be prepared in this particular specialized instructional technology approach. Therefore it is recommended that the teacher of simulation have a minimum preparation of at least one semester hour of college credit or its equivalent on the methodology of simulation teaching in driver and traffic safety education. The preparation should be so organized as to provide knowledge, experiences, and understanding of the simulation system. An outline of a suggested minimum course can be found in the Appendix. The following are the major topics for such a course:

1. Introduction to simulation.
2. Objectives.
3. Methods of instruction.
4. Equipment.
5. Evaluation.
6. Teaching practice.

MULTIPLE-CAR DRIVING-RANGE PLAN. The multiple-car driving-range plan has been in use since 1936. Today a large number of schools are using this laboratory plan to instruct students of driver education. Therefore it is necessary for the teacher to be prepared in this area of instruction. It is recommended that the teacher complete the minimum preparation of at least one semester hour of college credit or its equivalent on the methodology of multiple-car driving-range teaching. The content of such a course should contain these topics:

1. Objectives of an off-street program.
2. Advantages and disadvantages.
3. Administrative considerations.
4. Equipment.
5. Layout and design of driving range area.
6. Safety considerations.
7. Curricular aspects.
8. Laboratory experiences.

A complete outline for such a course is included in the Appendix.

IN-SERVICE EDUCATION

Regardless of whether or not the teacher has a background of a teaching minor or major in this field, he should continue to upgrade and enhance his background and professional status through continuous participation in various types of in-service educational programs. Through such programs he is able to keep up to date, become aware of new information and materials, and begin to assimilate new concepts and methods of instruction. Such experiences are provided by professional associations, colleges and universities, and state education departments. It is recommended that each year the teacher augment his background by enrolling in an additional academic course and attending at least one state and one national conference directly related to the field of driver and traffic safety education.

Advanced Course Preparation

Colleges and universities should provide several opportunities for teachers of driver education to enhance their professional backgrounds by enrollment in additional academic courses throughout the year. Such in-service improvement courses might be given through extension courses, advanced workshops or courses, specialized conferences, clinics, or institutes. Generally it would be necessary for such course offerings to be conducted in the evening and during the summer months, when the teacher has the opportunity to return to the campus.

Professional Conferences

Each year there are opportunities for the teacher to improve his professional background through attendance and participation in driver and traffic safety conferences. The teacher should endeavor to attend those conferences that are in his section of the state or nation each year.

NATIONAL CONFERENCES. There are two national conferences provided for the teacher of driver education that he should make an effort to attend. These are:

1. *Annual Conference of the American Driver and Traffic Safety Education Association.* ADTSEA sponsors annually a national conference that attracts driver educators from all parts of the nation. Since this is the only national professional association for teachers in this field, it is recommended that the teacher affiliate with ADTSEA and attend the annual conference that is generally held during the summer months. This association and its functions are discussed in more detail later in this chapter.

2. *National Safety Congress and Exposition.* Each year the National Safety Council sponsors the National Safety Congress and Exposition. The School and College Department of NSC sponsors a special program for teachers of driver education. This conference is held in Chicago in October. Specific program activities are available for the driver education teacher to give him an opportunity to supplement his knowledge and professional preparation in the field of driver and traffic safety education.

3. *Special Conferences.* At various times there are special conferences conducted around the nation which the teacher of driver and traffic safety education should make an effort to attend. The conferences are sponsored by such agencies as the Highway Users

Federation, National Highway Traffic Safety Administration, and the American Association of Motor Vehicle Administrators. Because of the nature of many such conferences, they are sometimes by invitation only. However, if the conference is not identified as an invitational conference, the teacher is at liberty to attend if he so desires.

Figure 5-3. Annual Conference State Driver Education Association (Photograph by Jack Berger, DASEANYS Publications Chairman)

STATE CONFERENCES. Generally in each state there are one or two conferences held on an annual basis for teachers of driver education. Such affairs afford the teacher an opportunity to attend a professional conference relatively close to home. Such conferences are sponsored by:

1. *State Driver and Safety Education Associations.* Forty-eight states now have a professional association for their teachers of driver and traffic safety education. Most of these associations provide an annual conference that gives the teacher an opportunity to participate on the state level in a program designed to meet his particular needs and interests. For information on these conferences, one should check with his state professional association of driver education needs.

2. *State Agencies.* From time to time various state agencies, such as a motor vehicle department, or department of education, or the governor, will sponsor a statewide conference of interest to teachers of driver education. The teacher should participate if the conference is applicable to his particular interest and will help him as a professional traffic safety specialist.

Professional Workshops

In addition to the conferences mentioned, there are specialized workshops made available to the driver educator. Such workshops are sponsored by a variety of associations and agencies. Following are some examples of special workshops held for the teacher of driver and traffic safety education.

NATIONAL WORKSHOPS. There are workshops that are sponsored by agencies concerned principally with traffic safety on the national level. Such workshops are conducted by the Highway Users Federation, American Association of Motor Vehicle Administrators, and various other associations and agencies. In view of the specialized nature of many such workshops, they are invitational conferences.

STATE WORKSHOPS. Statewide workshops for teachers that have a special interest in traffic safety are conducted in many states. Most often these are sponsored by the state driver and safety education association, the department of education, or the state motor vehicle department. These programs generally deal with statewide problems and are therefore often termed workshops or working conferences where specific concerns or problems are resolved regarding the conduct of a statewide traffic safety program.

LOCAL WORKSHOPS. Several of the state professional driver and safety education associations conduct one-day workshops that attempt to involve the teacher at the local level. For example, in the state of New York, the Driver and Safety Education Association of New York sponsors a series of one-day workshops each year. There are several of these workshops located conveniently around the state, so that every teacher of driver and traffic safety education has an opportunity to attend and participate in a workshop relatively close to home. Similar programs are conducted in Wisconsin, Illinois, and other states.

COLLEGE WORKSHOPS. Across the nation many colleges and universities sponsor workshops in the interest of traffic safety. In such workshops, consideration is given to current research trends, new publications, new policies and practices, and other current developments in the field of traffic safety.

Professional Literature

One of the best ways for the teacher of driver and traffic safety education to stay abreast of current developments in the traffic safety field is through professional reading. There are books, periodicals, and newsletters published annually or monthly. In addition to attending conferences and workshops, the teacher is encouraged to strengthen his professional growth through a substantial amount of reading on current literature each month. It is further recommended that the teacher subscribe or have access to the following basic periodicals:

1. *Traffic Safety*, published monthly by the National Safety Council, 444 North Michigan Avenue, Chicago, Ill., 60611. Subscription price is $7.50 per year.
2. *Journal of Safety Research*, published quarterly by the National Safety Council, 444 North Michigan Avenue, Chicago, Ill., 60611. Subscription price is $25.00 per year.
3. *Journal of Traffic Safety Education*, published by the California Driver Education Association for the American Driver and Traffic Safety Education Association, 1201 16th Street, N.W., Washington, D.C., 20036. One copy is given to ADTSEA members. Subscription price is $5.00 per year.

Each teacher of driver education should make an effort to develop a professional library that will enable him to become knowledgeable in the field of traffic safety as it relates to education, engineering, and enforcement. It is only through such knowledge that the teacher can appreciate and understand the traffic problem and the total program of traffic safety education that must be applied to the alleviation of the nation's traffic accident problems.

THE DRIVER EDUCATION PROFESSION

During the early days of the driver and traffic safety movement, teachers were recruited from many different disciplines. As a result, there was little concern or effort put forth toward the development of a professional group of people. However, as time passed and as teacher education standards continued to rise, individuals with a specific interest in the discipline of driver and traffic safety education became concerned about the development of professional organizations and associations that would deal with their specialized interests. A driver education section was organized in the National Safety Council; various state driver and safety education associations were organized; and more recently, the American Driver and Traffic Safety Education Association (ADTSEA) has emerged as the only national professional organization representing teachers of driver and traffic safety education. A professional association gains its strength through the attitudes and professional qualifications of its membership. Holding membership in an organization does not necessarily make an individual a professional driver and traffic safety educator. Nor is any field of endeavor classified as a profession simply because those who have similar interests call it a profession. A field of specialization or work accomplishes professional status only when it achieves certain qualities and characteristics. The following are generally considered to be the characteristics of a profession:[5]

1. The profession serves a distinctive and permanent social function in the community.
2. A profession has a highly specialized body of knowledge, complex enough to require a prolonged special education and a technique.

[5] Ed Williamson, "Driver Education—A Profession," *ADTSEA News and Views* (October–November 1963), pp. 1–4.

3. The members of the profession form professional associations or societies to improve standards and extend public acceptance.
4. A profession develops and follows a code of ethics.
5. A profession is characterized by professional behavior, attitudes, and workmanship of those who make up its membership.

Harcleroad has identified seven criteria of a profession. They are as follows:[6]

1. An intellectual technique.
2. Applications to practical affairs of man.
3. A period of long training.
4. A close-knit association of members with a high quality of communication between them.
5. A series of standards and an enforced statement of ethics.
6. An organized body of intellectual theory constantly expanded by research.
7. Active influence on public policy in its field.

The field of driver and traffic safety education meets the above criteria. However, before complete professional acceptance is realized by the driver educators of the nation, it is necessary for each individual working in the field to be affiliated with the professional association that is representing him. Moreover, it is incumbent upon each teacher to improve his public image in the betterment and acceptance of the driver education profession. Since this discipline is an integral part of the educational profession, all teachers should subscribe to the code of ethics of the education profession that was adopted by the National Education Association Representative Assembly in 1963.

Figure 5-4. Qualified Instructors Are Needed for Motorcycle Rider Instruction (Courtesy Safety Education Program, Texas A & M University)

[6] Fred Harcleroad, "We Must Base Our Profession on Social Needs," *Audiovisual Instruction* (June 1963), p. 283.

PROFESSIONAL ORGANIZATIONS

In order to develop a professional posture, individuals have banded together in various professional organizations for years. Several of these organizations were initiated for individuals who have a specific interest in the field of traffic safety. The following professional organizations are those that deal with matters related to traffic safety and therefore cater to those individuals who have this specialized professional interest.

American Driver and Traffic Safety Education Association

ADTSEA emerged after a meeting in 1956 of leaders from some 31 state driver and safety education associations. In 1957 a constitution and bylaws were approved, and officers were elected. After subsequent study ADTSEA was granted departmental status within the National Education Association in 1960. As an NEA department, ADTSEA benefited from the combined strength of the NEA when dealing with matters on important professional problems that are within the ADTSEA sphere of interest and competence. In 1975 ADTSEA became an independent association and is no longer affiliated with the NEA.

The purpose of the American Driver and Traffic Safety Education Association is to work toward the prevention of accidents by improving and extending driver and safety education in schools and colleges. The purpose of the association is in harmony with those of general education. To accomplish this purpose, ADTSEA is organized on a divisional basis. The following divisions serve the special interest of various people:

1. Division of Elementary Traffic Safety.
2. Division of Secondary Traffic Safety.
3. Division of Higher Education Traffic Safety.
4. Division of Traffic Safety Administration and Supervision.
5. Division of Traffic Safety Research.

An ADTSEA member may be affiliated with one or all of these divisions.

The association is financed basically through sustaining memberships, publications, and membership dues. The association conducts an annual conference for the benefit of its membership and provides several additional benefits, such as various publications, newsletters, packet service, and so on. The offices of ADTSEA are located at the National Education Association Headquarters Building, 1201 16th Street, N.W., Washington, D.C.

American Society of Safety Engineers

The American Society of Safety Engineers was organized in 1911 with the specific objective of the development of the safety engineering profession. Throughout the years it has maintained high membership requirements of both professional training and experience in the field of safety engineering. Associate memberships are granted to representatives of manufacturers of safety products. Today the society has 70 chapters across the nation and in Canada, with worldwide membership of approximately 8,000 persons. The society publishes a professional journal, *The Journal of the American Society of Safety Engineers*, and has offices in Chicago, Illinois.

Institute of Traffic Engineers

Founded in 1930, the Institute of Traffic Engineers is a professional engineering society. Today it has a membership in excess of 1,700 individuals professionally engaged in the traffic engineering field in all parts of the world. Membership requirements are based on education and experience that qualify persons to work with engineering problems related to planning, design, and operation of highway traffic facilities. *Traffic Engineering*, published monthly by the institute, develops standards and recommends practices in traffic engineering and participates in many joint traffic safety projects with other national organizations interested in traffic engineering. The Institute offices are in Washington, D.C.

State Driver Education Associations

In 1947 the first professional organization of driver and traffic safety education teachers was organized in Iowa. Since that date 41 states have organized professional statewide associations for their teachers of driver education. In general these associations publish newsletters, sponsor annual conferences and workshops, develop standards for statewide programs, assist in the development of adequate legislation to support traffic safety, and participate in various national conferences that pertain to policies and practices regarding the driver and traffic safety education program and profession. Most state associations elect officers on an annual basis, but they also maintain a permanent executive secretary who can be contacted throughout the year to receive new memberships or answer questions regarding the association. Therefore the teacher would have to make contact with his respective state association to become advised of its program and procedure for affiliation.

LIABILITY AND THE TEACHER

Every teacher in a school system is legally responsible for the safety of those students assigned to him. In the driver education program, the instructor should be vitally concerned about the role that he is to play in the conduct of his class. The driver education teacher is subject to the same rules of class management as is any other classroom teacher in the school. In addition he has the responsibility of a laboratory program. Anytime there is an accident or mishap involving the automobile used in the laboratory phase of the program, all involved can be subject to suits: the teacher, the student's parents, the owner of the automobile, or the Board of Education. The program of driver education enjoys common-law immunity throughout some 40 states. However, some states have abrogated their immunity laws and have at the same time made themselves liable for driver education accidents.

Teacher Responsibility

At the present time there appear to be few court decisions involving teachers or school districts for injuries sustained by students enrolled in a driver education course. However, this should not lead to a sense of false security on the part of the instructor. The instructor has a very serious responsibility as he works with groups of students throughout the day.

For a teacher to be held liable for an accident occurring during his driver and traffic safety education course, he must be found negligent. By definition, *negligence is the failure to act as a reasonable person, guided by ordinary conditions, would—or doing something that a prudent and reasonable man would not do.*[7] Therefore the jury would apply this definition to the factual situation at hand. The teacher can provide defense against liability resulting in accidents during a driver and traffic safety education course in these ways:

1. A sufficient background must be obtained in order to thoroughly understand the nature and scope of the traffic accident problem and those methods that can be utilized in the preparation of good traffic citizens.
2. Each lesson should be sufficiently planned based upon the prior experience and achievement of the individual students.
3. The teacher must provide continuous supervision at all times. In a classroom setting it may be permissible from time to time to leave the classroom unattended. However, at no time should a laboratory group be permitted to operate the practice-driving vehicle without the personal supervision of the instructor.

[7] N.E.A. Research Division for the National Commission on Safety Education, *Who Is Liable for Pupil Injuries?* (Washington, D.C.: National Education Association, 1962), p. 5.

Insurance Protection

It is wise for the teacher of driver and traffic safety education to be prepared for a liability suit even though he does his best to avoid accidents involving a practice-driving group. Boards of education and teachers should plan a type of insurance coverage necessary to protect fully the school district and the individual teacher.

BOARD OF EDUCATION. It is the responsibility of the Board of Education to obtain insurance protection that will provide liability for the school board, administrator, instructor, and other agents of the school who could be presumed to be involved. This type of protection is most frequently included under existing insurance programs of the school district. The legal counsel or their insurance adviser can suggest and advise proper coverage to the school administrator. If existing policies do not allow proper coverage, a separate policy should be purchased to cover this type of situation. Such a school district policy generally provides protection to both the student and the parent. It is recommended that adequate insurance be in force for both liability and property damage. The insurance adviser for the district should be consulted to determine adequate limits needed.

THE TEACHER. The instructor is usually protected from liable suits as an agent of the school district. However, for his own personal protection he may wish to explore this in some depth to determine the extent of the coverage on him and obtain advice relative to extended protection that he might obtain.

The classroom teacher of driver education can obtain liability protection in several ways:

1. A teacher-liability endorsement can be added to the teacher's comprehensive personal liability policy.
2. A personal liability policy can be written to provide the necessary teacher-liability protection.
3. The teacher's liability can be added by endorsement to the school board's policy.

In addition the teacher of the laboratory phase of the driver education program can obtain coverage through one of the following ways:

1. By adding to his present automobile liability policy a broad form coverage clause that protects him while driving other cars.
2. By purchasing a nonownership policy.
3. By including his name as an additional insured to the policy of the automobile used in the laboratory program.

Generally the cost of adequate insurance protection is not exorbitant. In most instances, it can be added to existing policies for a few additional dollars. Even though the amount may appear to be unnecessarily high, it is recommended that the teacher of driver education be thoroughly protected from any liable suit that may result from the teaching of a driver and traffic safety education course.

THE STUDENT. The secondary school student enrolled in driver education is generally protected by the school district policy while using the driver education vehicle, but not while driving other automobiles. Therefore it is suggested that parents make certain that the family automobile policy covers the student while driving other vehicles.

THE PARENT. In several states the parent assumes a specific liability when signing the student's learner permit. It is therefore important to know that their insurance policy provides protection to at least the amount of their legally assumed liability, because the assumed liability will apply to any car driven by the student, including the driver education vehicle. It is desirable that the parents have appropriate liability insurance protection in force.

Although cases dealing with rights and liabilities of the instructor of driver education are few, it is well for him to keep in mind the following points as he teaches his classes day after day:

1. Previous instruction, experience, knowledge of driving rules, and apparent mental and physical qualities of the student are important factors to be considered in making a preliminary estimate of his fitness to handle the car.
2. Careful consideration should be given to the area where the vehicle is to be driven during the course of instruction. This may depend to some extent upon the skill and ability of the beginner, as well as his driving judgment as ascertained by his actions or by preliminary investigation. It makes good sense to give initial driver instruction in areas where the likelihood of accident is remote.
3. Potentially hazardous situations should be avoided. This is one purpose of having the instructor present in the car. Alerting the driver to situations of potential danger is part of his duty, and his failure to exercise proper supervision in this respect will be negligent omission on his part.
4. When an emergency develops, the instructor should do what is reasonably possible to avert an accident or at least to minimize its consequences if it cannot be avoided entirely. He should be ready to seize the wheel, sound the horn, apply the brake, or take whatever measures are available at the moment if they become necessary.
5. Because the main purpose of having an instructor present in the vehicle during laboratory work is to provide available advice and counsel to the learner, the instructor must be careful to give the right kind of help when it is needed.
6. The instructor should remember that his is not merely a passive role. He has a positive duty to exercise reasonable care to prevent injury to the driver, passengers, himself, and other motorists and pedestrians.

Future of the Driver Education Profession

The future for the driver education profession appears to be very bright at the present time. To date it is reported that there are more than 54,000 teachers of driver and traffic safety education in the nation's secondary schools. It is recognized that some of these instructors are part-time and in all probability have a major interest in some other discipline. However, it seems certain that as schools continue to upgrade and expand their traffic safety programs, those instructors designated to assume teaching responsibilities shall be full-time instructors whose major interest shall be in the driver education program. Moreover, as the driver and traffic safety education program continues to grow in schools across the nation, the demand for highly qualified teachers will continue to be felt. To date, approximately 87 per cent of the nation's secondary schools are conducting programs of driver education that meet minimum recommended standards. Therefore as the last 13 per cent of the nation's schools move in the direction of organizing such programs, the need for driver educators will most certainly be increased.

Without question, those teachers who have a principal interest in driver and traffic safety education shall continue to band together in professional organizations. Therefore, as such growth is realized, the driver and traffic safety education profession shall grow in strength as well as in numbers. It is entirely possible that in the future there shall be 60,000 professionally trained teachers of driver and traffic safety education. Society will demand that the teacher of this discipline be as professionally prepared and oriented as for any other professional discipline in the nation's culture.

LEARNING ACTIVITIES

1. From the materials in this chapter and other resources, write a report on the development of teacher preparation and certification requirements for driver education in your state.
2. Compare the requirements for teacher certification for your state with those of six other states of comparable population. Identify similarities and differences between these programs and yours. Be prepared to discuss your findings in class.
3. Organize and participate in a 30-minute panel discussion on the topic, "Driver Education Teachers and Their Liability."
4. Contact your state's driver education association about its membership requirements. Report your findings to the class and encourage class members to become members.
5. Write a critique of a current issue of *Traffic Safety, Journal of Safety Research*, or *Journal of Traffic Safety Education*.

SELECTED RESOURCES

Aaron, James E., and Marland K. Strasser. *Driving Task Instruction—Dual-Control, Simulation, and Multiple-Car.* New York: Macmillan Publishing Co., Inc., 1974.

American Driver and Traffic Safety Education Association. *Policies and Guidelines for Preparation and Certification of School Safety Personnel.* Washington, D.C.: The Association, 1974.

Donigan, Robert L., and Edward C. Fisher. "Rights and Liabilities of Examiners, Instructors in Road Test Accidents," *Traffic Digest and Review* (January 1960).

Harcleroad, Fred. "We Must Base Our Profession on Social Needs," *Audiovisual Instruction* (June 1963), p. 283.

Hartman, Charles H. *Teacher Preparation Programs in Driver Education in Colleges and Universities of the United States.* Ed.D. Dissertation, Michigan State University, 1961.

National Highway Traffic Safety Administration. *Guide for Teacher Preparation In Driver Education—Secondary School Edition.* Washington, D.C.: The Administration (July 1974).

National Highway Traffic Safety Administration. *Statewide Highway Program Assessment—A National Estimate of Performance.* Washington, D.C.: The Administration (July 1975).

National Safety Council. *Driver Education Status Report 1972-73.* Chicago: The Council, 1974.

Chapter 6

Administering the Driver and Traffic Safety Education Program

OBJECTIVE: The student will be able to apply basic concepts of program administration to the development of an articulated classroom, and a dual-control, simulation, and multiple-car program of instruction.

Success of the driver and traffic safety education program is in large measure dependent on proper administration. Fundamentally the principles of administration that apply to all other areas of the school program apply to the administration of the school's driver education curriculum. The school administrator must assume full responsibility for the proper organization and administration of this program along with his other major administrative tasks. School administration is defined as *"all those techniques and procedures employed in operating the education organization in accordance with established policies."*[1] Because of his experience and training the teacher can be helpful as an adviser to the superintendent or principal.

THE ADMINISTRATOR'S ROLE AND RESPONSIBILITY

The administrator must assume many roles and responsibilities toward the conduct of the driver and traffic safety education program. Fundamentally these responsibilities lie in the areas of (1)

[1] Carter V. Good, *Dictionary of Education* (New York: McGraw-Hill Book Company, 1973), p. 13.

determination of administrative policy, (2) approval of budget allocations, (3) selection and placement of teachers, (4) determination of curricular offerings, (5) improvement of instruction, (6) assignment of responsibility for the driver education program, (7) procurement and use of vehicles and equipment, and (8) scheduling (probably the most important). Moreover, the administrator is responsible for the evaluation and success of the program content and instruction on a continuous basis. Also, he must assist in the development of a cooperative spirit between the school and community relative to the driver education program. The remainder of this chapter delineates various aspects of the organization and administration of the driver and traffic safety education program.

Administrative Policy

School programs develop and progress when administrative decisions are based upon written, approved policy determinations. Unless policies are clearly delineated, there will be confusion and unanswered questions regarding various aspects of the program. Without predetermined policies most decisions will be based upon expediency measures rather than on intelligent policy decisions.

There are many values in having predetermined policies regarding the organization, administration, instruction, and supervision aspects of the driver education program. By having written board of education approved policies, the following are achieved: (1) responsibility for program supervision and instruction is defined; (2) definite responsibility is assigned for the determination of budget allocations; (3) assignment of teachers is expedited; (4) a framework is established whereby the program can be developed in an orderly and intelligent manner; (5) efficiency in program development emerges; and (6) the objectives of the driver and traffic safety education program are more clearly achieved to the degree desired.

Determination of Legal Requirements

In the organization of the driver education program, the legal requirements for such a course are of major importance. In all states the offices of the superintendent of public education have established rules and regulations or policies regarding the conduct of all school programs. Such rules or policies have been established for the most part by legislation approved by the respective state legislature. Such legislative measures are to be found in school codes, state courses of study, or special bulletins published relative to the legal foundations of the driver and traffic safety education program of the state. The school administrator, safety supervisor, and teacher should be familiar with the legal foundations of the program in his respective state. The legal requirements of the state should be used to determine the nature and scope of the individual school district's driver and traffic safety education curriculum.

BUDGET AND FINANCING

One of the major responsibilities of the local board of education is the providing of adequate funds for the driver education program. Sufficient funds should be provided for this program by using the basic formulas applied in determining budget needs of all school programs.

A specific budget should be developed and approved. A fiscal officer should be designated in order that the budgeted funds be allocated and expended in a systematic and approved fashion. It is through the establishment of a budget that the program of driver and traffic safety education can be assured of adequate funds for this all-important phase of the school's curriculum. The following is a general discussion of the methods used to finance driver education programs across the nation.

Local and State Funds

Ideally the funds for the conduct of the driver and traffic safety education program should come from the same sources as the funds for all other school programs. It is reasonable to budget monies for driver education purposes from the local and state school tax monies. This is the proper approach in that the driver and traffic safety education program is part of the school's total curriculum.

Reimbursement Programs

During the past decade states have approved legislation that grants monies to the schools to help support the driver and traffic safety education program. Such programs are commonly referred to as reimbursement programs for driver education. The intent of such programs is to serve as an incentive to the local school districts toward the organization of quality driver and traffic safety education programs. The objective of a reimbursement program is to repay the school district a specific portion of the cost of instruction. Therefore the school invests relatively little of its local monies in the conduct of the driver education program. As of 1975 there were 35 states that had enacted driver education reimbursement legislation. It appears that in the years ahead most states will enact similar legislation. Figure 6-1 depicts those states with reimbursement programs.

DRIVER LICENSE FEE. One method of obtaining monies for driver education reimbursement programs is through an increase in the driver license fee. The additional money is placed in a special driver education fund and is allotted to the schools on a predetermined formula. In those states where such a program is operational, monies have been adequate to cover claims submitted by the schools.

VEHICLE REGISTRATION FEE. Some states accumulate funds for driver education purposes through an increase in the motor vehicle

1947 Delaware		Utah	1965 Tennessee
1952 Pennsylvania		West Virginia	to Hawaii
1953 California	1958	Wisconsin	1976 Iowa
1955 Florida	1959	Kansas	Montana
Louisiana	1960	Rhode Island	Nevada
Michigan	1961	Idaho	Ohio
1957 Connecticut		Maryland	Oklahoma
Illinois	1962	Mississippi	South Carolina
Indiana		Virginia	Texas
New Hampshire	1963	Nebraska	Vermont
North Carolina		Washington	
Oregon	1964	Alabama	
		(District of Columbia)	

Figure 6-1. States with Financial Support for Driver Education

registration fee. To date this has proven to be a successful method of obtaining monies to reimburse schools for their driver education program.

PENALTY ASSESSMENT PLAN. Another method used by states to obtain monies for driver education purposes is through a program identified as a penalty assessment plan. With such a plan an additional assessment is charged the traffic violator. A sliding-scale formula is used, so that as the fine increases, the additional penalty assessment increases also. In general the assessment is one dollar or more for each 10 or 20 dollars of a fine for a moving violation. The Stanley Act, approved by the California State Legislature in 1953, is perhaps the best example of this program in action. Apparently the concept of a reimbursement program has been a success in that all of the states with such a program in operation have experienced in their driver education programs a growth in quantity as well as in quality.

FEDERAL FUNDS. The Highway Safety Act of 1966 provides monies to each state to help support its highway safety activities. Driver education is one area of the Highway Safety Standards on which a great deal of federal monies have been spent. Driver education supervisors should contact the Governor's highway safety representative of the state to inquire about the eligibility requirements for the use of the state's highway safety monies.

SELECTION AND PLACEMENT OF TEACHERS

A major responsibility of the school administrator is that of selecting quality instructors. The teacher of driver and traffic safety education should be expected to meet the same high standards required of other teachers of the school. In Chapter 5 the background preparation is described, and it is suggested that the school administrator require the preservice education standards discussed in that chapter. In addition, the school administrator should be concerned with the following as he proceeds with the selection of a driver education teacher. The prospective teacher should have an appropriate capability in the following areas:[2]

[2] American Driver and Traffic Safety Education Association, *Policies and Guidelines for Preparation and Certification of School Safety Personnel* (Washington, D.C.: The Association, 1974), p. 9.

1. Ability to structure and implement driver education learning experiences and to identify and develop support materials related to the following modes:
   Regular classroom.
   Multimedia.
   Driving simulation.
   Off-street multiple-car driving range.
   On-street instruction.
2. Ability to assist students in examining and clarifying their beliefs, attitudes, and values as they relate to safety.
3. An understanding of the basic principles of motor vehicle systems, dynamics, and maintenance.
4. An understanding of the interaction of all highway transportation system elements.
5. Procedures and conditions for activating an emergency medical services system.
6. Demonstrated competence in motor vehicle operation and on-street instruction.
7. An understanding of the physiological and psychological influences of alcohol and drug abuse as they relate to the highway transportation system.
8. An understanding of due processes in the application of laws.
9. Ability to communicate effectively with appropriate agencies concerned with safety.
10. Understanding the frequency, severity, nature, and directions for prevention of accidents which occur to age groups while participating in various life activities.

ORGANIZATION OF PROGRAM

The program of driver education should be organized on the same basis as any other course in the school's curriculum. Those principles that apply to the supervision of program development and improvement of instruction are essentially the same as those utilized in the organization of the total school curriculum. The following is a detailed discussion of the factors that influence the organization of a quality program of driver and traffic safety education for the secondary school.

Supervisor of Driver and Safety Education

Every school should delegate the responsibility for the overseeing of the driver and safety education program to one qualified person. Studies have shown that if the program is to be properly organized and developed, specific responsibility must be delegated to one person, the supervisor of driver and safety education.[3]

[3] James E. Aaron, *A Study of Supervisory Practices in Safety Education in Selected Cities in the United States* (Ed.D. Dissertation, New York University, 1960).

THE RELATION OF DRIVER EDUCATION
TO THE SCHOOL TRAFFIC SAFETY PROGRAM

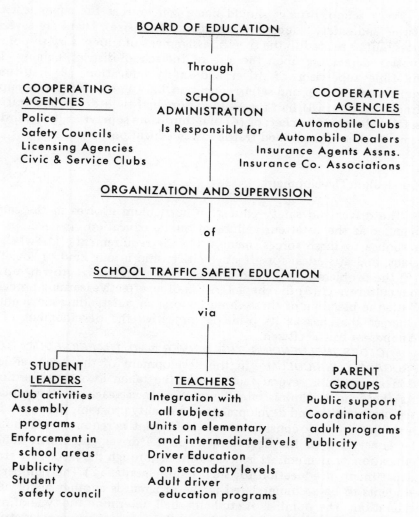

BOARD OF EDUCATION

Through

COOPERATING AGENCIES	SCHOOL ADMINISTRATION	COOPERATIVE AGENCIES
Police	Is Responsible for	Automobile Clubs
Safety Councils		Automobile Dealers
Licensing Agencies		Insurance Agents Assns.
Civic & Service Clubs		Insurance Co. Associations

ORGANIZATION AND SUPERVISION

of

SCHOOL TRAFFIC SAFETY EDUCATION

via

STUDENT LEADERS	TEACHERS	PARENT GROUPS
Club activities	Integration with	Public support
Assembly	all subjects	Coordination of
programs	Units on elementary	adult programs
Enforcement in	and intermediate levels	Publicity
school areas	Driver Education	
Publicity	on secondary levels	
Student	Adult driver	
safety council	education programs	

Figure 6-2. Suggested Organization for School Traffic Safety Education Program

The supervisor of driver and safety education should meet several requirements, including the following:

1. A Master's degree in driver and safety education.
2. A minimum of five years of teaching experience in driver and traffic safety education.
3. The requirements for a supervisory certificate, if required by the state.
4. Professional association with the American Driver and Traffic Safety Education Association and the respective state driver and traffic safety education association.

5. Administrative talent that is conducive to program development.
6. Personality qualities that are conducive to gaining the cooperation of teachers and community alike.

Every school district should name someone as the supervisor of driver and safety education regardless of its size. There are several possibilities related to the specific assignment of supervisory responsibilities, depending upon the size of the school district, namely (1) full-time supervisor of driver and safety education, (2) half-time supervisor of driver and safety education, half-time supervisor of pupil transportation; (3) half-time supervisor, half-time driver and traffic safety education teacher; or (4) one-third-time supervisor, two-thirds-time teacher of driver and traffic safety education.

Curriculum Development

The driver and safety education curriculum evolves in the same manner as the total curriculum of public education. It develops in response to three forces, namely (1) the requirements (knowledge, skills, and attitudes) for effective citizenship in our kind of society; (2) the problems, needs, and interests of the individual growing up in our culture; and (3) the characteristics of an effective learning process. With the blending of these three factors, an outstanding curriculum emerges that has as its principal objective the development of a competent traffic citizen.

FACTORS INFLUENCING THE DRIVER AND TRAFFIC EDUCATION PROGRAM CURRICULUM. In the development of the driver education curriculum, several factors must be taken into consideration. As the school administrator, supervisor, and teachers contemplate the organization and development of a quality program, the following must be taken into consideration. (1) Legislative requirements should be considered in the development of the driver and traffic safety education curriculum. It is best to check through the respective state department of education for such requirements. (2) The number of students to be accommodated in the program is another major consideration. The number of students shall determine the type of program as well as the scope of program for a particular school district. (3) The budget approved for the development of the program should be an initial deliberation. However, in those states where a reimbursement program is in effect, every school district should have ample financing to accommodate all of the eligible students desiring to enroll in the program. (4) The size of the school district will influence the type of program plan selected. For the small school a particular program plan may be suitable, whereas for the large school some other type of driver and traffic safety education program plan would be more desirable. (5) A study of teacher availability should be a part of the initial thinking on program development. Only those teachers who meet the certification requirements of the state should be assigned as teachers of driver and traffic safety education.

104

PROGRAM PLANS. The complete driver and traffic safety education program is comprised of a classroom phase integrated with a laboratory phase. The following describes each briefly, and they are described more fully in Chapter 11.

1. *Classroom Phase.* The classroom phase is an academically oriented classroom program that utilizes traditional teaching methods and techniques as well as field studies in traffic, individual study projects, and group discussion-decision techniques. It is recommended that this program be a minimum of one semester in length.

2. *Laboratory Phase.* The following are the four types of laboratory plans used in organizing laboratory instruction:

a. DUAL-CONTROL CAR. This approach to the teaching of the beginner driver is the original practice driving plan. An instructor plus two, three, or four students are placed in a dual-control vehicle, and instruction is given to each of the students on a rotating basis throughout the period of time assigned to this phase of the program.

b. SIMULATION. Driving simulation is a teaching method that uses an electromechanical simulator device to develop perceptual skills, practice adjustive driving procedures, and improve attitudes. The simulator is designed to represent the driver's compartment of the typical automobile, including controls, switches, gauges, and so on.

c. MULTIPLE-CAR DRIVING RANGE. The driving range approach includes an off-the-street driving area equipped with 8, 10, or 12 vehicles with an equal number of drivers under the supervision of one instructor. The range is for the development of fundamental skills, driving practice, and improvement of attitudes. A communication system maintains contact with all students.

d. FOUR-PHASED PROGRAM. This is a program that combines classroom instruction with dual-control, simulator, and multiple-car driving range in one comprehensive program. The best elements of each plan are selected for instructional purposes.

TIME STANDARDS. The recommended time standard for a complete driver and traffic safety education program is one full semester. In order for the objectives of the driver education program to be achieved, the classroom program should be comprised of some 90 hours of instruction, and the laboratory phase should be a minimum of 6 clock hours (but preferably 8 clock hours) of practice driving time per student. The minimum amount of time assigned to a complete program should be no less than 45 hours of classroom instruction and 6 clock hours of laboratory instruction per student.

COURSE CREDIT. The complete driver and traffic safety education program being offered in one semester period should grant one half Carnegie unit of credit to students who successfully complete this course. If it is necessary to reduce the amount of time given to each student, it is recommended that the basic Carnegie unit formula be applied in the awarding of credit to the student.

GRADE PLACEMENT. The driver education program should be placed at the grade level where most of the secondary school's population would be eligible to obtain a valid driver license upon completion of the course. From a psychological point of view, it is advantageous to offer the course at this time in that the student is at his peak in terms of interest and motivation. Therefore such interest and motivation can be used by the instructor to the advantage of developing wholesome attitudes toward the driving task. The opportunities for the development of a competent traffic citizen are enhanced at this point. In practice, the course is usually placed at the sophomore or junior level in the secondary school.

PROCUREMENT AND USE OF DRIVER EDUCATION VEHICLES. There are several methods that the school district may use in obtaining a vehicle for driver education purposes. The following is a brief description of those methods being used by the schools of the nation:

1. *Purchase.* The most satisfactory approach in obtaining a driver education vehicle is for the school to purchase the car. In view of the fact that the vehicle is a classroom on wheels, monies should be allocated for the purchase of this basic piece of equipment. Usually the school will be able to obtain such a vehicle at a reduced cost through a local dealer.

2. *Loan.* Through the cooperation of the automobile distributor, schools may obtain cars for driver education purposes on a free loan basis. Each of the cooperating dealers receives a $250 to $500 rebate from the manufacturer for each vehicle loaned to a school for driver education purposes. This rebate is to cover any dealer losses that might be incurred through the loan arrangement.

The American Automobile Association has a similar plan; the Association works with the individual school in the procurement of driver education vehicles on a loan basis from the local dealer. The basic difference is that the AAA does most of the contact work and basic arrangements through the dealer to the manufacturer in the assignment of the driver education vehicle. The dealer rebate applies with this arrangement also.

3. *Rental or Lease.* The school district may find that it is advisable to procure a car on a rental basis through a local dealer. In most instances, the school district pays a flat monthly rental fee for use of the car. All expenses are taken care of by the dealer in the rental price. It appears that this approach to the obtaining of a driver education vehicle is becoming more popular among the schools around the nation. Through a leasing arrangement, the school may obtain a car for an agreed time, paying a mutually agreed amount.

4. *Gift.* At various times service clubs, insurance associations, and other community groups give cars to schools for driver education purposes. Funds for such gifts are normally available through the organizations' community service budgets.

5. *Use of Vehicles.* Cars obtained for driver education programs are to be used for that purpose only. This is usually specified in the agreement signed by the dealer and the school administrator. Improper use or abuse of a loaned car is cause for the dealer to terminate the loan agreement.

SUGGESTED RIDER EDUCATION
UNIT LOAN AGREEMENT FORM

Dealership _____		Sponsoring Agency _____
Address _____		Address _____
City _____ State ____ Zip ____		City _____ State ____ Zip ____

DEALER AGREES:

- to provide, at no cost to the sponsor for the sponsor's exclusive use, properly equipped (to meet the State Motor Vehicle Code) motorcycles, and
- to provide basic maintenance under normal conditions of wear on the motorcycle(s) during the loan period at no cost to the sponsor.

VEHICLE IDENTIFICATION:

Unit   Make   Model   Identification (if available)

1 _____ _____ _____ _____

2 _____ _____ _____ _____

3 _____ _____ _____ _____

4 _____ _____ _____ _____

5 _____ _____ _____ _____

6 _____ _____ _____ _____

Total Number of Motorcycles Loaned: _____

Loan Period: From_____ To _____

SPONSOR CERTIFIES:

That the motorcycle(s) will be used exclusively for a motorcycle rider education program which meets all of the following criteria:

- is based on a curriculum or instructional guide approved by the State Department of Education, city school authorities, or military service officials (if offered on a military installation), or curriculum materials published and made available by the Motorcycle Safety Foundation; and
- is conducted by a qualified instructor who (1) has a valid operator's license (for auto and motorcycle); (2) has a good riding/driving record; and either (3) is a certified driver education teacher and has completed a college or university course in motorcycle teacher preparation; or, (4) has completed a course in motorcycle teacher preparation provided by other approved organizations which meet the instructional, course, and teacher certification requirements of the state.

SPONSOR FURTHER AGREES TO:

- use the motorcycle exclusively for the designated educational purpose;
- permit student operation of the motorcycles only in the presence of and under the direct supervision of a qualified instructor;
- require the use of approved safety helmets by all persons on the vehicle while it is in motion or may be set in motion;
- provide necessary "owner" maintenance on a regular basis as recommended in the owner's manual, arrange to have other maintenance performed periodically at the discretion of the dealer, and be responsible for damage or for maintenance beyond that which can normally be expected for the period of the loan;
- properly maintain the appearance of the motorcycle;
- provide insurance coverage for the protection of the dealer, the sponsor, the instructor(s), and the students; such insurance should include, but need not be limited to, $100,000/300,000 public liability, bodily injury, and $25,000 property damage; voluntary medical payment for operators and passengers, and physical damage to the motorcycle; and
- provide garaging to protect the vehicle from theft and environmental damage and degradation.

THIS AGREEMENT SHALL TAKE EFFECT WHEN SIGNED BY AUTHORIZED REPRESENTATIVES OF THE DEALER AND THE SPONSOR:

Dealer _____ Date:_____

　Name and Title (please print) _____

Sponsor _____ Date:_____

　Name and Title (please print) _____

SPONSOR INFORMATION

Type of Program:
____High School　　　　____Adult Education
____Private Driving School　____Civic Organization
____Police Department　　____Military
____Teacher Preparation　　____Other_____

Are you using curriculum materials developed by the Motorcycle Safety Foundation? ____Yes ____No

Other curriculum materials being used (please specify): _____

Length of program (hours):
Classroom _____ Range_____ On-Street_____

Has the instructor been certified to conduct motorcycle safety education training programs? _____Yes _____No

If yes, where? _____

Approximate number of students enrolled in the program: _____

Primary age range:
____14-17　　　　____26-35　　　　____mixed
____18-25　　　　____35 and over

How many programs are scheduled by your organization in a calendar year? _____

INSTRUCTIONS TO DEALER (for imprint by manufacturer):

MOTORCYCLE SAFETY FOUNDATION ● 6755 ELKRIDGE LANDING ROAD ● LINTHICUM, MD 21090
Distribution: White copy to dealer; Pink to Sponsor; Blue to MSF; Canary and Goldenrod to Manufacturer

Figure 6-3. Suggested Rider Education Unit Loan Agreement Form (Courtesy Motorcycle Safety Foundation)

If the major purpose of the driver and traffic safety education program is to enable the student to develop the ability to identify, predict, decide, and execute traffic situations in a manner that demonstrates proficiency in the driving task, then it is imperative that instruction be given priority in the organization and planning of the program. Organization for instruction is given in detail in Chapters 7 and 11.

This major purpose is contingent upon administrative decisions. It is well for the administrator to use the criteria presented in Chapter 7 as basic guidelines when selecting learning experiences for students of driver education. In addition to these criteria, there are several major functions to which the administrator should give attention if quality instruction is to result in the driver education program.

TEACHING LOAD. The teacher of driver and traffic safety education should be given a teaching load comparable to the load required of teachers of other subject matter. Since this program is an academically oriented subject, the teacher should receive the same treatment as other instructors employed by the school district.

SELECTING STUDENTS. It should be the goal of every school district to accommodate 100 per cent of the eligible students of their schools in driver education. However, if it is necessary to select students on a priority basis, the following are suggested as guides to the administrator and teacher: (1) students with a vocational need should be given first preference; (2) students who are the only driver possibility in a family should be given preference; and (3) students who are approaching or have just passed the legal minimum driving age should be given preference over graduating seniors or underaged students. Students who have been referred to the class by a traffic court official should also be given preference.

RECORDS AND REPORTS. A comprehensive and efficient record and reporting system should be organized and implemented by the teacher of driver education. It is essential that reports be accurate and kept up to date if they are to benefit the instructor in gaining an understanding of student progress, cost of instruction, and vehicle use. The following are suggested types of records and reports to be made by the teacher:

1. A student progress record form should be prepared for each student enrolled.
2. A permanent record form should be filed at the end of each semester to serve as a record of the student's accomplishments and a record for future reference.
3. A cost accounting form should be used to determine the cost of instruction in both the classroom and laboratory phases of the program.
4. A vehicle maintenance form should be used to record monthly and annual maintenance of the practice driving vehicle.

5. An accident record report should be available in each of the practice driving vehicles as well as in the files of the supervisor.
6. A vehicle use form should be utilized to determine who drives the vehicle and how many miles each driver is behind the wheel.
7. An approval letter and reply card for parents should be developed and placed on file when returned to the instructor.

INSTRUCTION PERMITS AND DRIVER LICENSES. Each student enrolled in the laboratory phase of the program must have a valid instruction permit or driver license if required by the state. Such a permit or license must be obtained before he is allowed to operate the practice driving vehicle. In most states it is illegal for an individual to receive driving instruction unless he has one of these two permits. Negligence could be proven against the instructor if the student were involved in a traffic accident while operating a practice driving car without a permit. The supervisor or instructor should check with licensing authorities for the requirements of his state in this regard.

ARTICULATION OF CLASSROOM AND LABORATORY PROGRAMS

As pointed out previously, the complete driver and traffic safety education program encompasses both classroom and laboratory instruction. Although the classroom phase is of definite value, it is recognized that if the objectives of the driver education program are to be accomplished, laboratory instruction must be an integral part of the total program. Each phase of the program complements the other, and therefore each phase may contribute to the success if the other is properly articulated. The absence of proper articulation destroys the effectiveness of both.

To accomplish the objectives of the driver education curriculum, the total program must be taught to the student during a minimum of one semester and no longer than one school year. This enables the instructor to develop the program on the same level as all other courses in the school curriculum and enhances the opportunities for the development of competent traffic citizens. It is imperative that close articulation of the classroom and laboratory phases be given high priority in the organization and administration of the driver and traffic safety education program. In no instance is it recommended that either phase of the program follow another phase after an extended period of time has elapsed. In those instances when close articulation of both phases is impossible on a concurrent basis, the classroom program should serve as the prerequisite to the laboratory program.

Scheduling

It is the responsibility of the school administrator to provide an adequate schedule for driver education. It is believed that the most effective way of teaching driver education is by scheduling it as a separate course. However, it is possible to schedule a course using the methods of integration and correlation. If the course is taught within another class subject, the content and quality of instruction must not be impaired, and an adequate allotment of time must be scheduled to meet state legal requirements.

The time scheduled for the classroom and laboratory sessions varies. Therefore the possibilities for effective articulation of both phases are deserving of the highest consideration. Based upon modern learning theories, many administrators and teachers believe that the most effective teaching and learning takes place when the total program is scheduled on a semester basis.

Between 48 and 60 students per semester are scheduled for one teacher in the typical driver education program. This number is flexible, depending on whether the school operates a dual-control car, simulator, multiple-car driving range, or four-phased program.

Teacher capacity or needs may be determined by applying the following formulas to the local school situation. In using the first formula these factors have been taken into consideration:

1. ———school days per year
2. ———teaching periods per day per instructor.
3. ———minutes per class period.
4. Four students per dual-control car per period.
5. ———students eligible for driver training per year.
6. Dual-control requirements:
   6 hours (24 periods) per student behind the wheel.

From this the following formula is derived:

$$\frac{\dfrac{\text{No. teaching periods}}{\text{day}} \times \dfrac{\text{No. days}}{\text{year}} \times \dfrac{\text{No. students}}{\text{period}}}{\dfrac{\text{No. of periods required}}{\text{student}}} = \text{No. students}$$

Another approach is suggested by Bishop in determining teacher capacity for dual-control, simulator, and range program.[4]

Instructor hours for a minimum 6 hours on-street are determined by the formula:

$$I = ST$$

I = Instructor hours
S = Number of students
T = Time for each student behind the wheel

Question: How many instructor hours are required to give 120 students 6 hours each of on-street experience?

[4] Richard W. Bishop, "Questions and Answers About Driving Simulators," *Safety Education* (December 1964), p. 11.

$$I = ST$$
$$I = 120 \times 6 = 720 \text{ hours}$$

Instructor hours for the *multiple-car-driving range* and the *simulator* program are determined by the formula:

$$I = \frac{ST}{U}$$

I = Instructor hours
S = Students
T = Time for each student behind the wheel or simulator or range car
U = Number of cars on the range, or the number of simulator units.

Therefore, the following formula will determine instructor hours required to give 120 students 12 hours of simulation, 8 hours behind the wheel on the multiple-car driving range, and 2 hours behind the wheel on-street.

$$I = \frac{ST}{U} \text{ (Simulator)} + \frac{ST}{U} \text{ (Range)} + ST \text{ (on-street}$$

$$I = \frac{120 \times 12}{12 \text{ (simulator units)}} + \frac{120 \times 8}{8 \text{ (cars)}} + 120 \times 2$$

$$I = 120 + 120 + 240$$

$$I = 480 \text{ hours}$$

In the Appendix there are a number of typical driver education schedules. These are flexible and can be adjusted to fit into most school situations.

RELATIONSHIP WITH STATE AGENCIES

In the conduct of the driver education program it is necessary to establish a desirable working relationship with various state agencies. Several state agencies have functions that relate to driver and traffic safety education programs. Therefore the administrator, supervisor, and teacher should become familiar with and understand the role that each of these agencies plays in the state's total traffic safety program, including driver education. The following is a brief discussion of some agencies that have responsibilities for certain aspects of the driver and traffic safety education program.

Department of Education

The state department of education has several responsibilities toward the conduct of the driver education program. The local school district should maintain a continuous contact with its respective state department of education so as to keep abreast of program requirements and considerations of policy changes. The state department of education is usually responsible for the following functions. It (1)

111

approves certification of driver education teachers; (2) establishes rules and regulations governing the conduct of the program; (3) establishes policies relating to legislative matters adopted by the state legislature; (4) supervises the program through a state director of driver and safety education; (5) evaluates local high school programs to determine accreditation; (6) administers the reimbursement program in operation in some 32 states; (7) develops state curriculum products to provide guidance to the local school system in the development of driver and safety education programs.

Motor Vehicle Department

Because most students (exception in some states) enrolled in the driver and traffic safety education program must have a valid student license (learner) permit or driver license, the local school district authorities should be familiar with that state agency responsible for the issuance of such permits. In each state there are specific policies that must be adhered to in obtaining licenses. A driver license division has the responsibility for the administration of the driver license laws of the various states. Each school district should be familiar with this particular state agency and keep abreast of any changes that may influence the driver and traffic safety education program.

Also, the local school districts must deal with the state agency responsible for the issuance of vehicle registration tags. In many states, there are specific rules and regulations established whereby the school district may obtain a special vehicle registration plate at a reduced cost to the school district. Generally there is a special vehicle license division within the motor vehicle department that has this particular responsibility.

Official State Traffic Safety Agency

Some states have a division of traffic safety within a state department concerned with highway safety that has some responsibility toward the conduct of the driver and traffic safety education program. In recent years, governors' highway safety representatives have been appointed to coordinate highway safety funding and project activities. Since federal funding may be available through this office, the eligibility requirements should be reviewed from time to time by the driver education supervisor. In other states, the highway patrol has some responsibility for driver education. They are responsible for the establishment of program standards and certification standards that apply to the teacher. In addition to these responsibilities, such groups are generally responsible for the state's official traffic safety program. Therefore, one of these may be the state agency that would contact the school from time to time so as to encourage them to better their driver education program as well as enter into a variety of traffic safety activities and projects throughout the school year.

112

LEARNING ACTIVITIES

1. Contact ten state departments of education and request program development standards for driver education. Develop a 15-minute presentation for the class.
2. Using the content of this chapter, develop a classroom and laboratory schedule to accommodate 60, 240, and 360 students of driver education per semester.
3. Organize an adequate driver education program budget for a school with 1,200 enrollment, three driver education teachers, and 350 students in driver education.
4. Participate in a group discussion on the topic, "The Role of the Supervisor of Driver and Safety Education."
5. Develop a set of administrative policies and practices to govern the conduct of a driver education program. Assume these are to be approved by a board of education.

SELECTED RESOURCES

Aaron, James E., and Marland K. Strasser. *Driving Task Instruction—Dual-Control, Simulation, and Multiple-Car.* New York: Macmillan Publishing Co., Inc., 1974.

American Driver and Traffic Safety Education Association. *Policies and Guidelines for Driver and Traffic Safety Education.* Washington, D.C.: The Association, 1974.

_____. *Policies and Guidelines for Motorcycle Safety Education: On-Street Riders.* Washington, D.C.: The Association, 1974.

_____. *Policies and Guidelines for Preparation and Certification of School Safety Personnel.* Washington, D.C.: The Association, 1974.

_____. *Policies and Guidelines for a School Safety Program.* Washington, D. C.: The Association, 1974.

Automotive Safety Foundation. *A Resource Curriculum in Driver and Traffic Safety Education.* Washington, D.C.: The Foundation, January 1970.

Kenel, Francis C. "A Driver Education Curriculum for the 70's," *Journal of Traffic Safety Education.* California Driver Education Association, Vol. XIX. No. 2 (January 1972), pp. 18-20.

McKnight, A. James, and Alan G. Hundt. *Driver Education Task Analysis, Volume I: Task Description.* Washington, D.C.: Department of Transportation, HS800-367, Hum RRO Technical Report 70-103 (November 1970).

State of Illinois. *Driver Education for Illinois Youth.* Springfield, Ill.: Safety Education Section, Office of the Superintendent of Public Instruction, 1972.

CLASSROOM INSTRUCTION

This part of the text deals with all aspects of the classroom phase of a total driver education program. The classroom program is an academically oriented course designed to teach knowledge concepts in the area of traffic safety. Classroom organization, teaching methods and techniques, and materials and equipment are discussed in depth for the benefit of all teachers, first year or experienced.

Included in Part II are the following chapters:

7. Organization of Classroom Instruction
8. Content of the Classroom Program
9. Teaching Methods and Techniques for Classroom Instruction
10. Classroom Materials and Equipment

Chapter 7

Organization of Classroom Instruction

OBJECTIVE: The student will be able to identify and apply those principles and concepts necessary to the development, organization, and teaching of a planned classroom instructional program.

The organizing, planning, and conducting of a quality classroom program is basic in achieving the driver and traffic safety education objectives identified in Chapter 3. Classroom driver education holds the key to the development of competent traffic citizens. Therefore it is essential that the administrator and teacher put forth a great deal of thought and effort when organizing this important subject.

One of the principal purposes of modern-day education is to develop cooperation among individuals and groups. Thus the position of classroom driver education is enhanced because it is uniquely suited to accomplish one of the major ends of general education, namely, that of cooperative effort on the part of society (especially as road-sharers). The youthful driver is a part of the traffic problem and should become a real part of the solution. Obtaining the driver license is the first legal recognition of adult responsibility. The driver education program is a laboratory for teaching democracy in the use of streets and highways. In preparing high school students to meet future needs of motor vehicle ownership and use, the school should recognize that the burden of such an accomplishment lies principally in the offering of the best classroom driver education program possible. This chapter will discuss the major considerations in the organization of a quality driver education classroom program.

ACADEMIC BASIS

School administrators, supervisors, and teachers should acknowledge the fact that a classroom driver education program is no different from any other classroom course included in the school curriculum. Therefore basic planning and organizing of the course should follow the same principles used when establishing all other school subjects.

Basic organization plans should call for an academic course in which (1) knowledge concepts are taught, (2) essential content is covered, (3) attitude concepts are presented, and (4) evaluation and testing are essential ingredients of a good classroom course. Moreover, it is a course in which modern instructional technology is used. These are characteristics of all academic subjects offered by the school. In a previous chapter the characteristics of a discipline were presented. It is worth mentioning here that classroom driver education meets the requirements to be classified as a regular school subject.

Course credit should be given to all students enrolled in driver education. Moreover, the teacher should give course grades that become a permanent part of the students' academic record. Discussion of course credit and grades was presented in greater detail in Chapter 6.

INSTRUCTIONAL PLANNING

The school that is alert to its responsibility for meeting the needs of youth is engaged continuously in the process of curriculum reorganization and improvement of instruction.[1] Evaluation and improvement of instruction should be approached as a partnership between the administration and teachers. This is necessary for the improvement of instruction, based on a common philosophy and purpose. This improvement of instruction generally results when driver education teachers are organized into a separate department. Teachers work best when they have common interests and strive to reach common goals, namely, developing courses of study and selecting textbooks and other teaching aids. Moreover, adequate classroom facilities, texts for each student, and appropriate classroom equipment contribute to the improvement of instruction.

Implementation of instruction in driver and traffic safety education should be a never-ending process if it is to keep pace with a dynamic and changing society. New modern methods of instructional technology are being introduced continuously. Therefore the school should be prepared to include these advanced techniques in today's driver education program. "Classroom procedures that encourage learning through discovery are one potential means of encouraging creative thinking, of stimulating interest and insight, and of helping pupils develop conceptual frameworks for the subjects they study."[2]

[1] Harold B. Alberty and Elsie J. Alberty, *Reorganizing the High School Curriculum* (3rd ed.; New York: Macmillan Publishing Co., Inc., 1962), p. 468.

[2] National Education Association, *Deciding What To Teach* (Washington, D.C.: The Association,1963) p. 45.

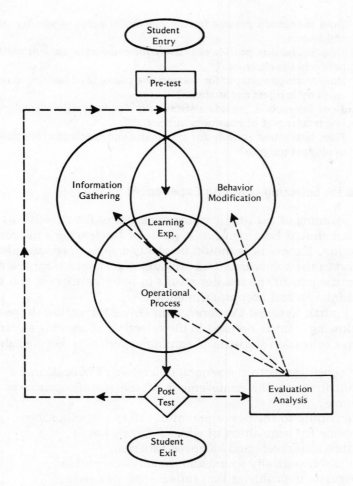

Figure 7-1. Instructional Configuration

Instructional planning should be taken as a serious and necessary aspect of the teacher's responsibility. To assist the teacher in the development of the best possible program of instruction the following criteria are suggested as guidelines:[3]

1. Does instruction make adequate provisions for all youths regardless of interest, intelligence level, or socioeconomic background?
2. Is instruction based on a dynamic conception of the learner and the learning process?
3. Is instruction concerned with the immediate and projected needs, problems, and interests of the students?
4. Does instruction provide effectively for learning through direct experience in the school and the community?
5. Is instruction designed to develop the ideals, attitudes, knowledge, and skills needed by all citizens in our traffic society?
6. Does instruction allow for utilization of modern instructional technology?

[3] Alberty and Alberty, op. cit., pp. 469-73.

7. Does instruction provide for use of a modern plan of unit teaching and learning?
8. Does instruction provide effectively for democratic student participation in the classroom?
9. Does instruction allow for cooperative planning of learning experiences by teachers and students?
10. Does instruction provide satisfactorily for instructional materials as a regular part of classroom instruction?
11. Does instruction provide for systematic and continuous evaluation of student progress?

Criteria for Selecting Learning Experiences

The planning of realistic learning experiences for students of driver education should be a significant phase of the teacher's instructional preparation. Experiences should be planned so as to enhance learning and assist in the achievement of program objectives. Haphazard planning on the part of the teacher results in poor instruction and lack of student interest and accomplishment.

The Fourth National Conference on Driver Education suggests that the following criteria be used in the selection of learning experiences for driver education students. Learning experiences selected should:[4]

1. Be consistent with the general objectives of education.
2. Contribute to the achievement of the specific purposes of the course.
3. Contribute to the development of safety consciousness.
4. Provide for acquisition of correct driving habits.
5. Insure a complete and balanced program.
6. Be psychologically sound and socially acceptable.
7. Originate in problems that reflect student needs.
8. Accommodate individual differences.
9. Motivate the student to continue in the maintenance and improvement of his proficiency as a safe driver and good traffic citizen.
10. Provide for and encourage student-centered activities.

Objectives of Classroom Instruction

All instruction in driver education should be designed to produce specific accomplishments. This implies that instruction is to be carefully thought out and planned for groups and individual students. The objectives of the classroom program are to do the following:

1. Teach knowledge concepts necessary for safe motoring.
2. Gain an understanding of the interrelationship between man, machines (vehicles), and environment.

[4] National Commission on Safety Education, *Policies and Practices in Driver and Traffic Safety Education* (Washington, D.C.: National Education Association, 1964), pp. 3–4.

3. Teach the concept of traffic citizenship.
4. Teach the values of wholesome driver behavior.
5. Stimulate interest and participation in efforts to improve traffic conditions through legislative measures, application of engineering principles, and support of enforcement functions.
6. Gain an understanding of how a motor vehicle functions.

Classroom experiences and activities planned for driver education students should be based on one or more of the objectives listed, for there is a close relationship between learning, classroom content, student accomplishments, and objectives.

Figure 7-2. Classroom Instructional System (Courtesy Scheib Industries, Inc.)

CLASSROOM STANDARDS

A classroom course in driver education should include a number of instruction hours comparable to that of other subjects in the school's curriculum. The recent national conference on driver education recommended "that the course consist of 90 hours of structured learning experiences."[5] Many school systems are meeting this standard, and it is recommended that school systems initiating driver education courses meet the full-semester requirement. In those instances when schools may wish to begin with a lesser number of hours, it is

[5] American Driver and Traffic Safety Education Association, *Policies and Guidelines for Driver Traffic Safety Education* (Washington, D.C.: The Association, 1974), p. 15.

121

suggested that a minimum of 45 hours of classroom instruction be given. This would mean the offering of a comprehensive nine-week classroom program.

In order to accomplish the stated objectives of driver education, it is necessary that a full-semester program be given to each driver education student. The education and training of competent, safe and efficient traffic citizens will result only from a program complete enough to allow the teacher to develop in depth the necessary knowledge, attitudes, and skills essential to performance of the driving task.

Classroom Organization Plans

The results of a driver and traffic safety education program are dependent on how the pattern of instruction is organized. Obviously some classroom organizational plans are more desirable than others. When a decision must be made concerning the establishment of a classroom course, administrators and teachers should consider (1) program objectives, (2) desirable course characteristics, and (3) recommended classroom standards.

SEPARATE COURSE. The most desirable way to organize classroom instruction is through a separate course. Classroom driver education is a course comparable to other classroom subjects offered by the school. Therefore it should be established with the same time standards as other courses in the school's curriculum. With such an organizational plan the teacher can develop a quality course that will motivate learning on the part of the student.

INTEGRATION. Another plan used in organizing classroom instruction is that of integration. In this plan, time is shared with another subject during the same period. For example, nine weeks of a semester are given to driver education and nine weeks to general science or social studies. Therefore each subject would be identified and receive equal amounts of time. In some instances the same teacher, if properly certified, would teach both subjects, whereas other situations might require two different instructors.

UNIT APPROACH. The unit approach to classroom teaching combines a unit of driver education instruction with that of some other subject. A block of time is allowed for the driver education unit. Needless to say, this would not be a comprehensive classroom program. Such instruction is not identified in the school's curriculum, and the teacher of the identified course would do the teaching.

CORRELATION. When instruction is offered through the method of correlation, the teaching of traffic safety occurs as the instructor finds the appropriate place and time to relate it to the content of another subject. Many times this is referred to as incidental teaching. It is assumed that the individual teacher will relate such facts and information as logical opportunities arise in the teaching of a course— for example, English, physics, or home economics. Thus, theoretically, traffic safety could be related to all courses included in the secondary school's curriculum.

Your Total Projected Path Of Travel Has 3 Parts:

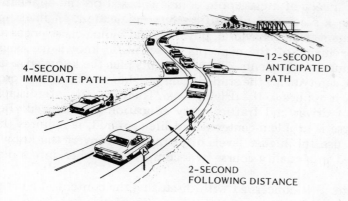

4-SECOND
IMMEDIATE PATH

12-SECOND
ANTICIPATED
PATH

2-SECOND
FOLLOWING DISTANCE

Vehicle Speed Should Be Determined by
Making Three Assessments Within an Area

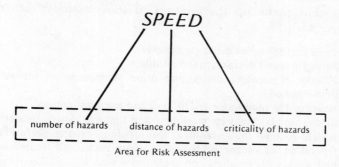

SPEED

number of hazards   distance of hazards   criticality of hazards

Area for Risk Assessment

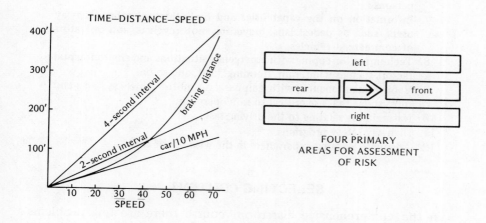

TIME–DISTANCE–SPEED

400'
300'
200'
100'

4-second interval
braking distance
2-second interval
car/10 MPH

10 20 30 40 50 60 70
SPEED

left

rear → front

right

FOUR PRIMARY
AREAS FOR ASSESSMENT
OF RISK

Figure 7–3. Classroom Instructional Concepts

123

KNOWLEDGE CONCEPTS TO BE TAUGHT

The concept of a classroom course is based on the application of the three E's concept of traffic safety—education, engineering, and enforcement. The behavioral, physical, and biological sciences are the basis for many of the concepts of scientific knowledge taught to driver education students. These concepts plus the knowledge unique to traffic safety helps the student gain insights into the traffic problem and how it applies to the driving task. Therefore the interdisciplinary nature of driver and traffic safety education is evidenced. Because the course is problem-centered and life-centered, it requires the student to use the higher levels of learning to convert the knowledge, presented in a quality course by a competent teacher, into a personal value.

Chapter 8 is concerned with discussing the content of a classroom course. In addition, suggestions are made relative to selected units of study. This section will identify concepts of fundamental knowledge that form the basis for the development of a classroom program. The following concepts are suggested by the National Conference on Safety Education as the basis for a classroom course. Knowledge concepts that make up the content of the classroom program are concerned with:[6]

1. Basic and advanced driving maneuvers.
2. Perceptual and decision-making skills.
3. Effects of alcohol, drugs, and other substances on the driving performance.
4. Rules of the road (state traffic laws and local ordinances).
5. Signs, signals, highway markings, and highway design innovations which require understanding for efficient driving performance.
6. Operation of motor vehicles on urban, rural, and limited-access highways with emphasis on techniques that will aid the driver in avoiding collisions, protect the driver and passenger in the event of a collision, and facilitate the transportation and care of injured persons.
7. Information on the capabilities and limitations of other highway users, such as pedestrians, bicyclists, motorcyclists, and operators of commercial vehicles.
8. Techniques for coping with emergency situations and environmental factors such as wind, rain, flooding, heat, and so on.
9. Vehicle maintenance, with emphasis on motor vehicle systems and subsystems that are critical to safe operation.
10. Natural laws relating to the driving task.
11. Highway safety programs.
12. Adequate learning experiences in the wise use of fuel.

SELECTING CONTENT

In the comprehensive classroom course there are few problems encountered by the instructor relative to the selection of content.

[6] Ibid., p. 17.

But the teacher in this type of situation is faced more with the decision of proper time allotments for the various units to be taught. Any one of the several high school texts identified in Chapter 10 is suitable for use in a semester program. Again the problem is one of giving priority to units deemed most important and awarding the proper number of class periods to such units.

Time allotments for classroom courses do vary from school to school. Therefore it is wise to use some reasonable guidelines to help adapt a textbook to the requirements of the individual course. Moreover, it must be kept in mind that a limited classroom schedule calls for limited textbook study and a curtailing of the use of class discussion, individual projects, resource persons, field trips, films or filmstrips, and other valuable aids to learning.

The teacher faced with deciding what content to include in a classroom course may find the following criteria useful in making such determinations:

1. Does the unit relate to a significant traffic problem involving youth?
2. Does the unit assist in the development of wholesome attitudes?
3. Does the unit help the student gain an understanding and appreciation of his role in traffic safety matters?
4. Can the unit selected be covered in depth in the amount of time available and allotted to the unit?
5. Does the unit contribute to the development of competent traffic citizens?
6. Will the unit chosen allow for student participation in the amount of time available?
7. What is the entry level of the student? Has the student had some predriver education experience?

Classroom schedules require the teacher to select the most pertinent content. The following section briefly presents various classroom organizational plans. The amount of content to be included depends on the number of classroom hours available.

Full Semester Course

A full semester's program provides an ideal time allotment for classroom work in driver education. Adequate time is available to cover the content of a classroom text. Moreover, the teacher has an opportunity to use group discussions, student projects, films and filmstrips, and many other worthwhile teaching aids. In addition, supplementary readings can be assigned, traffic surveys taken, and several other learning activities attempted. It is suggested that schools assign a full semester (90 hours) to the teaching of the classroom course in driver education.

Forty-Five-Hour Course

Many schools give only nine weeks (45 hours) to the teaching of the classroom driver education course. This time allows the teacher to develop a comprehensive classroom schedule. But obviously it does not allow for the covering of classroom content in the depth that is possible in the full semester course. Therefore, with limited time the teacher must develop priorities and select the most critical units to be taught.

With such a classroom schedule the teacher should do a superior job of planning to get maximum benefit from the time available for instruction. Moreover, instructional materials must be chosen with great care for maximum usefulness to the student and the accomplishment of program objectives.

Thirty-Hour Course

The least desirable classroom program schedule is one that calls for a minimum of 30 hours of instruction. The content needed for a sound program of teaching is severely curtailed. To do an adequate job with any one classroom unit, it is necessary to omit many units of instruction from the classroom schedule. Thus it is the responsibility of the teacher to choose units that will be most beneficial to the student. The criteria suggested earlier in the chapter should be consulted by the teacher faced with the problem of omitting valuable classroom units.

The use of instructional materials and other helpful classroom methods shall be limited by a lack of time. Without question, the teacher must plan his work well to make the course a worthwhile experience for students. Also, the teacher must do an outstanding job of teaching if program objectives are to be realized.

LEARNING ACTIVITIES

1. Survey the driver education programs of 15 secondary schools, and determine the type of classroom organizational plan used in each.
2. List the advantages of scheduling driver education over a full semester. Specifically identify those principles of learning that would be involved.
3. Develop a chart depicting the knowledge concepts that should be taught to students of driver education.
4. The improvement of instruction is necessary in the upgrading of driver education programs. Be prepared to discuss in class how you would go about doing this.

SELECTED RESOURCES

American Driver and Traffic Safety Education Association. *Policies and Guidelines for Driver and Traffic Safety Education.* Washington, D.C.: The Association, 1974.

Automotive Safety Foundation. *A Resource Curriculum in Driver and Traffic Safety Education.* Washington, D.C.: The Foundation (January 1970).

Gagne, Robert M. "Modern Learning Principles and Driver Education," *Concepts.* Hartford, Conn.: Aetna Life & Casualty Vol. 4, No. 2 (Spring-Summer 1971).

Gronlund, Norman E. *Stating Behavioral Objectives for Classroom Instruction.* New York: Macmillan Publishing Co., Inc., 1970.

Lauer, A. R. *The Psychology of Driving.* Springfield, Ill.: Charles C. Thomas, Publisher, 1972.

McKnight, A. James, and Bert B. Adams. *Driver Education Task Analysis, Volume III: Instructional Objective.* Washington, D.C.: Department of Transportation, PB202-247, Hum RRO Technical Report 71-9 (March 1971).

———. *Driver Education Task Analysis, Volume IV: The Development of Instructional Objectives.* Washington, D.C.: Department of Transportation, PB202-248, Hum RRO Report IR-DI-71-1 (March 1971).

Platt, Fletcher, N. *Operations Analysis of Traffic Safety.* Dearborn, Mich.: Ford Motor Company, 1959.

Strasser, Marland K., et al. *Driver Education: Learning to Drive Defensively.* River Forest, Ill.: Laidlaw Brothers, Publishers, 1973.

Chapter 8

Content of the Classroom Program

OBJECTIVE: The student will be able to identify the content of a classroom driver education program and use that knowledge in the development of appropriate instructional units.

A sound, comprehensive program of classroom instruction is essential to the attainment of the stated objectives of driver education. Program objectives are discussed in greater detail in Chapter 3.

It is in the classroom that the knowledge, understanding, and positive attitudes of social responsibility involved in the successful operation of a motor vehicle must be inculcated. This instruction must be reinforced by an integrated program of laboratory experience in the actual operation of a motor vehicle if the necessary habits and skills required to produce safer drivers are to be developed to the optimum. The laboratory phase of driver and traffic safety education is the practical application of classroom experiences to the driving task.

The development of proper driver attitudes cannot be achieved through preaching, moralizing, or attempting to force the student to accept the attitudes of the instructor, even if the attitudes of the instructor are above reproach. *The only way to develop sound attitudes is to provide types of learning experiences that will enable the student independently to develop positive attitudes based on his own thinking.* This will require a knowledge in reasonable depth of the many ramifications of the total traffic problem. It will require an opportunity for an interaction of the experiences of an entire class.

It will also require a sufficient period of time to permit the gradual evolution of the concept of a sense of social responsibility, with regard to the use of motor vehicles, to develop in the mind of each student. Russell I. Brown, President of the Safety Management Institute, has said that "Driver education offers one of the greatest opportunities to provide on-the-job experience in citizenship for our nation's youth."[1] It becomes readily apparent that if driver education is the laboratory of citizenship for youth, then the achievements of driver education can be realized fully only in classes small enough to facilitate spontaneous discussion of problems and of sufficient duration to permit the attainment of a broad knowledge and understanding of the basic elements of the traffic accident problem. It is for this reason that the National Conference on Safety Education stated that driver education courses "consist of 90 hours of structured learning experiences, scheduled over a full term."[2] Advanced driving courses should be available as reinforcement prior to leaving the secondary school.

This chapter will be concerned with an explanation of the necessary depth of understanding in a number of subject areas that a student must have in order to become a skilled driver and an acceptable traffic citizen. These areas will include the driver, the laws affecting driving, driving practices, the car, economics of driving, and several additional areas. The chapter will discuss only the nature and scope of these major topics. There is not sufficient space to deal in detail with each area. There are now a number of good high school driver education textbooks that treat the subject content of these areas in depth. A vast amount of pamphlet and periodical literature is also available. A number of these texts are listed in the selected resources at the end of this chapter. These texts will vary in the manner in which the content is treated and the emphasis placed on given areas, but most of them will deal in one way or another with the basic subject matter. Also most states have curriculum products for the teacher based upon an analysis of the driving task. However, it will be the responsibility of the teacher to supplement his own knowledge through advanced courses in driver education and related areas and through individual study. Driver and traffic safety education is a dynamic area of education, and a continuous study of current literature and new research findings is essential to keep up to date in the field. It will be the responsibility of each teacher to determine the time to allocate to the various topics as he develops his own course of study.

Each content area to be discussed will be organized in this manner: (1) the nature and scope of the problem will be defined, (2) its function in a comprehensive driver and traffic safety education class will be outlined, (3) the subject will be treated in brief, and (4) a listing

[1] The President's Committee for Traffic Safety, *Report of Regional Driver Education Workshops* (Washington, D.C.: The Committee, February 1964), p. 34.

[2] American Driver and Traffic Safety Education Association, *Policies and Guidelines for Driver and Traffic Safety Education* (Washington, D.C.: The Association, 1974), p. 15.

129

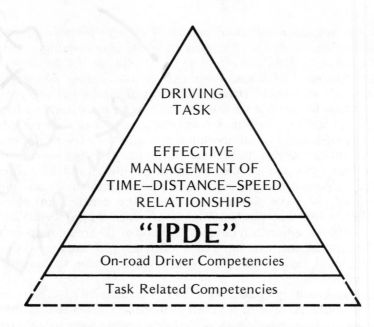

DRIVING
TASK

EFFECTIVE
MANAGEMENT OF
TIME—DISTANCE—SPEED
RELATIONSHIPS

"IPDE"

On-road Driver Competencies

Task Related Competencies

To Perfect "IPDE"
You Must Be ABle To:

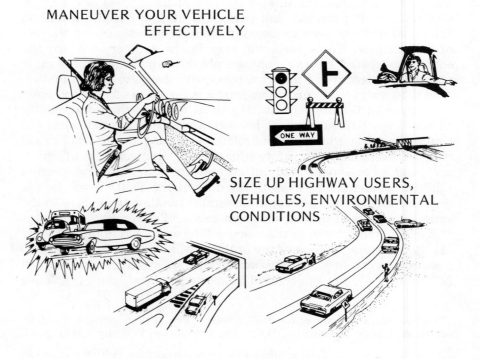

MANEUVER YOUR VEHICLE
EFFECTIVELY

SIZE UP HIGHWAY USERS,
VEHICLES, ENVIRONMENTAL
CONDITIONS

Figure 8-1. An IPDE Instructional Approach

of the topics will follow that should be included in the discussion of this subject area in the driver education classroom.

THE DRIVER

It has been said on many occasions that the driver is the most important single element in traffic safety. Thus, it is important for the informed traffic citizen to understand the nature of the characteristics of the driver and how they relate to the driving task. It is only through understanding personal physical and psychological capacities and limitations that the student will be able to apply the concept of defensive driving.

The classroom program in driver and traffic safety education must include information relating to the many facets of the driver. It should include the numerous responsibilities to be assumed in the safe operation of a motor vehicle, the physical capacities and limitations of drivers, the effects of alcohol and drugs on the judgment and performance of both drivers and pedestrians, and the mental and emotional capacities and limitations of both drivers and pedestrians.

Driver Responsibility

When a person accepts a driver license from his state government, he accepts a responsibility that will involve the lives and personal safety of millions of people, including himself. The manner in which he assumes that responsibility is of considerable significance to our entire society. This is particularly true of the young driver because of the comparatively bad driving record of his age group and because of the many burdens and anxieties that driving will create for the parents or guardians of teen-age drivers. The pattern of family living changes when the teenager begins to drive. This results in many social and economic adjustments for the entire family unit. A knowledge and understanding of this impact on family life should be made evident to the driver education student early in the course so that he will be able to interpret correctly the many aspects of driver education in terms of his own responsibilities. The young driver has a responsibility also to law enforcement agencies, driver license personnel, and to all users of the highways.

As an introductory unit of instruction in the course, this emphasis on personal responsibility in accepting a license to drive provides an opportunity to present a broad overview of the entire course. Each of the units of instruction in a driver education class is designed primarily to cause the student to realize fully his responsibilities as a safe driver and a good traffic citizen.

Requirements for driver licensing
Privilege of driving
Responsibilities to all other highway users
Responsibilities to governmental agencies
Impact on family living
Overview of driver education course

Mental and Emotional Characteristics

There is an increasing awareness today that the manner in which a driver accepts his driving responsibilities is a fairly good index of his total personality. It is, perhaps, a better indication of the type of person he is than his behavior under almost any other circumstances would reveal. A good indication of this is the fact that many personnel directors obtain the driving records of job applicants from departments of motor vehicles. They feel that a poor driving risk may be a poor employment risk as well.

It does not matter whether it is called driver attitude, driver psychology, driver personality, or some other name; there is concern with the relationship of human behavior and its manifestations in driving. Current research findings point to the existence of a positive correlation between a person's adjustment to other social forces and his adjustment to his driving responsibilities. The good citizen in the school, community, and business world is likely to be a good traffic citizen also. This will tend to become true to an even greater extent when a larger segment of our society, through driver and traffic safety education classes, becomes as well informed about the responsibilities of traffic citizenship as about responsibilities of citizenship in other aspects of daily life.

Drivers can be separated into the following broad, general classifications: problem drivers, superior or expert drivers, and average or casual drivers. Although the terminology related to these groups may vary, the concepts are the same.

Problem drivers are readily identifiable by their records of traffic accidents and convictions for moving violations maintained by motor vehicle departments. Although small percentagewise, they represent millions of licensed drivers in the nation. This group will tend to be, for the most part, maladjusted persons. They have tendencies toward the following: aggression toward society as a whole, manifestations of instability, resentment to any type of authority, egocentric behavior, failure to assume responsibility, lack of respect for the rights of others, emotionalism, lack of attention, exhibitionism, and other undesirable personal characteristics.

Superior drivers, again a comparatively small group, have the opposite characteristics of the problem driver. Their ability to adjust in a positive way to the many stresses and tensions of society permits them to become responsible drivers who can drive almost indefinitely without accidents or traffic violations.

The bulk of the driving population are just average or casual drivers. For the most part they are successful drivers. But through distraction from their driving tasks or pressures of everyday living they commit driving errors that often result in tragedy. To a large degree the problem drivers must be controlled through enforcement efforts or removal from the highways. The superior drivers will, by means of self-control or self-enforcement, continue to drive safely. The large majority of average drivers provide the greatest promise for traffic accident reduction through education. If they can be inculcated with attitudes of safe and responsible driving and a realization that a posture of dedicated responsibility and attention is required every minute behind the wheel, they can become successful, accident-free, superior drivers.

If young drivers are to drive as safely as their physical abilities will permit, it is important for them to comprehend these concepts. It is the responsibility of the driver educator to develop the feeling that safe driving is the desirable type of driving, and it should be the goal of every new driver. This is one of the most important units of instruction in a driver and traffic safety education class. Successful teaching here will lay the groundwork for a student's desirable achievement in other phases of the classroom and laboratory program.

Topics for Study

Attitudes
Attention
Emotional maturity
Courtesy
Driving fitness
Defensive driving
Accident repeaters
Self-control
The self-centered driver
Exhibitionism
Driver responsibility

Physical Characteristics

The physical condition of the driver has an important influence on the manner in which he will be able to operate his vehicle. This fact is of such concern to legislators that some states have enacted laws to strengthen license examinations and require examination of persons cited for numerous violations and those age 65 and over. It is important that drivers be familiar with the significance of physical condition and its relationship to safe driving.

The driver education student should learn of the physical limitations to safe driving so he will be more apt to use the appropriate precautions necessary when being overcome by fatigue or when visibility is dangerously limited. He must recognize also the significance of individual differences of drivers as revealed in the testing of vision. There is no stronger case to be made for defensive driving than the fact that other drivers vary greatly in their abilities to perceive emergency situations and to react to them with safety. Also, the student must understand his own physical limitations and learn to drive within a desirable margin of safety to compensate for them.

The classroom program in driver and traffic safety education should explore all phases of physical characteristics of drivers that relate to the safe operation of a motor vehicle. These will include such factors as vision, hearing, permanent and temporary disabling conditions, age, and reaction time. There are many corrective and compensative measures that can lessen the hazards of a number of these physical limitations.

An effective way to present the relationship of physical limitations to traffic safety is through the administration of psychophysical tests to members of the class. It was formerly thought that persons with superior vision, reaction time, and other physical qualities were superior drivers. However, research has revealed that this is not necessarily true. To drive most efficiently it is important to be physically fit, but even with the best physical condition it is important to use all of the accepted techniques of safe driving to prevent accidents.

Topics for Study

Physical limitations
Fatigue
Corrections and compensations
Individual differences in drivers
Traffic hazards caused by individual limitations
Vision
Hearing
Permanent and temporary disabilities
Age
Carbon monoxide poisoning
Physical disabilities

Effects of Alcohol and Other Drugs

The use of alcohol and other drugs by drivers and pedestrians constitutes a definite hazard on our streets and highways. Many studies have indicated that a high percentage of all fatal automobile accidents involve a drinking driver. "The largest year-long survey to date of post-mortem blood alcohol determination showed 62 per cent of the drivers responsible for accidents had been drinking and 53 per cent were under the influence of alcohol."[3] This percentage increases

[3] National Safety Council, *Accident Facts* (Chicago: The Council, 1975), p. 52.

134

considerably over holiday periods. The use of drugs in any form, from serious addiction to alkaloid narcotics to perscription drugs or tranquilizer pills, decreases driving efficiency and presents a serious problem on the road. Because of these effects, it is important that all drivers be made aware of this hazard. They should realize the physical and emotional effects that the use of alcohol and other drugs will have on themselves and the many other users of the highway, both drivers and pedestrians. This strengthens their comprehension of the need for defensive driving practices as protection from the unpredictable actions of drivers and pedestrians so impaired.

ALCOHOL. Although many persons use alcohol as a means of escape from tensions or pressures, it actually acts as a depressant rather than a stimulant. It will increase reaction time, release normal inhibitions, develop a false sense of confidence, and seriously impair judgment on the part of the driver or pedestrian. Dr. Ira Cisin says, "It is generally conceded that virtually any discernible amount of alcohol in the blood will be accompanied by a decrease in competence in the operation of a motor vehicle."[4] Because drinking, particularly to excess, is frequently motivated by deep-seated emotional causes, the drinking driver may well be a particular hazard to driving because of these manifestations of maladjustment. In some respects the drinking driver is a greater hazard than the "drunk" driver, because the latter will often be aware of his limitations and be overcautious in his driving.

There is need for greater control of the drinking driver. Most states have laws permitting the use of chemical tests to determine intoxication and the degree of impairment in driving. All states require the applicant for a driver license to sign a statement that he will submit to tests to determine intoxication when requested to do so or else surrender his license. These are known as *implied consent* laws, because the applicant gives his consent to take such tests before he receives his license to drive. There should be a more general use of these techniques as a means of providing greater traffic safety.

OTHER DRUGS. Like alcohol, the use of other drugs presents a serious hazard to safe driving. The use of drugs is frequently the result of emotional problems that would affect the person's driving efficiency even though drugs were not used. The traffic problem created by the addict is apparently not serious, perhaps because the typical addict does little driving. However, the use of pep pills, tranquilizers, and prescription drugs all have serious physical effects that make users of them serious traffic hazards. A combination of the use of alcohol and other drugs is perhaps the most serious condition of all.

Topics for Study

Alcohol, other drugs, and the accident problem
Physical effects of alcohol and other drugs

[4] Bernard H. Fox and James H. Fox, eds., *Alcohol and Traffic Safety* (Bethesda, Md.: National Institutes of Health, May 1963), p. 3.

Psychological effects of alcohol and other drugs
Drinking drivers vs. "drunk" drivers
Alcohol as an escape
False sense of confidence
Tranquilizers and prescription drugs
Drug addiction including alcoholism
A combination of alcohol and other drugs.

LAWS AFFECTING DRIVING

There are numerous laws, both natural and man-made, that have an important influence on the safe operation of a motor vehicle. Some authorities say that "in most motor vehicle accidents, improper driving of one kind or another contributes to the accident."[5] In approximately 70 per cent of all fatal traffic accidents, one or more of the drivers involved are found to be in violation of at least one traffic law. It is also true that a large number of these accidents involve drivers who have been violating some natural force that would inevitably lead to an accident. Because research shows that a lack of knowledge of traffic laws and safe driving practices is a characteristic of accident-involved drivers as compared to accident-free drivers, it would suggest that a sound accident prevention measure involved in the proper education of drivers would be an emphasis on a knowledge of both man-made and natural laws.

The ever-increasing mobility of drivers into all parts of the nation presents a constant reminder of the urgent need for more uniformity of traffic laws in the various states. The millions of traffic citations issued annually and the varying manner in which traffic enforcement is handled by both the police and the courts are testimony to the fact that there is need for greater self-enforcement on the part of drivers and a more coordinated legal enforcement of traffic laws. The well-prepared driver education student should have a thorough knowledge and understanding of the functions and responsibilities of making, observing, and enforcing traffic laws.

Natural Laws—Forces of Nature

There are certain forces of nature that demand strict obedience in driving. Failure to abide by these forces, or natural laws as they are often called, will result in the car's going out of control and will frequently result in a serious traffic crash. It is essential that driver and traffic safety education students be made thoroughly familiar with these natural forces and that such forces be heeded if the driver is to maintain control of his vehicle. It is unquestionably true that there are many accidents among particularly new and inexperienced drivers because they lack a fundamental knowledge of the effect of natural forces on the operation of an automobile under different types of road and traffic conditions.

[5] National Safety Council, op. cit., p. 48.

136

Particular attention should be given to the relationship of the effect of natural forces to such factors as speed, force of impact, stopping distances, types of road surfaces, and weather conditions. Many of these factors cannot be realistically experienced in the laboratory phase of the driver education program because of the extreme hazards involved. Therefore the teacher should make use of all possible examples, demonstrations, films, and other teaching aids and devices in order to make a lasting impact on the students concerning the significance of the effect of natural forces on safe driving.

Topics for Study

Friction
Centrifugal force
Inertia
Energy—potential and kinetic
Gravity
Force of impact
Speed and natural forces
Stopping distances

Man-made Laws

Because a sound knowledge of traffic laws and regulations and obeying them in driving are important factors in safe driving, they warrant particular emphasis in every driver education class. Instruction in traffic laws is important also because the student will have to know these rules to obtain a permit to receive laboratory instruction that may come very shortly after the beginning of the course. The grades students receive on the written portion of the driver license examination is also one simple and direct evaluation of the effectiveness of the teacher's instruction.

The objective of teaching the rules of the road should be *knowledge with understanding*. If the student understands the reason for the law and feels that it is a good law, necessary to maintain safety and a ready flow of traffic on the highways, he will learn it, retain it, and obey it. A study of uniform traffic laws as recommended by the National Committee on Uniform Traffic Laws and Ordinances in the Uniform Vehicle Code and the Model Traffic Ordinance will be helpful to develop proper student understanding of traffic laws and their importance to safe driving. These may well be the first steps to his becoming a safe driver. To accomplish this desired end with his students, a teacher must be positive in his own regard of the protective force of the law and have a thorough knowledge of traffic laws and ordinances in his state and city. In addition to the traffic laws, the student should be thoroughly instructed in other laws relating to motor vehicle operation and use, such as financial responsibility, obtaining a driver license, vehicle registration, and others.

Topics for Study

Obtaining a license
Right of way
Speeding
Pedestrian practices
Passing
Turning
Signaling
Signs, signals, and markings
Equipment regulations
Vehicle registration
Financial responsibility
Accident reports
Uniformity in traffic laws

Making, Observing, and Enforcing Laws

A more thorough understanding of the desirability of obeying traffic laws can be achieved through a study of the manner in which such laws are made, observed, and enforced. Basic concepts that should be established are that laws grow out of needs and that compliance with the traffic laws is the socially desirable thing to do.

Legislators are sensitive to the expressed wishes of their constituents. The best prospects of obtaining a sound program of traffic laws and ordinances with a desirable degree of uniformity in the various jurisdictions throughout the nation is through the demands of citizens. The best hope of a long-range program of public education is through the more than 3 million students in driver education classes each year.[6] Students should be informed about desirable uniform laws and the techniques of informing legislators of the wishes of citizens in this regard. As these young people become of voting age, they can provide a strong force of informed public opinion that can make desired uniformity a reality.

Traffic law enforcement is a two-phase program involving both self-enforcement and enforcement by the police and courts. The most effective approach is the development of a strong desire for self-enforcement on the part of every individual. Students completing a driver education course should have a strong conviction of the need for traffic law enforcement based upon knowledge and understanding of the necessity of all drivers to operate a motor vehicle in compliance with the law. It should be an objective of driver educators to release into the national pool of drivers every year millions of young drivers who will not need traffic police supervision to require compliance with traffic laws and ordinances.

[6] National Highway Traffic Safety Administration, *Statewide Highway Safety Program Assessment—A National Estimate of Performance* (Washington, D.C.: The Administration, July 1975), p. 94.

There will always be a small group of drivers who will lack the discipline or knowledge of traffic laws to insure compliance without police enforcement efforts. Driver and traffic safety education-trained students should form a large group of informed citizens to provide strong support of traffic law enforcement efforts as an important factor in reducing traffic accidents on our streets and highways.

Topics for Study

Origin of traffic laws
Need for modern, uniform traffic laws
The function of courts in traffic law enforcement
Public education for compliance with traffic laws
Legislating traffic laws
The Uniform Vehicle Code
The Model Traffic Ordinance
Self-enforcement of traffic laws
Police enforcement
Traffic control devices

SAFE-DRIVING PRACTICES

There is a great deal of information relating to safe-driving practices that can be taught in the classroom. Such information can be presented in lecture, discussion, and illustration, using chalkboard and magnetic board. This instruction can be supplemented with the many excellent films and film strips that describe the basic traffic maneuvers as well as advanced driving skills that are required for successful driving under both adverse and emergency driving situations. Many of these experiences are of such a nature that it is impractical to duplicate them under actual driving conditions in the car.

One of the advantages of classroom presentations is the fact that as many as 30 or more students can be instructed in this manner, whereas no more than four can be dealt with at a time in the car. It is, therefore, a greater economy of time to provide appropriate instruction in safe-driving practices in the classroom situation. However, careful attention should be paid to the development of a high degree of articulation of instruction between the classroom and the laboratory instruction. Uniform terminology should be adopted for use in both situations, and the same approach should always be followed to avoid confusion of students, particularly if different teachers are giving the classroom and the laboratory instruction.

Some of the areas of emphasis that can be included in classroom instruction in safe-driving practices are knowledge of the driving compartment, basic driving maneuvers, advanced driving maneuvers, adverse, special, and emergency situations, and safe- and energy-saving driving practices. Although they may be treated differently, most textbooks have materials related to these safe-driving practices.

The Driver's Compartment

A prime factor in getting the student started properly in behind-the-wheel instruction is to have him feel comfortable and at ease from the very beginning of his driving experience. A thorough knowledge of the many instruments and controls found in the driving compartment is a good beginning point to develop this attitude on the part of the student. Much of this information can be presented in the classroom with a larger group of students, thereby effecting an economy of time to provide additional opportunity for actual driving experience in the laboratory phase of the program.

Group instruction in orientation to the car should include achieving a comfortable position in the seat, properly adjusting seat in relation to foot controls, adjusting seat belt, shoulder harness, and mirrors, checking the brake, and locking the doors. The student should be familiar with the functions of the instruments and gauges, the control devices, the safety devices, and the accessories. With this understanding of functions developed in the classroom, an identification of the devices and controls in the driving compartment when the student first gets into the car is all that is necessary to prepare him for his first driving lesson.

Topics for Study

Instruments and gauges
Starting instruments
Control instruments
Safety instruments
Accessories
Steps in starting the engine
Seat belt and shoulder harness

Basic Maneuvers

The fundamental or basic maneuvers of starting, stopping, backing, turning, and parking are the first concern of the instructor with a beginning driver. If these basic maneuvers are learned properly, the student will be equipped, with the development of judgment gained through practice and experience, to become a skillful driver. The instructor must remember that the techniques of these basic skills are unfamiliar to the student. A thorough analysis and step-by-step explanation of the anatomy of these basic skills in the classroom situation will prepare the student to make much more satisfactory progress when he gets into the car for his laboratory instruction. If classroom instruction has preceded the laboratory phase of the program, the instructor should require the student to review these basic driving procedures, found in his textbook, prior to laboratory sessions on turning, parking, and other basic maneuvers. If the teacher follows these procedures, he will save valuable instructional time and enjoy a greater degree of achievement on the part of his students.

140

Topics for Study

Starting, stopping, and backing
Steering
Shifting gears
Turning
Parking
Driving on hills
Seeing habits

Advanced Maneuvers

When the student has completed a satisfactory degree of mastery of the basic maneuvers, he is ready to move to more advanced driving practices. These will deal largely with meeting the increasingly complex driving situations he will encounter as he gets into heavier traffic, both on city streets and country highways, depending largely upon the types of experience that will be available in any given school location. Metropolitan and rural areas provide quite different types of experience. However, regardless of traffic conditions, the student will need to practice such maneuvers in learning to adjust to the many, rapidly changing elements of the traffic pattern and acquiring the skills to meet them satisfactorily. The classroom provides an opportunity to prepare the student for these experiences. Through class presentation and discussion, assigned reading in the textbook, and visual presentations of chalkboard diagrams, slides, and films, the teacher is able to accelerate the student's progress in developing these necessary skills.

Topics for Study

Applying IPDE Concept
Adjusting speed to traffic flow
Following at proper distances
Maintaining space cushion
Changing lanes
Following traffic signs and signals
Observing the total traffic pattern
Adjusting to intersections
Observing pedestrians and cyclists
Keeping in lanes
Overtaking and passing

Adverse, Special, and Emergency Situations

There are many types of traffic situations that require special driving skills. These would include such things as adjusting to slippery road surfaces, driving on high-speed highways, or recovering from a skid. Some of these conditions are encountered in laboratory in-struction, whereas others are not because of the extraordinary hazards involved or the lack of available circumstances. However, the student should be aware of these conditions and provided with as much knowledge about how to confront them successfully as possible. Many of these conditions are treated very well in slide and film presentations. Others can be discussed and analyzed with the class. The instructor should make a special effort to include materials of this nature in the classroom phase of driver and traffic safety educa-tion. Emergency driving situations are dealt with effectively in driver simulator programs and on the multiple-car driving range facility.

Topics for Study

Emergency and evasive maneuvers
Motorcycle and traffic mix
Freeway problems and skills
Highway hypnosis and fatigue
Reduced visibility and night driving
Weather conditions
Road surfaces and conditions
Railroad crossings
Road construction and detours
Mountain driving
High water
Emergency stop on highways
Pulling out of a skid
Winter driving

Energy-Saving and Safe-Driving Practices

The manner in which a car is driven can have a measurable influence upon the safety and economy of its operation as well as its resale or trade-in value when the owner wishes to dispose of it. The way the brakes are applied can influence the life and safe condition of brake linings as well as affect tire wear. Quick starts and stops and emer-gency application of brakes can influence tire wear. Excessively high speeds increase gasoline consumption and, particularly in hot weather, cause greater wear on tires. The national 55 mph speed limit assists in the saving of the nation's fuel supply. There are ecological con-siderations that the driving teacher must teach the students. Bumping curbs or hitting objects or holes in the roadway will affect wheel alignment, which will lead to excessive tire wear and create hazardous mechanical conditions. All driving practices that tend to influence the safe mechanical condition or result in uneconomical operating costs for the driver should be considered in the driver education classroom.

Topics for Study

Ecology and driving
Driving and tire wear

142

Driving and gasoline consumption
Quick starts and stops
Avoiding striking objects
The economy of keeping the car in good mechanical condition
How high speeds affect safety and economy in driving
Economy and safety in proper use of brakes

THE CAR

Defective vehicles contribute materially to traffic crashes on the streets and highways of the nation. Although there is disagreement as to the actual percentage of accidents that can be attributed directly to faulty vehicles, it is a fact that this is either the primary cause or a contributing factor in a very large number of accidents. Some studies and inspection programs conducted in the past have found that "1 out of every 5 vehicles safety-checked needed service attention to one or more safe driving parts."[7] There are 32 states that require periodic motor vehicle inspections. In a recent year, over 70 million vehicles were inspected in these systems.[8]

It is not the purpose of a course in driver education to develop a skilled mechanic. However, it is necessary for each student to understand something of the complicated operations of the vehicle if he is to appreciate fully its limitations. To drive a vehicle beyond these limitations is to expose the operator and all other users of the highway to unusual hazards to their personal safety. The student should be familiar also with proper maintenance procedures. Although he probably will not perform the maintenance functions himself, he must know what preventive maintenance procedures are necessary to keep the vehicle in safe and efficient operating order at all times.

Construction

Opinions vary among driver educators concerning the knowledge of the mechanical operation of an automobile necessary for driver education students. In some foreign countries a proficiency in auto mechanics is a prerequisite to receiving a driver license. Many driver education teachers in America feel that no knowledge of mechanics is necessary to drive safely, and others feel that a knowledge of the mechanical operation is an aid to the student in learning the fundamental skills of safe driving. In any case, a knowledge of the fundamental principles of the operation of an automobile will be helpful to the teacher in answering student questions. Also, some knowledge of the operation of the car will no doubt be helpful to the student in understanding the limitations of the vehicle and in being aware of trouble signs that suggest the need for attention to keep the vehicle in safe and efficient operating condition.

[7] Auto Industries Highway Safety Committee, *Periodic Motor Vehicle Inspection* (Washington, D.C.: The Committee, 1960), p. 3.

[8] National Highway Traffic Safety Administration, op. cit., p. 114.

The classroom unit in automobile construction in driver education should be limited to the fundamental principles of the manner in which power is developed in the engine, how this power is transmitted to the drive wheels, and how the vehicle is controlled through steering and braking.

The automobile is an efficient mechanism designed to give many thousands of miles of safe and economic transportation. The manner in which it is driven will affect the efficiency and longevity of the engine, the rate of gasoline consumption, and the life of brakes and tires. An understanding of the operation of the vehicle is helpful to the student in developing driving practices that will conserve the car and impress on him the need for proper preventive maintenance procedures.

Topics for Study

Operation of the internal combustion engine
Ignition system
Electrical system
Cooling system
Power transmission
Steering system
Braking system
Design factors

Maintenance

The attention given to vehicle maintenance and the manner of maintenance have proven to be important factors of both safety and economy in commercial vehicle operations. This is also true in the use of private passenger cars, even though most modern cars do not require as frequent lubrication services as they did in the past. The most important preventive maintenance practice of the driver should be to read carefully the Owner's Manual that comes with each car and outlines clearly what maintenance functions should be performed and at what time intervals for that particular car.

Preventive maintenance should be a planned program of regular car care. There are routine procedures that should be followed each time gasoline is purchased, others to be completed at every lubrication, and still others at varying intervals, as prescribed in the Owner's Manual. Special attention should be given at times of seasonal changes or in preparation for a long trip. If proper air pressure is maintained, a system of rotation is followed, and proper driving procedures are used, tires will give much greater service. Maintenance attention should be given also to lights, batteries, brakes, the steering mechanism, and other parts that require periodic lubrication, adjustment, or replacement. The student should be made familiar with the various aspects of a continuous, planned maintenance program and how it can contribute to his safety and economy in driving.

Planning for preventive maintenance
The Owner's Manual
Routine maintenance procedures
Special maintenance procedures
Care of brakes
Tire care
The electrical system
The steering system
The cooling system
The power train
Meeting roadside emergency situations

THE ECONOMICS OF DRIVING

A well-informed user of the highways must have some knowledge of the fundamental economics of car ownership and use. The total investment in automobile transportation during the period of an active life-time is going to be one of a person's major expenditures, being nearly as much as he will spend for housing. If at least ten cents of every dollar that an individual will earn in his lifetime should be spent on the operation of motor vehicles, then he should be as informed as possible in ways that will lead his investment to the greatest safety, protection, and economy for him.

This section will deal with the economics and responsibilities of car purchase and ownership and the economic implications with regard to automobile insurance and financial responsibility law requirements. It will treat also the savings that can be effected through proper driving of the car and proper travel planning.

Car Ownership

Nearly every driver and traffic safety education student looks forward to the day when he will have a car of his own. However, very few of them have a realistic understanding of the legal and financial responsibilities of car ownership. In purchasing a used car, they frequently become the victims of unscrupulous practices that result in their paying excessive financing costs or purchasing a car with disguised mechanical deficiencies. Because these young people are generally unfamiliar with legal procedures, they frequently sign papers that they do not understand. Often this has disastrous financial results. Because many cars are sold from one young person to another and these cars are frequently altered considerably, they sometimes encounter serious problems involving proper motor vehicle registration.

The driver education class should prepare the student to encounter many of the unfamiliar problems involved in car ownership. He should know some of the qualities to look for in purchasing a car and the legal implications of sales contracts, interest charges, and automobile registration. This phase of the classroom program adapts itself particularly well to student projects involving these many ramifications of car ownership.

Topics for Study

Costs of car ownership and operation
Legal problems of a minor owning a car
Selecting a car, new or used
The sales contract
Financing the purchase of a car
Motor vehicle registration

Insurance and Financial Responsibility

Insurance protection is a virtual necessity for a responsible automobile owner or operator today. Because of the accident rate and the high cost of repairs, replacement, medical care, and other accident costs, the cost of insurance is substantial. It is particularly expensive for the teen-age driver because of the comparatively high rate and severity of traffic accidents in the teen-age group. However, because it has been shown that students who have received a complete course in driver education have fewer and less costly claims against insurance carriers, many companies offer reduced rates to students who have successfully completed an approved course. There are also reductions given by a number of companies to adults with good driving records. Because of the significant and costly role that automobile insurance plays in the life of nearly every driver, the driver education course should provide the student with an understanding of adequate insurance protection and its implications to the automobile owner. Because some type of financial responsibility law, including compulsory uninsured motorists protection, is in force in nearly every state in the nation, the student should be made aware of his obligations under such laws.

In some states, insurance agents' associations, in cooperation with driver educators, have prepared booklets on automobile insurance and financial responsibility laws specifically for use with high school driver education classes.[9] Several excellent films have been produced for this purpose also. A number of professional insurance people as well as insurance groups have made their services available as resource persons who appear in driver education classes to give authoritative presentations on this subject. By supplementing textbook treatment of the insurance problem with these many resources, the classroom teacher can make a significant contribution to the student's knowledge of this subject matter, which is of such primary importance to every driver and pedestrian.

[9] Illinois Insurance Information Service, *Automobile Insurance and Your Future, A Fact Book of Insurance Protection for Beginning Drivers* (Chicago: The Service, 1974).

146

Insurance terminology
How insurance rates are determined
Bodily injury liability
Property damage liability
Collision coverage
Comprehensive coverage
Medical payments insurance
Uninsured motorists coverage
Safe driver insurance plans
Financial responsibility laws
Accident reporting requirements under financial responsibility laws

Trip Planning and Economics

The automobile is such a common means of transportation for both business and pleasure that almost every person in the country will, at one time or another, make a long trip in a car. Accident records reveal that many such trips result in a disastrous traffic accident that was basically the result of a lack of proper planning. Frequently the cause may be listed as high speed, falling asleep at the wheel, highway hypnosis, faulty mechanical condition, faulty tires, or other apparent reasons. However, if sufficient time had been planned or the extent of the trip reduced, the driver might have been alert and avoided the accident. If the vehicle had been properly equipped and maintained, the accident might never have occurred.

This unit of instruction can deal with many things that have an important bearing upon the safety of the trip. It provides an excellent opportunity for group or class projects. The planning of a trip to include such factors as pretrip vehicle maintenance, adequate time allowance, rest stops for the driver, shortest and best route, accommodations en route, and costs can provide an interesting project and one that will contribute to safety in cross-country travel.

Topics for Study

Planning a route
Providing sufficient time
Making reservations
Pretrip car checkup
Estimating costs
Using road maps

CAUSES AND COSTS OF TRAFFIC ACCIDENTS

A basic concept of the social and economic dimension of the traffic accident problem in our society is essential if the student is to understand the significance of becoming a good traffic citizen. All of the elements of a total traffic safety program do not come into focus until their true meaning is spelled out in terms of human lives destroyed and the economic waste incurred. These impressive statistics were reviewed in some detail in Chapter 1 of this text from a historical point of view. However, to make this subject meaningful and of interest to high school students the statistics must be brought completely up to date and presented on state and local as well as the national level. *Accident Facts*, published annually, and the magazine *Traffic Safety*, published monthly, are National Safety Council publications that present the best sources of current national traffic accident statistics. State and local traffic safety agencies have current statistics available for use in driver education classes.

Although a considerable portion of the driver and traffic safety education class is devoted to a study of basic and reported causes of accidents, it is well to discuss accident causes in relation to social and economic costs. This brings into clearer perspective the fact that most traffic accidents are preventable and that the reduction of human failures that contribute so heavily to accidents should become a broad social objective of teen-age drivers.

Topics for Study

Traffic injuries and fatalities
Economic costs of traffic accidents
Social costs of traffic accidents
Basic causes of accidents
Role of under-25 driver

ENRICHMENT OR SUPPLEMENTAL UNITS

In addition to the groups of instructional units already discussed, there are a number of additional units that are of importance if the student is to become a well-educated traffic citizen. Some of these units are an integral part of nearly every driver education course, whereas others are enrichment units found generally only in more complete courses of instruction. These units of instruction will include the automobile in our society, highway and traffic engineering, what to do in case of an accident, the Highway Safety Act of 1966, and driving as a career.

The Automobile in America

There has probably been no more significant social or economic force in American life than the automobile. The influence of motor vehicle transportation is a determining factor in where we live, the social activities in which we engage, and the availability of food and other commodities, and the automotive industry employs, in one capacity or another, about 15 per cent of the wage earners of the nation.

148

The average teenager appreciates the meaning of an automobile in his daily life. However, he has little concept of the fact that the impact of this mode of transportation has been so recent in its development. A brief study of the evolution of the automobile and its significance in the twentieth century will lead to a better understanding of the nature of the traffic problems and the needs for an informed citizenry to promote effective solutions.

Topics for Study

Inventions, discoveries, and experimentation with automobiles
Social changes in a mobile society
Economic implications of improved transportation
Emergence of the traffic problem

What To Do in Case of an Accident

With the large number of traffic accidents in the nation every day there is a good possibility that nearly every student in the driver and traffic safety education classes will be involved in such an accident at some time during his life. What will be his responsibilities at such a time? Will he be able to meet this situation? Because of the likelihood of students being confronted with this experience it seems desirable that the driver education class should prepare them to meet their responsibilites at that time. Basically a person involved in an accident should do whatever is possible to care for any injured persons, obtain facts of the accident, and make the necessary reports to his insurance carrier and the public agencies involved.

Topics for Study

Emergency care of injured
Getting the facts of the accident
Witnessing statements
Withholding comments
Notifying police
Written reports for police agencies
Financial responsibility reports
Notifying insurance carrier

The Highway Safety Act of 1966

A comprehensive and problem-orientated program of attack on the nation's traffic crash problem by public officials is presented in detail in Chapter 18. This is the Highway Safety Act of 1966[10] which

---

[10] Section 101, Title 23, United States Code, *Highway Safety Act of 1966.* Public Law 89-564, 89th Congress, S. 3052, September 9, 1966.

grew out of the concerns of federal Congressional leaders for the rising traffic toll. The Act brings together 18 highway safety program standards that are to be used as a blueprint for a balanced program of legislation and performance activities upon which a state's highway safety effort is to be based.

Those persons supporting the Highway Safety Act recognize the fact that traffic safety cannot be achieved as the result of simple, one-phase, panacea activities on the national, state, or local level. Traffic safety is a complex problem that can be solved only by a planned and coordinated approach to the application of proven techniques of accident prevention and accident countermeasures to each problem area and on a continuous basis. The standards give public officials a framework around which to develop an aggressive traffic safety program based upon the most pressing identifiable priority needs.

The traffic accident problem has grown to its present dimension largely because of public apathy resulting from a lack of understanding of the significance and complexity of the problem. If driver and traffic safety education classes are to develop well-informed traffic citizens, they must provide a sound background in the need for a balanced approach to reducing traffic accidents in keeping with the recommendations of the Highway Safety Act.

Topics for Study

Background of the Highway Safety Act of 1966
Highway Safety Program Standards
Role of the National Highway Traffic Safety Administration
Role of Governor's Highway Safety Representative
Citizen support for traffic safety

Engineering

The planning of a system of streets and highways to handle the continually increasing volume of traffic is a costly, technical problem. The highway engineer must construct roads that will be safe and durable. The traffic engineer must design streets and highways that will handle the traffic with a minimum amount of congestion. He must also develop systems of signs, signals, and markings that will direct the driver with a minimum amount of confusion and delay. An understanding of the intricate problems of traffic engineering and the tremendous costs of developing an adequate highway system will provide the student with a broader understanding of the total problem of traffic control and safety.

Topics for Study

Highway planning
Financing highway construction
Design of highways
Traffic engineering
Traffic congestion in cities

150

Driving As a Career

There are more persons employed as commercial drivers in the United States than there are in any other job classification, with the possible exception of agriculture. In addition, the demands of the armed forces are such that most branches of the service now provide special courses of driver and traffic safety education for their personnel. Many high school students will have future driving responsibilities in one or the other of these areas. If students are properly indoctrinated with responsible attitudes toward driving and have acquired proper skills in their laboratory instruction, they will be immeasurably benefited in either a military or commercial driving career.

Topics for Study

Job opportunities in commercial driving
Driving requirements for bus drivers
Job requirements for commercial drivers
Safety training and supervision of commercial drivers

Pedestrians and Cyclists

Pedestrians and cyclists have always been an important aspect of the traffic problem. The rapid increase in the use of motorcycles and bicycles has increased traffic hazards considerably. The pedestrian and cyclist toll of fatalities constitutes more than one fourth of the annual traffic deaths. Because every driver education student is also a pedestrian and a large number of them ride either bicycles or motor-driven cycles at one time or another, it is important that they receive instruction in safe walking and riding practices. Emphasis should also be placed on the responsibility of drivers for the safety of pedestrians and cyclists.

The fatality rate of both very young and aged pedestrians is exceptionally high. It has also been found that a large number of pedestrians involved in traffic accidents, particularly at night, had been drinking. These are important facts in preparing young drivers to assume their responsibilities as safe users of the streets and highways.

Topics for Study

The pedestrian and cyclist problem
Age and pedestrians
The driver's responsibility
The pedestrian and cyclist at night
Safe pedestrian practices
Safe cycling practices
Laws governing the pedestrian and cyclists

151

LEARNING ACTIVITIES

1. Collect data on traffic crashes in your state. Develop a brief paper on how the accident rate of your state compares with states of comparable population.
2. Develop a paper on the topic, "Is driving a privilege or a right?" Present it to the class instructor for evaluation.
3. Develop a paper explaining how well the financial responsibility laws in your state protect the uncompensated motor vehicle accident victim. What changes in the laws would you recommend?
4. Given the content of this chapter and other selected resources, develop a teaching unit on the driving task and how it relates to the development of driving habits.
5. Prepare an evaluation check list that could be used in buying a used car. Go to a local automobile dealer and determine the effectiveness of such a check list in helping you select a car to meet your needs.

SELECTED RESOURCES

American Automobile Association. *Sportsmanlike Driving.* New York: McGraw-Hill Book Company, 1974.

Automotive Safety Foundation. *A Resource Curriculum in Driver and Traffic Safety Education.* Washington, D.C.: The Foundation, 1970.

Bishop, Richard W., et al. *Driving: A Task-Analysis Approach.* New York: Rand McNally & Company, 1975.

Halsey, Maxwell, et al. *Let's Drive Right.* Glenview, Ill.: Scott, Foresman and Company, 1972.

Lauer, A. R., et al. *Tomorrow's Drivers.* Chicago: Lyons and Carnahan, 1971.

Marshall, Robert L., et al. *Safe Performance Driving.* Lexington, Mass.: Ginn and Company, 1976.

McKnight, A. James, and Alan G. Hundt. *Driver Education Task Analysis, Volume III: Instructional Objectives.* Washington, D.C.: Department of Transportation, PB202-247, HumRRO Technical Report 71-9 (March 1971).

National Safety Council. *Accident Facts.* Chicago: The Council, published annually.

Strasser, Marland K., et al. *Driver Education: Learning to Drive Defensively.* River Forest, Ill.: Laidlaw Brothers, Publishers, 1973.

Chapter 9

Teaching Methods and Techniques for Classroom Instruction

OBJECTIVE: The student will be able to identify and select appropriate teaching methods and techniques for classroom instruction.

The driver education teacher should select, plan, and utilize methods of instruction according to their effectiveness in helping students achieve desired objectives. In the teaching of all subjects there is need for the instructor to apply methods and techniques that enhance learning through student motivation. The teaching-learning process is in large measure dependent upon proper selection and utilization of appropriate methods.

Instructors should choose methods that take personal needs of students into account. Moreover, accepted practice and learning theory suggest that teaching in driver education should be oriented positively. Negative instruction should be used sparingly and with discretion, although at times negative instruction may be desirable. Methods used should reflect teacher awareness of needs, interests, and maturity level of the individual classroom group. The teacher should attempt to strike a balance between the theoretical and practical aspects of a classroom program and should adopt methods that create among students the greatest possible motivation for learning.

Methods of instruction should be selected on the basis of their appropriateness for specific kinds of subject matter. Thus one method that may be successful for presenting one teaching unit may be ineffective in teaching another unit. In addition, new methods of instruction should be selected on the basis of appropriateness for specific kinds of classroom subject matter and because they represent an improvement in the quality of instruction.

153

For positive behavioral expectations to result, the teacher should plan carefully the driver education learning experiences. Moreover, a variety of teaching methods and techniques should be used to enrich learning. The complexity of the teaching-learning process has handicapped attempts to measure the relative merits of various methods. However, through a study and application of the principles of learning discussed in Chapter 4, the teacher is able to plan better for basic and related learning valuable to the achievement of driver education program objectives. Figure 9-1 depicts a number of concepts related to the value of several teaching techniques. The following is a brief discussion of some of these selected techniques.

Projects

The project approach to teaching may include interviews, opinion polls, creative writing, making models, and so on. The value of this approach is that it can be used to satisfy individual and group needs.

Surveys

The survey method allows the student, as an individual or group member, to examine a traffic situation carefully. First-hand experience is gained by doing this practical work. Such experience helps the student develop traffic citizen characteristics necessary for good driving.

Traffic or Accident Analysis

By the use of the traffic or accident analysis approach, attention is focused on basic driving concepts in a meaningful and interesting way. It helps the student develop the ability to sense a hazardous situation through the improvement of perceptual skill.

Resource Person

An expert is invited to the class to discuss a given topic related to the objectives of driver education. Student behavior attitudes can be influenced if the speaker knows his subject and makes an effective presentation.

Demonstrations

An excellent aid to understanding various skills maneuvers, forces of nature, or emergency evasive actions is the demonstration method. This is a combining of visual and hearing senses that motivates student interest and improves learning.

CRITERIA FOR SELECTION

Teachers have the specific task of selecting learning experiences for driver education students. Moreover, they have the responsibility of selecting appropriate methods and techniques that enhance learning and assist in the development of classroom units. Fundamentally, *method is the organization of materials in a teacher presentation to meet the learner's problems.* It is best for the teacher to use acceptable guidelines or criteria when choosing methods suitable to the subject matter being taught. The following are nationally recognized criteria for the selection of methods in driver education:[1]

1. The method provides for personal needs and individual practice of the learning involved in meaningful and realistic settings.
2. Positive teaching should be the general rule. Negative elements may at times make a contribution, but they should be kept to a minimum.
3. The teacher strikes a good balance between the practical and theoretical aspects of the program, and is endeavoring to adapt or slant each method used so as to create among the students the fullest possible motivation for learning.
4. An emphasis is placed on self-directed student activity as well as on the motivation and focusing of student effort toward further self-improvement.
5. The method should allow for the development and encouragement of cooperation in solving the traffic accident problem.
6. The method should allow for many specific details of the instructional program to be determined from a study by students and teachers of the overall environment or social setting in which the students live.

METHODS OF INSTRUCTION

Teaching methods contribute to the learning situation in two ways. First, they provide the means whereby a teacher is able to convey the course context to the class members, thereby fulfilling the objective of the course. The second way in which teaching methods contribute to the learning situation relates to the direct fulfillment of aims. That is, the teaching method itself fulfills one of the aims of the course.

Throughout this chapter the terms *methods* and *techniques* will be used continually. Whether these terms are sometimes used synonymously, each has a definite meaning and makes an individual contribution to the enhancement of learning.

"Teaching methods are the orderly procedures used by teachers to direct learners in developing knowledge and attitudes leading to the fulfillment of the teaching objectives." Whereas *"teaching techniques are the special details and refinements of the presentation which the teacher employs to make instruction more meaningful."*[2] It is desirable for the driver education teacher to use a combination of methods.

---

[1] State of Illinois, *Driver Education for Illinois High Schools* (Springfield, Ill.: Office of Public Instruction, 1963), p. 43.

[2] Marland K. Strasser, et al., *Fundamentals of Safety Education* (New York: Macmillan Publishing Co., Inc., 1974), p. 207.

PLANNING FOR LEARNING EXPERIENCES

Technique	Description or Example	Strengths	Problems
Role Playing	Two or more students act out a situation relating to a problem under discussion.	Stimulates analysis of a problem. Promotes better group understanding of interpersonal problems. Tends to bring out attitudes that might not otherwise appear.	Time-consuming. Students may lose sight of the goal. Must be well done.
Projects	May include interviews, opinion polls, creative writing, poster drawing, making models, etc.	Provides a means for satisfying group and individual needs.	May become an end in itself.
Use of Audiovisual Materials	Supplementary materials that need correlation with topics being studied. Not a teacher substitute. Films, slides, transparencies, etc.	Facilitates learning and retention. Can provide the same information to large groups of students.	May cover too much material too fast. Scheduling and cost.
Psychophysical Testing	Used primarily as an educational tool rather than as a screening device to evaluate fitness to drive. Tests may be purchased, borrowed, constructed, or improvised.	Stimulates interest. Helps teacher locate gross physical disabilities. Shows individual differences. Has good educational value.	Questionable validity of test results. Not prognosticating instruments except in the hands of a specialist.
Surveys	Examine a traffic situation closely through observation by teams of students.	Students get first-hand experience doing practical work in effective traffic citizenship.	Limited possibilities in rural areas.
Lecture	One person presenting facts and information on a predetermined subject.	Can provide material to large groups. May involve audience in highly motivated ideals. Can even influence attitudes.	No group participation. If used to excess or if done poorly, boredom and resistance may occur.
Traffic Situation and/or Accident Analysis	Students view a graphic description of a hazardous traffic situation or an accident and identify potential factors or causes.	Focuses attention on basic driving concepts in a meaningful and interesting way. Improves perceptual skill. Develops the ability to sense a hazardous situation.	Difficulty in ascertaining the underlying factors in an accident.

Figure 9–1. Planning for Learning Experiences in Driver Education (From *Policies and Practices for Driver and Traffic Safety Education*, 1964, pp. 55–56. By permission of National Commission on Safety Education, NEA)

Group Discussion (Decision)	The process in which students actively take part in examining a problem or concept. The instructor or student plays the role of moderator so that an orderly discussion is maintained. The group tries to reach a consensus or commitment. Panel. Forum.	Teacher can tell if group members understand and follow ideas. Unity or group belonging develops. Group exchanges experiences. Thinking is challenged. Individual attitudes may be changed or developed through group influence.	Time-consuming. Unrelated ideas may be discussed. May create tension. Group can draw wrong conclusion. Students may talk too much.
Field Trips	Entire class or small group visits police station, garage, traffic court, inspection station, etc.	Better understanding of a particular area. The instructor may learn with the students.	Cost, transportation, and for time problems frequently prohibit trips by entire class.
Resource Persons	A specialist with the necessary ability and knowledge presents information on a given topic related to the objectives of driver education.	A good method of influencing attitudes. Gives information in an area in which the instructor's knowledge may be limited.	Difficulty in obtaining and scheduling qualified persons.
Demonstrations	The use of real objects or models in presentation.	Aids in understanding driving maneuvers, such as steering, turning, parking, forces of nature, and emergency driving practice. Students enjoy and benefit by participating in demonstrations and watching fellow students participate.	Preparing suitable materials.
Educational Television	Short telecasts of basic material in driver education by a carefully selected teacher. The material is selected by classroom and studio teachers. Offered during school day through monitors in school building.	All students benefit from presentation by outstanding teacher. Students also benefit from equipment which is too expensive for each school. Instructor has adequate time for preparation. Gives classroom teacher more time to develop attitudes by reducing material to be covered. All students are able to learn from effective use of resource peoper. Uniform view of demonstrations for all students.	Scheduling. Cost. No interaction between teacher and student. Only available in few areas.

Figure 9-1. *(Continued)*

For learning to occur most efficiently and economically, it is essential that each teacher be skilled in a variety of methods and techniques. Methods are selected for (1) logical presentation, (2) best use of time, (3) variety (motivation and interest), and (4) related learning (content and attitudes). Therefore there is a direct relationship between objectives, content, and methods. The following guidelines may be of value in selecting methods, concepts, principles, and generalizations: [3]

1. One cannot effectively tell another how he shall think, feel, or act during a lifetime of independent operation in the traffic environment.
2. Authoritative approaches or implied force seldom produce permanent changes in driver behavior.
3. The value of lecture is often limited to providing students with factual information.
4. When development of desirable traffic behavior patterns is the primary purpose of a specific lesson, student-centered activities encourage participants to examine a variety of insights, reveal attitudes and beliefs, discuss probable results and arrive at a choice based on reasoning.
5. Individual differences among students should encourage teachers to use a variety of presentation techniques and methods.
6. Extensive or repeated presentations of gruesome collision scenes do more harm than good.
7. Safety concepts should be presented to students with a positive accent rather than a negative one.
8. Instructional techniques for in-car teaching should be flexible, with full recognition of individual differences in previous driving experience, eagerness to learn, physical coordination, composure, confidence, and attitude.

In the teaching of a classroom driver education course the teacher should be aware of new ideas or innovations that emerge from time to time. In recent years a number of advanced methods and techniques have been suggested for use in driver education. These new approaches to classroom instruction seem to be effective in the motivation of students and the enhancement of learning. The following sections attempt to describe briefly a number of recent developments related to instruction.

Group-Discussion Decision

Social psychologists and sociologists have developed a teaching method known as the group-discussion decision technique. This method has been proven to be very successful in the accomplishment of driver education program goals. Given the proper conditions plus capable leadership, students participating in such a discussion will look for facts, interpret facts, clarify their own thinking, and eventually modify their own conduct.

This is principally a method whereby students are allowed to discuss mutual problems of their age group and then make a unified,

[3] American Driver and Traffic Safety Education Association, *Policies and Guidelines for Driver and Traffic Safety Education* (Washington, D.C.: The Association, 1974), p. 24.

158

definite group decision that each member shall abide by in the conduct of their day-to-day affairs, particularly as it pertains to safety. Examples of how this technique can be effectively applied were developed by Sawers in a recent study. The following is one of the "discussion starters" developed to assist the teacher in learning how to apply the group-discussion technique:[4]

Situation

Think about some of the drivers you know, both experienced and inexperienced.

Suggested Categories for Questions

1. Drivers who are bad risks: the egotist, the show-off, the immature, the one who is never at fault, the little man in the big car, the bully.
2. Characteristics of the first-class driver: good judgment, attention, foresight, car control, self-control.
3. How attitudes can be improved: desire, knowledge, practice.

Suggested Questions

1. Do you know any good drivers? Why do you think they are good drivers?
2. What driving lessons are most needed by experienced drivers who already have their licenses?
3. Of the drivers you know, how many feel that they are good drivers? Why do they feel this way? Do you agree with them?

Sociodrama

Another technique in group dynamics that is applicable to driver education is sociodrama. This is the acting out of a problem by one or more students. A sociodramatic approach to learning should benefit a teacher, because it uses the group process in learning and personality development and thereby substitutes living or experience for what is often mere academic verbiage. It is agreed that this method can contribute to fundamental behavioral changes in individuals and such a teaching procedure can readily be learned by the teacher.

Role Exchange

The term *role behavior* refers to the kind of driving generally expected in accordance with the traffic laws, the road, and the traffic conditions of a particular place.[5] In the application of the role-exchange method, the driver puts himself in the place of the other driver by attempting to predict that driver's behavior from minute

[4] Kenneth T. Sawers, *Group Discussion Techniques for Driver Education* (New York: New York University, The Center for Safety Education, 1961), pp. 23–24. Used by permission of Center for Safety Education, New York University.

[5] Leo T. Mills, and J. V. Couch, *"Role Exchange—A Social Attitude Approach to Driver Education," ADEA News and Views* (Washington, D.C.: NEA, American Driver Education Association, 1962), 2, No. 3 (November), p. 3.

to minute. To do this successfully the driver using this approach must possess a substantial knowledge of traffic laws and rules of safe conduct for motor vehicle operation in order to predict driver actions accurately.

Team Teaching

Team teaching is a systematic arrangement wherein several teachers cooperatively instruct a group of students, varying the size of the student groups and procedures with the purposes of instruction. They spend staff time and energy in ways that will make the best use of their respective competencies.

Programed Instruction

Organized materials calling for an immediate response and being reinforced by immediate knowledge of current information is referred to as *programed instruction*. It is a method of teaching that calls for a tutor and a student—the tutor being a program that contains the kind of learning experiences that lead the learner through a set of specified behaviors designed and sequenced to make it more probable that he will behave in a given desired way.

The program may be linear or branching, and it may take the form of a book, scroll, separate sheets, motion film, slides, film clips, or combination of media. Its greatest strength is in verbal reinforcement of facts and development of concepts. Each student works at his own rate, and in well-developed programs he will be accurate 95 per cent of the time. Such accuracy of knowledge is the reinforcing element of the method. Many programs are constructed to permit a more experienced student to bypass information he already knows by moving to other content that meets his learning needs.

Large-Group Instruction

Because of the lack of space, pressure of numbers, a crowded curriculum, and financial considerations, large-group instruction is being used more extensively. In the hand of a master teacher with up-to-date equipment and materials this method can produce the desired results. However, in order to be of maximum value it should be followed by small-group discussions, other than in the car. Because driver education is attempting to modify and restructure human behavior, it is essential that instruction be personalized and kept on an individual basis. Each student participating in the large-group instruction should be given the opportunity to drive in the driver education car.

Television Teaching

The use of a broadcast or closed circuit television channel in group teaching permits highly qualified teachers and resource persons to reach a large number of students. Costly teaching resources, not ordinarily available to classroom teachers, can be utilized, and the total quality of the program will be enhanced by the use of this medium. A number of schools in Ohio, Florida, and New York have used this medium for classroom instruction.

Driving Simulation

Driving simulation programs utilize electromechanical devices in conjunction with programed audiovisual aids and can aid substantially in developing the student's ability to recognize, analyze, and correctly respond to traffic by:

1. Providing adjustive response practice under a wider variety of driving environments than are available near most schools.
2. Providing practice, in complete safety, in driving under adverse conditions, such as emergencies and foul weather.
3. Providing continuous and cumulative information on individual student performance.
4. Providing opportunity for the development of the basic manipulative skills in response to realistic portrayals of traffic environments.
5. Substantially eliminating time in which to become familiar with control in the dual-control car.

Although the use of simulation, as described in Chapter 11, is normally considered to be laboratory instruction, it can be classified as a classroom method.

Such innovations in teaching can stimulate the learner to grasp a higher degree of knowledge, influence attitudes, and modify student behavior. Recent innovations have led to more dynamic instruction. However, before such results occur, each method described here must be handled by a skilled teacher having a thorough understanding of the method and knowing how to use it successfully. Therefore the teacher must keep up to date and adopt the revised instructional pattern.

UNIT PLANNING

"Every alert teacher recognizes that he is faced with two basic problems: (1) to determine what concepts, skills, and attitudes the pupils are to have an opportunity to acquire in his course; and (2) to plan definite activities whereby each pupil according to his ability, aptitudes, and interests, may be able to achieve in some measure the desired objectives."[6] The teacher of driver and traffic safety education uses a teaching unit approach in the organizing of knowledge concepts for classroom instructional purposes. This is a plan to assist in determining unit objectives, content, methods, evaluative criteria, and the organization of the material in logical sequence to stimulate learning. Figure 9-2 depicts the organizational structure of a typical teaching unit, and the following briefly describes the makeup of its major parts.

UNIT PLAN OUTLINE

TITLE

GENERAL STATEMENT—

    A statement outlining the nature and content of the unit to be taught.

  I. Objectives of the Unit
    A. Lesson Objective
    B. Instructional Objectives

 II. Outline of Unit Content

III. Activities and/or Projects

IV. Evaluation Methods
    A. Test (Knowledge, etc.)
    B. Projects

 V. Bibliography
    A. For Teacher
    B. For Student

VI. Materials and Equipment
    A. Models
    B. Sound Films, Film Strips
    C. Posters, Charts, etc.

Figure 9-2. Unit Plan Outline for Driver Education

General Statement

The general statement describes the nature and general content of the unit to be taught. This is a statement that is clear and understandable so a person can easily gain an insight into what the unit is about.

Objectives of the Unit

In the development of a teaching unit, it is desirable to determine what objectives are to be accomplished. The unit objectives are

[6] Leon Brody and H. J. Stack, *Highway Safety and Driver Education* (New York: Prentice-Hall, Inc., 1954), p. 150.

closely related to the content covered and the activities assigned the students. There can be a *lesson objective* that briefly suggests some of the broader philosophical aims of the unit, and there can be *instructional objectives* that identify definite measurable accomplishments on the part of each student.

Outline of the Unit Content

The content to be covered in the teaching of the unit needs to be identified and outlined for the teacher's consideration. Knowledge concepts to be presented can be organized on a *topical* or on a complete *sentence* basis. In the former, key phrases or topics are noted, whereas with the latter, content items are developed in depth, using complete sentences. Either approach is desirable, but the teacher's personal background and experience will be the determining factor as to the approach used.

Activities and/or Projects

In this section of the unit, the instructor identifies the activities and projects that he anticipates assigning to students. The number will depend upon the length of the unit. The activities should assist in achieving the unit objectives. Such assignments should motivate students to work as individuals or as a group toward the betterment of the traffic accident problem.

Evaluation Methods

The teacher should plan the various types of evaluative measures to be used in evaluating student progress during and at the termination of the unit. By doing this the teacher will plan better the content covered and will seek to motivate students to learn. Tests, projects, and teacher observations are suggested as evaluative criteria.

Bibliography

Various references will be used in the development of all teaching units. In order to identify and remember these the teacher should list them as a part of the overall unit plan. Moreover, bibliographic references should be identified as being for the teacher or for the student, because some of the materials developed are to be used by the teacher and some by the student.

Materials and Equipment

To encourage learning, every instructor should use various instructional materials. These may be models, films (sound or silent), charts, magnetic traffic board, or other available aids. The use of such aids should be programed into the teaching unit as it is being organized. This eliminates confusion at the last moment, when an aid is needed to illustrate an important point. A list of the aids at the end of the unit plus an identification of sources is very helpful in planning the teaching unit.

The foregoing outlines the manner in which a teaching unit is organized. Each of the sections is an integral part of the unit when taught. The teacher should develop each unit as comprehensively as possible, including each step of the example given here.

STUDENT TRAFFIC SAFETY ACTIVITIES

There are many safety activities with instructional value that qualify as a method of instruction. These activities may be used to motivate predriver education students or to keep them interested after they complete the course. Hence there is a need for supplemental traffic safety activities that introduce students to safety problems and concepts at an earlier age and that offer them worthwhile projects in later years.

Student groups should accept primary responsibility in planning and carrying out student traffic safety activities. Moreover, a wide range of projects should be selected. Among those activities that could be planned are a safety conference, driver education club, voluntary vehicle check program, parking lot patrol, traffic court, assembly program, and driver education open house. All of these should be well planned, with an evaluation of results upon completion.

LEARNING ACTIVITIES

1. Plan a group discussion on a topic mutually agreed upon with your instructor. Assume the role of a teacher and use the group-discussion decision technique as a classroom practice teaching experience.
2. Participate in a debate on the subject, "The Value of Television Teaching in Driver Education."
3. Write a term paper on the subject of driving simulation and its worth in teaching beginning drivers.
4. Develop a comprehensive teaching unit on a subject assigned by your instructor. Use the unit outline discussed in this chapter as your guide.

SELECTED RESOURCES

Brethower, Dale M. *Programed Instruction: A Manual of Programing Techniques.* Chicago: Educational Methods, Inc., 1963.
Gagne, Robert M. *The Conditions of Learning.* New York: Holt, Rinehart and Winston, Publishers, 1970.
Mills, Leo T., and J. V. Couch. "Role Exchange—A Social Attitude Approach to Driver Education," *ADEA News and Views.* Washington, D.C.: NEA, American Driver Education Association, 1962 2, No. 3 (November), p. 3.

National Education Association. *Planning and Organizing for Teaching.* Project on the Instructional Program of the Public Schools. Washington, D.C.: The Association, 1963.

National Highway Traffic Safety Administration, *Guide for Teacher Preparation in Driver Education—Secondary School Edition.* Washington, D.C.: The Administration (July 1974).

National Transportation Safety Board. *Youth and Traffic Safety Education.* Washington, D.C.: The Board, Report No. NTSB–STS–71–3, 1971.

Sawers, Kenneth T. *Group Discussion Techniques for Driver Eudcation.* New York: New York University, Center for Safety Education, 1961, pp. 23-24.

State of Illinois. *Driver Education for Illinois Youth.* Springfield, Ill.: Safety Education Section, Office of the Superintendent of Public Instruction, 1972.

Strasser, Marland K., et al. *Fundamentals of Safety Education.* New York: Macmillan Publishing Co., Inc., 1973.

Tanner, Daniel. *Using Behavioral Objectives in the Classroom.* New York: Macmillan Publishing Co., Inc., 1972.

Chapter 10

Classroom Materials and Equipment

OBJECTIVE: The student will be able to identify and select appropriate materials and equipment for classroom instruction.

In the teaching of all subjects there is need for illustrative materials and equipment that will excite interest and make more meaningful the concepts being presented to the students. The extent to which appropriate materials and equipment are available and in use is an indication of the quality level of the teaching-learning process.

A status study identifies the wide variety of materials and equipment being used by driver educators in programs across the nation.[1] The most common equipment used for classroom instruction was psychophysical devices, projection equipment for films, traffic boards (magnets or flannel types), models, charts, road signs, and others. Figure 10-1 depicts the variety of equipment for both classroom and practice-driving instruction.

Instructional materials need to be selected and planned with great care if maximum benefits are to result. Therefore certain guiding principles regarding use are in order before any instructional materials can be applied effectively. The following are principles to help the teacher select materials:[2]

[1] Norman Key, *Status of Driver Education in the United States* (Washington, D.C.: National Education Association, 1960), pp. 42–47.

[2] Superintendent of Public Instruction, *Instructional Materials,* The Illinois Curriculum Program, (Springfield, Ill: Office of Public Instruction, 1963), pp. 10–11.

1. Improvement of instruction usually involves education media of some sort.
2. Educational media, to be educationally sound, must be used to promote the achievement of specific educational objectives only.
3. Educational media must be readily available from a physical standpoint.
4. Educational media must be readily available and usable from a psychological standpoint.
5. All educational media should be classified for placement in the total instructional program.
6. Educational media can be evaluated only in terms of (and through) their uses.

SPECIAL EQUIPMENT REPORTED REGULARLY USED IN CLASSROOM AND PRACTICE DRIVING INSTRUCTION BY LOCAL SCHOOL SYSTEMS

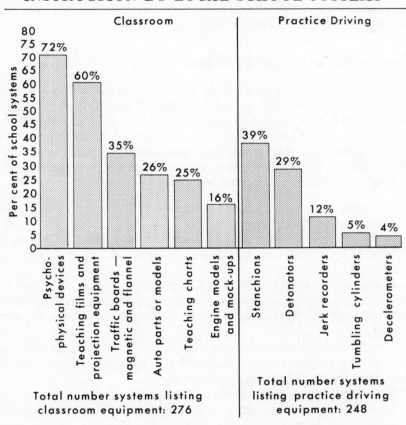

Figure 10-1. Equipment Used in Classroom and Practice Driving (From Norman Key, *Status of Driver Education in the U.S.*, 1960, p. 44. By permission of Norman Key and National Commission on Safety Education, NEA)

TEACHING ENVIRONMENT

If driver education is to be taught effectively, a proper environment is needed to complement the qualified teacher. Although nothing can substitute for good teaching, the effectiveness and morale of the best teacher is impaired in a poor atmosphere with makeshift facilities and equipment. With an ever-increasing number of students entering driver education each year, planning adequate facilities for the classroom phase is most important, especially because all students should receive such instruction before graduation.

The creation of an adequate teaching and learning environment requires the best of planning. Such planning will enable teachers to study carefully the present program in driver education and reestablish future goals. This presents an opportunity and a challenge to every driver educator in the field. The classroom facilities to be provided are usually dependent to a great extent on the kind of learning activities that take place in the classroom. The kinds of activities that may take place in the driver education classroom are presented here as a guide for planning local school facilities.

Student Activities Requiring Facilities

The student shall be involved in numerous projects and activities that will require classroom facilities. Each school is obligated to make available adequate facilities to enhance student learning. The following activities are characteristic of those engaged in by most driver education students. Therefore classroom facilities should be planned and organized with these suggestions, which might serve as guides to teachers, supervisors, administrators, and school boards.

1. Planning—helping to choose pertinent problems and working on short- or long-term approaches.
2. Making arrangements—helping schedule field trips, selections of committees and assignments, and sending out requests for information.
3. Using committees—organization, gathering information, obtaining group judgments, organization reports, preparing presentations using a variety of techniques, such as dramatics, panels, displays, and so on.
4. Using individual research—using library and community resources, inquiring of government and industry, sifting evidence, arriving at facts, making judgments, preparing results.
5. Reading—texts, supplementary literature.
6. Listening—to teacher, other class members, community resource persons, recordings.
7. Watching—demonstrations, displays, movies, film strips, diagrams.
8. Discussing—on basis of facts known and reported.
9. Constructing—drawing and designing models, posters, demonstration apparatus.
10. Practicing—skills on mockups or simulators.
11. Displaying—charts, models, reports, posters, demonstrations, in classroom, school assemblies, corridors, community stores.
12. Summarizing and reporting—individual or group study.
13. Storing—written reports, committee projects, collections, models, charts, posters, incomplete materials.

168

Teacher Activities Requiring Facilities

The teacher needs sufficient space and facilities to do a successful job of teaching. Adequate classroom facilities similar to those provided for other subjects should be provided for driver education. In order for the teacher to motivate students he must be enthusiastic and in the proper spirit to improve the classroom atmosphere. Adequate classroom facilities and equipment help to establish a proper learning environment. Activities, such as those listed, are daily experiences for the teachers. Therefore it is evident that good facilities are essential for a successful classroom program:

1. Planning—teacher's work, cooperative planning with students.
2. Explaining—to entire group, committees, individual.
3. Evaluating—oral or written testing.
4. Guiding—observing individual or group actions, counseling, referring to anecdotal or other records for each student.
5. Record keeping—attendance, supply forms, student progress forms, results of psychophysical testing.
6. Discussing—leading and participating in small groups or with entire group.

Special Features of the Classroom

Besides giving careful attention to the general location, size, and furnishing of a driver education classroom, the following features are suggested:

1. Space for testing, small committee work, and library area.
2. Table top cabinets for storing and displaying testing equipment and demonstration models.
3. Facilities for display of loose charts and maps.
4. Permanent picture screen and adequate electrical outlets.
5. Simulator classroom location convenient to the regular classroom.

The special features of the driver education classroom mentioned here are essential to the conduct of a quality classroom course. Moreover, these features and the facilities suggested for teacher and student activities are closely related.

INSTRUCTIONAL MATERIALS

The instructor has the responsibility of selecting appropriate materials for use in the driver education program. Efforts should be made to relate materials that will help meet the objectives of the complete program. Instructors should use certain guides or criteria when choosing classroom materials. The following criteria should prove helpful in performing this task:[3]

1. Does the material follow standards established by national and state policy organizations?
2. Are materials and equipment available from reputable publishers or manufacturers?
3. Does the material or piece of equipment help accomplish some objective that other material or equipment cannot?
4. Are materials up to date with the current philosophy of the traffic safety movement?
5. Will materials and equipment be used sufficiently to justify expenditure of funds?
6. Are materials written by reputable persons in the traffic safety field?

Texts

There are a number of textbooks from which the teacher may select a suitable one for classroom use. The following are the leading texts available at the present time. Each should be evaluated by the driver educator in order to choose the text that best fits the needs of his students and assist in achieving program aims. Listed alphabetically, some of the current texts available are:

American Automobile Association. *Sportsmanlike Driving*, 6th ed. New York: McGraw-Hill Book Company, 1974.

Bishop, Richard W., et al. *Driving: A Task Analysis Approach*. New York: Rand McNally & Company, 1975.

Center for Safety Education. *Driver Education and Traffic Safety*. Englewood Cliffs, N.J.: Prentice-Hall, Inc., 1967.

Halsey, Maxwell, et al. *Let's Drive Right*. Glenview, Ill.: Scott, Foresman and Company, 1972.

Paulowski, J., et al. *Tomorrow's Drivers*. Chicago: Lyons and Carnahan, 1971.

Strasser, M. K., et al. *Driver Education: Learning to Drive Defensively*. River Forest, Ill.: Laidlaw Brothers, Publishers, 1973.

Program goals, student needs, and psychological soundness are among the most important factors considered vital in the textbook selection process. Teachers and safety supervisors should evaluate texts before a final choice is made. The following questions may be asked in the evaluation of driver education textbooks:[4]

1. Are the goals of the textbook consistent with the school's objectives and philosophy?
2. Is the material rich in content, interesting, and well written?
3. Is the material well organized, objective, accurate, and presented with clarity?

[3] James E. Aaron and M. K. Strasser, *Driving Task Instruction—Dual-Control, Simulation, Multiple-Car* (New York: Macmillan Publishing Co., Inc., 1974), p. 136.

[4] Illinois Superintendent of Public Instruction, op. cit., p. 17.

170

4. Are the illustrations and other graphic materials well selected, well reproduced, and an integral part of the presentation?
5. Are teachers' manuals and other teaching materials provided?
6. Are the learning activities interesting and directed toward desired behavior?
7. Are the bibliographies of good quality and up to date?
8. Is the selection of content well balanced and in good proportion to the whole body of knowledge?
9. Are the concepts presented appropriate to the maturity level intended?

Periodicals

There are a number of periodicals with which the driver educator should be familiar. All issues carry information valuable to the instructor. New ideas, methods, techniques, and materials are generally announced and discussed in such publications. Therefore the teacher should subscribe to all of the periodicals listed here in order to enhance his professional background and keep abreast of current developments.

American Association of Motor Vehicle Administration Bulletin. Published by the Association, 1201 Connecticut Avenue, N.W., Washington, D.C. Devoted to the interests of State Motor Vehicle and Traffic Enforcement Officials. (Free)

Fleet Owner. Published monthly by the McGraw-Hill Publishing Company, Inc., 1221 Ave. of the Americas, New York, N.Y. ($9.00 yearly)

Highway Highlights. Published monthly by the Highway Users Federation, Public Information Department, 1776 Massachusetts Avenue, N.W., Washington, D.C. (Free)

Journal of Traffic Safety Education. American Driver and Traffic Safety Education Association, 1201 16th Street, N.W., Washington, D.C. Published by California Driver Education Association. (Free to ADTSEA members)

Journal of Safety Research. Published quarterly by the National Safety Council, 444 North Michigan Avenue, Chicago, Ill. ($24.00 yearly)

MSF: On The Move. Published six times each year by the Motorcycle Safety Foundation, 6755 Elkridge Landing Road, Linthicum, Md. (Free)

National Safety News. Published monthly by the National Safety Council, 444 North Michigan Avenue, Chicago, Ill. ($10.00 yearly)

Safety Maintenance and Production. Published monthly by the Alfred M. Best Company, Inc., 75 Fulton Street, New York, N.Y. ($7.00 yearly)

Status Report. Published bi-monthly by Insurance Institute for Highway Safety, 600 Watergate, Washington, D.C. (Free)

Today's Traffic. The monthly newsletter of the Traffic Section of the National Safety Council, 444 North Michigan Avenue, Chicago, Ill. (Free)

Traffic Engineering. Published monthly by the Institute of Traffic Engineers, 2029 K Street, N.W., Washington, D.C. ($10.00)

Traffic Quarterly. An independent journal for better traffic. Published by the Eno Foundation for Highway Traffic Control, Saugatuck, Conn. (Free to libraries)

Traffic Safety. Published monthly by the National Safety Council, 444 North Michigan Avenue, Chicago, Ill. ($7.00 yearly)

Transport Topics. Published weekly by the American Trucking Associations, Inc., 1424 16th Street, N.W., Washington, D.C. ($7.00 yearly)

General Traffic Safety References

The driver educator should have a substantial traffic safety library in order to develop personal knowledge and to serve as basic references in the development of classroom teaching units. By investing yearly a small amount of the school's driver education budget, an excellent professional library will materialize in a short number of years. The references mentioned here are those suggested for initial consideration in the development of such a library.

Aaron, James E., and M. K. Strasser. *Driving Task Instruction—Dual-Control, Simulation, and Multiple-Car.* New York: Macmillan Publishing Co., Inc., 1974.

American Driver and Traffic Safety Education Association. *Policies and Guidelines for Driver and Traffic Safety Education.* Washington, D.C.: The Association, 1974.

Automotive Safety Foundation. *A Resource Curriculum in Driver and Traffic Safety Education.* Washington, D.C.: The Foundation, 1970.

Brody, L., and H. J. Stack. *Highway Safety and Driver Education.* Englewood Cliffs, N.J.: Prentice-Hall, Inc., 1954.

Forbes, T. W., (ed.) *Human Factors in Highway Traffic Safety Research.* New York: John Wiley & Sons, Inc., 1972.

Institute of Driver Behavior. *Training Your Eyes for Expert Driving.* Detroit: The Institute, 1972.

Ladd, W. *Organization for Traffic Safety in Your Community.* Springfield, Ill.: Charles C Thomas, Publisher, 1959.

National Committee on Uniform Traffic Laws and Ordinances. *Model Traffic Ordinance.* Washington, D.C.: The Committee, 1972.

National Committee on Uniform Traffic Laws and Ordinances. *Uniform Vehicle Code.* Washington, D.C.: The Committee, 1972.

National Joint Committee on Uniform Traffic Control Devices. *Manual on Uniform Traffic Control Devices for Streets and Highways.* Washington, D.C.: U. S. Department of Commerce, Bureau of Public Roads, 1971.

National Safety Council. *Accident Facts.* Chicago: The Council, published annually.

Snellen, Robert C. *Vision and Driving.* The American Optometric Association, 1962.

Strasser, M., et al. *Fundamentals of Safety Education.* New York: Macmillan Publishing Co., Inc., 1973.

Free or Inexpensive Materials

A great quantity of inexpensive materials is available from private and public agencies. Most government agencies, state police, departments of education, highway departments, insurance groups, and automobile manufacturers are among those agencies with a wealth of material available for use in driver and traffic safety education programs. Several copies of materials dealing with the general traffic safety topics of seat belts, freeway driving, driver attitudes, forces of nature, and vehicle operation should be available for student use. The following list of free or inexpensive materials is representative of those available.

Allstate Insurance Company, Allstate Plaza, Northbrook, Illinois 60062; booklets: *Avoid Rear End Collisions, Expressway Driving Is Different.*

American Automobile Association, 8111 Gatehouse Road, Falls Church, Virginia 22042; write for bibliography of driver education and traffic safety materials.

American Association of Industrial Editors, 24 Fairfield Street, Montclair, New Jersey; booklet: *How To Tell the Traffic Story*

American Optical Company, Southbridge, Massachusetts 01550; brochure: *Survey of State Requirements for Motor Vehicle Operators.*

Association of Casualty and Surety Companies, 60 John Street, New York, New York 10038; booklets: *Common Sense Driving Pays Off, Driver Education in the Secondary School, How to Attack the Traffic Accident Problem in Your Community, Safety Film News, Traffic News and Views.*

Baltimore and Ohio Railroad Company, Safety Department, Baltimore, Maryland 21203; booklet: *Look, Listen, Live.*

Bear Manufacturing Company, Rock Island, Illinois 61201; booklet: *Periodic Motor Vehicle Safety Inspection.*

Birk and Company, Inc., Publishers, 270 Park Avenue, New York, New York 10017; booklet: *How To be an Expert Driver, as Told by the Experts.*

Federal Energy Administration, Washington, D.C. 20461; booklet: *Gas Mileage Guide for New Car Buyers.*

Ford Motor Company, The American Road, Dearborn, Michigan 48121; booklet: *The Big Plus—Seat Belts.*

General Motors Corporation, Department of Public Relations, Detroit, Michigan 48202; booklets: *How the Wheels Revolve, When the Wheels Revolve, Electricity and Wheels, A Power Primer, Optics and Wheels, Chemistry and Wheels, We Drivers, How To Avoid the Two-Car Crash.*

Also, charts: *Automobile Chassis, Automobile Progress, Stopping Distances for Different Road Conditions, Engine Efficiency, Four-Stroke Cycle and Flame Travel, Three-Speed Gear Transmission, Automobile Fuel System, Typical Gear Combinations, Rear Axle Assembly, Automobile Brake System.*

The B. F. Goodrich Company, Akron, Ohio 44309; booklet: *Tommy Gets the Keys.*

Highway Users Federation for Safety and Mobility, 1776 Massachusetts Avenue, N.W., Washington, D.C. 20036; booklets: *Highway Facts* (Published annually), and *What Freeways Mean to Your City.*

Metropolitan Life Insurance Company, 1 Madison Avenue, New York, New York 10010; booklets: *Accident Prevention Can Be Taught, How's Your Driving?*

Motor Vehicle Manufactures Association, 320 New Center Building, Detroit, Michigan 48202; booklets: *Motor Truck Facts* (Published annually), *Automobile Facts and Figures* (Published annually), *The Work Cars Do,* and *A Car Traveling People.*

National Association of Motor Bus Operators, 879 17th Street, N.W., Washington D.C. 20036; booklet: *Bus Facts* (Published annually),

National Committee on Uniform Traffic Laws and Ordinances, 1776 16th St., N.W., Washington, D.C. 20036; booklet: *65 Million Drivers Want Uniform Traffic Laws.*

National Highway Users Conference, National Press Building, Washington, D.C. 20005; booklets: *The Highway Transportation Story in Facts, Motor Manners.*

National Safety Council, 444 North Michigan Avenue, Chicago, Illinois 60611; Write for list of driver education and traffic safety materials.

Nationwide Insurance Company, 246 North High Street, Columbus, Ohio 43215; booklet: *Ten Common Driving Emergencies and How To Live Through Them.*

The Travelers Insurance Companies, Hartford, Connecticut 06115, booklet: *Annual Book of Street and Highway Accident Data.*

Projected Materials

Through the medium of projection, it is possible to bring a great variety of experiences into the classroom. The teacher has at his disposal all types of aids to support his instruction and enhance learning. By planning and using projection properly, the teacher may be assured that the objectives of the driver and traffic safety education course will be more fully realized.

MOTION PICTURES. Of all the projected materials for use in teaching, perhaps the most commonly used is the motion picture. Time can be compressed in sound films so that students may observe driving techniques over a wide range of driving environments. Many of the unnecessary details of explanation may be eliminated, because they can be observed and studied through meaningful experiences on films.

Films used in driver education are films that either (1) develop attitude; (2) give information (knowledge); or (3) develop skill. In films that develop attitude, attempts are made to involve the student emotionally, and films that give information and develop skill present criteria for distinguishing what constitutes good driving, compliance with traffic laws, or correct procedures for operation of the vehicle during performance of stops, starts, turns, maneuvers, and so on. "Evidence clearly supports the conclusion that films can teach factual information effectively over a wide range of subject matter content, age ranges, abilities, and conditions of use. . . . Furthermore, it is concluded that films can modify motivations, interests, attitudes, and opinions if they are designed to stimulate or reinforce existing beliefs of the audience."[5]

In the final analysis, the effectiveness of all instructional materials is in direct proportion to the ability and willingness of the teacher to use them successfully. Whether it is a sound film or one of the materials discussed further in this chapter, it is suggested that the teacher follows these steps:

1. Preview the film (or material).
2. Prepare the class.
    a. Suggest things to look for in the film (or material).
    b. Define any new words.
3. Show the film (or material).
    a. With as little disturbance of the class as possible.
3. b. In a room that is dark in order to focus students' attention on the screen.
    c. In a room that has proper temperature and ventilation.
4. Discuss and reshow if necessary.
    a. Discuss the film (or material).
    b. Test and evaluate information retained.
    c. Reshow if improper or incomplete concepts are formed.

[5] William H. Allen, *Audio-Visual Communication Research* (Santa Monica, Calif.: Systems Development Corporation, 1958), pp. 9, 14.

5. Follow-up steps.
   a. Show the relationship of the film (or material) content to the material being studied.
   b. Encourage students to develop activities that show they understand the concepts in the film (or material).

FILM STRIPS AND SLIDES. A film strip is a series of pictures on a piece of 35mm film. They can be sound or silent. Slides may be a piece of film mounted on cardboard, metal, or glass. Since these are inexpensive to make or purchase, they can be readily available for class use. Film strips and slides are among the most beneficial materials when it comes to enrichment of student learning. These materials can be used to illustrate lectures, demonstrations, or teacher presentations. Thus the driver education teacher can motivate student interest in traffic safety matters through the intelligent use of these selected materials.

OVERHEAD PROJECTIONS. The overhead projector is somewhat new to the driver education classroom. However, industry and the military have used them for many years. One advantage of such equipment is that it can be used in a lighted room. It has the distinct advantage of allowing the teacher to face the class and thus maintain eye contact with the students. Present-day transparencies for use in traffic safety education are available commercially or can be made locally by the school's photography department or commercial photographer.

OPAQUE PROJECTION. The opaque projector is a piece of equipment that has long been in use. In fact, it was developed before the electric light bulb. In the classroom the opaque projector can be used to project a photograph, page of a book, or any type of opaque material.

The classroom teacher who uses the opaque projector may present traffic safety material to the class that otherwise might not be presented due to lack of time or equipment with which to copy material. The driver education teacher should investigate the values of using opaque projections to give variety to classroom presentations and reinforce learning.

Selected Instructional Materials

In recent years a number of special instructional materials have been developed for use by driver education teachers. Each of these special purpose materials is designed to accomplish certain objectives of the driver and traffic safety education program. Following is a brief discussion of five of these innovations in driver education instructional materials.

TIME-LAPSE FILM STRIPS. One of the most effective instructional materials ever developed for use by driver educators is the time-lapse film strip series available from the Ford Motor Company. This is a combination of programed instruction with a time-lapse projection

175

technique. The 35mm film strip series presents driving maneuvers in short learning steps and is designed to reinforce each driving sequence through repetition of basic rules. A single driving situation is covered three times in each film strip. Each film strip is accompanied by a teacher's guide and a $33\frac{1}{3}$ rpm record keyed to the strip. Complete information regarding this series may be obtained from Ford Motor Company, Traffic Safety and Highway Improvement Department, The American Road, Dearborn, Michigan.

SINGLE-CONCEPT FILMS. A series of 8mm (also available in 16mm) silent films has been produced for use in teaching difficult traffic safety concepts. The series is built on a single-concept approach in order to assist the teacher in emphasizing specific difficult-to-teach items. Through this approach the instructor can present a complete, progressive picture of both environment and action, while making full use of the spoken word and employing whatever emphasis, pointing, stops, or references he may choose. Each of the eight films averages $4\frac{1}{2}$ to 5 minutes in length and is available for use with a cartridge-loading 8mm projector or typical 8mm or 16mm projector. The films are available from the American Oil Company, 910 S. Michigan Avenue, Chicago, Illinois.

FLASH-FILM METHOD. The approach of the flash-film method revolves around instruction of judgment through association with actual driving situations. A two-picture presentation highlights each situation. The first frame depicts an average driving scene. Class members are permitted to study this preapproach scene. Then the instructor asks the students to suggest possible responses to the scene. The class is then distracted and the teacher flashes the second or critical picture onto the screen by use of a tachistoscope. Each picture is shown on a predetermined time span and students are required to give a response immediately on a student participation form.[6] The values of this method are these: (1) It reduces driver mistakes through prior association; (2) it stresses the *necessity of 100 per cent attention* to the important task of driving; (3) it motivates trainee interest in accident awareness; (4) it helps develop mature attitudes in younger drivers; (5) it promotes *student participation;* (6) it is compatible with any teacher's schedule and is *low in cost;* and (7) it trains *visual perception and increases visual field.* The total set is composed of eight film strips organized on an elementary and advanced basis. Complete information regarding the flash-film method may be obtained from Safety Education Films, Inc., Minneapolis, Minnesota.

MULTIMEDIA TEACHING SYSTEM. The multimedia teaching system includes a motion picture projector, film strip slide projector, taped sound track, individual pushbutton responder boxes, and a master console control unit that scores all the students' answers. In using this system, the students view an accident or traffic situation, study alternative answers, and signal their decisions by pressing buttons on small response devices on the table in front of them.

[6] Safety Education Films, Inc., *Safer Driving* (Minneapolis, Minn.: Safety Education Films, Inc., 1956), pp. 10–11.

Figure 10-2. Drivocator System for Classroom Instruction (Courtesy Aetna Life & Casualty)

PERCEPTION OF DRIVING HAZARDS.   This is a relatively new program designed for use in high school driver education classes. The program involves training in perception of traffic hazards through time-limited exposure to a specially prepared film strip and the use of discussion procedures that contribute to the development of desirable attitudes. This program includes a series of three film strips: (1) Perception of Driving Hazards; (2) Limited Access Highway; and (3) Highways and Byways. The strips were developed by the Center for Safety, New York University. Copies of these may be obtained from the Shell Oil Company, Public Relations Department, 50 West 50th Street, New York, New York.

DRIVER SAFETY TRANSPARENCY SERIES.   This series is designed to provide the potential driver with knowledge necessary for safe driving. There are a total of 14 complete units in the series that actually show conditions and types of situations the driver will be confronted with and what his response should be. The transparencies are depicted on a screen through the use of the overhead projector. The complete series is composed of 91 basic transparencies, 109 attached overlays, creating 200 separately illustrated driving and traffic situations. Information regarding the availability of this series is available from Porto-Clinic Instruments Incorporated, 298 Broadway, New York, New York. Other distributors have similar sets available for purchase.

Film Sources

Nationwide, there are many sources from which driver educators may obtain traffic safety films. Following is a representative list of organizations and agencies where films are available.

American Automobile Association
Foundation for Traffic Safety
8111 Gatehouse Road
Falls Church, Virginia 22042

Aetna Life & Casualty
151 Farmington Avenue
Hartford, Connecticut 06115

AIMS Instructional Media Services
P. O. Box 1010
Hollywood, California 90028

Allstate Enterprises
Driver Education Services
Allstate Plaza, F3
Northbrook, Illinois 60062

American Safety Belt Council
1717 N. Highland Avenue
Hollywood, California 90028

Association Films, Inc.
512 Burlington Avenue
La Grange, Illinois 60525

Coronet Instructional Films
66 E. South Water Street
Chicago, Illinois 60601

Ford Motor Company
Film Library
The American Road
Dearborn, Michigan 48121

General Motors Corporation
Film Library, G. M. Bldg.
Detroit, Michigan 48202

Insurance Institute for Highway Safety
Watergate 600
Washington, D.C. 20037

International Film Bureau, Inc.
332 S. Michigan Avenue
Chicago, Illinois 60604

Modern Talking Picture Service, Inc.
1212 Avenue of the Americas
New York, New York 10036

Motion Picture Production Center
University of Illinois
501 S. Wright Street
Champaign, Illinois 61820

National Audiovisual Center
General Services Administration
Washington, D.C. 20409

National Safety Council
444 N. Michigan Avenue
Chicago, Illinois 60611

Professional Acts, Inc.
P. O. Box 8484
Universal City, California 91608

Safety Centers Inc.
25 Reservoir Avenue
Providence, Rhode Island 02907

Shell Film Library
50 W. 50th Street
New York, New York 10020

Southern Illinois University
Learning Resources Services
Carbondale, Illinois 62901

The Jam Handy Organization
2821 E. Grand Boulevard
Detroit, Michigan 48200

EQUIPMENT

Various classroom teaching units can be enriched through the proper use of equipment. There are many types of desirable classroom equipment that serve to illustrate concepts, emphasize difficult points, and in general motivate student interest in the unit.

178

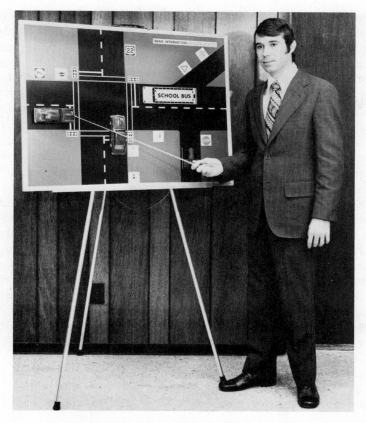

Figure 10-3. Magnetic Traffic Board for Classroom Instruction (Courtesy Bumpa-Tel, Inc.)

Types of Classroom Equipment

The following equipment is typical of the type used in classroom driver education classes. The successful use of this equipment is contingent upon the teacher's ability to integrate it into the unit at the most advantageous time. Furthermore, the instructor must have a definite purpose in mind to be accomplished from the use of classroom equipment. Equipment should not be used as "time fillers" or entertainment. The values of classroom equipment are closely related to the learning process.

PSYCHOPHSYICAL. "Reaction time, distance acuity, night blindness, and field of vision are psychophysical factors which could contribute to a person's ability to avoid accident-causing situations."[7] To evaluate these psychophysical characteristics, special testing devices are used to test individuals. These devices permit the teacher to

[7]Marland K. Strasser, et al., *Fundamentals of Safety Education* (New York: Macmillan Publishing Co., Inc., 1974), p. 460.

determine whether or not a student has normal abilities. Value can also be derived from the discussion of test results and how disabilities might influence one's driving performance. Sources for such equipment are identified later in the chapter.

FLANNEL AND MAGNETIC BOARD. The flannel and magnetic traffic boards have wide application in the area of traffic safety. Such equipment particularly enhances the demonstration of relevant traffic situations or traffic laws. Through the use of miniature cars the teacher may illustrate numerous traffic situations with ease on the diagrammed board provided. The flannel board is a versatile piece of equipment that lends itself to this through the use of teacher-made materials that adhere to the flannel surface.

MODELS AND CUTAWAYS. The use of three-dimensional models is invaluable in the presentation of complex mechanisms and principles. Models have significant application to the high school driver and traffic safety education program. In driver education they are of particular value in the instruction of the operating principles of the automobile and in the application of these principles to the driving task. By using cutaways, the teacher can show the actual parts of a mechanism in both size and material. Through the wise use of this equipment, students will quickly develop an understanding of difficult concepts and their application to driver education.

Equipment Sources

There are numerous sources where equipment for classroom use may be obtained. The following listing is representative of those sources that manufacture and/or distribute classroom equipment.

American Automobile Association
8111 Gatehouse Road
Falls Church, Virginia 22042

Bumpa-Tel, Inc.
P.O. Box 611
Cape Girardeau, Missouri 63701

Educational Device Company
Driver Testing and Training Equipment
Tecumseh, Michigan 49286

Instructive Devices, Inc.
147 Armistice Boulevard
Pawtucket, Rhode Island 02860

Intext
Driver Testing Equipment Division
925 Oak Street
Scranton, Pennsylvania 18515

Life Technology, Inc.
2361 Stanwell Drive
Concord, California 94520

Minnesota Automotive, Inc.
502 Patterson Avenue
Mankato, Minnesota 56001

Scheib Industries, Inc.
305 Hall Street, Box 244
Charlotte, Michigan 48813

Stromberg Hydraulic Brake
and Coupling Company
5453 Northwest Highway
Chicago, Illinois 60630

C. G. Zaun Sales
1340 Winchester Avenue
Glendale, California 91201

LEARNING ACTIVITIES

1. Contact 10 of the sources listed in the chapter and request sample copies of their free or inexpensive materials. The letter should specify the item(s) desired.
2. Visit five secondary schools with driver education programs. Use the equipment listed in Figure 10-1 to determine the scope of equipment available for classroom use. Be prepared to report your observations to the class.
3. Build a piece of classroom equipment that could be used in the teaching of a unit of instruction. Consult with your instructor before commencing the project.
4. Preview 10 driver and traffic safety education films at your campus audio-visual center. Write a report describing the content, value, and application of each.
   Prepare and make a classroom presentation on the topic, "The Values of a Classroom Driver Education Reference Library."

SELECTED RESOURCES

Aaron, James E., and Marland K. Strasser. *Driving Task Instruction—Dual-Control, Simulation, and Multiple-Car.* New York: Macmillan Publishing Co., Inc., 1974.

Allen, William H. *Audio-Visual Communication Research.* Santa Monica, Calif.: Systems Development Corporation, 1958, pp. 9, 14.

Backman, J. W. *How to Use Audio Visual Materials.* New York: Association Press, 1956.

Gronlund, Norman E. *Stating Behavioral Objectives for Classroom Instruction.* New York: Macmillan Publishing Co., Inc., 1970.

McKnight, A. James, and Bert B. Adams. *Driver Education Task Analysis, Volume III: Instructional Objectives.* Department of Transportation, PB202–247 (HumRRO Report 71-9) (March 1971).

National Highway Traffic Safety Administration. *Guide for Teacher Preparation in Driver Education—Secondary School Edition.* Washington, D.C.: The Administration (July 1974).

National Joint Committee on Uniform Traffic Control Devices. *Manual on Uniform Traffic Control Devices for Streets and Highways.* Washington, D.C.: U.S. Department of Commerce, Bureau of Public Roads, 1972.

Stack, Herbert J., and J. D. Elkow. *Education for Safe Living.* Englewood Cliffs, N.J.: Prentice-Hall, Inc., 1966.

Strasser, Marland K., et al. *Fundamentals of Safety Education.* New York: Macmillan Publishing Co., Inc., 1973.

PART

LABORATORY INSTRUCTION

In this section of the text the laboratory phase of a total driver education program is discussed in depth. Program content and organization supplemented with appropriate teaching methods and instructional aids are presented. Evaluation as applied to both laboratory and classroom instruction is treated in this section.

Included in Part III are the following chapters:

11. Organization of Laboratory Instruction
12. Content of Laboratory Program
13. Teaching Methods and Techniques for Laboratory Instruction
14. Materials and Equipment for Laboratory Instruction
15. Methods of Evaluation for Classroom and Laboratory Instruction

Chapter **11**

Organization of
Laboratory Instruction

OBJECTIVE: The student will be able to identify and apply those principles and concepts necessary to the development, organization, and teaching of a planned laboratory instructional program.

The National Conference on Safety Education defined *laboratory instruction* as "that portion of a driver education course, covering motor vehicle operation under real or simulated conditions, characterized by student learning experiences arising from use of electronic driving simulation equipment, an off-street multiple-car driving range, and/or on-street driving practice in a dual-controlled car under the direction of a teacher."[1]

The primary objectives of the laboratory program are the development of proficiency in the operational tasks and the development of perceptual processes. In the organization of the laboratory phase of the driver and traffic safety education program, it is imperative that the instructor keep foremost in his mind these two principal objectives. In addition, he should be aware of the overall objectives of the laboratory program as presented in Chapter 3.

The laboratory program is a well-planned and -designed program of instruction, so that the student is prepared systematically and intelligently to operate a motor vehicle safely. The instructor should be prepared to accomplish specific objectives each day that he is with a group of students. The laboratory program is a specific learning

[1] American Driver and Traffic Safety Education Association, *Policies and Guidelines for Driver and Traffic Safety Education* (Washington, D.C.: The Association, 1974), p. vii.

situation that must be as carefully structured as a classroom lesson. For the program to be successful the administrator and teacher alike must be aware of the need for considerable thinking and advance planning for each day's lesson.

SELECTING A PROGRAM PLAN

As the instructor contemplates the organization of a laboratory program, he must consider whether or not he is meeting recommended national or state standards, providing satisfactory experiences for the student, meeting needs of individual students, and developing a program that meets acceptable academic standards.

The instructor must consider many different factors when determining a laboratory plan. Some of the factors to be considered would include the following:

1. *RECOMMENDED STATEWIDE STANDARDS.* In every state there are recommended standards for the laboratory program. Such standards must be considered if the school is to meet accreditation standards. National standards recommend that a minimum of six hours of on-street instruction be given each student. However, many driver educators recommend a minimum of eight hours of such instruction for each student.

2. *PROGRAM BUDGET.* A primary consideration should be the amount of money available for the development of the laboratory program. The administrator and instructor should develop a budget that allows for the accommodation of all eligible students in the laboratory phase. In those states where reimbursement programs are in operation, schools seem to have adequate financing, but all need to consider the most economical way to teach the program.

3. *TEACHER AVAILABILITY.* The number of teachers available to assist in the conduct of the laboratory program must be given initial thought in overall program planning. The number of practice driving vehicles, the availability of driving simulators, or a multiple-car range will all be factors in determining teacher needs and availability. Also, each teacher should have training in the type of program he is to teach. Many states require additional certification of teachers in simulation and range instruction before they may teach that mode of instruction.

4. *SCHOOL SIZE.* In organizing the laboratory program plan, the number of students to be accommodated will be a major consideration. A rather small school would entertain the development of a dual-control practice-driving program, whereas it would be more feasible for a larger school to entertain the possibility of developing a simulation or multiple-car range laboratory program to be used in conjunction with the dual-control car.

5. *FACILITIES AND EQUIPMENT.* Various laboratory program plans require specific types of facilities and equipment. Therefore the instructor must give thought to the availability of such equipment as he plans the laboratory experiences for his students.

186

The content of the laboratory program should be planned with a great deal of care. It is important that a series of basic lessons be chosen and taught in a logical sequence. In Chapter 12 the content of the laboratory program is outlined and discussed in some depth; however, the following is a suggested daily lesson plan sequence that can be used by the instructor when preparing his daily lesson plans.

DAILY LESSON PLAN SEQUENCE

1. General Orientation
2. Basic Procedures
   a. Starting
   b. Shifting and placing car in motion
   c. Steering
   d. Stopping
   e. Simple left and right turns
3. Residential Driving
4. Developing Perceptual Skills
5. Driving in Reverse
6. Angle Parking; Turning Vehicle Around; Perpendicular Parking
7. City Practice Driving
8. Advance City Driving
   a. Starting and parking on hill
9. Driving on Rural Highways, State Highways, and at Higher Speeds
10. Expressway Driving
11. Driving Under Adverse Weather Conditions
12. Driving at Night
13. Emergency Maneuvers
    a. Changing a tire
14. Parallel Parking
15. Final Driver Performance Test

CONSIDERATION OF HIGHWAY TRAFFIC SITUATIONS

Driving involves the perceptual organization of complex stimuli and coordinated sequences of activity that must be accomplished within a given time in a given situation. In order to meet these situations, it is necessary that sequences or patterns of activity be learned by the beginning student.

In the planning of laboratory experiences for the driver education student, the instructor needs to be aware of the existence of the many traffic situations that influence driver performance. As the driver moves along the highway, he is confronted with a wide variety of situations or events. These include the roadway, signs, signals, other vehicles, weather conditions, and pedestrians. As the driver observes these various events from time to time, he must make pertinent decisions that influence his safety on the highway. Actions taken by the driver based on his decisions result in space-time relationship of vehicle position, direction, velocity, and acceleration.

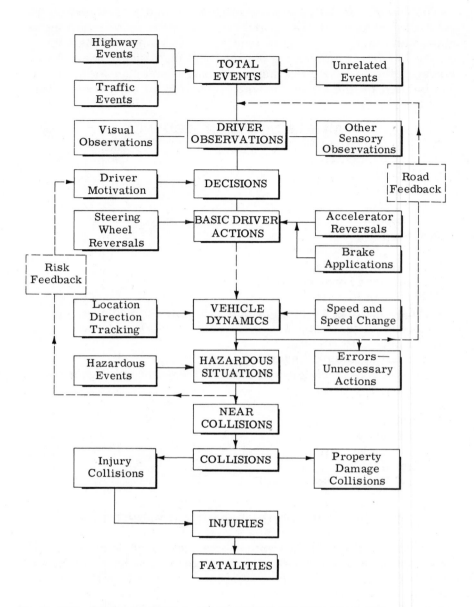

Figure 11-1. Schematic Diagram of Highway Traffic Situations (Courtesy Ford Motor Co., Traffic Safety and Highway Improvement Program)

At times the actions of the driver may be in error, causing undesirable movements of the vehicle and possibly leading to hazardous situations, near collisions, collisions, injuries, and fatalities. Figure 11–1 describes the total highway traffic situation and how it influences driver performance and subsequent vehicle control.

Fletcher N. Platt of the Ford Motor Company has developed a probability theory of highway traffic situations. This theory is reflected in Figure 11-1. In hopes of clarifying the theory, the following listing of highway traffic situation probabilities is presented.[2]

The Probability of Highway Traffic Situations

Highway and Traffic Events	A Hazardous Situation
—10 or more per second	—every hour or two
Driver Observations	A Near Collision
—2 or more per second	—once or twice a month
Driver Decisions	A Collision
—1 to 3 per second	—every 6 years of driving
Driver Actions	An Injury
—30 to 120 per minute	—every 40 years of driving
Driver Errors	A Fatality
—at least 1 every 2 minutes	—every 1,600 years of driving

In studying this listing of highway traffic situations and Figure 11-1, it is apparent that such events and their measurement are related to environment, driver operation, and vehicle dynamics as related to environment. In view of the fact that these highway and traffic events are inputs to the driver and are influenced by his attitude and his emotions, it is vital that in the planning of the laboratory phase of the driver and traffic safety education program the instructor make every effort to include instruction based upon the probability theory presented here. As the instructor plans the teaching of those lessons presented in Chapter 12, every effort should be made to relate the lessons to the material presented in this section.

LABORATORY PROGRAM PLANS

Eventually the supervisor and/or teacher must make a decision as to the type of laboratory program plan to be utilized in the school. Such a decision should be the result of critical and comprehensive study based upon the standards desired plus consideration of the materials presented in this chapter.

There are three principal ways to organize laboratory instruction. They are (1) dual-control car, (2) simulation, and (3) multiple-car driving-range plans. Each of these approaches has distinctive characteristics. It is necessary that the instructor consider these plans thoroughly before he decides which to use. Generally dual-control instruction is used in schools with 250 students or less per year eligible for driver education, and consideration should be given to a simulator or multiple-car driving-range program in schools with a number greater than this. The following is a discussion of each of these methods. Although each is presented separately, the simulator or multiple-car driving-range plan is always used in conjunction with the dual-control car plan.

[2] Fletcher N. Platt, *Traffic Safety Research: A Unique Method of Measuring Road, Traffic, Vehicle, and Driver Characteristics* (Dearborn, Mich.: The Ford Motor Company, 1962), p. 3.

Dual-Control Car

The dual-control car program emerged in the 1930s as the original laboratory program plan. This plan calls for direct instruction in a driver education vehicle in traffic under the supervision of a qualified instructor. The number of students assigned to each practice driving group should be from two to four individuals. Generally this instruction is given in traffic, and therefore no special instructional area is necessary. Each student is guided through the series of lessons outlined in Chapter 12. Consideration is given to individual progress, because all students do not progress at the same rate during the course of instruction.

The dual-control method has several advantages; however, it also has several disadvantages. The following is a listing of each of these considerations.

Advantages

1. Provides real traffic experience.
2. Provides direct instruction under the supervision of a qualified instructor.
3. Provides immediate application of lesson to the driving task.
4. Provides for planned logical learning sequences.
5. Provides for observation time that enhances the total laboratory learning process.

Disadvantages

1. Student-teacher ratio comparatively low.
2. Financial consideration when accommodating over 250 students per year.
3. Temptation to do nothing but drive in a restricted protective area.
4. Difficulty in locating satisfactory driving areas in large metropolitan cities.
5. Difficulty in guiding individual students based on personal needs.

Simulation

Throughout the past two decades simulation has become a familiar method of organizing laboratory instruction. It is a method similar to the one used by the Air Force and the aircraft industry for the training of pilots principally through the use of a simulator piece of equipment named the Link Trainer. The National Conference on Safety Education defined driving simulation as "group student learning experiences which permit individuals to operate vehicular controls in response to audio-visual depictations of traffic environments and driving emergencies. The electromechanical equipment provides for evaluation (by a teacher) of perceptual, judgmental, and decision-making performance of individuals and groups."[3] As indicated in this

[3] American Driver and Traffic Safety Education Association, op. cit., p. vii.

Figure 11-2. Students Receiving Simulation Instruction (Courtesy Idaho State University)

definition, a system such as this uses a piece of equipment known as a simulator. By definition, a *driving simulator is an electromechanical device designed to represent the driver's compartment of the automobile, including typical controls and gauges.* In a recent year there were 2,300 schools in 49 states giving instruction on driver simulators.[4] The basic components of the driving simulation system are as follows:

1. A basic piece of classroom equipment that represents the interior of a typical motor vehicle.
2. A set of programed films that assist one in the learning of fundamental driving skills and the application of these skills in typical and emergency driving situations.
3. A master control unit that scores student responses mechanically on a scoreboard or a master score sheet.
4. A 16mm projector adapted for use with the master control unit.

In determining whether a school should take advantage of the driving simulation system, consider the pros and cons of such a laboratory program. The following advantages and disadvantages are listed for consideration.

[4] National Highway Traffic Safety Administration, *Statewide Highway Safety Program Assessment: A National Estimate of Performance* (Washington, D.C.: The Administration July 1975), p. 95.

Advantages

1. Allows the teacher to schedule a larger number of students simultaneously.
2. Reduces the per capita cost of instruction.
3. Enables the teacher to instruct in emergency techniques.
4. Enhances the development of driver attitudes.
5. Allows student to practice drive in all types of traffic environments.

Disadvantages

1. Initial costs are sometimes prohibitive.
2. The instructor may become nothing more than a projection operator if he does not use the system properly.
3. Lack of real work movement and perspective.
4. Lack of 360° visual range.
5. Difficulty in the supervising of several students at the same time.
6. Lack of creativeness on the part of the instructor to use and interject other teaching methods that would enhance learning in the simulation system.

Driver Simulation Systems

Today there are two basic simulation systems in use in a substantial number of secondary schools across the nation. These two systems are (1) the Aetna Drivotrainer system, and (2) Allstate Good Driver Trainer system. These systems are either fixed installations or housed in mobile trailers and may be purchased or leased. Simulation can help develop the student's ability to recognize, analyze, and correctly respond to traffic by:

1. Providing adjustive response practice under a wider variety of driving environments than are available near most schools.
2. Providing practice, in complete safety, in driving under adverse conditions, such as emergencies, foul weather, and heavy traffic.
3. Providing continuous and cumulative information on individual student performance.
4. Providing an opportunity for development of basic manipulative skills in response to realistic portrayals of traffic environments.

AETNA DRIVOTRAINER SYSTEM. This system of training was introduced to the secondary schools in 1953. Since that time the Aetna Drivotrainer system has become familiar in the driver education laboratory program within the schools of the nation. It has proven to be quite effective in training students in the fundamental procedural skills of driving, development of perceptual processes, and enhancement of driver behavior.

The equipment for the Aetna Drivotrainer system is manufactured by Doron Precision Systems, Inc., Binghamton, New York. Information may be obtained from the manufacturer and from Aetna Life

Figure 11-3. Multiple-Car Facility (Courtesy Minnesota Highway Safety Center, St. Cloud State University)

Insurance Company, 151 Farmington, Hartford, Connecticut. In addition to providing equipment for permanent classroom installation, there are available mobile facilities that contain up to 16 Drivotrainer units that can be moved from school to school, based on the type of laboratory schedule the school develops.

A teacher's manual is provided that outlines each of the films and gives suggestions for effective use. Moreover, the teacher's manual serves as an effective program guide to the teacher in the development of the simulation system.

ALLSTATE GOOD DRIVER SYSTEM. In 1961 the Allstate Insurance Company announced the development of the Link Driving Simulator system to be made available to the secondary schools of the nation. This system of laboratory instruction is also manufactured by Doron Precision Systems, Inc.

SUMMARY OF DRIVING SIMULATOR FUNCTIONS

The following is a comparative summary of the Aetna Drivotrainer and the Link Simulator. It should be kept in mind that as models change, these specifications will change.

		Link Simulator	Drivotrainer
1.	Car Length	48" (base only)	58" (base only 48")
	Width	29"	26"
	Height	37-½"	39"
2.	Shift	Two	One
	Automatic	On column	On column
	Manual	On floor	On column
3.	Film Library	13 Films	20 Films
4.	Student Display	Yes	Yes
	Shifting	None	"Change Gears"
	Signals	"Turn Signal"	"Signal Left"
			"Signal Right"
	Accelerating	"Speed"	"Speed Up"
			"Slow Down"
	Steering	"Steer"	"Steer Left"
			"Steer Right"
	Braking	"Brake"	"Brake More"
			"Brake Less"
	Headlights	"Headlights"	None
5.	Printer	Optional (shows students making errors)	Optional (shows degree of student's actions right and wrong)
6.	Instant Reader	Usually optional (1 student at a time)	Yes (for multiple activities)
7.	Clutch	Functional	Functional
	Up	Not Recorded	Recorded
	Down	Not Recorded	Recorded
	Friction Point	Not Recorded	Recorded
8.	Brake—soft, medium, hard, pump		
9.	Engine	Engine noise; no recording	Simulator motor; on–off recorded
10.	Horn	Nonoperational	Operational and Recorded
11.	Total Checks	22	32
12.	Coding	Binary (on film)	Binary (on tape)
13.	Synchronization	Test code on film	Optical code on film
14.	Student Response	Optional, 10 Filmstrips	Basic system on Standard unit; full system optional with 20 filmstrips and projector
15.	Car Power	36V DC	28V DC
16.	Instructor's Manual	Approximately 220 pages	Approximately 360 pages
17.	Group Performance Meter	No	Yes

194

Multiple-Car Driving-Range Plan

Another approved laboratory program plan is the multiple-car driving range. This is a program whereby some of the behind-the-wheel instruction given to the individual student takes place on an off-the-street area that protects the student from the problems and hazards of a real traffic environment. However, a driving range does provide all of the typical driving situations that are necessary for the student to become a proficient beginner driver. By definition, the multiple driving range is an off-street area that simulates real world driving and uses a number of cars simultaneously to provide laboratory instruction under the supervision of one or more teachers. The area includes:

1. Space for development of fundamental skills.
2. Road surfaces wide enough for two-way and multiple-lane traffic.
3. Intersections, curves, and grades.
4. Lane markings, signs, and signals.
5. Configurations for good traffic mix.
6. A method of communication between teacher and students by radio, loudspeaker, or other effective means.[5]

The driver education supervisor should carefully evaluate the relative merits of the multiple-car method in determining whether or not the school should utilize this method. The following are given for consideration:

Advantages

1. Helps the student develop basic manipulative skills.
2. Helps the student develop independence.
3. Helps the student develop a sense of responsibility.
4. Allows the teacher to recognize and teach toward individual student differences.
5. Helps the student develop perceptual habits.
6. Provides flexibility, allowing for a wide variety of situations.
7. Allows the teacher to do a more efficient job of instruction.
8. Allows the student an opportunity to drive various makes and models of cars.[6]

Disadvantages

1. Initial construction costs may be prohibitive.
2. Appropriate number of instructional vehicles may not be available.
3. If the range is some distance from the school, traveling time will subtract from instructional time.

[5] American Driver and Traffic Safety Education Association, op. cit., pp. 20–21.

[6] Highway Users Federation for Safety and Mobility. *The Multiple-Car Method.* (Washington, D.C.: The Federation, 1972), p. 4.

Figure 11-4. Instructor Instructing Student on the Driving Range (Courtesy Florida State University, Traffic and Driver Improvement Program)

The multiple-car driving range is an open driving area used to practice basic skills and confidence driving. The open driving area has no layout stimulating various traffic situations and conditions.

An ideal driving range is developed on a two-acre tract of land. However, a suitable range program can be developed in an area approximately 400 feet by 200 feet.

In order for the range to be an economical operation, it is suggested that a minimum of eight vehicles be used in such a program and that the maximum be approximately 12.

The use of a multiple-car driving range has proven to be an effective means of offering laboratory instruction to secondary school students and adults alike. Each year, in some larger school systems across the nation, approximately 1,000 high school students and an equal number of adults receive instruction in the fundamentals of driving by this method of instruction.

Articulation of Various Methods

The most common articulation is between the dual-control and simulator. A team-teaching approach is used in numerous schools in order to strengthen the overall laboratory program. For example, one teacher will teach in the simulators while three or four others will teach in the cars, alternating days in the cars and simulators. For the most effective instruction, the student is first taught the lesson in the simulator, then practices in the car. However, in some school systems they have determined that the student receives better instruction if program articulation combines dual-control, simulation,

196

and multiple-car driving range into one comprehensive laboratory program. This approach seems to be feasible in that each of these approaches accomplishes specific goals. By combining all of the good features of each of these program plans, learning is more effective, and a better traffic citizen is developed.

SELECTION OF ROUTES

The instructor of a dual-control car program must give thought to the environment that best suits the type of lesson to be taught and the ability of the individual student. Moreover, he should consider the fact that it is best for the student to advance from an area that is relatively free of traffic congestion into an area that taxes and challenges the ability of the driver as he progresses through the course. At no time should a beginning student be immediately thrust into a complex and hazardous driving environment. The instructor should preplan routes in an attempt to avoid a liable suit. Moreover, the teacher should have routes filed with and approved by the administrator. This is especially important in the scheduling of night driving lessons. Also approval of public officials should be sought for lessons taught in various places in the city.

General Practice Areas

In the dual-control system, it is best for the instructor to have a traffic-free environment to present his first lessons. This enables the instructor to explain and satisfactorily demonstrate the lesson. The traffic-free area gives the student an opportunity to assimilate and practice the lessons being presented during this early phase of the laboratory program. After the introductory lessons, practice driving should be done on streets and highways relatively free of traffic. Such areas may be found in (1) quiet residential sections, (2) service drives adjacent to the school facilities, (3) abandoned fairgrounds, and (4) park roads.

Individual differences should be considered as lessons are presented day after day. As the student progresses in his ability to apply those lessons presented to him, and as he progresses in his ability to identify, predict, decide, and execute in various complex traffic environments, he should be allowed to practice-drive in areas where traffic is more prevalent and congested. Ultimately practice driving should take place on congested city streets in downtown areas, and on expressways, if available. Because students progress at different rates, the instructor may need to plan routes or practice-driving areas for two or three different levels of ability in any one group of practice-driving students. Though convenient for him, the teacher should not force all students, regardless of ability, to practice-drive in the same area. Moreover, the teacher should be aware of the fact that some students will never progress to the point of being able to drive safely in heavily congested traffic during a minimum six-hour course.

In selecting practice routes, the instructor should consider that along with practice driving in various traffic environments students need practice in making various maneuvers, especially left and right turns. Routes chosen should contain all types of traffic situations and experiences in meeting traffic with varying degrees of density and complexity in order for the student to become a proficient beginning driver. Much thought must be given to route selection prior to the beginning of the daily lesson and not after the practice-driving session has begun.

Skill Drill Areas

The instructor of a driver education laboratory class may desire to supplement his driving instruction by teaching a series of skill drills. The area should be entirely free of traffic and approved for school use. It is recommended that areas such as school parking lots, service drives adjacent to the schools, barricaded streets and highways, abandoned fairgrounds, or driving range area be used to facilitate such instruction. Such an area should be one that is accessible to the school and with lines painted on the surface to remain permanent for use throughout a school year. If areas having traffic are to be used, the supervisor could check with the local police department to gain their cooperation to limit and control the traffic using such a street or highway. Such an area should be used as an off-street practice area and not for a range program.

OBSERVATION TIME

One phase of the laboratory program that is significant and valuable to the individual student is the phase referred to as observation time. Observation time is defined *as that time a student spends in the back seat of a practice-driving vehicle observing the driving of another practice driver or the instructor.* Such time should be well planned by each instructor. This should not be considered a time when the individual student may relax, talk, study some other lessons, or take a nap. The student can gain considerable knowledge through the development of his powers of observation as another student is operating the motor vehicle on the streets and highways of the local community. The student's duty to observe cannot be overemphasized.

The following are suggested as possibilities for the instructor in planning the observation time.

1. Be prepared to ask timely questions regarding the driving environment or the performance of the student behind the wheel.
2. Develop a check list on which observing students may note the significant aspects of driver performance and of the traffic scene.
3. Have each student verbally evaluate the performance of the driver.
4. Have each student evaluate the performance of the other vehicle drivers observed in the practice-driving area.

198

5. Allow the students to discuss violations observed on the part of other drivers and to determine from the discussion the proper action that should have been taken by the driver.
6. Use an on-the-spot teaching method to point out good and poor features demonstrated by other drivers.

EMERGENCY LESSONS

In the planning of a laboratory program, it is desirable that time be allocated for preparing students to meet certain common driving emergencies. Such lessons are outlined in Chapter 12.

Emergencies can be classified into two different areas. These areas are (1) driving situation emergencies, and (2) car failures. In the former it is necessary for the student to know and to understand that when such emergency situations are present on the highway scene he must be prepared to dispose of such emergencies or apply the proper evasive action. With car failures, it is necessary for the driver to understand and know how to apply certain elementary corrective measures in order to place his vehicle into operating condition once again, or the driver should know what to do if he cannot correct the condition.

The teacher should be cautious and not present hazards beyond the capability of the student. Such an act could be interpreted as negligence.

GROUPING OF STUDENTS

As stated previously practice-driving groups contain between two to four beginning students. It is desirable from a learning point of view to group together students having comparable abilities. If possible, homogeneous grouping should take place before beginning practice-driving sessions. However, if this is not possible it is suggested that practice-driving groups be rearranged after students have been given several lessons and the instructor has had an opportunity to assess properly the level of achievement for each student at that point.

Practice-driving groups should be organized for instructional efficiency. The most desirable grouping arrangement is to have a maximum of two practice-driving students. This would mean one practice driver and one observer who could concentrate on every performance of the driver behind the wheel. However, the instructor may be required to accommodate up to a maximum of four students each period. If this is the case, students should be grouped so there are (1) four males, or four females in each of the groups, or (2) two males and two females in each of the groups, or (3) three females and one male in a group. One lone female should not be grouped with three males, because she may be at a disadvantage when working with three males, who presumably have a higher technical and mechanical ability when it comes to the motor vehicle. The driver education instructor never takes one lone female or male student if the lesson calls for a movement of the practice-driving vehicle away from the school building and premises. From a public relations point of view, this is not a recommended practice.

RECORDS AND REPORTS

It is sound teaching procedure to maintain proper records. Thus it is essential that a number of basic records and reports be maintained in a quality driver education program. In those states where the schools are involved in statewide reimbursement programs, records and reports will be required and the types specifically stated by the state agency responsible for administering the reimbursement program. However, it is good business practice and efficient management for the instructor to keep satisfactory records and reports for the program and for each student enrolled. The following are the suggested records and reports that are necessary in the conduct of a good laboratory program:

1. Individual student enrollment form.
2. Individual student daily progress report.
3. Class report form to note accumulation of practice-driving time.
4. Vehicle maintenance report forms.
5. Cumulative budget form that identifies expenditures related to the laboratory program.
6. Periodic maintenance chart reports for practice-driving vehicles.
7. Accident report forms kept in the practice-driving vehicle at all times.
8. A permanent record form for each student, filed at the end of the semester as a permanent school record for reference purposes at any time in the future.

SPECIAL STUDENTS

In the planning of the laboratory program, it may be necessary to accommodate special students. These may be students with (1) physical defects, (2) mental handicaps, or who are (3) problems to the school and the community. It is desirable that the instructor consult and work very closely with the school's guidance counselor, special education teacher, and others who might assist in working with these students. The driver and traffic safety education program is uniquely suited to work with such students, and the instructor should encourage these students to become part of the laboratory phase of the driver education program. The objectives of the driver education program are in harmony with the objectives of the programs that are specifically identified with handicapped students. Therefore driver education can play a major role in the rehabilitation or the development of a useful citizen by accommodating such students in the driver and traffic safety education program.

If these students are to be accommodated, the instructor should (1) evaluate closely the biographical background of the individual student, (2) be aware of specific physical or mental deficiencies, (3) discuss student's background with other instructors who may be assisting in the teaching of such students, and (4) preplan the course of instruction to be given the student. The instructor of driver education will strengthen his own program as well as gain favor with the school administration and the other disciplines in the secondary school's curriculum by developing a program for handicapped students. Therefore it is recommended that consideration be given to working with special education and school counseling personnel in order to develop a driver education program for special education students.

LEARNING ACTIVITIES

1. Plan a dual-control car laboratory program to accommodate 120 students. Assume that there are available one teacher and one practice-driving vehicle. Use schedules in Appendix as a guide.
2. Plan a simulation program for 360 students. Assume that you have a twelve-place simulator installation. Provide for three of the six total hours to be articulated with the dual-control plan.
3. Plan a multiple-car driving-range program to accommodate 240 students. Assume that you have 12 cars for use on the range. Provide for one hour of the six total hours to be articulated with the dual-control car plan.
4. Organize a check list that can be used by students who are observing another student drive.

SELECTED RESOURCES

Aaron, James E., and M. K. Strasser. *Driving Task Instruction—Dual-Control, Simulation, and Multiple-Car.* New York: Macmillan Publishing Co., Inc., 1974.

Bishop, Richard W. *Comparing the Effectiveness of Various Combinations of On-Street and Multiple-Car Driving Range Instructional Hours.* Tallahassee, Fla.: Florida State University, 1965.

Florida Department of Education. *Florida High School Driver Education Curriculum Guide.* Tallahassee, Fla.: The Department, 1974.

Highway Users Federation for Safety and Mobility. *The Driving Simulator Method.* Washington, D.C.: The Federation (April 1970).

_____. *The Multiple-Car Method.* Washington, D.C. The Federation (March 1972).

National Highway Traffic Safety Administration. *Driver Training Simulators, Ranges and Modified Cars.* Springfield, Va.: National Technical Information Services, 1971.

Platt, Fletcher N. *Traffic Safety Research: A Unique Method of Measuring Road Traffic, Vehicle, and Driver Characteristics.* Dearborn, Mich.: The Ford Motor Company, 1962, p. 3

Strasser, Marland K., et al. *Driver Education: Learning to Drive Defensively.* River Forest, Ill.: Laidlaw Brothers, Publishers, 1973.

Texas Education Agency. *Curriculum Guide for Multi-Car Driving Ranges.* Austin, Tex.: The Agency, 1970.

Chapter 12

Content of Laboratory Program

OBJECTIVE: The student will be able to select and apply appropriate content for the development of a dual-control, simulation, or multiple-car laboratory instructional program.

In the design of a quality driver and traffic safety education laboratory program, the instructor must give careful thought to the content of each lesson taught to beginning students. Consideration must be given to the inclusion of content that will develop operational skills, perceptual processes, and wholesome attitudes.

The role of a motor vehicle operator is to control the relationship of a vehicle to the roadway and traffic environment. Therefore the instructor should recognize that his responsibility in the preparation of beginner drivers is intimately related to the development of the driver's ability to "(1) identify any critical objects or changes in the environment, (2) predict possible future relationships or outcomes, (3) decide what to do, and (4) execute the decision."[1]

If these goals are to be achieved, then it should be recognized that laboratory instruction in driver education must develop five systems of skills and abilities that emerge as a coordinated driver system. This is vital if the beginner is to be capable of operating a motor vehicle in the traffic society of the twentieth century. The skills and abilities that make up the driver system are the following:

[1] Automotive Safety Foundation, *A Resource Curriculum in Driver and Traffic Safety Education* (Washington, D.C.: The Foundation, 1970), pp. 7-9.

1. *Motor skills*—operating and manipulating vehicle control devices.
2. *Perceptual or seeing skills*—seeing, receiving inputs from the total traffic environment, and proper interpretation of input data.
3. *Application of laws*—recognizing forces of nature and applying man-made laws that assist in disposing of collision courses or traffic violations.
4. *Accurate judgments*—estimating speeds, distances, decelerations, disposing of potential hazards, and predicting driver behavior.
5. *Properly timed and correct responses*—planning, deciding, reacting, and timing correct evasive action.

These must be developed into an integrated driver system by the motor vehicle operator. Teaching the driver to do this is the task of the driver education instructor.

The driver educator needs to recognize that the beginning driver shall face at least five different categories of driving situations. Therefore the learning and application of the skills and abilities presented should be taught with a variety of driving environments in mind. The principal types of driving situations that shall confront each student are as follows:

1. Residential areas with light traffic.
2. Heavy, complex city traffic including expressways.
3. Rural open highways, including superhighways.
4. Adverse conditions, including night driving.
5. Emergency situations.

Figure 12-1. Practice Driving Student Receiving In-Car Instruction (Courtesy Marshall University).

Without vision safe driving cannot be accomplished. Vision influences more than 90 per cent of the decisions that *are made behind the wheel of a moving automobile.*[2] This fact should be considered by the instructor as he plans the application of daily lesson plans.

The objective of any driving period is to transport persons or goods from a starting point to a destination. Basic factors in accomplishing this objective are (1) identifying the road surface, (2) avoiding striking any fixed objects en route, and (3) avoiding striking or being struck by any moving objects en route. The sensory stimuli received by the individual that permit him to achieve these three basic factors are largely visual.

During the performance of the driving task the eyes undergo a constant changing relationship with the traffic environment. They are always active and moving from other vehicles, highway conditions, roadway signs and signals, pedestrians, and bicyclists. Moreover, continuous observation of rear- and sideview mirrors, speedometer, and other vehicle gauges and controls is also in progress. Functionally the eyes undergo a continuous process of (1) detection—awareness of presence of something, (2) recognition—recognition of objects, and (3) dynamic relationships—realization of vehicle position, speed, and direction of travel. Also, visual discrimination involves the following capabilities:[3]

1. The ability to discriminate motion.
2. The ability to discriminate objects or parts of objects subtending small visual angles both near and far.
3. The ability to discriminate objects seen only in the peripheral fields of vision.
4. The ability to discriminate depth.
5. The ability to discriminate color.

Development of Seeing Habits

Individuals learn to see just as they learn to walk and talk. Every driver thinks he sees correctly. However, investigations report that four out of five drivers do not use their eyes correctly or have some faulty seeing habits. Because the purpose of seeing is to feed input data to the brain, it is extremely important that such data be correctly received, transmitted, and interpreted. Traffic accidents occur when a collision course is allowed to continue to impact or accident. A collision course is *defined as a dynamic situation in which two objects will collide if direction and acceleration of both continue unchanged.*

[2] National Academy of Sciences—National Research Council, *The Visual Factors in Automobile Driving* (Washington, D.C.: The Council, Publication 574, 1958), p. 17.

[3] National Academy of Sciences—National Research Council, ibid., p. 2.

In countless numbers of traffic accidents a collision course is allowed to continue because of delayed perception. Delayed perception seems to be caused by impediments of vision and inattentiveness. Impediments to vision are to be found within the individual drivers, vehicle, and environment. Inattentiveness is principally the result of preoccupation, distractions, and daydreaming. If collision courses are to be avoided, the driver must use knowledge and information already learned and stored in the brain. Moreover, accurate interpretation of other drivers' behavior is especially important. Therefore "the driver must 'see' and 'understand' the dynamics of the collision course to avoid an accident. It is then obvious that vision and intelligence are inseparable."[4]

The prediction of collision courses can be improved through proper training. The instructor of driver and traffic safety education should include this important training in the laboratory program. Proper seeing habits can be developed by teaching each beginner student to use the five habits developed by the Institute of Driver Behavior described as follows:[5]

1. *High aim steering*—learn to steer by occasional glances well ahead at the center of your intended driving path. Then center your vehicle in the right lane and eliminate low-aim, fixed-stare visual habits.
2. *Get the big picture*—the driving environment should be observed in total through use of central vision. Scan the entire scene, and do not fix vision on any one vehicle or other object. Observe other vehicles in relation to the ground. This assists in estimating speed and steering path.
3. *Keep eyes moving*—shift eyes frequently. A person sees only through a tiny cone of center eyesight. This cone is approximately 5 feet wide when looking 100 feet ahead. Unless the eyes are shifted often, a blank visual stare results. This habit is related to the big-picture habit discussed already. Check rear- and sideview mirrors as eyes scan the entire traffic environment.
4. *Leave yourself an out*—attempt to ride in a space cushion all the time. This could mean an adjustment of vehicle speed to avoid tailgating or the selection of a different lane. Be aware of an escape route to right, left, or onto the road shoulder. Moreover, adjust speed on hills, curves, in darkness, inclement weather, and for reduced visibility. Never allow yourself to be boxed in where you have no place to go in the event of errors on the part of other drivers.
5. *Make sure you are seen*—watch for cues of wrong moves and errors by other drivers. Do not rely on traffic laws or the assumption that you are seen by other drivers for protection. If in doubt, communicate with the other drivers by honking horn, flashing headlights, and using turn signals and brake lights.

[4] Robert C. Sneller, *Vision and Driving* (St. Louis: American Optometric Association, 1962), p. 3.

[5] Institute of Driver Behavior, *Training Your Eyes for Expert Driving* (Detroit: The Institute, 1957), pp. 4-10.

The content of the laboratory program developed in every school should include the application of these habits. For complete information and sample tests, contact Institute of Driver Behavior, 1380 Penobscot Building, Detroit, Michigan.

Scanning Pattern

Safe driving requires prompt and accurate perception of hazards and the correct prediction of their courses. To accomplish this it is necessary that the driver develop a scanning pattern that will enable him to detect and discern all events and cues presented in the traffic environment. Such a scanning pattern is the result of conscious effort to learn and apply the habits already mentioned.

The driver should develop the habit of scanning the entire traffic scene. Eyes should move from left to right in a continuous effort to assess potential hazards. In specific areas attention should be devoted to suspected or known hazards. An effort should be made to identify habit patterns of other drivers and check their vehicles in relation to the ground in order to ascertain steering path. Figure 12-2 suggests that a scanning pattern be developed that would allow the driver to check on about 300 degrees of the entire driving environment.

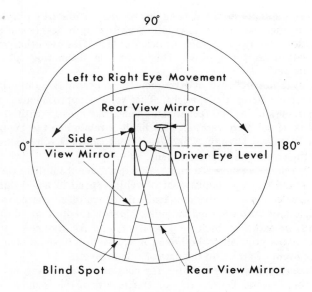

Figure 12-2. Driver Scanning Pattern

DEVELOPMENT OF PERCEPTION

Very closely related to the development of satisfactory vision habits for safe driving is the teaching of perceptual skills. Perception is related to but is more than vision and should not be confused with fundamental vision proneness.

206

A motor vehicle operator must be able to identify, comprehend, and interpret visual input data transmitted from the physical and social environments. This is made possible through the process of perception. It should be understood that the "principal medium of transmission may be visual, but auditory, tactile, kinesthetics, and/or other sensory mechanism may also be involved."[6] Perception performs the functions of (1) receiving and establishing awareness of incoming data, (2) sorting and organizing these data, and (3) making decisions resulting in proper action. This process, called perception, can be improved or sharpened in the individual. Laboratory instruction in driver education should develop perceptual skills to aid in the development of accident-free drivers.

Because the driver is constantly making decisions relating to numerous events observed during each mile of driving, it is important that these decisions be correct. The development of improved perceptual skills may be accomplished by (1) improving basic visual skills, (2) presenting a variety of vicarious experiences that will allow the beginner to see (recognize) and comprehend traffic situations, and (3) providing the driver with an understanding of the psychological factors (emotion and misconception) that may cause distortions in the perception of traffic situations. As related to the driving task, good visual habits can do the following:

1. Lengthen the perceptual distance which allows more time for decision and actions.
2. Assist automatically the driver in control of the car even though the driver is momentarily distracted at times.
3. Build a strong resistance to distracting events.
4. Reduce physical and mental strain which in turn reduces fatigue.
5. Give the driver a feeling of security and assurance.

Methods for improving perception are discussed in Chapter 13.

DUAL-CONTROL CAR DAILY LESSON SEQUENCE

The driver and his vehicle represent a man-vehicle system wherein the control relationship between man and the machine suggests a high degree of control performance. However, the occurrence of accidents and near accidents attests to the fallibility of the system. Therefore, as the driver educator organizes daily lesson plans, it should be borne in mind that the instructional process related to behind-the-wheel instruction is a highly organized and exacting procedure.

The following lessons plans are designed for use in those laboratory programs in which the dual-control car method of instruction is the principal way of teaching beginner drivers. However, all lessons have application to simulation and multiple-car driving-range programs as well.

[6] Leon Brody, "Teaching Perceptual Skills," *Safety Education Digest* (New York: New York University, The Center for Safety Education, 1957), p. 33.

High school instructors may wish to use some of the lessons in a different sequence than that presented. This is satisfactory; however, teachers should be alert to the fact that the sequence presented is logical and represents a successful alignment of daily lesson plans. Furthermore, the instructor must decide whether instruction of a particular unit requires one or more periods. This will vary with the length of the instructional period. Individual student progress must also be considered when determining the time allowed for a unit.

All of the following laboratory lessons are outlined for use in the automatic shifting vehicle, because this type of vehicle is used predominately in driver education classes. These are representative lesson plans, and others should be developed by direction from the instructor. For specific teaching methods and techniques, see Chapter 13.

DAILY IN-CAR LESSON PLAN NO. 1

BASIC PROCEDURES: 4 S's (STARTING, STEERING, SHIFTING, STOPPING); SIMPLE LEFT AND RIGHT TURNS

Required Entry Level

The student will demonstrate (1) proper predriving habits, (2) location and function of gauges, control instruments, and other devices on the vehicle, (3) shifting the selector lever and verbally explaining the function of each gear, and (4) proper procedure for leaving the vehicle.

Lesson Objectives

The student will demonstrate (1) procedure for starting the vehicle, (2) procedure for moving the vehicle forward, (3) procedures for making a left and a right turn, and (5) procedure for stopping the vehicle.

Specific Instructional Objectives	Learning Activities
1. The student will demonstrate the proper starting procedure.	1. The instructor will verbally review student to insure proper performance of these tasks.

CONTENT

Starting Procedure

   1. Park brake on.
   2. Place gear selector lever to "P" (Park position).
   3. Gas feed—depress accelerator lightly. (In many cases it may be necessary to consult the instruction or owner's manual for specific instructions relating to the use of the gas feed when starting the engine.)
   4. Ignition on.
   5. Check gauges.

EVALUATION

The instructor will visually check the student as he performs starting procedure.

2. The student will demonstrate the proper procedure for moving the vehicle forward away from curb.	2. The instructor will verbally review student as he performs the task.

CONTENT

Moving Car Forward (away from curb)

   1. Depress foot brake with right foot.
   2. Shift selector level to "D" position.

3. Release parking brake.
4. Check mirrors inside and out; check blind spot.
5. Signal to your left.
6. Check blind spot again.
7. Release foot brake.
8. Recheck traffic.
9. Move into nearest traffic lane.
10. Check traffic again.
11. Turn signal off.

EVALUATION

The instructor will visually check the student as he performs procedure for moving away from the curb.

3. The student will demonstrate the proper procedure for making a left turn.	**3.** The instructor will verbally review student as he performs left turn.
	The instructor will demonstrate the proper hand-over-hand steering to the left. The student will practice the procedure following the demonstration.

CONTENT

Left Turn

1. Get into proper lane.
2. Check traffic.
3. Signal.
4. Place right hand at 12 o'clock position.
5. Brake with right foot.
6. Check traffic again.
7. Check for pedestrians.
8. Turn hand-over-hand.
9. Look up intended path of travel; unwind steering wheel.
10. Accelerate—halfway around turn.
11. Resume safe speed—check traffic.

Hand-Over-Hand Steering to the Left

1. The off-side hand (right) starts near 12 o'clock at the top of the steering wheel and pulls it downward.
2. The other hand (left) reaches over the first one to get a new grip near the top of the wheel.
3. This kind of hand-over-hand motion is repeated until the steering wheel has been turned the required amount.

EVALUATION

1. The instructor will visually check student as he performs the left turn.
2. The student must perform 5 out of 5 good left turns.

210

3. The student must perform proper hand-over-hand steering while making the turn. (Visually checked by instructor.)

4. The student will demonstrate the proper procedure for making a right turn.	**4.** The instructor will verbally review student as he performs right turn. The instructor will demonstrate the proper hand-over-hand steering to the right. The student will practice this procedure following the demonstration.

CONTENT

Right Turn

1. Position car in right lane.
2. Check traffic.
3. Signal.
4. Place right hand near top of wheel.
5. Brake with right foot.
6. Check traffic again.
7. Turn hand-over-hand.
8. Release brake slightly.
9. Look up intended path of travel.
10. Unwind steering wheel naturally.
11. Accelerate.
12. Resume safe speed—check traffic.

Hand-Over-Hand Steering to the Right

1. The off-side hand (left) starts near 12 o'clock at the top of the steering wheel and pulls it downward.
2. The other hand (right) reaches over the first one to get a new grip near the top of the wheel.
3. The kind of hand-over-hand motion is repeated until the steering wheel has been turned the required amount.

EVALUATION

1. The instructor will visually check the student as he performs the right turn.
2. The student must perform 5 out of 5 right turns properly.
3. The student must perform proper hand-over-hand steering while making the turn. (Visually checked by instructor.)

5. The student will demonstrate proper procedure for stopping the vehicle.	**5.** The instructor will verbally review student as he performs the task.

CONTENT

Stopping the Car

1. Check mirrors.
2. Signal intentions.
3. Brake smoothly to stop.
4. Depress brake.

EVALUATION

The instructor will visually check student as he performs the task of stopping the car.

6. The student will demonstrate proper procedure for leaving the vehicle.	**6.** The instructor will verbally review the student as he performs the task.

CONTENT

Leaving the Car

1. Apply foot on brake and hold.
2. Set parking brake.
3. Shift selector to "P".
4. Turn key off and take out.
5. Unfasten seat belt and shoulder strap.
6. Check traffic before opening the door.
7. Lock doors.

EVALUATION

The instructor will visually check the student as he performs the task of leaving the car.

MEDIA AND RESOURCES

1. Driving Guide.
2. Anderson, William G. *In-Car Instruction: Methods for Teachers of Driver and Traffic Safety Education*. Reading, Mass.: Addison-Wesley Publishing Co., Inc., 1969.
3. Handouts, "Left Turn Procedures" and "Right Turn Procedures."

DAILY IN-CAR LESSON PLAN NO. 2

PERCEPTUAL DEVELOPMENT

Required Entry Level

The student will demonstrate (1) proper predriving habits, (2) location and function of gauges, control instruments, and other devices on the vehicle, (3) shifting the selector lever and verbally explaining the function of each gear, (4) proper procedure for starting the vehicle, (5) proper procedure for moving the vehicle forward, (6) proper procedures for making left and right turns, (7) procedures for stopping and securing the vehicle.

Lesson Objective

The student will explain and demonstrate effective visual habits for driving a vehicle.

Specific Instructional Objectives	*Learning Activities*
1. The student will state five ways good visual habits can aid in meeting the driving task more efficiently.	**1.** The instructor will verbally review the good visual habits.

CONTENT

Visual Habits

1. Can lengthen the perceptual distance which allows more time for decisions and actions.
2. Can assist, automatically, in control of the car, even though the driver is momentarily distracted at times.
3. Can build up a strong resistance to distracting events.
4. Can reduce physical and mental strain which in turn reduces fatigue.
5. Can give the driver a feeling of security and assurance.

EVALUATION

The instructor will listen as the student states the good visual habits and make additions and corrections when necessary.

2. The student will orally list the five steps included in the "Smith System," define each step and how it relates to the actual traffic condition, and demonstrate these steps while driving.	**2.** The instructor will verbally review the "Smith System" and how it relates to the driving task.

CONTENT

Smith System

1. Aim High in Steering

a. Look well ahead at your intended driving path.

b. Analyze traffic conditions before you get to any point of potential conflict.

2. Get the Big Picture

a. Be aware of both sights and sounds that are around your vehicle.

b. Make every attempt to see visually everybody and everything that is coming into your view.

3. Keep Your Eyes Moving

a. Move your eyes to look near, far ahead, to both sides, and in your rearview and outside mirrors.

b. Keep eyes moving in order to

(1) Spot approaching traffic hazards and have more time to adjust to them safely.

(2) Keep your eyes from getting tired.

4. Make Sure They See You

a. Use various controls to make sure other vehicles and pedestrians see your vehicle.

(1) Horn

(2) Headlights

(3) Turn signals

(4) Emergency flashers

5. Leave Yourself an Out

a. Leave yourself an escape route.

b. Allow adequate following distance.

EVALUATION

1. The instructor will quiz the students orally on the steps and significance of the "Smith System."

2. The instructor will visually check the students to make certain they are checking their mirrors, blind spots, and slowing down when potential hazards exist while driving.

---

3. The student will orally list the components involved with the IPDE concept, define each part and how it relates to the actual driving task, and demonstrate the concept while driving.

3. The instructor will verbally review the components of the IPDE concept.

The instructor will state examples for the student, having them identify situations, predict what is going to happen, decide what to do, and how they would execute that decision.

CONTENT

IPDE Concept

I — Identify the situation at hand. Look for any potential driving hazards (parked cars, pedestrians, children and their toys, rolling balls, and someone following them into the street).

P — Predict what may happen, predict the possible action of the identified objects (will the car pull out? will ball roll into street with someone running after it? will pedestrian move into your driving path?).

D — Decide what to do. Decide what action you should take (decelerate gradually or quickly, stop quickly or gradually, swerve).

E — Execute your decision. Perform the action you decided to take.

214

EVALUATION

The instructor will quiz the student orally on the components and significance of the IPDE components.

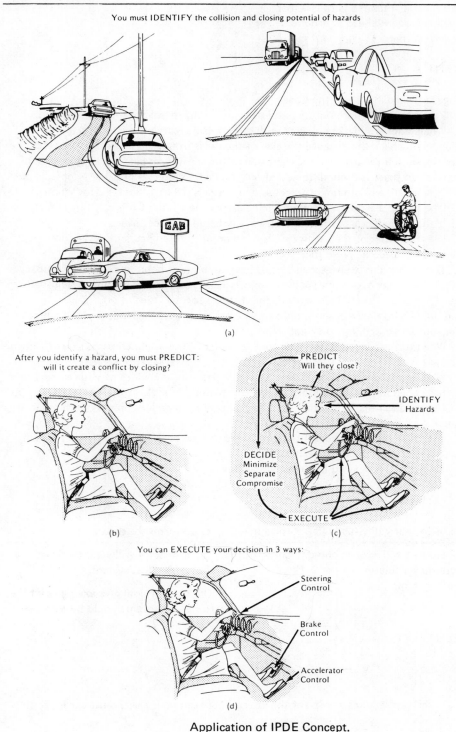

You must IDENTIFY the collision and closing potential of hazards

GAB

(a)

After you identify a hazard, you must PREDICT: will it create a conflict by closing?

(b)

PREDICT
Will they close?

IDENTIFY
Hazards

DECIDE
Minimize
Separate
Compromise

EXECUTE

(c)

You can EXECUTE your decision in 3 ways:

Steering
Control

Brake
Control

Accelerator
Control

(d)

Application of IPDE Concept.

| 4. The student will explain and demonstrate keeping the car in the middle of the lane or pathway by the intermittent focusing of central vision on the center of the intended path whether traveling straight ahead or around a curve or corner. | 4. The instructor will verbally review the procedure of keeping the car in the middle of the lane. |

CONTENT

Keeping Car in the Middle of the Lane

1. Focus central vision, both far and near, down the middle of the lane selected.

2. When lanes are marked, glance in the left outside rearview mirror and along left front fender to check the distance the side of the car is from road marking. Also, the instructor should tell the distance the right side of the car is from lane marking or edge of roadway. When space is limited, the car should be kept as close as possible to objects on the left. Lanes are a minimum of 9 feet and are usually 10 to 12 feet wide when marked.

3. When lanes are not marked, imagine a carpet the width of this car (6 to 7 feet) unrolling ahead of the car. Trucks and buses may be up to 8 feet wide.

4. Use the center of the pathway as a main point of reference, but never allow your central vision to become fixed there.

5. To develop the twelve-second visual lead or aim high habit, pick out a stationary feature of the roadway or some roadside object ahead at about the distance you usually look to. Then count the time in seconds that it takes for the front of your car to pass the selected point. The time elapsed should equal or exceed twelve seconds (at least a block in town, and one-fourth mile in rural areas).

6. When turning corners, aim high for the center of the intended path. Look through the turn.

7. When parking parallel to a curb, imagine a pathway the width of your car and next to the curb. Then line up the middle of your car with the middle of this pathway.

8. Use roadway marking, other cars, and objects as secondary points of reference (use quick glance only).

9. Put forth a determined effort to make greater use of fringe vision when focusing on the center of your intended pathway.

10. At night look beyond the head lamp spray.

EVALUATION

The instructor will visually check the student as he performs the driving task.

| 5. The student will explain and demonstrate the calculation of the 2–12 adjust system. | 5. The instructor will verbally review the 2–12 adjust system. The students will give examples where this 2–12 system should be used. |

CONTENT

2–12 Adjust

1. 2—The two seconds stands for the interval between your car and the car in front

of you. While driving at higher speeds you may want to increase this distance to 3 or 4 seconds. The way to calculate the 2 seconds is by picking out a stationary object in your path ahead. When the tail end of the car in front passes that object you count "1000–one, 1000-two"; if your car's front end reaches on 1000-two you have the proper distance. If you reach the object on 1000-one you are too close.

2. 12—The 12 seconds stands for how far ahead your eyes should be looking down the road. The way to calculate this is by picking out a stationary object in your path ahead and starting to count "1000–one, 1000–two . . . " until you reach 1000–twelve at which time the front end of your vehicle should be even with this object. If you have reached the object before you have reached 1000-twelve you are not aiming far enough down the road.

3. Adjust—The adjust means how you adjust the position of your vehicle within the traffic pattern. You can do this by accelerating, braking, and steering to adjust your position safely.

EVALUATION

The instructor will ask the student to verbally recite how the 2—12 adjust system is calculated and when it is used.

6. The student will demonstrate the procedure of checking one of the rearview mirrors or the instrument panel on the dash at least every 5 seconds in an urban area and at least every 10 seconds in a rural area while still maintaining proper lane control.

The student will demonstrate a head check in the proper direction prior to making a change of direction.

6. The instructor will verbally review the procedure for checking mirrors, instrument panel, and so on.

CONTENT

Checking Mirrors, Instrument Panel, and Directional Change

1. Use habit of small-scale shifting of head.
2. Check only one gauge or display at a time.
3. Employ the quick glance technique to maintain continuous awareness of traffic scene.
4. Make a quick headcheck to the blind spot before making lateral movements.

EVALUATION

The instructor will visually check the student as he performs the various perceptual checks.

7. The student will demonstrate the procedure for efficient scanning and search techniques by shifting his eyes and attention to a different section of the traffic scene at least an average of every 3 seconds.

7. The instructor will verbally review the scanning and search techniques.

The student will use commentary
driving as he performs the scanning
and search techniques.

CONTENT

Scanning and Search Techniques

1. Move the eyes regularly, in sweeping action, to each sector of the traffic scene.
Pause only a second or two on any one object.
2. Concentrate on the various sectors in proportion to the number of events or likelihood of hazards.
3. The search rate and pattern should vary with traffic conditions.
4. Use the ground-viewing habit. Scan near and far as well as to both sides.
5. Look through the glass areas of other vehicles for objects and events.

EVALUATION

The instructor will visually check the student's eye movement.

MEDIA AND RESOURCES

Hand out, "The Development of Effective Visual Habits for Driving," or similar material.

DAILY IN-CAR LESSON PLAN NO. 3

DRIVING IN REVERSE

Required Entry Level

The student will demonstrate (1) proper procedures necessary in starting and putting the car in motion, (2) making left and right turns, (3) stopping and securing the car, (4) scanning techniques for recognition of obstacles and potential hazards.

Lesson Objective

The student will demonstrate procedures for backing a car on a straight path as well as a turning path.

Specific Instructional Objectives	Learning Activities
1. The student will demonstrate preparatory steps for backing the car.	1. The instructor will verbally review preparatory steps for backing the car.

CONTENT

Preparatory Steps

    1. Bring the car to a complete stop.
    2. Depress the brake pedal to hold the car firmly in position.
    3. Move the selector lever to the R position.
    4. Check road and traffic conditions to be certain that they will permit the safe completion of the backing maneuver; be ready to delay or postpone the maneuver when necessary.

EVALUATION

The instructor will visually check the student while performing preparatory steps.

2. The student will demonstrate appropriate driver's position for moving the car backward on a straight path which best enables him to maintain control of the vehicle, accurately guide it on the intended path and observe events on both sides of intended path.	2. The instructor will verbally review the appropriate driver's position for moving the car backward on a straight path.

CONTENT

Appropriate Driver's Position

    1. Body turned slightly to the right.

2. Head turned all the way around to directly face the rear of car.
3. Right foot remains on the brake.
4. Left hand grasps the steering wheel at approximately 12 o'clock position.
5. Right hand and arm may be placed on top of the backrest.

EVALUATION

The instructor will visually check the student while performing the appropriate driver's position.

3. The student will demonstrate speed control skills while backing the car in a straight path.	3. The instructor will verbally review speed control skills.

CONTENT

Speed Control Skills

1. Gradually depress the accelerator pedal to put the car in motion.
2. Immediately move foot to brake pedal and control speed through gradual application and release of pedal.
3. Thereafter, use accelerator only as necessary to maintain the car's momentum.

EVALUATION

The instructor will visually check the student while performing the speed control skills.

4. The student will demonstrate tracking skills while backing the car in a straight path.	4. The instructor will verbally review proper tracking skills.

CONTENT

Tracking Skills

1. Know (in advance) the intended path over which the vehicle is to travel.
2. Look along the intended path and aim the car in the direction of the path.
3. Recognize when the car begins to deviate from the intended path and make the necessary steering corrections.

EVALUATION

The instructor will visually check the student while performing the proper tracking skills.

5. The student will demonstrate appropriate driver's position for moving the car backward on a turning path.	5. The instructor will verbally review student on the appropriate driver's position.

CONTENT

Appropriate Driver's Position

1. Head and shoulders turned in the direction in which rear end of car is to move.
2. Right foot remains on the brake.
3. Right hand at 12 and left at 3 when backing to the right.
4. Left hand at 12 and right hand at 9 when backing to the left.
5. Hand-over-hand technique is recommended for use in backing the car.

EVALUATION

The instructor will visually check for appropriate driver's position.

---

6. The student will demonstrate speed control skills while backing the car on the turning path.

6. The instructor will verbally review student on the appropriate speed control skills.

CONTENT

Refer to Content under Objective 3.

EVALUATION

The instructor will visually check the student while performing the speed control skills.

---

7. The student will demonstrate tracking skills while backing the car on a turning path.

7. The instructor will verbally review student on proper tracking skills.

CONTENT

Tracking Skills

1. Refer to Content under Objective 4.
2. Tracking on a backward turning path, the lateral movement of the front end of the vehicle is in the opposite direction from the rear end.
3. When backing into a driveway from a parking lane, the front end of the vehicle extends into the traffic lane during the course of the maneuver.
4. Hand-over-hand movements used in backing normally are restricted to the side of the steering wheel closest to the direction in which the vehicle is turning.

EVALUATION

Instructor will visually check student while performing the proper tracking skills.

MEDIA AND RESOURCES
1. Driving Guide.
2. Class notebook.
3. Anderson's "In-Car Instruction: Methods and Content."

DAILY IN-CAR LESSON PLAN NO. 4

CITY PRACTICE DRIVING

Required Entry Level

The student will demonstrate (1) predriving habits, (2) 4 S's (starting, shifting, steering, and stopping the car, (3) proper procedures for left and right turns, (4) concepts related to the Smith System (Lesson Plan No. 2) and IPDE, (5) perceptual skills involved in residential and light city traffic driving.

Lesson Objective

The student will demonstrate the ability to react properly to on-the-street situations (traffic signals, lane positioning, city speeds, right-of way) encountered while driving in a downtown city situation.

Specific Instructional Objectives	Learning Activities
1. The student will demonstrate general perceptual and decision-making skills needed to successfully drive in a city situation. The student will use commentary driving to demonstrate his awareness of these situations.	1. The instructor will verbally quiz the student and review the student on these skills as he drives.

CONTENT

Skills

1. Looking through the windows and underneath parked cars.
2. Timing traffic lights well in advance.
3. Selecting the best lane in terms of free-flowing traffic and meeting your specific driving needs.
4. Checking mirror every 5 seconds.
5. Looking for pedestrians and cross traffic when approaching and starting up at an intersection.

EVALUATION

1. Instructor will visually check the student as he performs these skills.
2. Instructor will listen to his commentary driving and make corrections when necessary.

2. The student will demonstrate proper procedure for correctly changing lanes.	2. The instructor will verbally review the student when performing the procedure and state any error made.

CONTENT

Lane Changing Procedure

1. Check mirrors (in and out).
2. Signal intentions.
3. Check blind spot (glance in direction you intend to turn).
4. Decide if safe.
5. Accelerate slightly, checking traffic again; looking over traffic and make slight turn.
6. Turn off signal indicator.
7. Maintain safe speed and proper lane position (center of intended path).

EVALUATION

The instructor will visually check the student as he performs the procedure.

---

3. The student will demonstrate precautions and procedures which should be taken once the lane is established.

3. The instructor will verbally ask the student to state some precautions and procedures which should be taken.

CONTENT

Precautions and Procedures

1. Keep in your own lane.
2. Ride out of other driver's blind spots.
3. Let others know your intentions in advance.
4. Move early enough to proper lane for turn or proper lane positioning.
5. Obey your lane signals.

EVALUATION

1. Instructor will visually check for precautions and procedures which should be taken.
2. The instructor will listen to the student state some of these precautions and procedures and make corrections or additions to explanation when necessary.

---

4. The student will demonstrate proper use of right, center, and left lanes when driving on either a one-way street or a multilane two-way street.

4. The instructor will verbally review the uses of these lanes.

The instructor will have the student state the uses of these lanes during the latter part of the lesson.

CONTENT

Proper Lane Usage

1. Right turn—slower-moving vehicles and right turns.
2. Center lane—through traffic; must signal when changing lanes.
3. Left lane—faster-moving traffic and left turn (possible pavement markings will mark left-turn lane).

EVALUATION

    1. The instructor will visually check the student's usage of lanes.

    2. The instructor will listen to student's explanation of lane usage and make corrections when needed.

5. The student will demonstrate proper procedures for making left turns in city traffic through the use of specialized lanes.	**5.** The instructor will verbally review these procedures.

CONTENT

Procedures for Left Turn Using Special Lane

    1. Get in proper lane well in advance.
    2. Check traffic situation.
    3. Signal (100 feet in advance).
    4. Brake.
    5. Check traffic and traffic signal.

EVALUATION

The instructor will visually check the student as he performs the procedure.

6. The student will demonstrate procedures which are to be followed when approaching the different components of a traffic signal.	**6.** The instructor will verbally review these procedures.

CONTENT

Components of Traffic Signal

    1. *Red*—stop at the cross line; remain until light turns to green.

    2. *Yellow*—warning that the signal is changing from green to red or red to green.

    3. *Green*—proceed, but not until it is safe to do so; yield to vehicles and pedestrians in the intersection first, then proceed.

    4. *Green arrow*—proceed in the direction that the arrow points; yield also to pedestrians.

EVALUATION

The instructor will visually check the student as he performs these procedures through the city area.

7. The student will demonstrate ability to adjust to various city speed limits by using his previous knowledge of the Smith System and IPDE.	**7.** The instructor will recite questions to the student in regard to speed zone signs which would alter the student's driving.

224

CONTENT

City Speed Zones

1. Signs are posted which state the speed limits.
2. In city traffic, the speed limit is 25 mph.
3. Traffic into the city will follow a 35–45 mph speed limit.
4. Obey the traffic speed zones; many times speed is being recorded by city police.

EVALUATION

1. The instructor will visually check the student's speedometer throughout the city.
2. The instructor will make corrections when student fails to answer speed zone questions correctly.

8. The student will demonstrate proper following distance for city traffic.	8. The instructor will verbally review the proper following distance when following another vehicle.

CONTENT

Following Distance

1. Two-second interval—when the car in front of you passes a certain point, you should be able to count one thousand one, one thousand two slowly prior to reaching that same point.

EVALUATION

The instructor will visually check to be sure student maintains proper interval.

9. The student will state reasons for maintaining this 2-second interval.	9. The instructor will verbally review these reasons with the student.

CONTENT

Reasons for Maintaining Interval

1. Gives one that space cushion needed to avoid potential hazards.
2. Gives the driver a good view of the back of the car in front of him.
3. Gives the driver some distance if the car in front rolls backward.
4. Gives the driver some measure of distance to move if the car in the rear is headed for a collision.

EVALUATION

The student should be able to state 3 out of 4 reasons for maintaining this proper following interval.

10. The student will demonstrate (if occasion arises) the correct procedure required when meeting or being	10. The instructor will verbally review the procedure with the student in regard to emergency vehicles.

overtaken by emergency vehicles
with their warning devices in
operation.

CONTENT

Emergency Vehicle Procedures

1. Yield right-of-way.
2. Slow down gradually.
3. Pull to the right side of the street and stop if possible.
4. Wait until vehicle is past.
5. Check for other emergency vehicles.
6. Check traffic, signal, pull into traffic at safe speed.
7. DO NOT FOLLOW EMERGENCY VEHICLES!

EVALUATION

1. The instructor will visually check the student if situation arises.
2. If situation does not arise, the instructor will check student by asking him to state these procedures.

11. The student will demonstrate precautions necessary to observe the right-of-way of pedestrians.	**11.** The instructor will verbally review these precautions.

CONTENT

Pedestrians' Right-of-Way

1. On right or left turn, yield to pedestrians the right-of-way and allow them free access.
2. Yield to possible jaywalkers who feel they must cross streets at places other than the intersection.
3. Yield right-of-way to blind people—they will have a white cane.
4. Yield to pedestrians at a bus stop.
5. Yield to pedestrians at railroad crossings or stations when in heavy traffic—they are in a rush.
6. Yield to pedestrians already in the intersection who have violated the wait sign; you must yield the right-of-way.

EVALUATION

The instructor will visually check the student to make sure he is observing the right-of-way to pedestrians.

MEDIA AND RESOURCES

1. Driving Guide.
2. Link Instructor Manual, "Complex Traffic."
3. Commentary driving.
4. Dual-control car.
5. "Rules of the Road"—your state.

DAILY IN-CAR LESSON PLAN NO. 5

DRIVING ON RURAL HIGHWAYS, STATE HIGHWAYS, AND AT HIGHER SPEEDS

Required Entry Level

The student will demonstrate (1) predriving habits, (2) 4 S's (starting, shifting, steering, and stopping the car), (3) proper procedures for left and right turns, (4) driving in reverse, (5) starting and stopping on a hill, (6) concepts related to the Smith System and IPDE in relation to residential driving, city driving.

Lesson Objective

The student will demonstrate precautions and procedures which can be taken to aid him in driving safely and efficiently on rural highways, state highways, and at higher speeds.

Specific Instructional Objectives	Learning Activities
1. The student will demonstrate the proper procedures for approaching and passing slow-moving farm or road repair equipment. The student will use commentary driving as he performs the task.	1. The instructor will verbally review the procedure. The procedures will be done in a drill situation unless the actual situation arises.

CONTENT

Procedures

1. Slow as you approach equipment to give yourself the opportunity to analyze the situation.
2. If equipment is wider than the road, in order to pass, slow down.
3. Sound horn to alert driver of your presence.
4. Observe his actions; in most cases he will pull over or wave you around him.
5. Accept this assistance cautiously; check to make sure the path is clear before passing.

EVALUATION

1. The instructor will visually check the student as he performs skill under drill situation (or real if situation arises).
2. The instructor will listen to his commentary driving and make correction when necessary.

2. The student will demonstrate and state precautions which can be taken to avoid the highway hazard of animals. The student will use commentary driving as he performs the task.	2. The instructor will verbally review precautions. The procedures will be done in a drill situation unless the actual situation arises.

CONTENT

Precautions

1. Be alert for signs posted to warn motorist that such hazards exist.
2. Slow down when you see such a sign.
3. Be ready to stop at any time.

EVALUATION

1. The instructor will visually check the student as he performs the skill under drill situation (or real if situation arises).
2. The instructor will listen to the student's commentary driving and make corrections when necessary.

3. The student will demonstrate the procedures for approaching a school bus. The student will use commentary driving as he performs the task.	3. The instructor will verbally review procedures. The procedures will be done in a drill situation unless the actual situation arises.

CONTENT

Procedures

1. Drivers seeing a school bus should slow, anticipating a possible stop.
2. Drivers behind the bus and approaching in opposite lane must stop when the bus is loading and unloading passengers.

EVALUATION

1. The instructor will visually check the student as he performs skill under drill situation (or real if situation arises).
2. The instructor will listen to the student's commentary driving and make corrections when necessary.

4. The student will demonstrate precautions which should be taken when passing a roadside stand. The student will use commentary driving as he performs the task.	4. The instructor will verbally review precautions.

CONTENT

Precautions

1. Be alert for other vehicles that may suddenly swing off the highway or onto it.
2. Slow slightly and scan area carefully.

EVALUATION

1. The instructor will visually check the student's eye movement and speed.
2. The instructor will listen to the student's commentary driving and make corrections when necessary.

5. The student will demonstrate procedures for dodging chuckholes in the road.	**5.** The instructor will verbally review the procedures.

CONTENT

Procedures

1. Be alert for such holes.
2. Scan well the area ahead.
3. If you see a hole in the road ahead, prepare to slow down or dodge it.

EVALUATION

The instructor will visually check the student as he performs the skill.

6. The student will demonstrate precautions which should be taken when driving on gravel and dirt roads.	**6.** The instructor will verbally review these precautions.

CONTENT

Precautions

1. Slow down to avoid veering into loose gravel.
2. If you are traveling behind a car that kicks up dust, slow down until the car is far enough ahead not to bother your visibility.
3. Don't try passing if dust hinders clear visibility.

EVALUATION

The instructor will visually check the student's speed and scanning techniques while driving on gravel or dirt roads.

7. The student will demonstrate precautions which should be taken when driving on a blacktop road.	**7.** The instructor will verbally review these precautions.

CONTENT

Precautions

1. Reduce speed.
2. Don't make any abrupt maneuvers (stopping, turning).
3. Be careful of road when it is wet because it becomes slippery.

EVALUATION

The instructor will visually check the student's speed and scanning techniques while driving on a blacktop road.

---

8. The student will demonstrate procedures for approaching road repairs.

The student will use commentary driving as he performs the task.

8. The instructor will verbally review procedures.

The procedures will be done in a drill situation unless the actual situation arises.

CONTENT

Procedures

   1. Slow down.
   2. Follow directional signal whether it is a flagman or detour.
   3. If it does require a detour, road may be unpaved, bumpy, and dusty; adjust your speed for conditions to maintain greatest control of your vehicle.

EVALUATION

   1. The instructor will visually check the student as he performs the skill under drill situation (or real if situation arises).
   2. The instructor will listen to the student's commentary driving and make corrections when necessary.

---

9. The student will demonstrate the procedures for approaching intersections and crossroads on the highway and country roads.

The student will use commentary driving as he performs the task.

9. The instructor will verbally review procedures.

The procedures will be done in a drill situation unless the actual situation arises.

CONTENT

Procedures

   1. Approach with caution.
   2. Be alert for cars which may enter into your traffic lane with little or no warning.
   3. If the intersection is unmarked and visibility is obscured by vegetation, signs, or any other obstruction, come to a complete stop, check traffic, and then proceed.

EVALUATION

   1. The instructor will visually check the student's braking, speed control, and scanning techniques as he performs skill under drill situation (or real if situation arises).
   2. The instructor will listen to the student's commentary driving and make corrections when necessary.

---

10. The student will demonstrate general procedures related to the proper speed which should be maintained while driving on the highway.

10. The instructor will verbally review these procedures.

CONTENT

Procedures

1. Never go faster than is reasonable under the existing conditions.
2. Try to maintain the speed at which most cars are traveling; if you drive too slowly, cars bunch up behind you.
3. When you can see that cars are bunching up ahead, hang back and let the congestion clear.

EVALUATION

The instructor will visually check the student's speed so that he does maintain a safe and efficient speed while driving on a highway.

11. The student will demonstrate and explain the 2–12–adjust concept as it is related to driving.	11. The instructor will verbally review the concept.
	The instructor will have the student count his following distance and concentration point.

CONTENT

Two Concept

1. The proper following distance which should be maintained is a 2–second interval between you and the car you are following.
2. When the car ahead of you passes a certain point, you should be able to count 1000-one, 1000-two very slowly prior to reaching that same point.

Twelve Concept

1. Down the road pick a point such as the crest of a hill or bend in the road at the distance that you normally concentrate your attention while driving.
2. Count off the seconds 1000-one, 1000-two . . . that it takes you
to travel to that fixed reference point.
3. Be able to count to 1000-twelve prior to reaching that point.
4. Think of the 2-12 concept as optimum goals though there may be exceptions to the concept.

Adjust

1. Use acceleration, braking, steering to adjust your position in traffic.
2. Once you have developed the habit of vigilant scanning through the use of the 2-12-second time rules, you'll not only see "traps" but will have more time to adjust lane position and/or following distance.

EVALUATION

1. The instructor will visually check the student as he performs the 2-12 concept.

2. The instructor will listen to the student count his following distance and concentration point.

12. The student will demonstrate the proper procedures for pulling off the side of the highway. (Use commentary driving.)	**12.** The instructor will verbally review these procedures.

CONTENT

Procedures

    1. Unless it is an emergency, find a location where you can stop well off the traveled portion of the road.
    2. Decide on a proper location.
    3. Signal to your right well in advance.
    4. Reduce speed gradually.
    5. Pull off the road carefully, keeping car under control (completely off the traveled portion of the road).
    6. Activate your emergency flashers.
    7. Keep all passengers from the traffic side of the car and from in front and behind it.

EVALUATION

    1. The instructor will visually check the student as he performs the skill.
    2. The instructor will listen to the student's commentary driving describing the procedures and make corrections where necessary.

13. The student will demonstrate procedures for approaching and going through a narrow roadway or over a narrow bridge. The student will use commentary driving as he performs the task.	**13.** The instructor will verbally review these procedures.

CONTENT

Procedures

    Time your approach to the narrow place or bridge so the cars go through it one at a time, easily, safely, and pleasantly.

EVALUATION

    1. The instructor will visually check the student as he performs the skill.
    2. The instructor will listen to the student's commentary driving and make corrections when necessary.

14. The student will demonstrate procedures for passing another vehicle on a roadway.	**14.** The instructor will verbally review these procedures.

232

The student will use commentary
driving as he performs the task.

CONTENT

Procedures

1. Check to see that there is enough clearance ahead to permit safe passing.
2. Look for signs and pavement markings (if there is a solid yellow line next to the road center line, on your side, it is illegal for you to cross it to pass; you may cross a broken white line, even if there is a solid yellow line on the side of the white line away from you; notice any signs or markings that may be appropriate).
3. When you move left to look ahead be sure you are not too close to the vehicle ahead of you (maintain the proper interval).
4. Look ahead very carefully before you start to pass (look for any possible hazards).
5. Check your inside and outside rearview mirrors and blind spots.
6. Give the proper turn signal to show your intentions.
7. Accelerate and check traffic again.
8. Sound your horn to let driver know that you are passing him (at night click bright lights on and off).
9. When you can see the whole car that you just passed in your rearview mirror signal your intentions to return to the proper lane.
10. Return to the proper lane after passing.
11. Turn off signal and resume a safe speed.

EVALUATION

1. The instructor will visually check the student as he performs the skill.
2. The instructor will listen to the student's commentary driving and make corrections where necessary.

---

15. The student will demonstrate the proper procedure for rounding a curve.

The student will use commentary driving as he performs the task.

15. The instructor will verbally review the procedures.

CONTENT

Procedures

1. Be alert for road signs indicating curves.
2. Slow down prior to entering the curve.
3. Do your braking before you reach the curve (if the curve becomes sharper ahead or you misjudged the curve and/or your speed, then brake as necessary).
4. Slow down to sufficient speed so that your sight distance will not be shorter than your stopping distance.
5. Stay in your own lane on your side of the road on curves.
6. Increase speed slightly when you are halfway through the curve.

EVALUATION

1. The instructor will visually check the student as he performs the skill.
2. The instructor will listen to the student's commentary driving and make corrections where necessary.

16. The student will demonstrate the procedures for crossing a railroad track with or without a mechanical device. The student will use commentary driving as he performs the task.	**16.** The instructor will verbally review these procedures.

CONTENT

Procedures

1. Slow down and be ready to stop (stop within 50 feet of the crossing but no closer than 15 feet from the nearest track).
2. Check left and right for any sign of an approaching train before you cross the tracks.
3. If automatic device activates while you are in the middle of the tracks, clear the crossing as quickly as possible.
4. If one train has passed, check for the approach of a second train.

EVALUATION

1. The instructor will visually check the student as he performs the skill.
2. The instructor will listen to the student's commentary driving and make corrections where necessary.

17. The student will demonstrate proper precautions for driving on hills. The student will use commentary driving as he performs the task.	**17.** The instructor will verbally review these precautions.

CONTENT

Precautions

1. Be sure to stay in your *own lane*.
2. Reduce speed.
3. Be alert for any hazard which may make it necessary for you to take evasive actions to avoid a collision.
4. Do not pass another vehicle near or on the crest of a hill.
5. If you are going up a steep hill in a standard-shift car in high gear, shift into a lower gear.
6. When you go downhill, keep your foot off the accelerator, apply a little pressure on the brake early before your car has gained momentum.
7. When you descend a steep hill, shift to low or second to give the engine more braking power.

234

8. In going downhill, never coast with the gearshift or selector in neutral or clutch disengaged or the ignition switched off.

EVALUATION

1. The instructor will visually check the student as he performs the skill.
2. The instructor will listen to the student's commentary driving and make corrections where necessary.

MEDIA AND RESOURCES

1. "Driver Education, Learning to Drive Defensively," by Strasser, Eales, and Aaron (Laidlaw, 1973).
2. Driving Guide.
3. Commentary driving.
4. Dual-control car.

DAILY IN-CAR LESSON PLAN NO. 6

EXPRESSWAY DRIVING

Required Entry Level

The student will demonstrate (1) predriving habits, (2) 4 S's (starting, shifting, steering, and stopping the car), (3) proper procedures for left and right turns, (4) driving in reverse, (5) starting and stopping on a hill, (6) concepts related to the Smith System and IPDE in relation to residential driving, city driving, rural driving, highway driving.

Lesson Objective

The student will demonstrate the ability to enter, maneuver, and exit an expressway safely and efficiently.

Specific Instructional Objectives	Learning Activities
1. The student will demonstrate precautions which should be taken in preparing him and the car prior to entering an expressway.	**2.** The instructor will verbally review these precautions.

CONTENT

Precautions

1. Check gas.
2. Check oil.
3. Check tires.
4. Check windshields and surrounding windows.
5. Check map.

EVALUATION

The instructor will visually check student as the precautions are taken.

2. The student will state and demonstrate the general ideas listed here while driving on the expressway.	**2.** The instructor will verbally review these ideas.

CONTENT

General Concepts

1. Avoid bunching.
2. Avoid the speed differential.
3. Avoid abrupt movements.
4. Beware of your highway neighbors.

EVALUATION

1. The instructor will visually check the student to assure that he is performing concepts listed above.

2. The instructor will listen to the student state concepts and make corrections where necessary.

3. The student will demonstrate the procedure for entering the ramp and moving onto the acceleration lane of the expressway.	**3.** The instructor will verbally review the procedure.

CONTENT

Procedure.

1. Speed approximately 25 mph on the ramp.
2. Glance over left shoulder to determine the traffic pattern.
3. Signal left.
4. Time approach onto the acceleration lane to fit into a gap in the traffic.
5. Enter acceleration lane.
6. Quickly accelerate to match expressway speeds (50–55 mph).
7. Glance over left shoulder.
8. Move from acceleration lane onto the expressway.
9. Turn left signal off.
10. Maintain expressway speeds.

EVALUATION

The instructor will visually check student as he enters expressway (speed, acceleration).

4. The student will use the Smith System and the IPDE concept while driving on the expressway.	**4.** The instructor will verbally review the procedures in relation to expressway driving.

CONTENT

Smith System

1. *Aim High in Steering*—Occasional quick glances at center of your intended driving path (¼ mile down the road).
2. *Get the Big Picture*—Look from side to side and develop fringe vision that helps to make judgments of speed, distance, and direction; watch all objects—moving or apt to move—for a quarter mile down the expressway.
3. *Keep Your Eyes Moving*—Keep glancing nearby, far ahead, to the side, and in the rearview mirror; never fix your eyes on any one object (avoid expressway hypnosis).
4. *Leave Yourself an Out*—Leave yourself a space cushion, a place to go to avoid an accident.
5. *Make Sure You Are Seen*—Make eye contact with the other driver or pedestrian; don't count on traffic laws to keep you out of an accident.

IPDE Concept

    I—Identify. Identify the type of hazard.
    P—Predict. Predict what is going to happen.
    D—Decide. Decide what action would be the best.
    E—Execute. Execute that action safely and efficiently.

EVALUATION

The instructor will visually check student's head movement, mirror check inside and out, and blind spot checks.

5. The student will demonstrate the proper following distance which should be maintained on an expressway.	**5.** The instructor will verbally review following distance which should be maintained.

CONTENT

Following Distance

1. The following distance should be doubled in regard to regular following distance. Instead of 2 second-interval, increase interval to 4 seconds.
2. *Four-Second Interval.* When a car in front of you passes a certain point, you should be able to count one thousand-one, one thousand-two, one thousand-three, one thousand-four slowly prior to reaching that same point.

EVALUATION

The instructor will visually check to make sure the student maintains the proper interval.

6. The student will demonstrate the proper procedures for passing a slower-moving vehicle traveling in the right lane on an expressway.	**6.** The instructor will verbally review the proper passing procedures.

CONTENT

Passing Procedures

1. Maintain proper following distance (double normal distance).
2. Check blind spot and mirrors.
3. Signal intentions left.
4. Check left blind spot again.
5. When path is clear proceed into left lane.
6. Remain in passing lane until vehicle passed is clearly visible and a safe following distance behind.
7. Check blind spots.
8. When path is clear signal intentions right.
9. Return to right lane.

10. Turn right signal off.
11. Maintain a safe speed in right lane.

EVALUATION

Instructor will visually check student as he performs the passing procedures.

7. The student will demonstrate two procedures for allowing a merging car to enter the expressway.	**7.** The instructor will verbally review these procedures.

CONTENT

Procedure #1 (remaining in right lane)

1. Check mirrors for following vehicles.
2. Signal a slowing-down maneuver by slightly pumping brakes.
3. Slow to provide a slot for the merging car to enter expressway safely and efficiently.

Procedure #2 (lane change)

1. Check left blind spot and mirrors.
2. If path is clear, signal left.
3. Again check left blind spot.
4. When path is clear, move into left lane.
5. Turn left signal off.
6. Check right blind spot to make sure the merging car is clear and proper following distance behind.
7. Signal right when path is clear.
8. Recheck blind spot to right and when path is clear move into right lane.
9. Turn right signal off.

EVALUATION

The instructor will visually check student performance of skill and his judgment of using the two procedures at the proper instances.

8. The student will demonstrate procedure which should be taken when approaching an accident scene on an expressway. The student will use commentary driving to explain procedure.	**8.** The instructor will verbally review the procedure. The procedure will be done in a drill situation unless the actual situation arises.

CONTENT

Procedures for Approaching an Accident Scene

1. Check mirrors.
2. Signal problem situation to cars following you by pumping brakes slightly.
3. Slow gradually, and cautiously pass the scene of the accident.

EVALUATION

1. The instructor will visually check the student's performance of the procedure.
2. The instructor will listen to the student's commentary driving and make corrections where necessary.

---

9. The student will state the meaning of "highway hypnosis" and list preventive measures which can be used to avoid becoming hypnotized.

   The student will demonstrate some of the preventive measures which can be taken.

9. The instructor will verbally review the meaning and preventive measures which can be taken against highway hypnosis.

CONTENT

Highway Hypnosis

Driver's eyes become fixed in certain places, and his mind is no longer alert to the traffic situations moving about him. It is probably the result of boredom—driving at the same speed with similar environment for a long period of time.

Preventive Measures That Can Be Taken

1. Keep eyes moving.
2. Stop the car and get a cup of coffee or just get out of the car and walk around.
3. Chew gum.
4. Turn on the radio.
5. Talk with someone in the car.

EVALUATION

1. The instructor will visually check the student as he takes precautions against highway hypnosis.
2. The instructor will listen to him state these precautions and make corrections where necessary.

---

10. The student will demonstrate the procedures for leaving an expressway using the deceleration lane and exit ramp.

10. The instructor will verbally review the procedures.

CONTENT

Exit Procedures

1. Check blind spots and mirrors.
2. Signal right.
3. Glance right again.
4. Enter deceleration lane (*DO NOT SLOW* before entering deceleration lane).
5. Slow preparing to enter exit ramp (25–30 mph).

240

6. Establish safe speed as you exit on ramp.
7. Turn right signal off when no longer needed.

EVALUATION

1. The instructor will visually check the procedure demonstrated by the student.
2. The instructor will check student's head movements.

MEDIA AND RESOURCES

1. Aetna Teacher's Manual for "Expressway Excellence."
2. Driving Guide.
3. Commentary driving.
4. Dual-control car.
5. Handout on expressway driving.

DAILY IN-CAR LESSON PLAN NO. 7

DRIVING UNDER ADVERSE WEATHER CONDITIONS

Required Entry Level

The student will demonstrate (1) predriving habits, (2) 4 S's (starting, shifting, steering, and stopping the car), (3) proper procedures for left and right turns, (4) driving in reverse, (5) starting and stopping on a hill, (6) concepts related to the Smith System and IPDE in relation to residential driving, city driving, rural driving, highway driving, and expressway driving, (7) procedure for correcting a skid.

Lesson Objective

The student will demonstrate the proper precautions and procedures which should be taken when driving in snow, ice, rain, fog, or any other adverse weather condition.

Specific Instructional Objectives	*Learning Activities*
1. The student will demonstrate procedure to aid him in preparing for adverse weather conditions.	**1.** The instructor will verbally review these precautions with the student.

CONTENT

Precautions

1. Check to see if headlights are working, clean, and adjusted properly.
2. Check for clean windshield.
3. Check to be sure driver's physical vision is good.
4. Check windshield wipers.
5. Check window washers.
6. Check defroster and heater.
7. Check tires (may want to put snow tires on).
8. Check brakes for stopping efficiency.
9. Check for the following equipment:
   a. Tire chains
   b. Sand or traction mats
   c. Small snow shovel
   d. Ice scraper
   e. Snow brush
   f. Flashlight

EVALUATION

The instructor will visually check the student as he makes checks.

2. The student will demonstrate precautions to take while driving in adverse weather (especially snow, ice, etc.)	**2.** The instructor will verbally review these precautions.

The student will use commentary driving as he performs the task.

The precautions will be done in a drill situation unless the actual situation arises.

CONTENT

Precautions

1. Press accelerator very gently to prevent tires from slipping or skidding.
2. Avoid sudden, abrupt turning of the steering wheel; steer smoothly.
3. Brake earlier than would be necessary on dry, clear road and apply the brakes lightly in pumping action.

EVALUATION

1. The instructor will visually check the student as he performs skill under drill situation.
2. The instructor will listen to the student's commentary driving and make corrections when necessary.

3. The student will demonstrate procedure for going up a hill grade in adverse weather.

The student will use commentary driving as he performs the task.

3. The instructor will verbally review the procedure with the student.

The procedure will be done in a drill situation unless the actual situation arises.

CONTENT

Procedure for Going Up an Uphill Grade

1. Gain enough speed to get over the hill.
2. If it is necessary to downshift, do it before you start up the hill.
3. Notice far ahead of you if there are any vehicles on the hill blocking the way.
4. If there are vehicles on the hill, stop before you reach the beginning of the upgrade because you may have to stop halfway up the upgrade and not be able to get started again.
5. Don't follow a line of cars up an upgrade because if one car gets stopped and can't make it up the hill the rest of the cars can't move either. Slow down, let car ahead proceed over the crest of the hill.

EVALUATION

1. The instructor will visually check the student as he performs skill under drill situation.
2. The instructor will listen to the student's commentary driving and make corrections when necessary.

4. The student will demonstrate the procedure for "rocking" the car to maneuver it from snow, ice, or sand.

4. The instructor will verbally review these procedures

The student will use commentary driving as he performs the task.

The procedures will be done in a drill situation unless the actual situation arises.

CONTENT

"Rocking" Procedures

1. Keep the front wheels of the car straight so they will stay in their own tracks.
2. Move it first over its own tracks if possible (may be forward or backward depending on how the car was moving just before it stopped).
3. May improve chances of starting by brushing sand or snow away in the tracks for a foot or two in front or in back of each wheel; then start the car gently in that direction.
4. Be patient; the car may only move a foot or two on the first "rock" before the snow or sand stops it.
5. Immediately as the first movement ends, apply light power in the opposite direction.
6. Move car in that direction as far as it will go.
7. Just as the motion stops, apply power in the opposite direction.
8. Rock the car back and forth to increase the length of its flattened track.
9. Continue rhythm until car is finally rocked free.

EVALUATION

1. The instructor will visually check the student as he performs the skill under drill situation.
2. The instructor will listen to the student's commentary driving and make corrections when necessary.

---

5. The student will demonstrate precautions which can be taken to lessen the hazards of ice spots on an otherwise clear road.

The student will use commentary driving as he performs the task.

5. The instructor will verbally review the procedure with the student.

The procedure will be done in a drill situation unless the actual situation arises.

CONTENT

Precautions for Ice Spots

1. Look ahead of the car for icy spots on an otherwise clear road.
2. Leave a long distance ahead of your car and brake before you get to the icy spot.
3. Beware of ice forming on bridges, overpasses, or on shady places on the road.
4. Passing vehicles can be hazardous; will need *longer* clear distance ahead than normal.
5. Be patient; when passing is hazardous don't pass.

EVALUATION

1. The instructor will visually check the student as he performs the skill under drill situation.

2. The instructor will listen to the student's commentary driving and make corrections when necessary.

6. The student will demonstrate precautions which should be taken when driving in the rain. The student will use commentary driving as he performs the task.	**6.** The instructor will verbally review these precautions. The precautions will be done in a drill situation unless the actual situation arises.

CONTENT

Precautions for Driving in Rain

1. Be careful when rain first begins because the oil on the road may make the road slick and hazardous.
2. Be alert for hazards which are hidden by the rain.
3. Increase following distance to allow extra stopping distance.
4. Apply brakes gently with a pumping action.
5. Don't make abrupt or sharp turns.
6. Keep windshield and all window glasses free from mud, dust, and anything else that may obstruct vision.
7. If rain darkens the environment, use your headlights to make sure you are seen.
8. If windows fog, open vent or window and turn on the defroster.

EVALUATION

1. The instructor will visually check the student as he performs the skill under drill situation.
2. The instructor will listen to the student's commentary driving and make corrections when necessary.

7. The student will demonstrate precautions which can be taken while driving in fog. The student will use commentary driving as he performs the task.	**7.** The instructor will verbally review these precautions with the student. The precautions will be done in a drill situation unless the actual situation arises.

CONTENT

Precautions for Driving in Fog

1. When there is fog the best rule to remember is "stay off the road unless the trip is absolutely necessary."
2. If you must drive in fog, drive very slowly; always drive at a speed at which you can stop in the assured clear distance.
3. Use headlights on low beam to make sure you are seen.
4. Don't stop on the traveled portion of the road.
5. Stop by flashing your brake lights on and off a number of times well in advance of stopping.
6. Stay as far right as you can.

7. Watch the edge of the road so you can keep your bearings as to your position on the road.

8. Be ready for sudden appearance of pedestrians, bicycles, or anything.

9. If fog is in patches slow down *before* you enter it.

EVALUATION

1. The instructor will visually check the student as he performs the skill.

2. The instructor will listen to the student's commentary driving and make corrections when necessary.

8. The student will demonstrate precautions which should be taken to avoid skidding.	8. The instructor will verbally review these precautions.

CONTENT

Precautions

1. When starting out in bad weather make braking tests at low speeds.
2. Avoid depressing the clutch in a standard-shift when road surface is slippery.
3. Avoid sudden acceleration, turns, starts, and stops.
4. Pump brakes gently to come to a stop.
5. Avoid shifting to lower gears in automatic or gearshift cars.

EVALUATION

The instructor will listen to student state precautions which can be taken (make additions or corrections).

9. The student will demonstrate procedure which should be taken if the car goes into a skid. The student will use commentary driving as he goes through the procedure.	9. The instructor will verbally review procedure. The procedure will be done in a drill situation unless the actual situation arises.

CONTENT

Procedure

1. Don't apply the brakes.
2. Follow your impulse to keep the car going straight. If the rear skids to the right, turn right; if left, turn left to bring the front in line with the back.
3. When the front of the car is even with the back, straighten the wheel.
4. Release the accelerator gradually.

EVALUATION

1. The instructor will visually check the student as he performs the skill under drill situation (may not be possible to perform skid).

246

2. The instructor will listen to the student's commentary driving and make corrections when necessary.

MEDIA AND RESOURCES

1. "Driver Education—Learning to Drive Defensively," by Strasser, Eales, and Aaron (Laidlaw, 1973).
2. Aetna Driving Manual, "Good Driving in Bad Weather."
3. Dual-control car.
4. Commentary driving.

DAILY IN-CAR LESSON PLAN NO. 8

DRIVING AT NIGHT

Required Entry Level

The student will demonstrate (1) predriving habits, (2) 4 S's (starting, shifting, steering, and stopping the car), (3) proper procedures for left and right turns, (4) driving in reverse, (5) starting and stopping on a hill, (6) concepts related to the Smith System and IPDE in relation to residential driving, city driving, rural driving, highway driving, and expressway driving.

Lesson Objective

The student will demonstrate the proper procedures which should be taken to drive safely and efficiently during nighttime hours or any time visibility is limited because of a storm or heavy cloud covering.

Specific Instructional Objectives	*Learning Activities*
1. The student will verbally identify the location and function of control instruments and other devices which are pertinent when driving at night.	**1.** The instructor will verbally review the function and location of the instruments and devices.

CONTENT

Control Instruments

1. *Gear selector*—device which indicates what gear the car is in; should be illuminated when driving at night to ensure placing the car in the correct gear.
2. *Gauge indicators*—indicate physical condition of the car; should be illuminated when driving at night to stay aware of the physical condition of the car.
3. *Ignition switch*—key is inserted to start vehicle; should be illuminated for a period of time to aid the driver in starting the car.

Other Devices (location varies with make of vehicle)

1. *Headlight switch*—turns headlights on.
2. *High beam indicator*—indicates when headlights are on high beam.
3. *Dimmer button*—controls the high and low beam of the headlights.
4. *Light switches*—switches controlling any inside light such as map light, etc., found within the car.

EVALUATION

The instructor will visually check the student as he locates the control instruments and devices and listen to the explanation of their function, making corrections when necessary.

2. The student will demonstrate the proper procedures when using the	**2.** The instructor will verbally review these procedures.

248

high and low beam headlights while driving at night.

The student will use commentary driving as he performs the task.

The procedures will be performed in a drill situation if there is little or no possibility of actually driving at night.

CONTENT

Using High and Low Beam Headlights

1. Keep your headlights properly adjusted to gain maximum visibility.
2. If your headlights are on high beam when a car is approaching from the opposite direction, change your lights to low beam to avoid blinding the other driver.
3. Use low beam lights when following another vehicle to avoid blinding the driver from the reflection of your lights on his mirrors, windshield, and window glass.
4. If the driver of an approaching vehicle fails to depress his headlights to low beam, you may give him a hint; while he is still a considerable distance from you, "flick" your headlights to high beam and immediately back to low beam (sometimes people do not realize they are using high beam).
5. *NEVER* switch your headlights to high beam because an approaching driver fails to switch his headlights to low beam.

EVALUATION

1. The instructor will visually check the student as he performs the skill.
2. The instructor will listen to the student's commentary driving and make additions or corrections when necessary.

3. The student will state and demonstrate the proper procedure to follow when another driver fails to dim his headlights.

The student will use commentary driving as he performs the task.

3. The instructor will verbally review the procedure when another driver fails to dim his headlights.

The procedure will be performed in a drill situation if there is little or no possibility of driving at night.

CONTENT

When Driver Fails to Dim Headlights

1. Keep your own headlights on low beam.
2. Look at the edge of the road, not into the lights.
3. Drive slowly.
4. Switch to high beam after he has passed.

EVALUATION

1. The instructor will visually check the student as he performs the task.
2. The instructor will listen to the student's commentary driving and make additions or corrections when necessary.

4. The student will state two reasons why speed should be reduced when driving at night.	**4.** The instructor will verbally review the reasons for speed reduction.

CONTENT

Reasons for Speed Reduction

    1. Posted daylight speeds do not make allowances for specific road conditions and headlight range.

    2. Darkness and glare reduce visibility, thus making hazards more difficult to detect.

EVALUATION

    The instructor will listen as student states the reasons for speed reduction and make additions or corrections when necessary.

5. The student will state three visual difficulties unique to night driving.	**5.** The instructor will verbally review these visual difficulties.

CONTENT

Visual Difficulties

    1. Small scope of vision provided by headlight beam.
    2. Distraction from reflected light.
    3. Visibility characteristics of light vs. dark objects.

EVALUATION

    The instructor will listen as the student states the three visual difficulties and make additions and corrections when necessary.

6. The student will state and demonstrate precautions which should be taken when driving at night.	**6.** The instructor will verbally review these precautions. The procedures will be performed in a drill situation if there is little or no possibility of driving at night.

CONTENT

Precautions

    1. Allow more stopping distance.
    2. Look longer
       a. When entering traffic.
       b. When turning.
       c. When backing.
    3. Lengthen following distance.
    4. Always use turn signals well in advance of turn.

EVALUATION

The instructor will visually check the student as he performs the precautions.

7. The student will state and demonstrate specific precautions which should be taken when driving at night in city traffic.

7. The instructor will verbally review these precautions for city driving at night.

CONTENT

Precautions in City Traffic

1. Use low beam headlights.
2. Watch carefully for other cars' signals and leave room for their maneuvers.
3. Watch pavement parkings.
4. Watch for traffic signals obscured by glare.

EVALUATION

The instructor will visually check the student as he performs the precautions.

8. The student will state examples of nighttime driving hazards on open highways and in the city.

8. The instructor will verbally review these examples of nighttime driving hazards.

CONTENT

Nighttime Driving Hazards on Highways

1. Road repair barricade.
2. Pedestrians (light- vs. dark- colored clothes).
3. Disabled vehicle (value of carrying a flare or using emergency flashers).
4. Cross traffic.
5. Difficulty of seeing signs (using high beam helps).

Nighttime Driving Hazards in the City

1. Glare distraction
   a. On the car's hood.
   b. In the rearview mirror.
2. Car doors opening.
3. Pedestrians stepping into the street.

EVALUATION

The instructor will listen as the student states the nighttime driving hazards and make corrections when necessary.

MEDIA AND RESOURCES

1. "Driving After Dark," Allstate Good Driver Trainer Program Instructor's Manual.
2. "Driver Education—Learning to Drive Defensively," by Strasser, Eales, and Aaron (Laidlaw, 1973).

DAILY IN-CAR LESSON PLAN NO. 9

EMERGENCY MANEUVERS: CHANGING A TIRE

Required Entry Level

The student will demonstrate (1) predriving habits, (2) 4 S's (starting, shifting, steering, and stopping the car), (3) proper procedures for left and right turns, (4) driving in reverse, (5) starting and stopping on a hill, (6) concepts related to the Smith System and IPDE in relation to residential driving, city driving, rural driving, highway driving, and expressway driving.

Lesson Objective

The student will demonstrate proper procedures for meeting various emergency situations when driving under different conditions, (emergency parking, blowout, changing tire, accelerator pedal jammed, brake failure, steering problem, lighting failure, hood flies up, stalling on a railroad crossing, car catching fire, car pulling into your lane head on, being forced off the roadway, pushing and pulling another car, and skidding.)

Specific Instructional Objectives	*Learning Activities*
1. The student will demonstrate procedures for emergency parking.	1. The instructor will verbally review procedures.
The student will use commentary driving as he performs the task.	The procedures will be done in a drill situation unless the actual situation arises.

CONTENT

Emergency Parking

1. Pull car completely off the road out of the line of traffic.
2. If you need help, tie a white handkerchief to door handle or antenna.
3. Raise the hood of the car.
4. Turn on the emergency flashers.
5. If at night, place a flare or reflector 100 feet in front of your car and 200 feet to the rear of your car.
6. If at night, do not stand between the car's taillights and oncoming traffic.

EVALUATION

1. The instructor will visually check the student as he performs the skill under drill situation.
2. The instructor will listen to the student's commentary driving and make corrections when necessary.

2. The student will demonstrate procedure that should be taken when a blowout occurs.	2. The instructor will verbally review this procedure.

The student will use commentary driving as he performs the task.

The procedure will be done in a drill situation unless the actual situation arises.

CONTENT

Blowout

1. When it occurs grasp the steering wheel tightly with both hands.
2. Remain calm and do not slam on the brakes.
3. Steer in a straight line and reduce speed gradually by removing foot from accelerator.
4. After vehicle is under control and speed is reduced begin to apply brakes very lightly.
5. Check traffic to left, right, and behind.
6. Signal right.
7. Ease the car completely off the road and out of the line of traffic.
8. Secure car, making sure parking brake is on.

EVALUATION

1. The instructor will visually check the student as he performs the skill under drill situation.
2. The instructor will listen to the student's commentary driving and make corrections when necessary.

3. The student will demonstrate procedure which should be taken when changing a flat tire.

The student will use commentary driving as he performs the task.

3. The instructor will verbally review procedure.

The procedure will be done in a drill situation unless the actual situation arises.

CONTENT

Changing Flat Tire

1. Remove the spare tire from its storage place together with the tools you will need and place them next to the wheel to be replaced.
2. Place block in front and rear of the wheel diagonally opposite the wheel to be replaced to keep the car from moving.
3. Pry off the hub cap from wheel to be replaced; use either screwdriver or the handle of the jack.
4. Loosen the wheel lugs slightly with the socket wrench.
5. Follow directions for the placement of the jack under the car.
6. Check ground to make sure it is solid where jack is to be placed; you may want to place wooden block under jack to keep it secure and straight on the ground.
7. Raise car until flat tire is clear of the ground.
8. Remove the wheel lugs and place them either in the hub cap or some other safe place to avoid losing one.
9. Pull the flat tire off.

254

10. Place the spare wheel on (may have to raise jack more to aid wheel in clearing the ground).

11. Replace lugs by hand and tighten the lugs with a socket wrench to position the spare tire.

12. Lower the car and tighten lugs with wrench until tire is securely in place.

13. Replace the hub cap with a sharp blow of your hand.

14. Store the damaged tire and your equipment.

15. As soon as possible have the damaged tire replaced or repaired.

EVALUATION

1. The instructor will visually check the student as he performs the skill under drill situation.

2. The instructor will listen to the student's commentary driving and make corrections when necessary.

4. The student will demonstrate procedures which should be taken when the accelerator pedal of the car jams. The student will use commentary driving as he performs the task.	**4.** The instructor will verbally review procedures. The procedures will be done in a drill situation unless the actual situation arises.

CONTENT

Accelerator Pedal Jams

1. Try to free pedal by raising it with your foot if there is no immediate danger.

2. Shift car to neutral or depress clutch.

3. If you do not have power steering, turn off your ignition switch (if you have power steering and turn the switch off, the steering will become very difficult, so grip wheel tightly).

4. Use the braking force of the dying engine to bring your car to a safe stop.

5. Even if the car is parked and accelerator jams, switch off ignition because uncontrolled revolutions in the engine can blow it apart.

EVALUATION

1. The instructor will visually check the student as he performs the skill under drill situation.

2. The instructor will listen to the student's commentary driving and make corrections when necessary.

5. The student will state procedures which can be taken to prevent brakes from fading.	**5.** The instructor will verbally review procedures which can be taken.

CONTENT

Procedure for Fading Brakes

1. If brakes begin to fade stop car occasionally and allow brakes to cool.

2. If in mountainous country, downshift and use braking power of the engine to slow your car.

3. Use good-quality brake fluid.
4. Try pumping brakes to build up pressure in brake lines.

EVALUATION

The instructor will listen to the student state procedures which can be taken to prevent brakes from fading and make corrections.

---

6. The student will demonstrate procedures which can be taken when brake failure occurs.

The student will use commentary driving as he performs the task.

6. The instructor will verbally review procedures.

The procedures will be done in a drill situation unless the actual situation arises.

CONTENT

Brake Failure

1. Pump brakes to build up pressure in brake line.
2. Hold parking brake release and slowly apply parking brake.
3. Downshift your car so drag of engine will slow your car down (if manual, shift to the next lowest gear, then as you slow, shift to the lowest gear).
4. Pull off the road by using proper procedures and get out of the line of traffic.

EVALUATION

1. The instructor will visually check the student as he performs the skill under drill situation.
2. The instructor will listen to the student's commentary driving and make corrections when necessary.

---

7. The student will state symptoms which can warn the driver of possible steering problems and what to do if he discovers one.

7. The instructor will verbally review symptoms.

CONTENT

Symptoms

1. Excessive play when turning the wheels.
2. Shimmy in the front end of the car.
3. Car tends to drift to one side of the road.

What to Do If You Discover One

1. Pull off the road and check for yourself.
2. If you cannot fix trouble, drive to the nearest garage and have the steering checked.

EVALUATION

1. The instructor will listen to student state symptoms and make corrections when necessary.

2. The instructor will also make necessary corrections of student's statements of what to do if he discovers one of these.

---

8. The student will demonstrate procedures which should be taken if there is a failure of power steering system.

   The student will use commentary driving as he performs the task.

8. The instructor will verbally review procedure.

   The procedure will be done in a drill situation unless the actual situation arises.

CONTENT

Failure of Power Steering

1. Check steering wheel; it will become rather difficult to turn.
2. Grip wheel firmly.
3. Reduce speed.
4. Proceed at once to a garage for repairs.

EVALUATION

1. The instructor will visually check the student as he performs the skill under drill situation.
2. The instructor will listen to the student's commentary driving and make corrections when necessary.

---

9. The student will demonstrate procedure which should be taken if there is a sudden lighting failure.

   The student will use commentary driving as he performs the task.

9. The instructor will verbally review procedure.

   The procedure will be done in a drill situation unless the actual situation arises.

CONTENT

Procedure for a Lighting Failure

1. Take heed of dimming and flickering lights; you may have light failure.
2. If one occurs slow down.
3. Flash your brake lights.
4. Pull off the road.
5. Turn on emergency flashers.
6. Walk to or call for assistance if you cannot locate the trouble.

EVALUATION

1. The instructor will visually check the student as he performs the skill under drill situation.
2. The instructor will listen to the student's commentary driving and make corrections when necessary.

10. The student will demonstrate procedures which can be taken when the hood flies up on the car.

The student will use commentary driving as he performs the task.

10. The instructor will verbally review procedures.

The procedures will be done in a drill situation unless the actual situation arises.

CONTENT

Hood Flies Up on Car

1. Remind service station men to shut it tightly each time it is open.
2. If it does fly up while driving, look under the center of it or out the left window.
3. Slow down.
4. Carefully pull onto the shoulder and stop.
5. Close hood tightly.

EVALUATION

1. The instructor will visually check the student as he performs the skill under drill situation.
2. The instructor will listen to the student's commentary driving and make corrections when necessary.

---

11. The student will demonstrate (as much as possible under drill conditions) the procedures which should be taken if car stalls on the railroad crossing.

The student will use commentary driving as he performs the task.

11. The instructor will verbally review procedures.

The procedures will be done in a drill situation unless the actual situation arises.

CONTENT

Stall on a Railroad Crossing

1. Make sure speed is at least 10 mph when you start across the tracks to have enough momentum so your car could coast across tracks.
2. If you do stall on tracks, get everyone out quickly.
3. Before you try to start the engine, look for trains in both directions.
4. If you see one, get out and leave the car.
5. If none is in sight, try to start engine but look for trains every half second.
6. If the tracks curve enough to cut off your view to less than a mile, don't stay in the car.
7. Get out of the car and try to push it off the tracks.
8. If a train should come suddenly, run off the tracks toward the direction from which the train is coming so that the train won't push the car onto you.

EVALUATION

1. The instructor will visually check the student as he performs the skill under drill situation.

2. The instructor will listen to the student's commentary driving and make corrections when necessary.

---

12. The student will demonstrate procedures which should be taken if the car catches fire.

The student will use commentary driving as he performs the task.

12. The instructor will verbally review procedures.

The procedures will be done in a drill situation unless the actual situation arises.

CONTENT

Car Catches Fire

1. Have a fire extinguisher in your car.
2. If you don't have one, try throwing dirt, mud, or snow on the blaze (use a hub cap to carry water from a ditch or stream if the fire doesn't have too great a start).
3. If the fire is out of control, get a safe distance away from the car, at least 50 feet, as the gas tank may explode.

EVALUATION

1. The instructor will visually check the student as he performs the skill under drill situation.
2. The instructor will listen to the student's commentary driving and make corrections when necessary.

---

13. The student will demonstrate procedures which should be followed if a car pulls into his lane head on.

The student will use commentary driving as he goes through the procedures.

13. The instructor will verbally review procedures.

The procedures will be done in a drill situation unless the actual situation arises.

The drill will mostly be explanation instead of action in this case.

CONTENT

Meeting a Car Head On

1. If there is a shoulder, you have a fair chance to make it; pull to the right before the other driver gets the same idea.
2. If there is no shoulder, the ditch is preferable to a head-on collision; try to angle into ditch gradually; turn and drive along it until you can stop.
3. If a line of cars is on your right, head for even a small gap in it, blowing a steady blast of the horn in the hope the driver of the car behind can slow and let you in.

EVALUATION

1. The instructor will visually check the student as he performs what he can of the drill.
2. The instructor will listen to the student's commentary driving and make corrections when necessary.

| 14. The student will demonstrate the procedures which should be taken if he runs off the pavement.

The student will use commentary driving as he performs the task at a fairly slow speed. | 14. The instructor will verbally review procedures.

The procedures will be done in a drill situation. |

CONTENT

Running Off the Road

1. Grip the steering wheel firmly; the shoulder, which is not as smooth as the pavement, will tend to turn your front wheels to the right. If only your right front wheel drops off the pavement, steer so that both your front and back wheels are on the shoulder. Do not turn sharply back onto the pavement, because this might produce a skid or turn the car over.

2. Do not apply the brakes, because this increases a tendency to skid. Ease up on the accelerator to slow down gradually; continue down the highway with two wheels on the shoulder until you slow down.

3. Pump the brake when you are going slow enough so there is no tendency to skid.

4. When you have slowed down, and cars are not coming either way, ease back on the pavement. If the shoulder is much lower, turn your wheels rather sharply, but keep your speed low, and don't jerk the wheels back. This could make your car cross into the oncoming lane and collide head on with a car there.

EVALUATION

1. The instructor will visually check the student as he performs the skill under drill situation.

2. The instructor will listen to the student's commentary driving and make corrections when necessary.

| 15. The student will state precautions which can be taken to avoid skidding. | 15. The instructor will verbally review these precautions. |

CONTENT

Precautions

1. When you start out in bad weather make braking tests at low speeds.
2. Avoid depressing the clutch in a standard-shift when road surface is slippery.
3. Avoid sudden acceleration, turns, starts, and stops.
4. Pump brakes gently to come to a stop.
5. Avoid shifting to lower gears in automatic or gearshift cars.

EVALUATION

The instructor will listen to the student state precautions which can be taken (make additions or corrections).

16. The student will demonstrate procedure which should be taken if the car goes into a skid.

The student will use commentary driving as he goes through the procedure.

16. The instructor will verbally review procedure.

The procedure will be done in a drill situation.

CONTENT

Procedure for a Skid

1. Don't apply the brakes.
2. Follow your impulse to keep the car going straight. If the rear skids to the right, turn right; if left, turn left to bring the front in line with the back.
3. When the front of the car is even with the back, straighten the wheels.
4. Avoid using the clutch. Keep the car in DRIVE or in THIRD.
5. Release the accelerator gradually.

EVALUATION

1. The instructor will visually check the student as he performs the skill under drill situation (may not be possible to perform skid).
2. The instructor will listen to the student's commentary driving and make corrections when necessary.

---

17. The student will state and demonstrate precautions which should be taken by each passenger in the car if a crash is unavoidable.

17. The instructor will verbally review these precautions.

CONTENT

Precautions

1. Driver—keep control of the car and steer up to the last instant. Then turn off the ignition to lessen the chance of a fire.
2. Front Seat Passenger—fold your arms over your face and press against the dash.
3. Back Seat Passenger—fold your arms over your face and press against the back of the front seat.
4. All occupants—fasten seat belts and shoulder restraints before you start driving.

EVALUATION

1. The instructor will visually check student as he demonstrates procedures.
2. The instructor will listen to the student's commentary driving and make corrections when necessary.

DAILY IN-CAR LESSON PLAN NO. 10

PARALLEL PARKING

Required Entry Level

The student will demonstrate (1) predriving habits, (2) 4 S's (starting, shifting, steering, and stopping the car), (3) proper procedures for left and right turns, (4) driving in reverse, (5) angle parking and perpendicular parking, (6) starting and stopping on a hill, (7) concepts related to the Smith System and IPDE in relation to residential driving, city driving, rural driving, highway driving, and expressway driving.

Lesson Objective

The student will demonstrate the proper procedures for approaching, entering, and leaving a parallel parking space safely and efficiently.

Specific Instructional Objectives	*Learning Activities*
1. The student will locate a proper parallel parking space.	**1.** The instructor will verbally review these procedures.

CONTENT

Location of a Parallel Parking Space

    1. Find a parallel parking space.
    2. Slow down.
    3. Signal for a stop.
    4. Decide if the space is large enough (at least a 2-foot and preferably a 3-foot leeway in front of and behind your car).

EVALUATION

The instructor will visually check the location selected.

2. The student will demonstrate scanning and assessment procedures which should be made prior to initiating the entering maneuver.	**2.** The instructor will verbally review these scanning and assessment techniques.
The student will use commentary driving to describe his scanning and assessment techniques.	

CONTENT

Scanning and Assessment Techniques

    1. Scan for obstacles and potential obstacles along the intended path—do not begin the maneuver until the intended path is clear.

262

2. Scan well along an intersecting traffic lane for approaching vehicles—do not begin the maneuver until the lane is clear.

3. Continuously scan along the intended path for obstacles and potential obstacles.

4. Check the movement of the front end of the vehicle in relation to obstacles at the side of the path.

EVALUATION

1. Instructor will visually check the student's head movements and mirror and blind spot check.

2. Instructor will listen to the student's commentary driving and make corrections when necessary.

---

3. The student will demonstrate the procedure for entering a parallel parking space.

The student will use commentary driving as he performs this task.

3. The instructor will give the student verbal cues to aid him in performing a successful entrance into a parallel parking space.

CONTENT

Procedure for Entering a Parallel Parking Space

1. Signal a slowdown and stop beside the car ahead, about 2 feet away and with your back bumpers even.

2. Shift to REVERSE; check traffic all around you. Then back slowly while you quickly and continuously turn the steering wheel to the right. Aim the tip of your right rear fender toward the right rear corner of the space.

3. As your front doorpost passes the back bumper of car ahead and your right rear wheel is in the approximate center of the parking space, quickly straighten the wheels and continue to back straight.

4. When your front bumper is even with the other car's back bumper, quickly turn the steering wheel to the left as far as it will go, while you back slowly to the car behind without touching it. Watch its left headlight, with which your left taillight will now line up. Your right rear wheel will be within a foot of the curb, not against it. Just before your car stops, straighten your wheels.

5. Slowly pull forward, turning right, as needed, to bring your car parallel to curb. If wheels are turned, let the car creep forward as you straighten wheels and center your car in the space.

EVALUATION

1. The instructor will visually check the student's entering procedure.

2. The instructor will listen to the student's commentary driving and make corrections when necessary.

---

4. The student will demonstrate procedures which should be taken when leaving a parked car.

4. The instructor will verbally review procedures taken.

CONTENT

Leaving a Parked Car

1. Keep brake pedal down.
2. Shift to park.
3. Set parking brake.
4. Turn off and lock ignition.
5. Withdraw the key from ignition.
6. Release foot brake.
7. Close windows.
8. Lock doors.
9. Get out on curb side.
10. Lock curb side door.
11. Take key.

EVALUATION

The instructor will visually check student leaving car on curb side.

---

5. The student will demonstrate proper procedures for leaving a parked car on the street side. (This may be necessary at some time.)

5. The instructor will verbally review procedures taken.

CONTENT

Leaving a Parked Car from Street Side

1. Check the outside mirror.
2. Look over your shoulder out the left-side windows (if you are parked near a corner, watch for turning cars).
3. If no cars are coming, open door, but continue watching for cars.
4. Get out and move quickly to the curb.

EVALUATION

The instructor will visually check student leaving car on street side.

---

6. The student will demonstrate procedures for reentering a parked car from curb side (street side).

6. Instructor will verbally review procedures taken.

CONTENT

Reentering Car

1. Always unlock door and enter from the curb side whenever possible.
2. If not possible, reenter on street side by carefully checking traffic, unlocking door (continue to check traffic), and enter the car as quickly as possible.
3. Perform all predriving habits.

EVALUATION

Instructor will visually check student reentering the parked car (both curb side and street side).

---

7. The student will demonstrate procedures for leaving a parallel parking space.

The student will use commentary driving as he performs this task.

7. The instructor will give the student verbal cues to aid him in performing this maneuver successfully.

CONTENT

Procedures for Leaving a Parallel Parking Space

1. Start car and shift to REVERSE.
2. Go straight back until your car is almost touching the bumper of the car behind you.
3. Signal for a left turn. Move forward, turning sharply to the left. Stop to look ahead while still in the parking space, front wheels pointing left.
4. Move forward slowly, turning wheels to right again when halfway out of parking space. Check traffic front and rear and make sure that both the front and back of your car can clear the car ahead of the space you are leaving.

EVALUATION

1. The instructor will visually check the student's leaving procedures.
2. The instructor will listen to the student's commentary driving and make corrections when necessary.

MEDIA AND RESOURCES

1. "Let's Drive Right" by Maxwell Halsey and Richard Kaywood.
2. "In-Car Instruction: Methods and Content," by Anderson.
3. Driving Guide.
4. Commentary driving.
5. Dual-control car.

DAILY IN-CAR LESSON PLAN NO. 11

FINAL DRIVER PERFORMANCE TEST

Required Entry Level

The student will demonstrate (1) predriving habits, (2) 4 S's (starting, shifting, steering, and stopping the car), (3) procedures for left and right turns, (4) driving in reverse, (5) angle parking, (6) perpendicular parking, (7) starting and parking up and downhill with and without a curb, (8) skills involved in driving in residential area, city, rural area, highway, expressway, and under adverse weather conditions and at night, and (9) skills related to different emergency maneuvers.

Lesson Objective

The student will demonstrate to the best of his ability the following skills which entail the final driver performance test.

Specific Instructional Objective	*Learning Activities*
1. The student will demonstrate the necessary maneuvers and skills involved in performing the following skills efficiently and safely.	1. The instructor will verbally instruct the student to perform the various skills at a given time.
The student will accumulate a minimum of 40 points in order to pass the Final Driver Performance Test.	

EVALUATION

The instructor will rate the student 1 through 6 depending on the student's performance of each skill or maneuver. 0 = excellent, 1 = very good, 2 = good, 3 = average, 4 = satisfactory, 5 = fair, 6 = poor. In order for the student to pass he must obtain a 3.5 score or better on all performance.

Comments on student's overall performance and progress:

_____

AARON-STRASSER DRIVER PERFORMANCE TEST   Copyright 1966

NAME_____   TEACHER_____

CLASS_____   DATE_____

Test Item		Score		Test Item		Score	
	Trial	Poor	Fair		Trial	Poor	Fair
1. Predriving Checks	1.	2	1	16. Right Turns	1.	2	1
	2.	4	3		2.	4	3
	3.	6	5		3.	6	5
2. Start	1.	2	1	17. Attention	1.	2	1
	2.	4	3		2.	4	3
	3.	6	5		3.	6	5
3. Backing	1.	2	1	18. Start on Hill	1.	2	1
	2.	4	3		2.	4	3
	3.	6	5		3.	6	5
4. Use of Clutch	1.	2	1	19. Parallel Parking	1.	2	1
	2.	4	3		2.	4	3
	3.	6	5		3.	6	5
5. Use of Accelerator	1.	2	1	20. Angle Parking	1.	2	1
	2.	4	3		2.	4	3
	3.	6	5		3.	6	5
6. Shifting	1.	2	1	21. Use of Footbrake	1.	2	1
	2.	4	3		2.	4	3
	3.	6	5		3.	6	5
7. Steering	1.	2	1	22. Use of Mirror	1.	2	1
	2.	4	3		2.	4	3
	3.	6	5		3.	6	5
8. Stopping	1.	2	1	23. Stop Sign	1.	2	1
	2.	4	3		2.	4	3
	3.	6	5		3.	6	5
9. Lane Position	1.	2	1	24. Turn About	1.	2	1
	2.	4	3		2.	4	3
	3.	6	5		3.	6	5
10. Lane Changing	1.	2	1	25. Traffic Lights and Signs	1.	2	1
	2.	4	3		2.	4	3
	3.	6	5		3.	6	5
11. Speed Control	1.	2	1	26. Perpendicular Parking	1.	2	1
	2.	4	3		2.	4	3
	3.	6	5		3.	6	5
12. Intersection Observation	1.	2	1	27. Defensive Driving	1.	2	1
	2.	4	3		2.	4	3
	3.	6	5		3.	6	5
13. Right of Way	1.	2	1	28. Use of Eyes	1.	2	1
	2.	4	3		2.	4	3
	3.	6	5		3.	6	5
14. Following	1.	2	1	29. Scans Traffic	1.	2	1
	2.	4	3		2.	4	3
	3.	6	5		3.	6	5
15. Left Turns	1.	2	1	30. Attitude	1.	2	1
	2.	4	3		2.	4	3
	3.	6	5		3.	6	5

Scoring		Deductions	Poor	Fair	Total
Above Average	0 to 10	First Trial			
Good	11 to 25				
Average	26 to 40	Second Trial			
Fair	41 to 55				
Failure	56 to 70	Third Trial			

INSTRUCTIONS

Aaron-Strasser Driver Performance Test

Introduction

The Aaron-Strasser Driver Performance Test is designed to measure driver ability while operating a motor vehicle in traffic. It may be used throughout the course in driver education and as a final examination. It allows for an assessment of driver errors on a periodic basis that can be used by the instructor for determining future lessons to correct the errors identified.

Administering the Test

The test form allows for the testing of drivers on *three* separate occasions. These are identified as *Trial* on the test form. To record errors on the Driver Performance Test, draw a line through the value of the item in the proper column (*Poor* or *Fair*). At the conclusion of each test period, deductions should be totaled. Total deductions should be compared with the Scoring Chart to rank students.

It is suggested that a two-mile testing route be established and that up to 15 minutes be allowed for completion of the Driver Performance Test.

Teacher Comments:

CONTENT SIMULATION PROGRAM

In Chapter 11 it was pointed out that driving simulation offers several important long-range benefits to the school's driver education program. Aided by the simulation technique, the beginner student receives instruction that cannot be reproduced in any other fashion. Therefore the content of a driving simulation system is unique in providing experience that produces a driver capable of adapting to a variety of traffic environments. The following sections outline the content of the two simulation systems in use today in a substantial number of the nation's secondary schools. In each instance the content is compatible with dual-control car and multiple-car driving-range programs. For methods and techniques used with simulation, refer to Chapter 13.

AETNA Drivotrainer System

The Aetna Drivotrainer system is composed of a basic film series that presents fundamental skills and then progresses through a planned, logical sequence of instruction into advanced and complex experiences. Each film is carefully programed and is a complete unit in itself. Therefore each film may be used separately for specific student or group needs, review, or retraining. Average running time is approximately 18 minutes. Films and component equipment are designed to accommodate any number of drivotrainer units to a maximum of 25. However, most installations in use today have been planned for 8, 10, 12, or 16 units. The following is a complete listing of films being used in the Aetna Drivotrainer System plus supplementary simulation films. The first 16 films are based on the IPDE concept.

1. Basic Control Tasks
2. Fundamental Turning Maneuvers
3. I.P.D.E.
4. Identifying and Predicting
5. Separating and Compromising Risks
6. Managing Space and Time
7. Crossing-Joining-Leaving
8. Interacting with Traffic
9. The Decision is Yours
10. Hazard Perception
11. Handling Emergencies
12. Expressways
13. Mixing With Motorcycles
14. Split-Second Decisions
15. Crash Avoidance
16. Driver Performance Test

17. You and the Drivotrainer System
18. Shifting Skill
19. A Drive in a Manual Shift Car
20. A Drive in an Automatic Shift Car
21. Blending in Traffic
22. Backing Safely
23. Perfect Passing
24. Angle Parking and Turning Maneuvers
25. Traffic Strategy
26. ABC's of Parallel Parking
27. Special Driving Techniques
28. Driving Emergencies
29. Safe Highway Driving
30. Expressway Excellence
31. Good Driving in Bad Weather
32. Road Check

Figure 12-3. Simulator for Laboratory Instruction (Courtesy Doron Precisions Instruments, Inc.)

Link Driving Simulator System

The Link Driving Simulator is a practice-driving simulator system that utilizes a unique set of training films, designed to develop safe and mature beginner drivers. The film series incorporates programed learning situations that simulate realism in the driving task. The system uses progressive teaching principles that reinforce learning on the part of the student.

Installed in a classroom setting, the films and component equipment can accommodate up to a maximum of 25 units. Most installations today are using approximately 12 to 16 simulators per classroom. The following is a complete list of the films being used in the Link Driving Simulator System:

1. You Take the Wheel
2. The Art of Turning
3. Perceptive Driving
4. Moderate Traffic
5. Intermediate Traffic
6. Control
7. Complex Traffic
8. Hit the Highways
9. Limited Access
10. Hazardous Situations
11. A Formula for Traffic Survival

OPTIONAL FILMS

12. Winterproof Your Driving
13. Special Maneuvers
14. Shift for Yourself
15. Expressways Are Different
16. Drive in Review

Simulator Lesson Sequence

The lesson plans that follow are representative of those used in each of the simulation systems described previously. Additional lesson plans should be developed at the direction of the instructor. Selected film lesson plans are included from both the Aetna Drivotrainer System and the Link Driving Simulator System.

AETNA FILM LESSON NO. 1

BLENDING IN TRAFFIC

Required Entry Level

The student will demonstrate (1) predriving habits, (2) 4 S's (starting, shifting, steering, and stopping), (3) left and right turns, (4) lane changes.

Lesson Objective

The student will demonstrate the proper procedures involved for entering a street from a private driveway, making lane changes, driving on multilane highways, yielding to oncoming vehicles, yielding to emergency vehicles, driving on one-way streets, and obeying the directions of a police officer.

Specific Instructional Objective	Learning Activities
1. The student will orally list the five steps included in the Smith System, define each step and how it relates to actual traffic conditions, and demonstrate these steps while driving under simulator conditions.	1. The instructor will write the five steps on the chalkboard and verbally review how they relate to actual traffic conditions.

CONTENT

Smith System

1. Aim High in Steering
   a. Look well ahead at your intended driving path.
   b. Analyze traffic conditions before you get to any point of potential conflict.
2. Get the Big Picture
   a. Be aware of both sights and sounds that are around your vehicle.
   b. Make every attempt to see visually everybody and everything that is coming into your view.
3. Keep Eyes Moving
   a. Move your eyes to look near, far ahead, to both sides, and in your rearview and outside mirrors.
   b. Keep eyes moving in order to
      (1) Spot approaching traffic hazards and have more time to adjust to them safely.
      (2) Keep your eyes from getting tired.
4. Make Sure They See You
   a. Use various controls to make sure other vehicles and pedestrians see your vehicle:
      (1) Horn
      (2) Headlights
      (3) Turn Signals
      (4) Emergency flashers
5. Leave Yourself an Out

272

a. Leave yourself an escape route.

b. Allow adequate following distance.

EVALUATION

1. The instructor will quiz the students orally on the steps and significance of the Smith System.

2. The instructor will visually check the students to make certain they are checking their mirrors, blind spots, and slowing down when potential hazards exist while driving under simulator conditions.

2. The student will demonstrate the procedures to follow when preparing to enter a highway from a private driveway.	2. The instructor will orally ask the student to state the proper procedures for entering a highway from a private driveway. The instructor will use the magnetic traffic board to demonstrate this.

CONTENT

Entering a Highway from a Private Driveway

1. Stop before the crosswalk.
2. Yield to pedestrians.
3. Move forward; stop; and check traffic from both directions.
4. If clear, enter highway and accelerate.

EVALUATION

1. The instructor will ask the student to orally state the procedures for entering a highway from a private driveway.

2. The instructor will visually check the students to make certain they demonstrate the proper procedures for entering a highway from a private driveway while under simulator conditions.

3. The student will identify and orally explain the meaning of a "moving slot" in traffic and demonstrate the procedure for entering a highway and blending with the existing traffic flow.	3. The instructor will demonstrate the procedure for blending with existing traffic on the highway by using the magnetic traffic board. The film narrator will explain the procedure for blending with existing traffic.

CONTENT

Blending with Traffic

1. A moving "slot" is an opening in the traffic flow that is of adequate size to allow a safe entry into the traffic flow.

2. Enter the "slot" and accelerate to the average speed at which the other traffic is moving.

EVALUATION

The instructor will quiz the students to see if they know the meaning of a traffic "slot."

4. The student will orally explain the procedure for using multiple-lane highways and demonstrate this procedure under simulation conditions.	4. The instructor will verbally review this procedure and demonstrate it using the magnetic traffic board.

CONTENT

Use of Multiple-Lane Highway

1. Purposes of Multilane Highway
   a. The left lane is the turning lane for vehicles preparing to make a left turn.
   b. The center lane is the "thru lane"; it reduces your exposure to the hazards of entering and exiting traffic from both sides.
   c. The right lane is for slower traffic and those vehicles making a right turn.
   d. A channelizing island is a special lane for vehicles making a left or right turn.
2. Points to remember when using multiple-lane highways:
   a. Use proper procedure when changing lanes.
   b. Never cut across more than one lane at a time.
   c. Stay out of another driver's blind spot.

EVALUATION

1. The student will orally state the procedure for using multiple-lane highways.
2. The instructor will visually observe the students to make certain they demonstrate the proper procedure for making a lane change.

5. The student will demonstrate the proper procedure for getting out of the path of an emergency vehicle.	5. The instructor will "still-frame" the projector and orally state the procedure for getting out of the path of an emergency vehicle.

CONTENT

Emergency Vehicle

1. You must yield the right-of-way to all emergency vehicles which are using sirens, lights, or a combination of both.
2. The law requires traffic to pull over to the right-hand edge of the highway and stop, if possible, until the emergency vehicle has passed. Do NOT block intersections.

EVALUATION

1. The instructor will ask the student to orally state the procedure for getting out of the path of an emergency vehicle.
2. The instructor will visually observe the student to make sure he performs the proper procedure while driving under simulator conditions.

274

6. The student will demonstrate the proper procedure involved in making a left turn from a two-way street onto a one-way street while driving under simulation conditions.

6. The instructor will verbally explain and demonstrate using the magnetic board the proper procedure for making a left turn from a two-way street onto a one-way street.

CONTENT

Turning from a Two-Way onto a One-Way Street

1. Turn from nearest left lane to nearest left lane in the direction you are traveling.

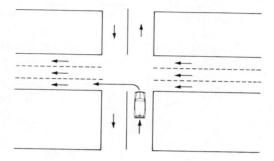

EVALUATION

The instructor will visually observe the students to make certain they are performing the procedures properly.

7. The student will demonstrate the proper procedure when approaching a police officer directing traffic at a stop sign while under simulation conditions.

7. The instructor will still-frame the projector and state the procedure to follow when approaching a police officer directing traffic.

CONTENT

Police Officer Directing Traffic

1. If a policeman is directing traffic, the right-of-way laws do not apply, and drivers must do as the officer instructs them.
2. The policeman's directions have precedence over a traffic signal or traffic sign.

EVALUATION

The instructor will visually observe the students to make certain they demonstrate the proper procedure for obeying the policeman's directions at the intersection.

8. The student will demonstrate the proper procedure when approaching or overtaking a bus while driving under simulation conditions.

8. The instructor will allow the narrator to explain the procedure for approaching and overtaking a bus.

275

CONTENT

Overtaking a Bus

1. Reduce speed.
2. Check traffic, signal, change lanes.
3. Cover brake when passing and blow horn if necessary.

EVALUATION

The instructor will visually observe the students to make certain they reduce speed, change lanes properly, and cover brake when passing the bus.

9. The student will demonstrate the proper procedure involved in stopping and starting on an uphill grade.

9. The instructor will allow the film narrator to explain the procedures involved in stopping and starting on an uphill grade.

The instructor will still-frame the projector and explain this procedure.

CONTENT

Stopping and Starting on an Uphill Grade

1. Brake to a complete stop.
2. Keep foot on brake and apply park brake.

Starting

1. Have accelerator down slightly.
2. Make certain park brake is "off."
   · 3. Accelerate to proper speed.

EVALUATION

The instructor will visually observe the students as they perform the proper procedure for stopping on an upgrade to allow a vehicle to proceed and prepare to move forward after the vehicle has passed.

MEDIA AND RESOURCES

1. Aetna film, "Blending in Traffic."
2. "Blending in Traffic." Instructor's Manual.
3. Magnetic traffic board.
4. Chalkboard.
5. Flashlight pointer.
6. Rules of the Road.
7. Driving Guide.
8. "In-Car Instruction: Methods and Content," by William G. Anderson.

AETNA FILM LESSON NO. 2

A DRIVE IN AN AUTOMATIC-SHIFT CAR

Required Entry Level

The student will identify the various controls on the Aetna Drivotrainer System, demonstrate the predriving habits and starting and stopping the vehicle.

Lesson Objective

The student will demonstrate the correct procedures required to put the vehicle in motion, stopping the vehicle, making right and left turns and simple lane changes.

Specific Instructional Objectives	*Learning Activities*
1. The student will demonstrate the proper predriving habits.	1. The instructor will verbally review these predriving habits.

CONTENT

Predriving Habits

1. Check around the car (simulator in this case).
2. Enter from curb side (right side).
3. Check and lock all doors.
4. Insert key.
5. Adjust seat.
6. Adjust head restraint.
7. Adjust mirrors (blind spot devices).
8. Fasten seat belt and shoulder strap.

EVALUATION

The instructor will visually check the students as they perform these procedures.

2. The student will demonstrate shifting the selector lever and verbally explain the function of each gear.	2. The instructor will verbally review the function of each gear.

CONTENT

Gear and Its Function

1. *Park*—transmission is locked, and the car cannot be rolled forward or backward; may be used when car is stationary, not in motion.
2. *Reverse*—moves the car backward.
3. *Neutral*—transmission is not locked, and the car can be rolled forward and backward; may be used to restart the car quickly while it is in motion.
4. *Drive*—moves the car forward.
5. *Drive 1 and 2*—used to move the car forward up steep hills or in sand or mud.

The instructor will visually check the students as they move the selector lever and listen for proper explanation of gears.

---

3. The student will demonstrate, using the driving simulator, the correct procedure in starting a vehicle.

3. The student will practice starting a vehicle by use of the driving simulator.

CONTENT

Starting

1. Check to make sure parking brake is on.
2. Selector level should be in "*P*" position.
3. Depress accelerator pedal to floor once, then release.
4. Turn ignition on.
5. Check gauges.

EVALUATION

The instructor will visually check the student as he performs the starting procedures.

---

4. The student will demonstrate the correct procedures for placing the vehicle in motion and pulling it away from the curb.

4. The instructor will verbally review these procedures.

The film narrator will verbally review the procedures.

CONTENT

Placing Vehicle in Motion and Away from Curb

1. Depress foot brake with right foot—hold it.
2. Shift selector lever to "*D*" position.
3. Release parking brake.
4. Check mirrors, inside and out.
5. Give left signal.
6. Check traffic, looking over the left shoulder (checking blind spot).
7. Release foot brake; accelerate slowly.
8. Recheck traffic (look to front first, then check blind spot again).
9. Move into nearest traffic lane.
10. Check traffic again.
11. Turn signal off.

EVALUATION

The instructor will visually check the students as they perform the procedures.

---

5. The student will demonstrate the proper procedures for a right turn.

5. The instructor will verbally review the procedures and demonstrate them on the magnetic board.

The student will practice these procedures, using the driving simulators, by following the verbal commands of the instructor.

CONTENT

Right Turn

1. Position vehicle in farthest right lane well in advance of turn.
2. Check the traffic including both mirrors.
3. Signal right at least 100 feet in advance of turn in business district, residential area (200 feet in other areas, rural highway, expressway).
4. Brake with right foot (slow down as necessary).
5. Check traffic again (look left-right-left).
6. Check for pedestrians.
7. Turn by hand-over-hand method, maneuvering vehicle into lane farthest to the right.
8. Release brake; look up intended path of travel.
9. Accelerate gradually about halfway around the turn and start unwinding steering wheel.
10. Resume safe speed—check traffic.

EVALUATION

The instructor will visually check the students as they perform the right turn.

6. The student will demonstrate the proper procedures for a left turn.	**6.** The instructor will verbally review the procedures and demonstrate them on the magnetic traffic board. The student will practice these procedures, using the driving simulators, by following the verbal commands of the instructor.

CONTENT

Left Turn

1. Position vehicle in proper lane well in advance.
2. Check traffic continuously (mirrors, intended path).
3. Signal left (100 feet in urban; 200 feet rural highway, expressway).
4. Brake with right foot (slow down as necessary).
5. Check traffic again (look left-right-left).
6. Check for pedestrians and oncoming traffic; yield if necessary.
7. Path is clear; begin hand-over-hand turning to the left.
8. Release brake, look up intended path of travel.
9. Accelerate gradually about halfway around the turn and begin unwinding steering again.
10. Resume speed, check traffic, turn off signal.

EVALUATION

The instructor will visually check the students as they perform the left turn.

7. The student will demonstrate the proper procedures for making a lane change.	**7.** The instructor will verbally review these procedures and demonstrate them on the magnetic traffic board.

CONTENT

Lane Change

1. Check mirrors, in and out.
2. Check blind spot.
3. Signal intentions.
4. Recheck traffic in mirrors and blind spot.
5. Accelerate slightly (checking traffic again and intended path).
6. Turn slightly in the direction of lane you desire to enter.
7. Turn signal off.
8. Maintain safe speed and proper lane position.

EVALUATION

The instructor will visually check the students as they perform the lane changes.

8. The student will demonstrate the proper procedures for stopping the vehicle.

8. The instructor will verbally review these procedures.

   The student will practice these procedures, using the driving simulator, by following the commands of the instructor.

CONTENT

Stopping

1. Check mirrors.
2. Signal intentions.
3. Brake smoothly to stop.
4. Depress brake.

EVALUATION

The instructor will visually check the students as they perform the task of stopping the car.

9. The student will demonstrate the proper procedures for leaving the car.

9. The instructor will verbally review these procedures.

   The student will practice the procedures, using the driving simulator, by following the commands of the instructor.

CONTENT

Leaving the Car

1. Apply foot on brake and hold.
2. Set parking brake.

3. Shift selector to "P."
4. Turn key off and take out.
5. Unfasten seat belt and shoulder harness.
6. Check traffic before opening the door.
7. Lock doors.

EVALUATION

The instructor will visually check the students as they perform the task of leaving the car.

MEDIA AND RESOURCES

1. Aetna film, "A Drive in an Automatic Shift Car."
2. "A Drive in an Automatic Shift Car" Instructor's Manual.
3. Magnetic traffic board.
4. Chalkboard.
5. Flashlight pointer.
6. Driving Guide.

AETNA FILM LESSON NO. 3

HIGHWAY DRIVING

Required Entry Level

The student will demonstrate (1) predriving habits, (2) 4 S's (starting, shifting, steering, stopping the car), (3) right and left turns, (4) those perceptual skills necessary for moderate and intermediate traffic situations.

Lesson Objective

The student will perform those skills necessary for safe highway driving such as proper procedures for entering the highway, proper passing techniques, pulling off the road in an emergency, and executing those perceptual skills of the 2–12 adjust, and Smith System necessary for safe driving.

Specific Instructional Objective	*Learning Activities*
1. The student will verbally review the meaning of the 2–12 adjust system and how to calculate it while driving.	1. The student will give examples of when this 2–12 system should be used. The instructor will use the chalkboard to demonstrate how to calculate the 2–12 adjust while driving.

CONTENT

2–12 Adjust

1. 2—the 2 seconds stands for the interval between your car and the car in front of you. While driving at higher speeds you may want to increase this distance to 3 or 4 seconds. The way to calculate the 2 seconds is by picking out a stationary object in your path ahead. When the tail end of the car in front of you passes that object you count 1000–one, 1000–two; if your car's front end reaches that stationary object on 1000–two you have the proper following distance.

2. 12—the 12 seconds stands for how far ahead your eyes should be looking down the road. The way to calculate this is by picking out a stationary object in your path ahead and starting to count 1000–one, 1000–two, . . . until you reach 1000–twelve at which time the front end of your vehicle should be even with this object. If you have reached the object before you have reached 1000–twelve you are not aiming far enough down the road.

3. Adjust—the adjust means how you adjust the position of your vehicle within the traffic pattern. You can do this by accelerating, braking, and steering to adjust your position safely.

EVALUATION

The instructor will ask the students to verbally recite how the 2–12 adjust system is calculated and when it is used.

2. The student will list and explain the five points of the Smith System.

2. The instructor will write on the chalkboard the five points and verbally review how they relate to highway driving.

CONTENT

Smith System

1. Aim High in Steering—look at least 12 seconds down the road ahead and pick out potential hazards.
2. Get the Big Picture—search the entire environment ahead which will affect your driving situation.
3. Keep Your Eyes Moving—aim high in steering, check mirrors (every 5 sec.), check gauges, check both sides of vehicle.
4. Leave Yourself an Out—try to predict what the potential hazards are, avoiding all possible hazards (such as 2-sec. interval, being ready to pull off the road, braking, etc.).
5. Make Sure You Are Seen—never drive in a person's blind spot if you can help it—use your lights, turn signals, backup lights, emergency flashers, and horn when necessary.

EVALUATION

The instructor will ask the students to recite the five points of the Smith System and give an example of how they will use these points in highway driving.

3. The student will give a definition of the "danger zone" and demonstrate the proper scanning pattern for this area.

3. The instructor will verbally review the definition of the "danger zone" and the scanning pattern.

The instructor will use the flashlight pointer to point this area out during the film.

CONTENT

Danger Zone

The area directly ahead and to the left and right of the vehicle.

Scanning Pattern

1. Glance down the road.
2. Glance left, checking road and area to the left.
3. Glance right, checking area to the right.
4. Check for potential hazards in all areas and be prepared for possible defensive action.

EVALUATION

The instructor will have the students orally define the "danger zone" and demonstrate the proper scanning pattern.

4. The student will orally explain the proper procedure for a basic passing maneuver as well as demonstrate the technique during the film.

4. The instructor will verbally review the procedures for passing and demonstrate them using the magnetic traffic board.

CONTENT

Passing

1. Maintain a safe following distance (at least 100 ft.).
2. Check traffic (ahead and in both mirrors).
3. Check blind spot.
4. Signal left.
5. Check traffic again—in other lane, ahead, mirrors, and blind spot.
6. Accelerate smoothly into the left lane.
7. Check traffic ahead and behind (turn off signal).
8. Accelerate and build at least 15 mph superiority over the car you are passing.
9. Point of decision—look at traffic ahead; if clear go ahead; if not, pull back into original lane.
10. Pass the vehicle—turn right, turn signal on.
11. Check traffic ahead in both lanes; check mirrors.
12. Check blind spot. When you see the front left headlights of the car you passed in your rearview mirror it is safe to pull back into your lane smoothly.
13. Turn off signal—resume safe speed—check traffic.

EVALUATION

The instructor will visually check the students as they perform the passing maneuver.

5. The student will list the areas where passing is forbidden by law.

5. The instructor will verbally review these areas.

CONTENT

Areas Where Passing Is Forbidden

1. When a yellow stripe is on your side of the road.
2. Within 100 feet of an intersection or a R.R. crossing.
3. Within 500 feet of a curve or crest of a hill.

EVALUATION

The instructor will ask the students to orally list the areas where passing is forbidden by law.

6. The student will demonstrate the proper procedure for entering a highway.

6. The instructor will use the magnetic traffic board to demonstrate the procedure for entering the highway, and verbally review that procedure.

284

CONTENT

Entering the Highway

1. Turn signal on.
2. Stop before entering highway, check traffic left, right, ahead.
3. Anticipate potential hazards (cars passing at intersection, etc.).
4. When clear, make the turn into the proper lane.
5. Accelerate without delay to a safe driving speed.
6. Check traffic ahead, mirrors, blind spot for possible hazards.

EVALUATION

The instructor will visually check students as they perform skill.

7. The student will demonstrate the proper speed control techniques used when approaching a curve.	7. The instructor will verbally review these techniques and demonstrate them, using the magnetic traffic board.

CONTENT

Speed Control Techniques

1. When entering a curve, reduce speed.
2. Check for possible hazards.
3. Approximately halfway through the turn, increase speed.
4. Follow through the curve and then resume normal speed.

EVALUATION

The instructor will visually check the students as they perform the speed control techniques.

8. The student will demonstrate the proper speed control techniques used when approaching a hill or crest.	8. The instructor will verbally review these techniques and demonstrate them, using the magnetic traffic board.

CONTENT

Speed Control Techniques

1. Reduce speed when approaching a hill.
2. Check for possible hazards at the top of the hill or just over the crest.
3. After the area is checked and the path is clear, resume normal speed.

EVALUATION

The instructor will visually check the students as they perform the speed control techniques.

9. The student will demonstrate the proper procedure for pulling off the highway when it is necessary to do so.	9. The instructor will verbally review the procedure and demonstrate it, using the magnetic traffic board.

CONTENT

Pulling Off the Highway

1. Turn on signal at least 100 feet in advance.
2. Make sure you are in the nearest lane to the side of the road.
3. Check traffic—mirrors, blind spot.
4. Pump brakes to warn drivers behind you that you are going to stop.
5. Slow down gradually, turn wheels off the road, and come to a complete stop after you are completely off the road (as far as you can safely be).
6. Shift to park, apply parking brake, turn emergency flashers on.

EVALUATION

The instructor will visually check the students as they perform the maneuver.

10. The student will demonstrate the proper procedure used for pulling back onto the highway after pulling off.	10. The instructor will verbally review the procedure and demonstrate it, using the magnetic traffic board.

CONTENT

Pulling on the Highway

1. Turn off emergency flashers and release park brake.
2. Check traffic (front, behind, and blind spot).
3. Signal left.
4. Recheck traffic (front, behind, and blind spot).
5. Proceed forward, gradually pulling vehicle back onto the road.
6. When all four tires are on the highway, turn signals off.
7. Resume normal driving speed.

EVALUATION

The instructor will visually check the students as they perform the maneuver.

11. The student will demonstrate and explain procedures for driving on dusty gravel roads.	11. The instructor will verbally review the procedure.

CONTENT

Driving on Gravel Roads

1. Remember that traction, braking, and steering of vehicle are reduced.
2. Reduce speed.
3. Slow and stop, if necessary, when dust impairs vision, and stay to the right.
4. Be prepared for hazards and traffic entering road from crossroads.
5. There is a lack of road signs; thus be ready to yield at any time.

EVALUATION

1. The instructor will visually check the students to make certain they follow the procedures to drive on gravel roads.

2. The students will orally explain these procedures, and the instructor will make corrections when necessary.

MEDIA AND RESOURCES

1. Aetna film, "Safe Highway Driving."
2. "Safe Highway Driving" Instructor's Manual.
3. Chalkboard.
4. Magnetic traffic board.
5. Flashlight pointer.

AETNA FILM LESSON NO. 4

EXPRESSWAY EXCELLENCE

Required Entry Level

The student will demonstrate (1) predriving habits, (2) 4 S's (starting, shifting, steering, and stopping the car), (3) proper procedures for left and right turns, (4) proper procedures for lane changes, (5) recognition of potential and immediate traffic hazards while driving in moderate traffic, intermediate traffic, complex traffic, and highway traffic.

Lesson Objective

The student will demonstrate the ability to enter, maneuver on, and exit an expressway safely and efficiently.

Specific Instructional Objective	Learning Activities
1. The student will state precautions which should be taken in preparing himself and the car prior to entering an expressway.	1. The instructor will verbally review these precautions and write them on the chalkboard prior to the beginning of the film. The narrator of the film will review the procedures.

CONTENT

Precautions

1. Check gas.
2. Check oil.
3. Check tires.
4. Check windshields and surrounding windows.
5. Check maps.

EVALUATION

The student will list five precautions to be taken prior to entering an expressway.

2. The student will demonstrate the procedure for entering the ramp and moving onto the acceleration lane of the expressway.	2. The instructor will verbally review the the procedures. The instructor will mechanically check speed maintained by the student on the entrance ramp.

CONTENT

Entering Expressway

1. Speed should be approximately 25 mph on the ramp.

2. Glance over left shoulder to size up the traffic pattern.
3. Signal left.
4. Time approach onto the acceleration lane to fit into a gap in the traffic.
5. Enter acceleration lane.
6. Quickly accelerate to match expressway speeds (55 mph is suggested in the film).
7. Glance over left shoulder.
8. Move from acceleration lane onto the expressway.
9. Turn left signal off.
10. Maintain expressway speeds.

EVALUATION

1. The instructor will mechanically check speed maintained by the student.
2. The instructor will visually check the students as they perform the procedure.

3. The student will demonstrate the ability to use the Smith System and the IPDE concept during the film by using commentary driving when the student enters the expressway at "New Haven and West" during the film.

3. The instructor will use the flashlight pointer to accentuate various hazards on the expressway.

The instructor will verbally discuss some of these hazards during the summary following the film.

CONTENT

Smith System

1. Aim High in Steering—make occasional quick glances at the center of your intended driving path.
2. Get the Big Picture—look from side to side and develop fringe vision that helps to make judgments of speed, distance, and direction; watch all objects—moving or apt to move—for a quarter mile down the expressway.
3. Keep Your Eyes Moving—keep glancing nearby, far ahead, to the side, and in the rearview mirror; never fix your eyes on any one object.
4. Leave Yourself an Out—leave yourself a "space cushion," a place to go to avoid an accident.
5. Make Sure You Are Seen—make eye contact with the other driver or pedestrian; don't count on traffic laws to keep you out of an accident.

IPDE

1. *I*dentify—identify the type of hazard.
2. *P*redict—predict what is going to happen.
3. *D*ecide—decide what action would be the best.
4. *E*xecute—execute that action safely and efficiently.

EVALUATION

1. The instructor will listen to the student's commentary driving and make comments or corrections when necessary.

2. The instructor will visually check the students as they perform the procedure.

3. The instructor will mechanically check braking, signals, steering, etc., as the students react to hazardous situations.

4. The student will demonstrate the three-point technique (4–12-adjust) to position himself in traffic on an expressway.	**4.** The instructor will verbally review the 4–12-adjust theory. The instructor will use the flashlight pointer to demonstrate the 4–12-adjust theory.

CONTENT

Following Distance (4)

1. The following distance should be doubled in regard to the regular following distance. Instead of a 2-second interval, it should be increased to a 4-second interval.

2. Four-Second Interval—when a car in front of you passes a certain point, you should be able to count one thousand–one, one thousand–two, one thousand–three, one thousand–four prior to reaching that same point.

Point of Concentration Down the Road (12)

1. Again you should pick a fixed point down the road at about the distance that you normally concentrate your attention.

2. Twelve-Second Interval—you should be able to count one thousand–one, one thousand–two . . . one thousand–twelve prior to reaching that point.

Adjust

1. This means how you adjust the position of your vehicle within the traffic pattern.

2. You can accelerate, brake, and steer to adjust a hazardous position into a safe one.

EVALUATION

The instructor will visually check to make sure the student makes proper adjustments to the 4– and 12–second intervals.

5. The student will demonstrate the proper procedures for passing a slower-moving vehicle traveling in the right lane on an expressway.	**5.** The instructor will verbally review the passing procedures. The instructor will demonstrate the procedures, using the magnetic board.

CONTENT

Passing

1. Maintain proper following distance (4–second interval).
2. Check blind spot and mirrors.
3. Signal intentions left.
4. Check left blind spot again.

5. When path is clear, proceed into left lane.

6. Remain in passing lane until vehicle passed is clearly visible and a safe following distance behind.

EVALUATION

The instructor will visually check the students as they perform the skill during the film.

6. The student will demonstrate two procedures for allowing a merging car to enter the expressway.	**6.** The instructor will verbally review these procedures prior to the film. The instructor will use the flashlight pointer to bring merging cars to the student's attention.

CONTENT

Procedure #1 (remaining in right lane)

1. Check mirrors for vehicles behind you.
2. Signal a slowing-down maneuver by slightly pumping brakes.
3. Slow to provide a slot for the merging car to enter expressway safely and efficiently.

Procedure #2 (lane change)

1. Check left blind spot and mirrors.
2. Path is clear; signal left.
3. Again check left blind spot.
4. Path is clear; move into left lane.
5. Turn left signal off.
6. Check right blind spot to make sure the merging car is clear and proper following distance behind.
7. Signal right.
8. Recheck blind spot to right and when path is clear, move into right lane.
9. Turn right signal off.

EVALUATION

The instructor will visually check the student's performance of the skills.

7. The student will demonstrate procedures which should be taken when approaching an accident scene on an expressway.	**7.** The instructor will verbally review these procedures. The instructor will use the flashlight pointer to accentuate the accident scene portrayed in the film. The instructor will mechanically check the student's ability to pump the brake.

CONTENT

Approaching an Accident Scene

1. Check mirrors.
2. Signal the problem situation to cars following you by pumping brakes slightly.
3. Slow gradually and cautiously pass the scene of the accident.

EVALUATION

1. The instructor will visually check the student's performance of the procedures.
2. The instructor will mechanically check the student's ability to pump the brakes.

8. The student will state the meaning of "highway hypnosis" and will write three preventive measures which can be used to avoid becoming hypnotized.

8. The instructor will verbally review the meaning of highway hypnosis and three preventive measures which can be taken.

CONTENT

Highway Hypnosis

Driver's eyes become fixed in certain places and his mind is no longer alert to the traffic situations moving about him. It is probably the result of boredom—driving at the same speed with similar environment for a long period of time.

Preventive Measures That Can Be Taken

1. Keep eyes moving.
2. Stop the car and get a cup of coffee or just get out of the car and walk around.
3. Chew gum—turn on the radio.
4. Talk with someone in the car.

EVALUATION

1. The student will orally define "highway hypnosis."
2. The student will orally list 3 of the 4 preventive measures that can be taken to avoid this state.

3. The instructor will visually check the students to make sure they are not fixing their eyes on a specific point during the film.

9. The student will demonstrate the procedures for leaving an expressway, using the deceleration lane and exit ramp.

9. The instructor will verbally review the procedures.

The instructor will mechanically check speed maintained by the student.

CONTENT

Exit Procedures

1. Check blind spots and mirrors.
2. Signal right.
3. Glance right again.

4. Enter deceleration lane (*DO NOT SLOW* before entering deceleration lane).
5. Slow preparing to enter exit ramp (25–35 mph).
6. Establish a safe speed as you exit on the ramp.
7. Turn right signal off when it is no longer needed.

EVALUATION

1. The instructor will mechanically check the speed maintained by the students, using the instructor's control console.
2. The instructor will visually check the student's head movements.

MEDIA AND RESOURCES

1. Aetna film, "Expressway Excellence."
2. "Expressway Excellence" Instructor's Manual.
3. Chalkboard.
4. Driving Guide.
5. Flashlight pointer.
6. Aetna teacher's console.

AETNA FILM LESSON NO. 5

INTRODUCTION TO IPDE

Required Entry Level

The student will demonstrate (1) predriving habits, (2) 4 S's (starting, steering, shifting, and stopping the car), (3) proper procedures for left and right turns, (4) proper procedures for backing, (5) proper procedures for lane changes, (6) functioning knowledge of the Smith System.

Lesson Objective

The student will (1) define and state the meaning of each component of the IPDE concept, (2) demonstrate proper reaction to residential hazards using the IPDE concept, and (3) demonstrate proper reaction to city driving hazards using the IPDE concept.

Specific Instructional Objectives	*Learning Activities*
1. The student will define and state the meaning of each component of the IPDE concept prior to the beginning of the film.	1. The instructor will verbally review the components of the IPDE concept.

CONTENT

IPDE Concept

    1. Definition of IPDE—a thought process that you and every other driver should use to improve your chances of collision-free driving.
    2. Relationship of IPDE to the Driving Task
        a. *I*dentify—identify critical objects and conditions in the traffic environment.
        b. *P*redict—predict changes and possible conflicts in traffic picture.
        c. *D*ecide—decide on an appropriate defensive response.
        d. *E*xecute—execute the response needed to adjust the speed and direction of your vehicle.

EVALUATION

The instructor will listen as the student defines IPDE and how it relates to the driving task and make corrections when necessary.

2. The student will use commentary driving to identify, predict, decide, and execute proper reactions to various potential hazards found within a residential area.	2. When the film narrator suggests having the students perform commentary driving, the instructor will select several students to use the IPDE concept in performing this task.
	The instructor will ask the student to identify the proper speed limit suggested in the residential section of the film.

The instructor will use the flashlight pointer to emphasize hazards in the residential area.

The instructor will still-frame the projector if the student fails to interpret the traffic situation properly or identify the pertinent hazards.

CONTENT

Potential Hazards Found Within a Residential Area

1. Children playing and running into the street.
2. Cars backing out of driveways.
3. Animals.
4. Children and adults riding bicycles.
5. Pedestrians.
6. Poorly arranged intersections.
7. People driving carelessly near their homes.

EVALUATION

The instructor will listen to the commentary driving and make additions or corrections when necessary.

3. The student will use commentary driving to identify, predict, decide, and execute proper reactions to various potential hazards encountered during city driving.

3. The instructor will select several students to use commentary driving during the city driving sequence.

The instructor will ask the student to identify the proper speed limit suggested during the city driving section of the film.

The instructor will use the flashlight pointer to emphasize hazards during city driving.

The instructor will still-frame the projector if the student fails to interpret the traffic situation properly or identify the pertinent hazards.

CONTENT

Potential Hazards Encountered During City Driving

1. Parked cars pulling out in front of you.
2. Delivery vehicles.
3. Pedestrians walking from between parked cars.
4. Drivers failing to use turn signals.
5. Construction work.
6. Cars changing lanes incorrectly.

EVALUATION

The instructor will listen to the commentary driving and make additions or corrections when necessary.

MEDIA AND RESOURCES

1. Aetna Drivotrainer System film, "Introduction to IPDE."
2. Still-frame on projector.
3. Flashlight pointer.
4. Commentary driving.

AETNA FILM LESSON NO. 6

SEPARATING AND COMPROMISING RISKS

Required Entry Level

The student will demonstrate (1) predriving habits, (2) 4 S's (starting, shifting, steering, and stopping the car), (3) proper procedures for left and right turns, (4) proper procedures for lane changes, (5) proper procedures for driving in reverse, (6) concepts related to the Smith System and IPDE concept in relation to residential driving, city driving, rural driving, and highway driving.

Lesson Objective

The student will demonstrate and/or state (1) IPDE concept, (2) difference between separating and compromising risks, (3) hazards created by parked cars, and evasive maneuvers against these hazards, (4) reason for adjusting to traffic flow, (5) proper procedures for approaching a yellow traffic signal, (6) conditions which prohibit passing, (7) practical use of separating and compromising risk theory.

Specific Instructional Objective	Learning Activities
1. The student will define the IPDE concept.	1. The instructor will review the IPDE concept.

CONTENT

IPDE Concept

I—Identify hazards or potential hazards through the use of visual clues and prime and secondary search areas.

P—Predict what type of hazards or potential hazards are going to arise.

D—Decide what you, as the driver, are going to do to keep the potential hazard from becoming an accident.

E—Execute the action you decided upon safely and efficiently.

EVALUATION

The instructor will listen as the student defines IPDE and make additions or corrections when necessary.

2. The student will define the difference between separating and compromising risks and the relation these theories have to the IPDE concept.	2. The instructor will verbally explain the difference between separating and compromising risks.

CONTENT

Separating Risks

1. Separating risks is a means of distinguishing or being able to identify different risks

and hazards involved in driving situations and adjusting speed to separate the conflicts. The perceptual concept of IPDE is related to separating risks in that you must *search* for the different risks and *identify* their significance to you as a driver.

Compromising Risks

1. Compromising is a means of allowing a space cushion between your car and the hazards creating the greatest danger. Compromising is related to IPDE in that a decision has to be made to determine the hazard of the greatest danger. After the decision is made, the proper maneuver should be executed.

EVALUATION

1. The instructor will listen as the student defines separating and compromising risks and how they relate to the IPDE concept.
2. The instructor will make corrections and additions when necessary.

3. The student will state hazards created by parked cars and suggest procedures which can be taken to decrease the risk of these hazards.	**3.** The instructor will review the hazards of parked cars and procedures which can be taken to decrease the risks of these hazards.

CONTENT

Hazards Associated with Parked Cars

1. Car doors opening.
2. Pedestrians emerging from between cars.
3. Parked cars pulling out in front of you.

Procedures to Decrease the Risks of These Hazards

1. Adjust speed.
2. Change lanes.
3. Place foot in caution position if necessary.
4. Use good scanning techniques; check for brake lights, exhaust, people inside of car, backup lights, or any other sign which may indicate the car is about to move.
5. Check through windshield or underneath vehicle for signs of pedestrians.

EVALUATION

1. The instructor will listen as the student states potential hazards created by parked cars and procedures to take which may indicate the car is about to move.
2. The instructor will make corrections or additions when necessary.

4. The student will state the main reason for adjusting to the traffic flow.	**4.** The instructor will verbally review the reason. The instructor will use the flashlight pointer during the film to state examples of proper traffic flow.

CONTENT

Reason for Adjusting to Proper Traffic Flow

Maintaining pace with the traffic flow decreases the risk of a rear-end collision.

EVALUATION

The instructor will listen as the student states the reason and make any corrections and additions necessary.

---

5. The student will state and demonstrate the proper procedures when approaching a traffic signal that has just turned yellow.

5. The instructor will review these procedures.

The instructor will use the flashlight pointer to demonstrate this situation.

CONTENT

Approaching a Yellow Traffic Signal

1. Prepare to stop.
2. If your car has already entered the intersection and you are unable to stop without increasing the risk of a rear-end collision, accelerate and continue through intersection.

EVALUATION

The instructor will listen as the student explains the procedures and make corrections and additions if necessary.

---

6. The student will state conditions which prohibit you from performing the proper passing maneuvers.

6. The instructor will review the conditions when passing is not allowed.

The instructor will use the flashlight pointer to demonstrate these.

CONTENT

Examples When Passing Is Not Permitted

1. Within 100 feet of a railroad crossing or an intersection.
2. When a yellow strip is in your lane and/or a "Do not Pass" sign marks the area.
3. On hills.
4. On curves.
5. Any time the lane you plan to pass into is obstructed or lacking excessive site distance.

EVALUATION

The instructor will listen as the student describes examples when passing is not permitted and make corrections or additions when necessary.

---

7. The student will demonstrate using the separating and compromising risk theory by using commentary driving during the second sequence of the film.

7. The instructor will use the flashlight pointer to emphasize specific hazards during the second sequence of the film.

The instructor will still-frame the projector if the student misinterprets the traffic situation.

The instructor should select 3 or 4 different students to demonstrate their use of this theory during the second sequence of the film.

The instructor should remind students to check speed limit signs and perform frequent mirror checks.

CONTENT

Commentary Driving

1. The student will verbally describe the traffic situation behind, beside, and in front of the vehicle.
2. The student should explain how compromising and separating risks can minimize these hazards.

EVALUATION

The instructor will listen as the student describes the traffic situation and make corrections or additions when necessary.

MEDIA AND RESOURCES

1. Aetna Drivotrainer System film, "Separating and Compromising Risks."
2. Flashlight pointer.
3. Still-frame on the projector.
4. Commentary driving.

AETNA FILM LESSON NO. 7

CRASH AVOIDANCE

Required Entry Level

The student will demonstrate (1) predriving habits, (2) 4 S's (starting, shifting, steering, and stopping the car), (3) proper procedure for left and right turns, (4) driving in reverse, (5) proper procedures for passing another vehicle, (6) concepts related to the Smith System and IPDE in relation to residential driving, city driving, rural driving, highway driving, and expressway driving, (7) procedures for correcting a skid.

Lesson Objective

The student will demonstrate (1) concepts relating to the IPDE system in relation to crash avoidance, (2) proper procedures for an escape right, (3) proper procedures for an escape left, (4) the brake and hold position.

Specific Instructional Objectives	Learning Activities
1. The student will verbally state and define the significance of the IPDE concept prior to the beginning of the class.	**1.** The instructor will verbally review this concept.

CONTENT

IPDE Concept

I—Identify the situation at hand. Be aware of potential driving hazards (cars stopping short, approaching car crossing into your lane, parked cars, etc.).

P—Predict what is going to happen and what are the most advantageous escape routes.

D—Decide what is the best action to take (decelerate gradually or quickly, escape right, escape left, brake and hold position).

E—Execute your decision.

EVALUATION

The instructor will quiz the student orally on the components and significance of the IPDE concept.

2. The student will demonstrate the proper procedure for an escape right during the film.	**2.** The film narrator will verbally explain driving situations requiring an escape right.
	The instructor may reverse the film to review any crash avoidance sequence.

CONTENT

Escape Right

1. This escape is usually the most desirable to avoid an accident.

301

2. Controlled braking—brake firmly but avoid locking the brakes.

3. Swerve to the right, onto the unobstructed shoulder or right lane area, to avoid a collision.

EVALUATION

The instructor will visually check the student as he performs right escape procedure. Check (1) braking, (2) steering.

3. The student will demonstrate the proper procedure for an escape left during the film sequence.	**3.** The film narrator will verbally explain driving situations requiring an escape left.
	The instructor may reverse specific film segments to review any crash avoidance sequence.

CONTENT

Escape Left

1. Keep a close check on traffic situation: oncoming cars or obstructed path to the left.
2. Controlled braking—brake firmly but avoid locking brakes.
3. Swerve to the left, onto unobstructed lane, to avoid collision.

EVALUATION

The instructor will visually check the student as he performs the left escape procedure. Check (1) braking, (2) steering.

4. The student will demonstrate the brake and hold position during the film sequence.	**4.** The film narrator will verbally explain driving situations requiring the brake and hold position.
	The instructor may reverse specific film segments to review any crash avoidance sequence.
	The instructor should impress on the students the fact that many times they have a choice as to the severity of the collision, such as hitting the rear of the car ahead, having a head-on collision, or hitting a pedestrian.

CONTENT

Brake and Hold Position

1. Controlled braking—brake firmly but avoid locking brakes.
2. Hold wheels straight.
3. Maintain lane position.
4. Use this procedure when both your left and right escape are obstructed.

EVALUATION

The instructor will visually check the student as he performs the brake and hold position. Check (1) braking, (2) steering wheel held straight.

MEDIA AND RESOURCES

1. Aetna Drivotrainer System film, "Crash Avoidance."
2. Reversing the film.

LINK FILM LESSON NO. 1

YOU TAKE THE WHEEL

Required Entry Level

    (1) Valid driving permit.

Lesson Objective

    The student will demonstrate (1) predriving habits, (2) procedure for starting the car, (3) procedure for pulling out from the curb, (4) procedure for returning to the curb, (5) procedure for securing the simulator.

Specific Instructional Objectives	*Learning Activities*
1. The student will demonstrate the proper predriving habits.	**1.** The instructor will verbally review the predriving habits.
	The instructor will verbally explain the function of the student warning panel.

CONTENT

Predriving Habits

    1. Enter car safely (from the curb side, if possible).
    2. Lock all doors.
    3. Place key in ignition.
    4. Adjust seat.
    5. Adjust mirrors, inside and out (in simulator adjust blind spot devices so student can see center of screen clearly).
    6. Fasten seat belt and shoulder belt.
    7. Check to make sure parking brake is on.
    8. Place foot on brake.
    9. Put selector lever in *Park* or *Neutral*.

EVALUATION

    The instructor will visually check the student as he performs the predriving habits and make corrections when necessary.

2. The student will demonstrate the correct starting procedures.	**2.** The instructor will verbally review these procedures.
	This procedure will also be covered by the film narrator.

CONTENT

Starting Procedure

    1. Depress and release accelerator pedal.

304

2. Place foot firmly on brake pedal.

3. Turn key on (hold for a moment and then release; oil light should go off and temperature gauge should start registering when simulator is on.)

4. Shift selector lever to drive.

5. Release the parking brake.

EVALUATION

The instructor will visually check the student as he performs the starting procedures and make corrections when necessary.

3. The student will demonstrate the procedures for pulling car away from the curb.	**3.** The instructor will verbally review these procedures. These procedures will also be covered by the film narrator.

CONTENT

Pulling Car Away from the Curb

1. Carefully check traffic.
2. Signal intentions to pull away from the curb.
3. Check both inside and outside mirror; check left blind spot.
4. Check front.
5. Release foot from brake and proceed forward.
6. Steer slightly to the left.
7. Center car in proper lane.
8. Turn off signal.

EVALUATION

The instructor will visually check the student's head movement, signaling procedures, and steering procedure and make corrections when necessary.

4. The student will demonstrate the procedures for approaching an un-controlled intersection.	**4.** The instructor will verbally review the procedures. These procedures will also be covered by film narrator.

CONTENT

Approaching an Uncontrolled Intersection

1. Check left.
2. Check right.
3. Check rear traffic.
4. When path is clear, proceed with caution.

EVALUATION

The instructor will visually check the student's head movement.

5. The student will demonstrate the procedures for returning to the curb.	5. The instructor will verbally review these procedures.
	These procedures will also be covered by film narrator.

CONTENT

Returning Car to the Curb

1. Signal intentions for pulling over to the curb.
2. Check traffic; inside and outside mirror and blind spot.
3. Check front.
4. When traffic is clear, turn slightly to the right and back left.
5. Brake to a slow stop.
6. Turn signal off.
7. Apply parking brake.
8. Shift selector lever to *Park*.

EVALUATION

The instructor will visually check the students as they perform the procedures.

6. The student will demonstrate the procedures for securing the car.	6. The instructor will verbally review these procedures.
	These procedures will also be covered by film narrator.

CONTENT

Securing the Car

1. Place foot on brake.
2. Shift to park.
3. Apply parking brake.
4. Turn key off.
5. Unfasten seat belt and shoulder belt.
6. Check traffic.
7. Leave car safely.
8. In the simulation lab, refasten seat belt in simulator seat.

EVALUATION

The instructor will visually check the students as they perform the procedures and make corrections when necessary.

MEDIA AND RESOURCES

Link film, "You Take the Wheel."

LINK FILM LESSON NO. 2

PERCEPTIVE DRIVING

Required Entry Level

The student will demonstrate (1) predriving habits, (2) 4 S's (starting, shifting, steering, and stopping the vehicle), (3) simple right and left turns.

Lesson Objective

The student will explain and demonstrate how the Smith System, the IPDE concept, visual clues, prime and secondary search areas, potential hazards, actual or real hazards, and preventive and evasive actions relate to the driving task.

Specific Instructional Objectives	Learning Activities
1. The student will verbally list and demonstrate the five steps of the Smith System, and tell how each relates to the driving task.	1. The instructor will list on the chalkboard and discuss the five concepts of the Smith System and review how each relates to the driving task.

CONTENT

Smith System

1. Aim High in Steering
   a. Look well ahead at your intended path.
   b. Analyze traffic conditions before you get to the point of potential conflict.
2. Get the Big Picture
   a. Be aware of the sights and sounds around your vehicle.
   b. Do your best to see everybody and everything in your view.
3. Keep Your Eyes Moving
   a. Move your eyes to look near, far ahead, to both sides, and in your inside and outside rearview mirrors.
4. Make Sure They See You
   a. Use your horn, headlights, turn signals, and emergency flashers to make sure the person in the other vehicle sees you and knows what your actions will be.
5. Leave Yourself an Out
   a. Leave yourself an escape route.
   b. Allow adequate following distance.

EVALUATION

1. The instructor will ask the student to verbally list and describe the five concepts of the Smith System.
2. The instructor will visually check the student as he demonstrates these five concepts during the film.

2. The student will define and relate the importance of the IPDE concept of perceptive driving.

2. The instructor will list the IPDE concepts on the chalkboard and explain how each relates to the driving task by using the simple example of a vehicle approaching an intersection.

The student will discuss the importance of each subtask in producing safe maneuvers.

CONTENT

IPDE Concept

1. Search—observational behavior used to cite the presence or absence of critical characteristics of the driving environment.
2. Identification—classification of the critical characteristics.
3. Prediction—estimation of the future states of the environment and the vehicular system from presently available information.
4. Decision—cognitive selection of response alternatives based on information gained from 3, prediction.
5. Execution—implementation of particular psychomotor output activities (apply brakes, release accelerator, signal, etc.).

EVALUATION

The student will define, in writing, the five concepts that IPDE denotes and explain how each relates to the driving task.

3. The student will define (a) visual clues; (b) prime search area; (c) secondary search area; (d) potential hazard; (e) actual or real hazard; (f) preventive action; and (g) evasive action.

3. The instructor will write the terms on the chalkboard and explain each term as it relates to the driving task prior to the beginning of the film.

The instructor will demonstrate examples of each term in the film through the use of the flashlight pointer.

The instructor will still-frame the projector at an appropriate segment, and ask the students to identify each of these terms.

CONTENT

1. Visual clues—any element in the environment that indicates a potential hazard or where it could occur.
2. Prime search area—the area in the environment that could present the most immediate conflict with your driving.
3. Secondary search area—any other area in the environment that is dependent upon the prime search or eventually could become the prime search area.
4. Potential hazard—anything that has the ability to cause conflict with your driving.

5. Actual or real hazard—anything that actually causes conflict with your driving.

6. Preventive action—an action by the driver to prevent any potential involvement in an accident situation.

7. Evasive action—a response to a situation in an attempt to avoid involvement.

EVALUATION

The instructor will ask the student to define these terms orally.

4. Upon completion of the first two segments of the film and during the third segment, the student will verbally identify, predict, decide, and discuss possible execution actions, depending upon the driving situations presented.

4. The instructor will still-frame the film and ask the student to identify the possible hazard, predict what difficulty this hazard might cause concerning the driving task, decide what the best action would be, and then execute that action.

CONTENT

1. Identify—through the use of visual clues and the prime search area.

2. Predict—in the prime search area what the potential hazards are or where they might possibly occur.

3. Decide—what you, as a driver, are going to do to keep the potential hazard from becoming an actual hazard.

4. Execute—the action of your decision.

EVALUATION

1. The instructor will visually check the students as they react to the various traffic situations and make corrections when necessary.

2. The instructor will listen as the student verbally identifies, predicts, decides, and explains a possible execution for the various traffic situations.

MEDIA AND RESOURCES

1. Link film, "Perceptive Driving."
2. Movie projector.
3. "Perceptive Driving" Instructor's Manual.
4. Chalkboard.
5. Flashlight pointer.

LINK FILM LESSON NO. 3

CONTROL

Required Entry Level

The student will demonstrate (1) predriving habits, (2) 4 S's (starting, shifting, steering, and stopping the car), (3) proper procedures for left and right turns, (4) proper procedures for lane changes, (5) driving in reverse, and (6) recognition of potential and immediate traffic hazards while driving in intermediate traffic.

Lesson Objective

The student will demonstrate (1) verbally listing the IPDE concept, (2) verbally stating the two control actions, (3) defining a set of given terms, (4) using the 2-second "space cushion" and reasons for maintaining this interval, (5) procedure for stopping at a stop sign when view is obscured "on back," (6) use of the four-phase traffic lights, and (7) passing a construction site.

Specific Instructional Objectives	*Learning Activities*
1. The student will verbally list and explain all the components involved in the IPDE concept and relate each component to a realistic driving situation.	1. The instructor will verbally review the IPDE concept. The instructor will list the IPDE components on the chalkboard.

CONTENT

IPDE Concept

*I*dentify—Identify hazards or potential hazards through the use of visual clues and prime and secondary search areas.
   *P*redict—Predict what type of hazards or potential hazards are going to arise.
   *D*ecide—Decide what you, as the driver, are going to do to keep the potential hazard from becoming an actual hazard.
   *E*xecution—Execute safely and efficiently the action you decided upon.

EVALUATION

The instructor will listen as the student orally lists the components of the IPDE concept and make corrections when necessary.

2. The student will state the only two control actions that can be used when responding to hazards.	2. The instructor will verbally review these control actions.

CONTENT

Control Actions

   1. Speed adjustment—adjust speed to meet the driving environment safely and efficiently.

2. Vehicle position—position your vehicle to maneuver safely and efficiently through the traffic environment.

EVALUATION

The instructor will listen as the student states these control actions and make corrections when necessary.

---

3. The student will verbally define the following list of terms prior to the beginning of the film.

3. The instructor will list the terms on the chalkboard prior to the beginning of the film.

The instructor will verbally quiz the students on these terms prior to the film and after.

CONTENT

Definition of Terms

1. *Clue*: any element that indicates a hazard or where it may come from.
2. *Hazard*: anything that *is* or *has* the ability to conflict with driving.
3. *Risk Assessment*: a driver's determination of which hazards present the greatest and least danger.
4. *Control Factors*: the use of speed adjustment and/or vehicle position to reduce danger when dealing with hazards.
5. *Space Cushion*: the front, rear, or lateral distance between a vehicle and another object.

EVALUATION

1. The instructor will listen as the student defines the terms and make corrections when necessary.

---

4. The student will demonstrate and explain the 2–second "space cushion" interval and give reasons for maintaining that interval.

4. The instructor will verbally review the 2–second interval.

CONTENT

2–Second Interval

The 2 seconds stands for the time/distance interval between your car and the car in front of you. The way to calculate the 2 seconds is by picking out a stationary object in your path ahead. When the back end of the car in front of you passes that stationary object you count 1000-one, 1000-two; if your car's front bumper reaches that point at 1000-two, you have the proper distance. If you reach the object on 1000-one you are too close.

Reasons for Maintaining 2-Second "Space Cushion."

1. To avoid potential hazards.
2. To give an adequate view of the signal intentions of the car in front of you.

3. To give some usable distance if the car in front rolls backward.

4. To allow some measurable distance to move the car forward to avoid a rear-end collision.

EVALUATION

The instructor will visually check the student and listen as he states the reasons for maintaining the 2–second interval.

5. The student will demonstrate the procedure for stopping at a stop sign when view is obscured by bushes.	**5.** The instructor will verbally review the procedure.

CONTENT

Stopping at a Stop Sign When View Is Obscured by Bushes

1. Come to a complete stop behind the crosswalk.
2. Roll forward until view is clear.
3. Check traffic carefully.
4. Continue forward.

EVALUATION

The instructor will visually check the student as he performs the skill.

6. The student will demonstrate and verbally explain the use of the four-phase traffic light.	**6.** The instructor will verbally review the four-phase traffic light.
	The instructor will use a scale model of a traffic light, if one is available, to demonstrate its use.

CONTENT

Four-Phase Traffic Signal

1. Red—Stop.
2. Yellow—Caution, prepare to stop.
3. Green—Check traffic in all directions and proceed.
4. Green with directional arrow—If in turning lane, proceed in the direction the arrow is pointing.

EVALUATION

1. The instructor will visually check the student as he performs the skill.

2. The instructor will use the scale model to check the student's ability to distinguish between the parts of the traffic signal.

312

7. The student will demonstrate the proper procedures for approaching and passing a construction site.	7. The instructor will verbally review these procedures.

CONTENT

Approaching and Passing a Construction Site

1. Slow your speed by releasing accelerator.
2. Prepare to stop by pressing lightly on the brake, reducing the speed and warning any driver behind you of a potential hazard.
3. Cautiously pass the construction site.
4. When path is clear, resume proper speed.

EVALUATION

The instructor will visually check the student as he performs the skill.

8. The student will demonstrate his ability to recognize potential and immediate hazards by using commentary driving during the Review Sequence of the film.	8. The instructor will use the flashlight pointer and still-frame the projector to emphasize specific hazards during the Review Sequence. The instructor will still-frame the projector if the student fails to recognize or analyze the hazard properly.

CONTENT

Commentary Driving

The student will verbally state the potential and immediate hazards that he observes in the driving environment during the Review Sequence of the film.

EVALUATION

The instructor will listen to the commentary driving and make corrections when necessary.

MEDIA AND RESOURCES

1. Link film, "Control."
2. "Control" Allstate Good Driver Trainer Instructor's Manual.
3. Flashlight pointer.
4. Model traffic light.
5. Still-frame on the projector.

LINK FILM LESSON NO. 4

COMPLEX TRAFFIC

Required Entry Level

The student will demonstrate (1) predriving habits, (2) 4 S's, (3) driving in reverse, (4) left and right turns, (5) right- and left-lane changes, (6) knowledge of traffic signs, (7) knowledge of how the Smith System and the IPDE concept relate to the driving task.

Lesson Objective

The student will identify potential danger areas in heavy city traffic, demonstrate correct procedures for special traffic control devices in congested traffic areas, explain and demonstrate proper procedures for safe multiple-lane driving, and execute proper steps when meeting the common "unexpected pedestrian."

Specific Instructional Objectives	*Learning Activities*
1. The student will list and discuss six good perceptual techniques when driving in complex traffic.	1. The instructor will verbally review these techniques and list them on the chalkboard.

CONTENT

Perceptual Techniques

1. Looking through the windows and underneath parked cars.
2. Timing traffic lights well in advance.
3. Selecting the best lane in terms of free-flow traffic.
4. Checking mirrors and blind spot carefully.
5. Looking for pedestrians and cross traffic when approaching and leaving an intersection.
6. Using the "caution position" (foot covering brake, reduce speed) when approaching a potential hazard.

EVALUATION

1. The student will list six perceptual techniques when driving in complex traffic.
2. The instructor will visually check the student as he performs these techniques during the film segment.

2. The student will define each part of the 4-phase traffic signal and demonstrate the proper procedure for approaching a 4-phase traffic signal, a flashing red traffic signal, or a flashing yellow traffic signal.	2. The instructor will use a model 4-phase traffic signal to define and explain what procedure should be taken when approaching such a signal.
	The instructor will use the flashlight pointer, during the film, to demonstrate a 4-phase traffic signal.

CONTENT

Four-Phase Traffic Signal

1. Red—Stop, remain until light changes and traffic clears.
2. Yellow—Warning signal light is changing from green to red; prepare to stop.
3. Green—Check traffic, then proceed.
4. Green arrow—proceed in the direction of the arrow (check traffic and turn with caution).

Flashing Lights

1. Red flashing light—Come to a complete stop, check traffic, then proceed.
2. Yellow flashing light—Yield to cross traffic (you may have to come to a complete stop before proceeding), check traffic carefully, then proceed.

EVALUATION

1. The student will orally define the meaning of the four-phase traffic signal.
2. The instructor will visually check the student to make certain he is using the correct procedure.

3. The student will verbally explain what a reversible lane is and how it functions.	3. The instructor will use the magnetic traffic board to explain what a reversible lane is and how it functions.
	The instructor will use the flashlight pointer to demonstrate a reversible lane during the film.

CONTENT

Reversible Lane

1. A lane which may be either open or closed to a particular lane of traffic depending on the density of the traffic flow.
2. Red X—indicates lane may not be traveled in.
3. Green Arrow—indicates lane may be traveled in.

EVALUATION

The instructor will listen to the student verbally explain what a reversible lane is and how it functions and make corrections when necessary.

4. The student will explain what clues to observe when approaching parked cars to avoid possible hazards.	4. The instructor will verbally review these clues and explain how each can aid in avoiding hazards.
	The instructor will use the flashlight pointer to bring these clues to the students' attention during the film.

CONTENT

Clues

1. Doors opening.
2. Exhaust fumes.
3. Backup lights or brake lights.
4. Pedestrians (look for them through windows of and beneath parked cars).

EVALUATION

The instructor will listen as the student explains what clues to observe concerning parked cars and make corrections when necessary.

5. The student will state five reasons why he should constantly check his rear-view mirror.	**5.** The instructor will verbally review these reasons and list them on the chalkboard.

CONTENT

Five Reasons to Check Rearview Mirror

1. To remain aware of the traffic behind you.
2. To remain aware of vehicles changing lanes.
3. To make sure it is safe for you to change lanes.
4. To remain aware of pedestrians and bicycles that are behind you or beside you.
5. To watch for emergency vehicles.

EVALUATION

1. The student will orally state five reasons to constantly check the rearview mirror.
2. The instructor will visually check the student to make sure he is aware of traffic situation behind them.

6. The student will state and demonstrate the proper procedures concerning proper lane usage.	**6.** The instructor will verbally review these procedures and explain how each is important in avoiding traffic conflict.

CONTENT

Lane Usage

1. Remain in your own lane during turns.
2. Do not drive in the blind spot of other vehicles, and look for other drivers in your blind spot.
3. Always signal intentions well in advance.
4. Plan well ahead before execution of a lane change.
5. Obey traffic signals which affect your lane of traffic.
6. Position vehicle in the proper lane to meet your needs:
   a. Right lane usually turns right.
   b. Center lane usually is through traffic.
   c. Left lane usually turns to the left.

EVALUATION

1. The instructor will listen as the student states the procedures concerning lane usage and make corrections when necessary.

2. The instructor will visually check the student during the film to ensure proper lane usage.

MEDIA AND RESOURCES

1. Link Film, "Complex Traffic."
2. "Complex Traffic" Instructor's Manual.
3. Chalkboard.
4. Magnetic traffic board.
5. Driving Guide.
6. Flashlight pointer.

LINK FILM LESSON NO. 5

LIMITED ACCESS

Required Entry Level

The student will demonstrate (1) predriving habits, (2) 4 S's (starting, shifting, steering, and stopping the car), (3) left and right turns, (4) lane changes to the right and left, (5) passing on a two-lane road, (6) recovering vehicle properly when it has run off the road, (7) listing components of the Smith System and IPDE and explain how they apply to the real driving situation.

Lesson Objective

The student will demonstrate (1) concepts related to the IPDE concept, (2) proper procedure for entering and exiting from a limited access roadway, (3) proper procedure for making a lane change, (4) proper procedure for passing a construction zone, (5) proper procedure for making an emergency stop on a limited access roadway, (6) proper lane usage on a limited access roadway, (7) the danger of driving in a pack and the way to avoid this situation, (8) ability to recognize and analyze traffic situation by using commentary driving.

Specific Instructional Objective	*Learning Activities*
1. The student will define and demonstrate the 2–12-adjust formula.	**1.** The instructor will verbally explain the 2–12-adjust formula.
	The instructor will have the students calculate the 2–12-adjust formula.

CONTENT

2–12-Adjust

1. 2—the two seconds stand for the time/distance interval between your car and the vehicle in front of you. The way to calculate the 2-second interval is by selecting a stationary object in your path ahead. When the tail end of the car in front of you passes that object, you count 1000-one, 1000-two. Your car's front end should not reach that stationary object *before* 1000-two or you are maintaining insufficient following distance for the speed you are traveling.

2. 12—the 12-second interval represents how far ahead your eyes should be scanning down the roadway. To calculate the interval select a stationary object, in your path ahead, which correlates with your point of aim down the roadway. Begin counting 1000–one, 1000–two . . . until you reach 1000–twelve, at which time the front end of your vehicle should be even with this object.

3. Adjust—The adjust means how you adjust the position of your vehicle to maintain the safest position within the traffic pattern. You can adjust your position by accelerating, braking, and steering.

EVALUATION

1. The instructor will visually check the student as he performs the 2-12 adjust concept.

2. The instructor will listen to the student calculate the 2-12 adjust concept and make corrections or additions when necessary.

2. The student will demonstrate the proper procedure for entering the entrance ramp and moving onto the acceleration lane of the expressway.	2. The instructor will verbally review the procedures. The instructor may want to review precautions which should be taken prior to entering an expressway before the film.

CONTENT

Entering Expressway

1. Locate correct entrance ramp well in advance.
2. Maintain suggested ramp speed.
3. Glance over left shoulder to size up the traffic pattern.
4. Signal left.
5. Time approach onto the acceleration lane to fit into a gap in the traffic.
6. Enter acceleration lane.
7. Quickly accelerate to match expressway speeds.
8. Glance over left shoulder.
9. Move from acceleration lane onto the expressway.
10. Turn left signal off.
11. Maintain expressway speeds.

EVALUATION

The instructor will visually check the student as he enters expressway (signaling, acceleration).

2. The student will demonstrate the proper procedures for making a lane change to the left and to the right.	3. The instructor will verbally review the procedures. The instructor will use the magnetic traffic board to demonstrate the procedures.

CONTENT

Lane Changing to the Left

1. Check mirrors (inside and outside).
2. Signal intentions left.
3. Check blind spot (over left shoulder).
4. Decide if it is safe.
5. Accelerate slightly, check traffic again, and make slight turn to the left.
6. Turn off left signal indicator.
7. Maintain safe speed and proper lane position.

Lane Changing to the Right

1. Check mirrors (inside and outside).
2. Signal intentions right.
3. Check blind spot (glance over right shoulder).
4. Decide if it is safe.
5. Accelerate slightly, check traffic again, and make slight turn to the right.
6. Turn off right signal indicator.
7. Maintain safe speed and proper lane position.

EVALUATION

The instructor will visually check the student as he performs the skill.

4. The student will state three hazards which may result while passing through a construction zone.	**4.** The instructor will verbally review these hazards.

CONTENT

Construction Site Hazards

1. Traffic slowing as they enter construction zone.
2. Last-minute lane changing, especially from the lane that is closed or obstructed.
3. Construction workers who are preoccupied with their work, not alert to the traffic moving around them.

EVALUATION

The instructor will listen as the student states the hazard and make corrections or additions when necessary.

5. The student will state the correct procedure for making an emergency stop on a limited access roadway.	**5.** The instructor will verbally review this procedure.

CONTENT

Pulling Off the Roadway

1. Signal intentions to pull off roadway.
2. Check traffic.
3. Begin decelerating.
4. Gradually pull off roadway onto the shoulder.
5. Stop completely, secure vehicle, and turn on emergency flashers.

Pulling Back on the Roadway

1. Turn off emergency flashers.
2. Signal intentions to return to roadway.
3. Check traffic.

4. When path is clear, begin accelerating.
5. Gradually pull off the shoulder back onto the roadway.
6. Position the car in the farthest right lane and accelerate to expressway speeds.

EVALUATION

The instructor will listen as the student explains emergency stopping procedure and make corrections or additions when necessary.

6. The student will state the proper use of the right, center, and left lane on a multiple-lane highway.	**6.** The instructor will verbally review the proper lane use of a multiple-lane highway. The instructor will use the magnetic traffic board to demonstrate the lane usage.

CONTENT

Right Lane

1. Slower-moving traffic.
2. Entering and exiting traffic.

Center Lane

1. Through moving traffic.
2. Passing slower-moving traffic in the right lane.

Left Lane

1. Faster–moving traffic.
2. Passing slower–moving traffic in the center and right lane.

EVALUATION

The instructor will listen as the student explains proper lane usage and make corrections or additions when necessary.

7. The student will state advantages of proper lane usage.	**7.** The instructor will verbally review the proper usage.

CONTENT

Advantages of Proper Lane Usage

1. Using center or left lane reduces the risk of cars that are entering and exiting from the roadway.
2. Increases sight distance.
3. Provides a space cushion around your vehicle to avoid potential hazards.

EVALUATION

The instructor will listen as the student states these advantages and make corrections or additions when necessary.

8. The student will state the main danger of driving in a pack and ways to avoid this situation.	8. The instructor will verbally review the danger of driving in a pack and review ways to avoid this situation.

CONTENT

Danger of Driving in a Pack

The possibility of having a rear-end collision increases greatly if you are forced to stop quickly.

Ways to Avoid the Pack Situation

1. Accelerating.
2. Changing lanes.
3. Exiting from roadway.
4. Decelerating.

EVALUATION

The instructor will listen as the student explains the danger of driving in a pack and ways to avoid this situation and make corrections or additions when necessary.

9. The student will demonstrate the proper procedure for exiting an expressway.	9. The instructor will verbally review the exiting procedure. The instructor will use the magnetic traffic board to demonstrate this procedure.

CONTENT

Exiting an Expressway

1. Select the correct exit well in advance.
2. Get into proper lane for exit well in advance.
3. Check traffic.
4. Signal intentions to leave expressway well in advance.
5. Decelerate after turning into deceleration lane.
6. Slow to posted exit ramp speed.
7. Assume a safe speed; adjust speed to the new traffic flow.

EVALUATION

Instructor will visually check the student as he performs the skill.

10. The student will demonstrate his ability to recognize and analyze traffic situations on a limited access roadway by using commentary driving during the third sequence of the film.	10. The instructor will use the flashlight pointer and still-frame the projector to emphasize specific hazards during the third sequence of the film.

322

The instructor should select eight
different students to perform this
procedure.

CONTENT

Commentary Driving

1. The student will verbally describe the traffic situation behind, beside, and in front of his vehicle.
2. The student should also discuss possible "outs" to avoid collisions and all potential hazards.

EVALUATION

The instructor will listen as the student describes these traffic situations and make corrections when necessary.

MEDIA AND RESOURCES

1. Link film, "Limited Access."
2. "Limited Access," Allstate Good Driver Trainer Instructor's Manual.
3. Flashlight pointer.
4. Still-frame on the projector.
5. Magnetic traffic board.

LINK FILM LESSON NO. 6

A FORMULA FOR TRAFFIC SURVIVAL

Required Entry Level

The student will demonstrate (1) predriving habits, (2) 4 S's (starting, shifting, steering, and stopping the car), (3) left and right turns, (4) right- and left-lane changes, (5) the ability to spot hazards and potential hazards on residential, rural, and expressway roads by using the Smith System and IPDE concept.

Lesson Objective

The student will demonstrate the IPDE process and its application to residential, rural, and expressway driving environments presented in the film sequence.

Specific Instructional Objective	*Learning Activities*
1. The student will state the IPDE concept and explain how it is used to analyze traffic situations.	1. The instructor will demonstrate how to use the IPDE concept when analyzing traffic situations by using the introduction section of the film.

CONCEPT

IPDE Concept

I—Identify potential and immediate hazards in the traffic environment.
P—Predict how these potential and immediate hazards could affect your driving pattern.
D—Decide what reaction would be best to take to avoid any traffic conflicts.
E—Execute your decision.

EVALUATION

The instructor will listen as the student explains how IPDE can be used to analyze traffic situations and make corrections when necessary.

2. The student will demonstrate proper IPDE analysis when encountering traffic conflicts in residential areas.	2. The instructor will verbally review these conflicts during the first film sequence.

CONTENT

Conflicts Encountered in Residential Driving

1. Car pulling out in front of you.
2. Cars failing to maintain proper following distance.
3. Failure to yield to vehicles in left lane when turning left from right lane.
4. Failure to execute correct right-of-way procedure at a four-way stop.
5. Improper lane-changing procedures.

EVALUATION

The instructor will visually check student as he encounters traffic conflicts in residential areas.

3. The student will demonstrate proper IPDE analysis when encountering traffic conflicts in rural areas.	3. The instructor will verbally review these conflicts during the second film sequence.
	The instructor will use the flashlight pointer to indicate various traffic conflicts encountered in rural areas, during the second film sequence.

CONTENT

Rural Conflicts

1. Poorly regulated side roads.
2. Hills causing limited sight distance.
3. Cars swerving across the center line.
4. Cars failing to maintain proper following distance.
5. Cars using unsafe passing procedures.
6. Cars stopping too abruptly, causing potential rear-end collisions.

EVALUATION

The instructor will visually check the student as he encounters traffic conflicts on rural roadways.

4. The student will demonstrate proper IPDE analysis when encountering traffic conflicts during expressway driving.	4. The instructor will verbally review these conflicts during the third sequence of the film.
	The instructor will use the flashlight pointer to indicate various traffic conflicts encountered in expressway areas during the third film sequence.

CONTENT

Conflicts Encountered in Expressway Driving

1. Cars entering and exiting the expressway.
2. Cars using improper lane-changing procedures (crossing several lanes at once).
3. Passing large trucks and vehicles which have side mirrors.

EVALUATION

The instructor will visually check the student as he encounters traffic conflicts on the expressway.

5. The student will use commentary driving to demonstrate his ability to analyze traffic situations using the IPDE concept during the fourth film sequence.	5. The instructor will use the flashlight pointer and still-frame the projector to emphasize the correct IPDE analysis procedures.
	The instructor will still-frame the projector to allow the student to analyze the traffic situation.

CONTENT

Commentary Driving

1. The student will verbally state the potential and immediate hazards that he observes in the driving environment during the fourth film sequence.
2. The student will use the IPDE concept to analyze this sequence.

EVALUATION

The instructor will listen to the commentary driving and make corrections when necessary.

MEDIA AND RESOURCES

1. Link film, "A Formula for Traffic Survival."
2. "A Formula for Traffic Survival," Allstate Good Driver Trainer Instructor's Manual.
3. Flashlight pointer.
4. Still-frame on the projector.

CONTENT MULTIPLE-CAR DRIVING RANGE

The multiple-car driving-range program is designed to develop competent drivers with a minimum of interference from conflicting traffic. Such a program is conducted over an established period of time and provides planned learning experiences for the beginner in logical and progressive sequences. Instruction begins with the development of basic skills and proceeds to the learning of more complex tasks and maneuvers. The instructor demonstrates the lesson, and then the students practice in the cars. In such an environment the student develops confidence, individual responsibility, and ability in making decisions. The typical multiple-car driving-range program uses 8, 10, or 12 vehicles at a time. One instructor can handle this program if he is properly trained and uses well-organized daily lesson plans. In general the content of the range program is similar to the content of the dual-control car program presented earlier in this chapter. Such instruction on a range would be developed principally on an "exercise" basis. A driver in his car needs to interact with others so some degree of traffic mix is important on a range. Automatic-shift vehicles would be used all the time. If available, standard-shift cars might be used at times in some more advanced lessons. The following is a suggested basic sequence of lessons for use on a multiple-car driving range:

Figure 12-4. Multiple-Car Program in Operation (Courtesy Highway Traffic Safety Center, Michigan State University)

Multiple-Car Lesson Sequence

1. Orientation
   a. Forward Movement
   b. Stopping and Securing
   c. Left Turn
2. Right and Left Turns
3. Introduction of Two-Way Traffic
4. Backing and Turning
   a. Steering
   b. Tracking
5. Parking
   a. Angle
   b. Perpendicular
   c. Three-point Turnabout
6. Merge, Diverge, and Blending in Traffic
7. Passing Maneuvers
8. Parallel Parking
   a. Turnabouts
9. Review and Evaluation
10. Emergency Techniques
    a. Skid Control
    b. Serpentine
    c. Evasive
    d. Controlled Braking
    e. Off-Road Recovery
    f. Blowout

The lesson plans that follow are designed to be used in a multiple-car program. Each are compatable with dual-control and simulation instruction. A selected group of lessons are included. Other lesson plans may be developed with your instructor.

MULTIPLE-CAR LESSON NO. 1

ORIENTATION: FORWARD MOVEMENT, STOPPING AND SECURING, LEFT TURN

Required Entry Level

The student will demonstrate the (1) predriving habits, (2) starting procedures, and (3) orally explain the left-turn procedures and securing the car.

Lesson Objective

The student will demonstrate (1) smooth start, (2) stop, (3) left turn, (4) securing his car.

Specific Instructional Objectives	*Learning Activities*
1. The student will orally list range rules and predriving procedures.	1. The instructor will introduce the students to the driving range, and a student will demonstrate the predriving procedures.

CONTENT

1. The instructor will explain that a driving range is an "Off-street Multiple-Car Range" which gives students experience driving in specific situations without the worry of conflicting traffic.

2. The instructor will read the rules of the range that are to be followed by all students at all times. (Hand out—see **page 332**).

3. The instructor will pick one student to demonstrate the proper predriving procedures.
   a. Unlock door.
   b. Enter car safely.
   c. Put proper key in ignition (do not force).
   d. Adjust seat.
   e. Adjust headrest.
   f. Adjust mirrors.
   g. Adjust ventilation.
   h. Fasten safety belt and shoulder harness.
   i. Turn key to "On" position and prepare to take orders from the radio.

EVALUATION

The instructor will orally quiz students on all procedures covered.

2. The student will perform smooth starting and stopping of the vehicle at the commands of the instructor.	2. The instructor will establish communications with the student. The students will start the cars and follow the instructions of the teacher who will have them drive to the far end of the range.

CONTENT

1. The teacher will give instructions to the students to start the cars.
2. Beginning with one car at a time, the teacher will have the students start the lesson at one end of the range and move slowly down the range stopping at certain intervals until they come to the last set of cones.
3. Starting and stopping the vehicle
    a. Shift to "P."
    b. Turn the key to the start position and release.
    c. Touch the accelerator lightly.
    d. Check the instrument panel for red lights.
    e. Place the right foot on the brake pedal.
    f. Shift to "D."
    g. Check around the car.
    h. Release the park brake—foot brake.
    i. Let the car ease forward by touching the accelerator pedal lightly.
    j. Press slowly but firmly on the brake to come to a complete stop.
    k. Students will be instructed to brake with the right foot only.

EVALUATION

The instructor will visually check the students as they perform the task.

3. The students will demonstrate proper left turns, using the hand-over-hand procedure.	**3.** The students will turn left around the cones at the corners of the range. This activity will continue as long as time permits.

CONTENT

1. The instructor will give commands as follows to help the students proceed around the range:
    a. Proceed to the corner.
    b. Turn to the left using the hand-over-hand procedure around the cone.
    c. Straighten the wheel using the hand-over-hand procedure.
    d. Each student will be instructed to follow, being sure to stay at least three car lengths behind the car in front.

(*Note*: The instructor should review orally the hand-over-hand procedure.)

EVALUATION

The instructor will observe the student's progress as he moves around the range.

4. The student will secure the vehicle and safely leave the range area.	**4.** The student will stop the car and secure it when instructed to do so.

CONTENT

1. The student will follow the instructions of the teacher with regard to stopping and securing the vehicle:
    a. Place the right foot on the brake.

b. Bring the vehicle to a complete stop.

c. Shift to "P."

d. Turn the key to the lock position.

e. Set the park brake.

f. Remove the key from the ignition.

g. Remove the seat belt.

h. Check around the car.

i. Open the door and leave the car safely.

j. Place the key in the left-door keyhole.

EVALUATION

The instructor will visually check the students as they perform the task.

MEDIA AND RESOURCES

1. Multiple-car driving range.
2. Motor vehicles available.
3. Chalkboard.
4. Radio transmitter.

PROBLEM AREAS

1. Hand-over-hand and reverse hand-over-hand procedure.
   a. Using steady pressure to accelerate and stop smoothly.
   b. Becoming used to the radio for direct communication.

SAFETY CENTER

SOUTHERN ILLINOIS UNIVERSITY

Rules of the Driver Education Range — Teacher Responsibility

1. Range supervisors and other staff members should adhere to the same rules for range use as the beginning drivers.

2. A teacher should perform the range lesson himself prior to the class period.

3. A thorough explanation of the range lesson should be given to the group of beginning drivers, either in a classroom or on the range itself.

4. A demonstration shall be made of each range lesson, consisting of having a student drive while the teacher talks him through, with the remainder of the class paying strict and close attention.

5. Previously demonstrated procedures, maneuvers, and exercises should always be reviewed.

6. The car radios should be checked for frequency and volume with your particular communication system *before* class.

7. The instructor's communication with students:
   a. Have students turn on ignition, but do not start engines.
   b. Call each car by number, having each student respond by a short horn.
   c. Always address students by car number.
   d. Talk briefly and clearly.
   e. Repeat each communication statement.
   f. Be positive in your comments; resist being negative constantly.
   g. Do not use sarcasm or profanity.
   h. Do not berate students over the radio.
   i. If severe correction is necessary, stop student and discuss the problem personally, not over the radio.

MULTIPLE-CAR LESSON NO. 2

RIGHT AND LEFT TURNS

Required Entry Level

The students will demonstrate and orally describe the skills and procedures involved in (1) the predriving habits, (2) starting of the vehicle, (3) moving the vehicle forward, (4) coming to a smooth stop, (5) left-hand turn and the correct recovery procedures, (6) observing the rules concerning the range, and (7) securing the vehicle.

Lesson Objective

The students will perform (1) right-hand turns with the hand-over-hand method and recovery method, (2) proper following procedures, (3) the use of appropriate turn indicators when necessary, and (4) right- and left-hand turns alternately, using proper steering and recovery methods.

Specific Instructional Objectives	Learning Activities
1. The student will orally list the correct predriving procedures and perform them on their respective cars.	1. The instructor will ask the students to orally list the correct predriving procedures and then the students will perform on their own the required procedures.

CONTENT

List of procedures for the predrive, and the starting of the vehicle. This is a review of the previous lesson.

EVALUATION

The instructor will listen to the oral explanations and when the students are in the cars, check over the radio if they have performed the procedures. Is the motor running? Is the car in park when trying to start?

2. The student will drive the car slowly forward to a set point, smoothly brake to a complete stop, and put the car in park, waiting for further instructions.	2. The student will physically demonstrate the proper procedures for forward motion and smooth proper braking.

CONTENT

1. Release brake pedal.
2. Lightly accelerate to move straight ahead.
3. Slow down by taking foot off the accelerator.
4. Push down on brake easily until a complete stop is reached.
5. Put car in "P" and put on parking brake.
6. Leave car running and wait for further instructions.

EVALUATION

The instructor will observe the movement of the cars.

PROBLEM AREAS

1. Accelerating too fast.
2. Braking too sudden or too fast.

3. The students will review left-hand turns and recovery procedures, and specifically, hand-over-hand method with the use of turn signals.

3. The student will physically demonstrate the proper method for the left turn and recovery and use of turn signals by driving around the outside edge of the range.

CONTENT

1. Accelerate slowly forward.
2. At the cones turn left; hand-over-hand steering, braking when necessary.
3. Recover hand-over-hand.
4. Proceed this way around the range.

EVALUATION

The instructor will visually observe the movement of the cars and make corrections over the radio when necessary.

PROBLEM AREAS

1. Not using indicators.
2. Turns too sharp.
3. Recovery too slow.
4. Improper spacing of the cars.
5. Not using hand-over-hand method.

4. The student will physically perform right–hand turns, using turn signals and hand–over–hand steering method.

4. The student will perform the right–turn procedures with their cars.

CONTENT

1. Accelerate slowly forward.
2. Apply right–turn indicator.
3. Release accelerator and gently brake before the turn.
4. Turn hand-over-hand and recover the same way.
5. Resume speed after turn and follow this procedure at every cone.
6. Maintain proper following distance.

EVALUATION

The instructor will visually observe the vehicles and the students, correcting mistakes when necessary.

PROBLEM AREAS

1. Not using turn indicators.
2. Too sharp turns.
3. Recovery too slow.
4. Improper spacing of cars.
5. Not using hand–over–hand method.

5. The students will drive their cars around the range safely making right and left turns at the prescribed points on the modified figure eight and serpentine pattern while maintaining correct turning and driving technique.

5. The instructor will demonstrate to the class and over the radio the manner in which the drill is to be done. The class will then drive the pattern.

CONTENT

1. Turn left using the proper techniques when told to do so by the instructor.
2. After recovery, turn right at the prescribed point.
3. Stay in single-file order, following the car in front of you but keeping adequate spacing.
4. Yield to the last few cars.
5. Follow the pattern until given further instruction.

EVALUATION

The instructor will visually check the vehicles for proper student performance, making corrections when necessary.

PROBLEM AREAS

1. Straggler.
2. Confusion.
3. Turns too sharp.
4. Recovery too slow.
5. Not using indicators.
6. Improper spacing.
7. Not using hand-over-hand method.

MEDIA AND RESOURCES

1. Range.
2. Layout of range.
3. Cars.
4. Cones.
5. Chalkboard.
6. Transmitter.

MULTIPLE-CAR LESSON NO. 3

INTRODUCTION TO TWO-WAY TRAFFIC

Required Entry Level

The student will demonstrate (1) predriving habits, (2) vehicle control (starting, shifting, steering, and stopping), (3) left- and right-turn procedures with proper signaling and recovery techniques.

Lesson Objectives

The student will demonstrate the proper procedures for (1) making proper lane placement of the vehicle, (2) making left and right turns while driving in two-way traffic, (3) observing all traffic signs (stop, yield, railroad), (4) obeying all regulations that are pertinent to the driving scene.

Specific Instructional Objective	*Learning Activities*
1. The student will demonstrate the proper technique for making a left turn in two-way traffic while driving a vehicle on the driving range.	1. The instructor will observe each student making a left turn. The instructor will have the student continue practicing left turns until he can perform the maneuver adequately in two-way traffic.

CONTENT

1. The student must signal at least 100 ft. before preparing to turn left in urban areas, and 200 ft. in rural areas. (See your state's "Rules of the Road.")
2. The vehicles should be positioned in the most favorable position for making each turn. (Turn from the right-hand lane into the right-hand lane when driving in two-way traffic.)
3. The driver must obey all traffic regulations.
4. The driver must yield to all vehicles in the oncoming lane.
5. Before making a turn the driver should check left, check right, check blind spots, check left again, and then make the turn.
6. The student will reduce speed before making the turn, braking slightly; he should accelerate slightly after completing the turn.
7. The driver should use the hand-over-hand method for both turning and recovering during a turn.

EVALUATION

The instructor will visually assess the student's ability to successfully complete a left-turn maneuver.

2. The student will demonstrate the proper technique for making a right turn in two-way traffic while driving on the range.	2. The instructor will observe each student making a right turn. The student will continue to practice right turns until he can perform the maneuver safely while driving under two-way traffic conditions.

CONTENT

1. The student must signal at least 100 ft. before making a turn in urban areas, and 200 ft. in rural areas.
2. The vehicle should be positioned in the most favorable position for making each particular turn.
   a. The driver should turn from the nearest right-hand lane into the nearest right-hand lane.
   b. The right turn is more difficult to perform because the driver is not as sure of the position of his vehicle. When making the turn the driver should look ahead into the lane and not over the right fender.

3. The driver should obey all traffic regulations.
4. Before turning right the driver should check left, right, check blind spots, left again, and then make the turn.
5. The driver should use the hand-over-hand method for both turning and recovery.

EVALUATION

The instructor will visually check and evaluate each driver's performance while making right turns.

---

3. The student will demonstrate the knowledge of traffic regulations by making the proper responses to stop, yield, and railroad signs while driving on the range.

3. Each student will encounter a stop, yield, and railroad sign while driving on the range.

The instructor will correct all improper student responses. Students must continue to practice unacceptable maneuvers until they are correct.

CONTENT

1. Stop Sign, Octagon (eight-sided). Color: red and white.
   a. Make a complete stop at the marked line.
   b. If there is no stop line, stop before entering the crosswalk on your side of the intersection.
   c. If there is no crosswalk line, stop behind an imaginary line behind the sidewalk (implied line).
   d. If there is no crosswalk, stop before entering the intersection at a point from which you can best see the oncoming traffic.
   e. After stopping, yield to all pedestrians and other traffic that has entered the intersection ahead of you.
2. Yield Sign, Triangle (three-sided). Color: old—yellow and black; new—red and white.
   a. The student must slow down to a speed that is reasonable for existing conditions and stop if necessary.
   b. If the driver must stop, he must observe all regulations pertaining to that situation.
   c. The driver must always yield the right-of-way to pedestrians.
3. Railroad Sign, Round. Color: black and yellow.
   a. The driver should look, listen, and slow down.
   b. The driver should roll down the window and listen for a whistle or roar which would indicate an approaching train.

c. The driver should stop for a flashing signal, lowered crossing gate, or flagman.

d. The driver must stop no more than 50 or less than 15 feet from the nearest rail. He should stop at the yellow cross line.

e. Passing is prohibited within 100 ft. of railroad crossing. This is denoted by a yellow "no passing" line.

EVALUATION

The instructor will observe that each student identifies and responds to each sign correctly.

4. The student will exhibit general driving skills by driving in the right-hand lane, keeping a following distance of two car lengths, and performing independent maneuvers while driving on the range.	4. The student will be instructed to perform these general skills in the pre-driving discussion. The instructor will correct each student when it is determined that his techniques are faulty.

CONTENT

1. The driver must be able to keep his vehicle in the right-hand lane (drivers who cannot perform this requirement will perfect this maneuver before they may continue to drive in two-way traffic).

2. Drivers must keep at least two car lengths' distance between vehicles:
   a. Use the 2-second approach.
   b. Keep about one-half the distance of the driving range between each vehicle.

3. Some drivers will be allowed to choose the sequence in which they will perform the range maneuvers:
   a. The more confident and competent drivers will be allowed freedom of the driving range.
   b. Other students will perform the maneuvers only when given specific instructions by the instructor.

EVALUATION

The instructor will observe that the students keep the minimum vehicle distance between cars and that the students are properly performing the range maneuver.

MEDIA AND RESOURCES

1. 36 cones 28 inches.
2. 50 cones 18 inches.
3. Four stop signs.
4. Two yield signs.
5. One railroad sign.
6. Three to twelve automobiles.
7. Driving range.

MULTIPLE-CAR LESSON NO. 4

BACKING AND TURNING

Required Entry Level

The student will demonstrate (1) predriving habits, (2) starting, shifting, steering, stopping the vehicle, (3) left and right turns into proper lanes, (4) ability to track proper lane, (5) ability to respond to traffic signs, (6) ability to signal.

Lesson Objective

The student will demonstrate (1) proper procedures involved in the use of a left-turn lane, (2) safe driving on one-way streets, (3) backing in a straight line, (4) backing 90° to the left, and (5) backing 90° to the right.

Specific Instructional Objective	*Learning Activities*
1. The student will demonstrate turning into proper lanes, proper tracking procedures, and proper reaction to traffic signs. This is a review of the previous lesson.	1. The instructor will have the student orally list the steps of turning into proper lanes, tracking, reacting to traffic signs. The instructor will walk the student through the proper lanes, tracking, reacting to signs.

CONTENT

1. Drivers will maintain at least one car-length space cushion, even when stopped.
2. Drivers must yield to oncoming traffic when turning left.
3. Drivers must come to a complete stop at all stop signs.
4. Drivers must yield to traffic from left and right at yield signs.
5. Drivers should always use turn signals.
6. Hands should be on steering wheel at 9–3 position.
7. Hand-over-hand method should be used at all turns.

EVALUATION

1. The instructor will observe the students turning, tracking, observing signs.
2. The instructor will ask the students questions about turning, tracking, observing signs.

2. The student will demonstrate the proper procedure for use of the left-turn lane.	2. The instructor will walk the students through the left-turn lane and explain the proper usage. The instructor will demonstrate the left-turn lane by a diagram.

CONTENT

1. Signal for turn.
2. Prepare to stop.
3. Check mirror and blind spot (to left).
4. Move into center lane.
5. Obey traffic control.
6. Perimeter road one-way to the left.

EVALUATION

1. The instructor will orally quiz the students on the proper usage of the left-turn lane.
2. The instructor will visually observe the students, correcting their errors and stressing their good points.

3. The student will demonstrate the proper procedures for the use of a one-way street.

3. The instructor will walk the student through the intersection and a one-way street.

The instructor will demonstrate by diagram the one-way street.

CONTENT

1. The one-way is counterclockwise completely around the track.
2. Vehicles go only one direction in this lane.
3. Whenever coming to the "T" intersection the driver must turn left.
4. Proper tracking procedures must be used.

EVALUATION

1. The instructor will quiz the students on the use of the one-way street.
2. The instructor will visually observe the students using the one-way street.

4. The student will demonstrate proper procedures for straight backing, 90° backing to the left, 90° backing to the right.

4. The instructor will walk the student through the procedures for backing.

The instructor will explain the methods of steering for the various backing maneuvers.

CONTENT

1. Be certain your car is in *Reverse*.
2. Check all around you before starting to back.
3. Look where you are backing.
   a. Straight—over right shoulder and out rear window.
   b. Left—over left shoulder and out left rear window.
   c. Right—over right shoulder and out right rear window.
   d. Occasionally check all around.
4. Back car very slowly; use gas only if car does not move.
5. Use hand-over-hand technique.
6. Be certain wheels are straight before starting to back and are straight after completing maneuver.
7. Exit backing area at the same place as entered.

340

EVALUATION

1. The instructor will quiz the students on the procedures of backing.
2. The instructor will observe the students executing the backing procedures.

MEDIA AND RESOURCES

1. Driving range.
2. Cars.
3. Cones.
4. Traffic signs.
5. Chalkboard.

PROBLEM AREAS

1. Each student must know his car number.
2. All steering should be hand-over-hand.
3. Students must keep proper following distance.
4. Students might be confused by the various cones and lanes.
5. Instructor must keep track of all the cars on the spread-out range.
6. Students must make only left turns from left-turn lane.
7. Students must not make right turns from the "T" intersections.
8. Students must be looking in proper places when backing.

MULTIPLE-CAR LESSON NO. 5

MERGE, DIVERGE, AND BLEND IN TRAFFIC

Required Entry Level

The student will adequately perform the following driving tasks: (1) predriving habits, (2) vehicle control, (3) left and right turns using proper signal and blind spot techniques, (4) perform lane changes safely, (5) follow directions or instructions.

Lesson Objective

The student driver will safely perform all the maneuvers that are pertinent to blending with traffic (lane changes, entering acceleration lane, entering deceleration lane) while operating a driver education vehicle during a range exercise.

Specific Instructional Objective	*Learning Activities*
1. After the instructions, the student will demonstrate the correct procedures for making a lane change while driving on the range.	1. The instructor will walk the student through a lane change maneuver. The student will perform numerous lane changes during the range exercise.

CONTENT

    1. Give appropriate signal for left or right turn.
    2. Check rear- and sideview mirrors.
    3. Check traffic in front and behind in the lane which you intend to enter.
    4. Check blind spots.
    5. Turn steering wheel slightly in the direction in which you intend to turn, and then move smoothly into the appropriate lane.
    6. Turn off signal because the slight turn of the wheel may not automatically do it.
    7. Be sure there is room to make lane change prior to reaching the end of the range.
    8. Be alert for extra drivers that will simulate hazardous driving situations.

EVALUATION

The instructor will visually assess each student as he is operating a vehicle on the range. The instructor will make both negative and positive appraisals of the student's activities.

2. The student driver will perform a deceleration maneuver while operating a vehicle on the range.	2. The instructor will have another instructor lead the student through the first deceleration maneuver. The student will have some prior experience in the deceleration maneuvers while driving on the range.

CONTENT

1. Give a right-hand signal prior to entering the deceleration lane.
2. Check rear- and sideview mirrors.
3. Check blind spots.
4. Wait until after you have entered the deceleration lane to slow speed.
5. Make turn onto deceleration lane and then slow speed.
6. Continue driving and blend with traffic.
   a. Slow so as not to alter traffic flow.
   b. Speed up so as not to create a hazard.
7. Judge the speed of other vehicles and adjust your speed
to match the movement of the general traffic flow.

EVALUATION

The instructor will attempt to visually observe and evaluate the student driver.

3. The student driver will demonstrate the correct technique for using the acceleration lane to enter the traffic flow on the range.	**3.** The instructor will have the maneuver demonstrated for the students. The student driver will perform acceleration maneuvers while driving on the range.

CONTENT

1. Give a proper left-hand signal.
2. Check traffic of the lane into which you intend to enter.
3. Check rear- and sideview mirrors.
4. Check blind spots.
5. Judge the speed of oncoming traffic and adjust the speed of your vehicle so that you may enter traffic without creating a hazard.
6. Continue well out into the acceleration lane and then blend with traffic.
7. Move smoothly into the correct lane.
8. Check to be sure that turn signal is off.
9. Immediately survey the traffic scene for any new hazards that may occur.

EVALUATION

The instructor will visually evaluate the student's performance of this maneuver.

4. The student will blend smoothly with traffic while operating a vehicle on the range.	**4.** The student will be required to blend with traffic while performing this range exercise. There will be other drivers on the range simulating hazards that may make blending in traffic difficult.

CONTENT

1. Continually search and scan the traffic scene for vehicles entering and exiting the traffic scene.

2. Be alert for traffic signs which will indicate position of acceleration and deceleration lanes.

3. Slow and allow an entering vehicle to merge ahead of your car.

4. Speed up and allow the vehicle to enter behind you.

5. Change lanes and allow the driver to enter beside you.

6. Be alert for drivers who fail to signal.

7. Be alert for drivers who may pull directly into your path.

8. Be alert for drivers who have missed their exit and have stopped or are illegally backing up.

EVALUATION

The instructor will visually assess the student's performance while operating a vehicle on the range.

MEDIA AND RESOURCES

1. 65 cones.
2. Motor vehicles.
3. Driving range.
4. Radio transmitter.
5. Student range lesson sequence.

PROBLEM AREAS

1. Some students may find this exercise difficult, thus upsetting the flow of traffic.
2. Some students tend to slow speed prior to entering traffic.
3. Drivers must be sure they see other vehicles merging into their lane of traffic.

344

MULTIPLE-CAR LESSON NO. 6

PASSING MANEUVERS

Required Entry Level

The student will demonstrate (1) predriving habits, (2) starting procedures, (3) left and right turns, (4) use of traffic controls, (5) lane changes.

Lesson Objective

The student will demonstrate proper procedures for passing another vehicle on a one-way street and a two-way street.

Specific Instructional Objectives	*Learning Activities*
1. The student will demonstrate the proper procedure for safe passing on a one-way street.	1. The range will be set up with two lanes in the same direction. The instructor will demonstrate the maneuver by walking the students through the maneuvers and then instruct the students to go to the cars and perform all the predriving maneuvers. The students will work in pairs. Upon the instruction of the teacher the students will begin to move the cars slowly in the right-hand lane.
	Car 2 will be instructed to pass car 1; 4, to pass 3; 6, pass 5. The students will then be in reverse position.
	Now numbers 1, 3, and 5 will be instructed to pass, and so on around the range.

CONTENT

1. Establish safe following distance until passing is safe (about 100 feet).
2. Check assured distance ahead.
3. Check traffic behind, in front, and to the sides, using inside and outside mirrors.
4. Turn on directional signal (left).
5. Check blind spot.
6. Accelerate smoothly into the left lane.
7. Build a 15 mph superiority over the car you are passing.
8. Check traffic ahead and behind; decide if you can make it.
9. Tap horn.
10. Turn on right signal.
11. Keep in passing lane.
12. Check right blind spot.
13. Return to right lane.
14. Turn off signal; resume safe speed.

EVALUATION

The instructor will visually check the student's ability to successfully complete a passing maneuver.

---

2. The student will demonstrate the proper procedure for safe passing on a two-way road with passing zones and oncoming traffic.

2. About halfway through the class period the students will be instructed to secure their vehicle inside the range.

The instructor will demonstrate the procedure for passing on a two-way street with the assistance of two of the other instructors. At the end of the demonstration the students will be instructed to drive around the range, 3 in one direction and 3 in the other. The two instructors who helped with the demonstration will be asked to drive very slowly around the range—one in each direction. The instructor will ask the students to pass these cars, using the proper procedure.

CONTENT

1. Establish safe following distance until passing is safe (about 100 feet).
2. Check for passing zone and passing signs (double-yellow or single-yellow line).
3. Check distance ahead for oncoming traffic in the left lane.
4. Turn on directional signal (left).
5. Check blind spot.
6. Accelerate smoothly into the left lane.
7. Build a 15 mph superiority over the car you are passing.
8. Check traffic ahead and behind; decide if you can make it.
9. Tap horn.
10. Turn on right signal.
11. Keep in passing lane until the vehicle being passed is seen in your inside mirror.
12. Check right blind spot.
13. Return to right lane.
14. Shut off signal; resume safe speed.

EVALUATION

The instructor will visually check the student's ability to successfully complete a passing maneuver.

MEDIA AND RESOURCES

1. Multiple-car driving range.
2. Motor vehicles.
3. Radio transmitters.

PROBLEM AREAS

1. May not signal.
2. May not check blind spot.
3. May pass too slowly and not return to proper lane before reaching the end of the range.
4. Lead car may not go slow enough.

MULTIPLE-CAR LESSON NO. 7

REVIEW AND EVALUATION

Required Entry Level

The student will demonstrate all pertinent procedures for controlling the vehicle safely and efficiently.

Lesson Objective

The student will adequately perform (1) predriving procedures, (2) procedures for securing the vehicle, (3) left and right turns, (4) tracking in two-way traffic, (5) backing (straight and turn procedures), (6) driveway turnabouts, (7) angle and perpendicular parking procedures, (8) passing procedures. The primary evaluation will center on the backing and passing maneuvers. The student will indicate his proficiency or deficiency by the driving habits exhibited during the review lesson.

Specific Instructional Objective	Learning Activities
1. The student will demonstrate the proper predriving habits while operating the driver education vehicle during the review exercise.	1. The instructor will tell the students that they will be checked on predriving procedures. The instructor will check and correct all errors.

CONTENT

1. Put key in ignition and turn to "On" position.
2. Turn radio to "On" position to receive instructions.
3. Adjust seat so that you can reach pedals.
4. Adjust headrest.
5. Adjust all mirrors.
6. Lock all doors and lower one rear window a small distance.
7. Fasten seat belt and shoulder restraint.
8. Wait for instructor to give additional instructions.

EVALUATION

The instructor will use the radio to check that the students have turned the radio to the "On" position; then he will visually check each driver individually.

2. The student driver will follow the correct procedure for securing a vehicle at the end of the range lesson.	2. The student will be required to secure the vehicle. The instructor will check each vehicle at the end of the lesson.

CONTENT

1. Completely stop the car before putting gearshift lever in P (park).
2. Turn the key to lock position and remove the key.
3. Remove seat belt.
4. Check all traffic before opening the door.
5. Leave the key in the driver's door—be sure all doors are locked.

EVALUATION

The instructor will check each car after the vehicle has been secured.

3. The student will demonstrate the correct procedures for performing a correct left turn while operating a vehicle on the range.	**3.** The student will have performed this maneuver many times prior to the lesson. The student will be reminded that he is to be checked on this maneuver.

CONTENT

1. The student must signal at least 100 ft. before preparing to turn left in urban areas, and 200 ft. in rural areas.
2. The vehicles should be positioned in the most favorable position for making each turn (turn from the right-hand lane into the right-hand lane when driving in two-way traffic).
3. The driver must obey all traffic regulations.
4. The driver must yield to all vehicles in the oncoming lane.
5. Before making a turn the driver should check left, check right, check blind spots, check left again, and then make the turn.
6. The student will reduce speed before making the turn, braking slightly; he should accelerate slightly after completing the turn.
7. The driver should use the hand-over-hand method for both turning and recovering during a turn.

EVALUATION

The instructor will visually assess each student as he performs a left-turn maneuver on the range.

4. The student will make a correct right-turn maneuver during the review session on the range.	**4.** The student has performed this maneuver previously in prior range lessons. He will be informed that he is to be checked on the procedure.

CONTENT

1. The student must signal at least 100 ft. before making a turn in urban areas, and 200 ft. in rural areas.
2. The vehicle should be positioned in the most favorable position for making each particular turn.

a. The driver should turn from the nearest right-hand lane into the nearest right-hand lane.

b. The right turn is more difficult to perform because the driver is not as sure of the position of his vehicle. When making the turn the driver should look ahead into the lane and not over the right fender.

3. The driver should obey all traffic regulations.

4. Before turning right the driver should check left, right, check blind spots, left again, and then make the turn.

5. The driver should use the hand-over-hand method for both turning and recovery.

EVALUATION

The instructor will visually observe the student's performance while driving on the range.

---

5. The student will make a correct response to all traffic regulations posted on the range.

5. Various traffic signs will be posted at desired points.

The student will be informed of their location and that he is to observe the signs.

CONTENT

1. Stop Sign—Octagon (eight-sided). Color: red and white
   a. The driver must make a complete stop at the marked line.
   b. If there is no stop line, the driver must stop before entering the crosswalk on his intersection.
   c. If there is no crosswalk line, the driver should stop behind an imaginary line behind the sidewalk (implied line).
   d. If there is no crosswalk, the driver should stop before entering the intersection at a point from which he can best see the oncoming traffic.
   e. After stopping, the driver must yield to all pedestrians and other traffic that has entered the intersection ahead of him.
2. Yield Sign—Triangle (three-sided). Color: old—yellow and black; new—red and white
   a. The student must slow down to a speed that is reasonable for existing conditions, and stop if necessary.
   b. If the driver must stop, he must observe all regulations pertaining to that situation.
   c. The driver must always yield the right-of-way to pedestrians.
3. Railroad—Round. Color: black and yellow
   a. The driver should look, listen, and slow down.
   b. The driver should roll down the window and listen for a whistle or roar which indicate an approaching train.
   c. The driver should stop for a flashing signal, lowered crossing gate, or flagman.
   d. The driver must stop no more than 50 or less than 15 feet from the nearest rail. He should stop at the yellow cross line.
   e. Passing is prohibited within 100 ft. of railroad crossing. This is denoted by a yellow "no passing" line.

EVALUATION

The instructor will visually observe the student's performance while driving on the range.

6. The student will demonstrate the ability to blend smoothly with two-way traffic.

6. The student has performed previously in two-way traffic.

The instructor will inform the students that they will be evaluated in two-way traffic.

CONTENT

1. The driver must continually search and scan the traffic scene for vehicles entering and exiting the traffic scene.
2. The driver should be alert for traffic signs which will indicate the position of acceleration and deceleration lanes.
3. The driver may slow and allow an entering vehicle to merge ahead of his car.
4. The driver may speed up and allow the vehicle to enter behind him.
5. The driver may wish to change lanes and allow the driver to enter beside him.
6. The driver should be alert for drivers who fail to signal.
7. Some drivers may not check traffic and pull directly into the path of your vehicle.
8. The student should be alert for drivers who have missed their exit and have stopped or are illegally backing up.

EVALUATION

The instructor will observe the students' performance and give verbal instructions that might help them perform the maneuver.

---

7. The student will perform the correct procedure for backing the driver education vehicle in a straight line on the range.

7. The instructor will verbally review the backing procedure that has been previously given.

CONTENT

1. Be certain your car is in *Reverse*.
2. Check all around you before starting to back.
3. Look where you are backing.
   - a. Straight—over right shoulder and out right rear window.
   - b. Left—over left shoulder and out left rear window.
   - c. Right—over right shoulder and out right rear window.
4. Back car very slowly; use gas only if car does not move.
5. Use hand-over-hand technique.
6. Be certain wheels are straight before starting to back, and are straight after completing maneuver.
7. Exit backing area at the same place as entered.

EVALUATION

The instructor will observe the students' performance and give verbal instructions which might help them perform the maneuver.

---

8. The student will perform the proper technique for making a left 90° backing turn maneuver while operating a vehicle on the range.

8. The instructor will verbally review the 90° backing maneuver during the introduction.

The instructor will verbally give instructions to the students while they are performing the maneuver if it seems necessary.

CONTENT

1. Check all traffic before starting the backing maneuver.
2. Be sure car is in *Reverse*.
3. Look over left shoulder and out left rear window.
4. Back slowly.
5. Use only hand-over-hand method, turning the wheel to the left.
6. Keep looking back until the car is stopped.
7. Use proper signal for exiting.

EVALUATION

The instructor will visually assess the student's performance.

---

9. The student will perform the proper technique for making a right 90° backing turn while operating a vehicle on the range.

9. The instructor will verbally review the maneuver during the review introduction.

The students will be required to perform the backing maneuver during the lesson.

CONTENT

1. Check all traffic before starting the backing maneuver.
2. Be sure car is in *Reverse*.
3. Look over right shoulder and out right rear window.
4. Back slowly.
5. Use hand-over-hand steering while turning wheel to the right.
6. Keep looking back until the car is stopped.
7. Use proper signal for exiting.

EVALUATION

The instructor will observe the student performing the maneuver and make corrections during the maneuver.

---

10. The student will perform a serpentine maneuver both forward and backward while operating a vehicle on the range.

10. The instructor will explain the procedures for making the maneuver.

The maneuver will be demonstrated before the students attempt it.

CONTENT

1. The driver will give proper signal, left or right.
2. The driver will turn the vehicle into the proper position and drive around each of three orange cones, being careful not to touch them with the car.

3. The car must stop, the driver must look out rear window, put the selector lever into the "R" and back out being sure to avoid hitting the three orange cones.

4. Before entering two-way traffic again, the student should stop, check traffic, back slowly, turning wheel to right.

5. When vehicle is in proper position, the driver should signal, check traffic, and continue to desired destination.

EVALUATION

The instructor will visually assess the student's performance and attempt to make the needed corrections as they occur.

11. The student will demonstrate the proper procedures for entering and exiting an angle parking area while operating a vehicle on the range.	**11.** The instructor will verbally review the procedures. The instructor will verbally assist students who seem to need help.

CONTENT

Approach

1. Position car as far left as possible.
2. Check traffic and brake gently.
3. Signal intentions (right).
4. Slow to safe speed for entrance.
5. When front wheels are opposite the nearest edge of the parking space, stop, and check space before pulling into it.
6. Steer right using correct hand-over-hand steering method.
7. As car moves into center space, straighten wheels.
8. Continue forward slowly.
9. Stop before touching curb.
10. Set park brake.
11. Shift to park "P."

Leaving

1. Shift to reverse (holding foot brake; release parking brake).
2. Check traffic to rear continuously.
3. Back slowly, cautiously (maintain straight position).
4. Stop and check traffic both left and right.
5. Continue backing (when front bumper clears rear bumper of car on your left).
6. Steer hard right.
7. Back into the lane you will be traveling in and preset the wheels before stopping (keep looking back until coming to a complete stop).
8. Shift to drive "D."
9. Check traffic.
10. Accelerate to proper speed.

EVALUATION

The instructor will visually observe the student's performance of the maneuver and attempt to make the necessary corrections.

12. The student will correctly enter and exit from a perpendicular parking area while operating a driver education vehicle on the range.	12. The instructor will verbally review the procedures. The instructor will verbally assist students who may need help.

CONTENT

Entering Perpendicular Parking Space on the Right

1. Check traffic.
2. Activate right directional signal; show hand signal at least 100 feet in advance.
3. Slow down to less than 5 miles per hour and position your car at least 10 feet or more from the parked car on the right side of the route, street, or parking area.
4. Just before the front wheels of your car are opposite the near edge of the parking space, steer full right quickly in the space. Make sure your foot is in the caution position when entering the space.
5. Enter space slowly, making sure wheels are straightened, and stop about one inch from the curb. Ease pressure on brake, allowing front wheels to touch curb gently.

Leaving a Perpendicular Parking Space on the Right

1. Back out only when traffic is clear.
2. Be cautious when performing this procedure because the rear end of the car has to come far out into traffic before the steering wheel can be turned.
3. When the front bumper of your car is even with the rear bumper of the car parked beside you, turn wheels full right.
4. When your car is completely clear of the car beside you, put vehicle in "Drive" and drive forward slowly, straightening your wheels.

EVALUATION

The instructor will visually observe the student's performance during the maneuver and attempt to make all necessary corrections.

13. The student will overtake and pass another vehicle while operating a driver education vehicle on the range.	13. The instructor will review the passing procedures prior to the lesson. The instructor will give the specific instructions during the passing sequence.

CONTENT

1. The student will establish a safe following distance until passing is safe.
2. The student will check assured distance ahead.
3. The student will check traffic behind him by use of inside and outside mirrors.

354

4. The student will activate left directional signal.
5. The student will glance over left shoulder to check blind spot.
6. The student will simultaneously accelerate, glance left, and steer into passing lane.
7. The student will tap horn.
8. The student will put on right directional signal.
9. The student will continue in passing lane until vehicle being passed is seen in inside mirror.
10. The student will glance over right shoulder.
11. The student will return to right lane, turn signal off, and adjust speed.

EVALUATION

The instructor will observe the student's performance during the lesson.

MEDIA AND RESOURCES

1. Motor vehicles.
2. Driving range.
3. Radio transmitter.
4. Information derived from prior lesson plans.

PROBLEM AREAS

1. The student will have difficulty performing the backing maneuver.
2. Some drivers will still not be performing basic procedures: signaling, head check, etc., every time.

MULTIPLE-CAR LESSON NO. 8

EMERGENCY TECHNIQUES

Required Entry Level

The student will demonstrate all skills necessary to operate a motor vehicle safely and efficiently under normal driving conditions.

Lesson Objective

The student will demonstrate (1) skid control maneuver, (2) serpentine maneuver, (3) evasive maneuver, (4) controlled braking, (5) off-road recovery, (6) blowout.

Specific Instructional Objectives	*Learning Activities*
1. The student will demonstrate the proper procedures for the skid control maneuvers.	1. The instructor will make sure the students completely understand the procedure. The instructor will demonstrate the skid control maneuver. The instructor should emphasize that the brake and throttle are not used to correct a skid.

CONTENT

1. The hands should be at 9 and 3 on the steering wheel.
2. With the vehicle in a curve, the instructor will initiate a braking skid, cornering skid, or power skid.
3. Immediately the student should back off the throttle and steer in the direction of the skid.
4. As soon as the vehicle responds to the skid correction, the student must countersteer in the opposite direction until the front wheels are as straight as possible and continue in his original path. He should be prepared to correct for a "second" skid if it should occur.

EVALUATION

The instructor will visually check the student's performance and make necessary corrections.

PROBLEM AREAS

1. Does not ease up on accelerator.
2. Hits brakes and locks wheels.
3. Tries to use the accelerator to control the skid.
4. Responds slowly to the first skid, allowing the vehicle to go beyond point of control.
5. Oversteers on first skid and cannot correct in time to catch the second skid.

6. Cannot distinguish in which direction the back end is skidding, and therefore either does nothing or turns in the wrong direction.

2. The student will demonstrate the proper serpentine maneuvers.	2. The instructor will make sure the students completely understand the procedure.
	The instructor will demonstrate the serpentine maneuver.
	The instructor should emphasize proper hand positioning, throttle control, timing, and rhythm.

CONTENT

1. The student will enter the course at a speed selected by the instructor, usually 20 mph to start.
2. The student will drive through the course, maintaining his speed and passing as close to the cones as possible.
3. At the end of the course the student will turn around and repeat the exercise from the other direction.
4. The course is repeated at increasing speeds until the student can no longer drive the vehicle through the course successfully.

PROBLEM AREAS

1. Understeers, hitting the cones with the front wheel.
2. Oversteers so the vehicle keeps swinging farther and farther out and can't negotiate the last few cones.
3. Fails to maintain speed.
4. Moves hands on steering wheel and loses his reference point.
5. Comes in at too wide an angle on the first cone, which sets the car up wrong for the remaining cones.
6. Steers too early or too late.

3. The student will demonstrate the proper procedures for performing evasive maneuvers.	3. The instructor will make sure the student completely understands the procedures.
	The instructor will demonstrate the evasive maneuvers.
	The instructor should emphasize correct hand positioning, and that the brakes are not to be used.

CONTENT

1. The student should accelerate down the approach lane at a speed determined by the instructor, usually 25 mph.
2. At the double cue cone, the student will attempt to evade the barrier without braking. The direction and initiation of the evasive maneuver will be determined by the instructor, using a verbal command of right or left.

3. After the student evades the barrier, he will brake to a stop, turn around, and proceed to the beginning of the course. Speeds increase with each successful run up to 35 mph.

4. The maneuver should be repeated, with the instructor giving the direction cue at random until he is satisfied that the student has acquired the skill to perform an effective evasive maneuver.

PROBLEM AREAS

1. Turns wrong way each time—usually caused from anticipating the direction.
2. Steers and countersteers late—wipes out course.
3. Overapplies throttle.
4. Poor hand position—fights the steering wheel.
5. Panic brakes and slides through barrier.
6. Oversteers, causing the vehicle to hit both sides of the cone lane.
7. Attempts to go in wrong direction and then tries to recover. Once the student has committed the vehicle in one direction he should continue in that direction. He cannot recover in time to make any corrections.

4. The student will demonstrate the proper procedure for controlled braking.	4. The instructor will make sure the student completely understands the procedure.
	The instructor will demonstrate the controlled braking maneuver.
	The instructor should emphasize that brakes are to be used to the point just before lockup.

CONTENT

1. The student will proceed down the approach lane at a speed selected by the instructor, usually 25–35 mph.

2. At the double cue cone, the instructor will give a verbal command to initiate braking and to evade the barrier.

3. At the command, the student should steer the vehicle to evade the barrier, and simultaneously brake. As soon as he clears the first barrier, he should steer back to the right-hand lane to evade the second, and come to a complete stop in the shortest possible distance.

PROBLEM AREAS

1. Locks brakes and thereby loses steering control.
2. Oversteers and cannot make it back to the right in time to miss the second barrier.
3. Understeers and hits the first barrier.
4. Anticipates the cue and brakes too soon.
5. Does not come to a complete stop at the end of the course.
6. Fails to return to the right lane.

5. The student will demonstrate the proper procedure for an off-road recovery.	5. The instructor will make sure the student completely understands the procedure.

CONTENT

1. The student will accelerate down the cone-marked lane at a predetermined speed.

2. At the beginning of the curb, the student will drop the right wheels off the edge while maintaining speed, or straddle the curb as he approaches.

3. The student will center the vehicle over the curb so the wheel has room to turn.

4. Halfway down the curb the student will turn the wheel approximately 90° left, depending on the vehicle and speed.

5. As soon as the student feels or hears the right front wheel hit the curb, he must immediately steer back to the right to maintain lane position.

6. The student should slow up, brake to a stop, and answer any questions.

7. The student should turn around and run the exercise the other way, dropping the left wheels off the edge. The procedure is the same except the steering directions are reversed.

8. The student should repeat the exercise until his performance is satisfactory.

---

6. The student will demonstrate the proper procedure for a blowout.	6. The instructor will make sure the students understand the procedure.
	The instructor will demonstrate the blowout procedure.
	The instructor should emphasize that the student should *not* hit the brakes when the tire blows out.

CONTENT

Straight-Line Blowout—Right Front

1. The student will proceed down the cone-marked course at a speed selected by the instructor, usually 25 mph.

2. Midway in the course, the instructor will blow the right front tire.

3. The student should take his foot off the accelerator, without braking, and steer to the left just enough to maintain lane position. Steering left is necessary to overcome the pull to the right caused by the right front tire increasing its rolling resistance.

4. After the student has slowed down and has control of the vehicle, he will brake gently to a stop.

5. The student will repeat the exercise until the instructor is satisfied with his performance.

Straight-Line Blowout—Right Rear

1. The student will proceed down the cone-marked course at a speed selected by the instructor, usually 25 mph.

2. Midway in the course, the instructor will blow the right rear tire.

3. The student should take his foot off the accelerator, without braking, and hold the steering wheel straight. In this type of blowout, if he steers right or left, he will cause the car to start to sway from side to side.

4. After the student has slowed down and has control of the vehicle, he will brake gradually to a stop.

5. The student will repeat the exercise until the instructor is satisfied with his performance.

Note: After the student has acquired skill in straight-line blowouts, then run the course and blow the front and rear at random.

PROBLEM AREAS

1. Panic brakes, thereby losing steering control.
2. Oversteers on either front or rear causing the vehicle to leave the lane.
3. Does not steer for a front blowout and runs off to the right.
4. Student cannot determine which tire has blown and therefore steers in the wrong direction or does not steer at all.

Blowout in a Curve—Right Front

1. The student will proceed down the cone-marked curve course at a speed selected by the instructor, usually 25 mph.
2. In the curve, the instructor will blow the right front tire.
3. The student should take his foot off the accelerator, without braking, and he will have to increase his left steering input in order to maintain his position in the lane. This is necessary because the right front tire has increased its rolling resistance and lost its cornering ability, thereby creating a pull to the right.
4. The student should repeat the exercise until he has mastered the skill of handling a right front blowout in a curve.

Blowout in a Curve—Right Rear

1. The student will proceed down the cone-marked curve course at a speed selected by the instructor, usually 25 mph.
2. In a curve, the instructor will blow the right rear tire.
3. The student should take his foot off the accelerator, without braking, and he will have to take some of his left steering out in order to correct for the skid started by the blown rear tire. As soon as he has corrected the skid, he will then add more left steer in order to maintain his lane.
4. After the student has slowed down and has the vehicle under control, he will brake gently to a stop.
5. The student will repeat the exercise until the instructor is satisfied with his performance.

Note: After the student has acquired skill in handling blowouts in a curve, then run the course and blow the front and rear tires at random.

PROBLEM AREAS

1. Panic brakes, thereby losing steering ability.
2. Does not add steer left on a right front blowout, causing the vehicle to run out of the lane to the right.
3. Oversteers to the left on a front blowout, running into the oncoming lane.
4. Oversteers both directions on a rear blowout, causing the car to spin out.
5. Does not correct for the skid started by the right rear blowout; spins out.
6. Does not steer at all, but just holds the wheel straight, and runs right off course.

360

7. Does not take his foot off the accelerator pedal.
8. Student cannot determine which tire has blown; therefore, steers the wrong way.

MEDIA AND RESOURCES

General Motors Proving Grounds, Vehicles Dynamics Laboratory, *Advanced Driver Education Course Training Manual*, 1971. (See next page.)

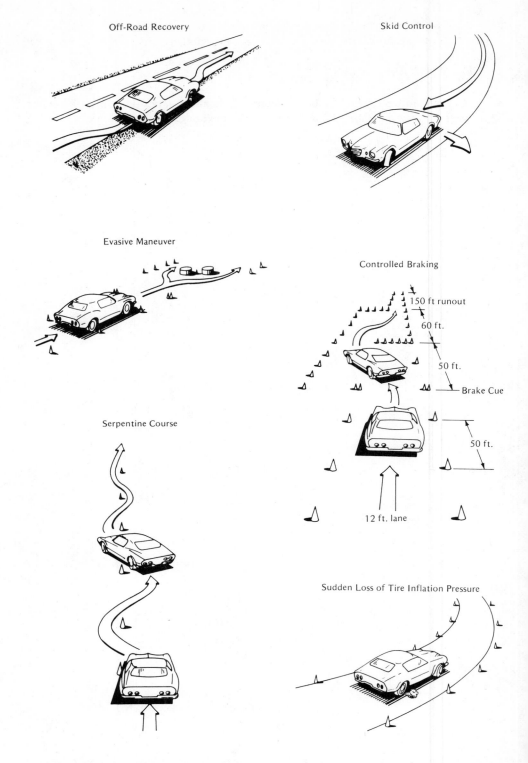

Off-Road Recovery

Skid Control

Evasive Maneuver

Controlled Braking

150 ft runout

60 ft.

50 ft.

Brake Cue

50 ft.

Serpentine Course

12 ft. lane

Sudden Loss of Tire Inflation Pressure

Emergency-evasive maneuvers. (Courtesy General Motors Proving Grounds)

LEARNING ACTIVITIES

1. Given the selected resources at the end of this chapter, write a research report on the topic, "The Value of Driving Simulation in the Development of Accident-free Drivers."
2. Use the Aaron-Strasser Driver Performance Test on page 267, and evaluate the driving ability of 15 drivers. Summarize your conclusions in a report to the instructor.
3. Participate in a panel discussion considering the subject, "The Role of Perception in the Driving Task."
4. Visit a school with a simulator or multiple-car driving-range program. Interview a teacher and observe the school's program in operation. Report orally to the class your impressions of the program visited.

SELECTED RESOURCES

Aaron, James E., and Marland K. Strasser. *Driving Task Instruction—Dual-Control, Simulation, and Multiple-Car.* New York: Macmillan Publishing Co., Inc., 1974.

American Automobile Association. *Practice Driving Guide.* New York: McGraw-Hill Book Company, 1970.

Anderson, William G. *In-Car Instruction: Methods and Content.* Reading, Mass.: Addison-Wesley Publishing Co., Inc., 1968.

Center for Safety Education. *Driver Education and Traffic Safety.* Englewood Cliffs, N.J.: Prentice-Hall, Inc., 1967.

Esarey, Melvin, et al. *Guides for Practice Driving.* Glenview, Ill.: Scott, Foresman and Company, 1972.

McKnight, A. James, and Bert B. Adams. *Driver Education Task Analysis, Volume III: Instructional Objectives.* Department of Transportation, PB202-247 (HumRRO Report 71-9) (March 1971).

Paulowski, J. G., and Duane R. Johnson. *Tomorrow's Drivers.* Chicago: Lyons and Carnahan, 1971.

Sneller, Robert C. *Vision and Driving.* St. Louis: American Optometric Association, 1962.

State of Illinois. *Driver Education for Illinois Youth.* Springfield, Ill.: Safety Education Section, Office of the Superintendent of Public Instruction, 1972.

Strasser, Marland K., et al. *Driver Education: Learning to Drive Defensively.* River Forest, Ill.: Laidlaw Brothers, Publishers, 1973.

Chapter 13

Teaching Methods and Techniques for Laboratory Instruction

OBJECTIVE: The student will be able to identify and select appropriate teaching methods and lesson management techniques and apply them to dual-control, simulation, or multiple-car lesson preparation and instruction.

The application of modern instructional techniques is essential in the conduct of a successful driver education laboratory program. It has been aptly stated that if you are teaching today the same as you were 10 years ago, in all probability you are out of date and teaching many concepts using the wrong approach. Recent investigation into the feasibility of teaching methods suggests that there are many methods and techniques that may be used successfully in behind-the wheel instruction. Therefore each instructor must be aware of the variety of methods available if these methods are to be properly applied when considering student needs and concepts to be taught.

In the selection of laboratory teaching methods, it is imperative that the teacher make every effort to select methods that will enhance learning on the part of the individual student. Each student learns and responds in accordance to a pattern that is peculiar to his personality, prior experience, and motivations of the moment. A practice-driving group cannot be thought of as a stereotype, nonflexible body that will react in exactly the same fashion regardless of which student is behind the wheel.

The teacher should make the most effective use of instruction time. Teaching in the laboratory phase requires the best of teachers. The greatest application of applied adolescent psychology takes place during the conduct of the laboratory program. Further, the instructor must recognize individual differences in students if instruction is to be effective. Moreover, a teacher uses certain methods better than others; therefore he should choose those methods that best suit his personality and ability.

The laboratory phase is a projection of the classroom phase. Students are given an opportunity to apply the knowledge and attitudes learned in the classroom to complete the process of becoming a safer driver and more competent traffic citizen.

This chapter shall identify methods and techniques used by driver educators across the nation. These methods should be utilized in the teaching of the lessons outlined in Chapter 12.

TEACHER-STUDENT RAPPORT

Driver education teachers should be aware of the fact that many factors influence student performance while behind the wheel. For example, the relationship between teacher and student is very important. The teacher should be firm in his approach, yet understanding and patient. Students should be given instructions with the expectation that these will be practiced.

The teacher may also use his voice to advantage when instructing. Voice inflections give approval or disapproval to student actions. Teachers should make wise use of the voice tone, depending on the individual student and his needs. Generally the voice should be firm and pleasant.

Students who are observing practice driving from the back seat should be assigned specific tasks. This is a part of the laboratory program; therefore observing students should be an integral part of all instruction and practice driving. Students should not be allowed to read or do work for other classes. This is distractive, and students do not gain the full benefit of practice-driving lessons.

CRITERIA OF SELECTION

In the application of instructional technology, the instructor should keep in mind the threefold purpose of the laboratory phase of the driver education program: (1) development of operational skills, (2) development of perceptual processes, and (3) development of decision-making processes. This suggests that the driver educator must develop within the student a broad concept of the driving task. Emphasis should be placed on experiences that develop knowledge, attitudes, emotional stability, and acts of driving that involve problems and decision making. In a recent study, Bishop concluded that "automobile operation is predominatly a perceptual task."[1]

[1] Richard Bishop, *Case Studies of One Car Accidents Involving Young Drivers* (Tallahassee, Fla.: The Florida Institute for Continuing Studies, 1963), p. 41.

The selection of teaching methods should be undertaken with a great deal of care. It is wise for the instructor to use guidelines to assist in the selection of methods that enrich the learning process. The following are suggested as criteria for the instructor to use in the selection of appropriate methods and techniques. The methods selected should do the following:

1. Emphasize the broad concept of the driving task.
2. Enhance the development of perceptual processes.
3. Emphasize the development of correct operational skills.
4. Be applicable to a variety of traffic environments.
5. Emphasize a positive approach in preference to a negative approach.
6. Apply to the local traffic scene.
7. Emphasize self-directed activity on the part of the student.
8. Provide for individual differences.
9. Challenge the student's capabilities.

LESSON PRESENTATION

Each practice-driving lesson should be a well-planned and carefully thought-out procedure. In this manner the student is guided through a logical instructional pattern that enhances his ability to grasp the lesson being taught. The following is suggested as a pattern for the instructor to follow in presenting each daily lesson plan.[2]

1. *Preparation*—Success or failure of each laboratory lesson is dependent on the amount of preparation made by the instructor prior to the beginning of each lesson period.
2. *Presentation*—The instructor should give a clear explanation of the lesson to be taught. This assists the student in gaining an understanding of the lesson plan for that day. (Should not be too lengthy.)
3. *Demonstration*—The instructor should follow the presentation of the lesson with a skilled demonstration. The demonstration should follow precisely the explanation given to the student.
4. *Practice*—The student should be given an opportunity to practice each lesson presented and demonstrated to him. This is practice under the direct supervision of the instructor.
5. *Evaluation*—After each lesson has been completed the instructor and student should evaluate student progress for that lesson. This is done to determine shortcomings and areas for needed improvement.

In the practice-driving sessions, the teacher should give *instructions* before the car is put into motion. He then should begin giving *directions* to the student after the car is in motion. It is best to allow the student to drive about two blocks before directions are given to him. This time period lets the student become oriented to driving.

[2] Leon Brody and Herbert S. Stack, *Highway Safety and Driver Education* (New York: Prentice-Hall, Inc., 1954), pp. 234–35.

Figure 13-1. Communication by Instructor on Multiple-Car Facility (Courtesy Highway Traffic Safety Center, Michigan State University)

The five-step method presented here will assist the instructor in organizing the daily lesson plans outlined in Chapter 12. By using such an approach, the instructor enhances the opportunity of achieving the objectives listed for each practice-driving program period.

Part Versus Whole Method

From a learning point of view it is best to present procedures or concepts one step at a time or one part at a time. By doing this the beginning student is able to grasp one idea or a portion of an overall procedure before he is required to relate an entire procedure to the driving task. The learning principle that an individual can learn a part better than a whole supports this teaching approach. However, in the use of an automatic shifting vehicle, it is possible to relate the procedures of starting, steering, and stopping almost simultaneously.

STUDENT FEEDBACK. Each lesson is strengthened if the student is required to relate back to the instructor the procedure or concept being taught. This approach verifies the fact that the student has committed to memory the lesson and at the same time reinforces the instruction given by the teacher.

TEACHER AIDS. The teacher should have available various instructional aids for laboratory teaching. Valuable aids include a clipboard, small chalkborad, small traffic board, pad of paper (for diagraming), and a supply of pencils and chalk.

Teacher Position

During the presentation and demonstration phases of the lesson, the instructor should occupy the seat behind the wheel. However, he should so position himself that students may clearly hear all instructions, and so he has adequate vision. Another approach is for the teacher to instruct from the right front seat. A skilled instructor can explain and demonstrate from this side. This approach saves time in changing drivers.

When a student is behind the wheel, the teacher should sit straight, arms forward, with the left arm in a position ready to grasp the steering wheel if it becomes necessary to do so. This position enables the instructor to observe the student, check traffic, and use the sideview mirror with a minimum of effort. The feet should be stationed in a position to use the dual brake in emergencies. The position of the teacher should permit him to observe the eyes of the student behind the wheel. The use of a small eye check mirror will assist in observing the student's eyes.

The instructor should be alert to mannerisms that will distract the student. These should be eliminated in order for the student to perform at his best during laboratory sessions.

Use of Dual Control

The dual-control brake, clutch (in manual-shift cars), accelerator, and decelerameter are installed in driver education vehicles principally for emergency use by the instructor. These controls should not be used excessively, but if the instructor is in doubt he should not hesitate to use them. The teacher should do everything possible to prevent a student from losing control of the car and becoming involved in an accident.

In some instances the beginning student may be assisted by use of dual-control clutch or accelerator at the appropriate time. The teacher should not overdo this because the student may come to rely upon the teacher too much and therefore never master some procedure or technique being taught.

METHODS FOR DUAL-CONTROL LESSONS

Many times the reason for the success or failure of an individual student to grasp and apply the lesson taught is dependent in large measure on the method of presentation. The instructor should be prepared to suggest and demonstrate techniques that will help a seemingly hopeless student master a particular procedure. Each person enrolled in the laboratory program does not respond according to a predetermined pattern assumed correct by the teacher. The instructor must be prepared to give additional assistance to students when the initial presentation and subsequent practice seems to be in need of enrichment and clarification. It should never be presumed that each student learns exactly the same way as all other students.

The following suggested methods and techniques are identified to help the teacher in presenting the daily lessons outlined in the previous chapter. These suggestions are to be used principally with dual-control lessons. However, they can be applied to lessons being presented by simulator instruction or on a multiple-car driving range.

PREDRIVING PROCEDURES

In the development of a safe and efficient traffic citizen, there are several procedures that may be stressed prior to the starting of the engine and placing the car in motion. These procedures are as follows:

1. Use check list to insure that students follow procedures taught.
2. Emphasize use of standard terminology when referring to vehicle control or steps in lesson procedure.
3. Stress the use of seat belts and shoulder harness. Never permit car to start until seat belts and shoulder harness are fastened.
4. Establish rotation plan for efficiency in movement of students in and out of car.
5. Adjust seat belt with seat as far to rear as possible. This places head and shoulders farther away from the dash-impact area.
6. Seat student in comfortable position.

Basic Skills

It is essential that fundamental skills be mastered by each student. The following are suggested to help the instructor do a better job of accomplishing this end:

1. Teach the position of hands and feet in the performance of many basic operating skills through classroom mimetic drills.
2. In manual-shift car, emphasize that the clutch places a car in motion.
3. In automatic-shift car, emphasize that the accelerator places a car in motion.
4. Inform the student that clutch control is learned more readily by hesitating at the friction point.
5. Teach students to listen for engine hum. If engine roars, too much pressure has been placed on accelerator. The engine should hum for a smooth takeoff.
6. In shifting, point out that for second and third gears, palm should be down; for first and reverse gear positions while stopped, palm is up.
7. Exert hand and arm pressure away from the body while shifting into second or third gears.

Steering

Students differ in their ability to steer properly during beginning stages of instruction. These hints may be helpful in teaching students correct steering habits:

1. Place tape on steering wheel to define area where hands should be placed.
2. Use classroom simulator or vehicle mockup for initial instruction.
3. Sight up center of traffic lane several feet in front of vehicle. Do not stare at one spot or other object.
4. Do a figure eight around a two-block area to give student concentrative steering and turning practice.
5. Remind the student that the car moves in the direction that the steering wheel is turned.
6. In some instances, combine steering practice, both forward and backward, because this sometimes helps the student better understand the techniques involved.
7. In steering around curves, have the student pull down with left hand for left movements and pull down with right hand for right movements.
8. To prove need for steering control with both hands, have student steer with one hand in center of wheel. Grab wheel, and the student experiences how little control he has with one hand. Emphasize that his experience would be similar if he hit a hole, bump, an object, or had a blowout.

9. Emphasize the need to keep his eyes moving and scanning the total driving environment.
10. Use hand-over-hand technique while turning corners. Allow steering wheel to return in hand in order for front wheels to straighten. On most modern vehicles, the steering wheel returns automatically when released.

Braking Procedures

The ability to stop smoothly and efficiently represents the possession of a high degree of skill on the part of the learner. Some tips to help the teacher develop this skill in the beginner student are as follows:

1. Place a milk bottle on the floor of the car. If the car is stopped smoothly, the bottle will remain upright.
2. Place a line of stanchions on the roadway. Let the student drive toward them and stop as close to the stanchions as he can.
3. Have the student make frequent stops at trees, signs, poles, and driveways.
4. Instruct the student to use a pumping action on brake in order to retain steering control.
5. In manual-shift vehicle, compare distance brake pedal is pressed down in contrast with the clutch pedal.
6. Have student relax pressure on brake pedal a moment before the vehicle comes to a complete stop.
7. If left foot is used to brake, position the foot over the brake pedal at all times.
8. At a speed of 20 to 25 miles per hour, have the student press clutch pedal down to demonstrate that it has no braking power when disengaged.

Turning

One of the more difficult maneuvers to perform is the turning of corners. The ability to turn properly involves the relating of steering, turning, and seeing habits to the path to be followed. The following steps will be useful in teaching the beginner driver:

1. If possible, use a simulator or classroom mockup for initial learning.
2. Emphasize that a slower speed allows the driver to correct mistakes, whereas at faster speeds the prompt correction of faulty action is severly limited.
3. Stop the car in the middle of a turn (when no traffic is present) and have students observe position of car in relation to lane and opposite position where another vehicle might be positioned.
4. Emphasize that to turn left or right the driver's vision should be concentrated on the intended path of travel, and the steering wheel is moved approximately one full revolution.

5. When releasing wheel to straighten up, never take hands off wheel. Some pressure should be exerted in order to eliminate straightening up too fast.
6. Use small chalkboard in car and draw path vehicle should travel. Have students commit the procedure to memory. Ask student to talk his way through turn.

Maneuvering

Ability to maneuver the car in a variety of traffic situations is dependent upon the fundamental skills developed by the student. The following are points that may be emphasized by the teacher in an effort to develop maneuvering ability in the beginner:

1. Vehicle control through slow speeds should be emphasized. Student should learn to make car inch along by slight accelerator pressure or slipping the clutch in a manual-shift vehicle.
2. In all maneuvers the left foot should be placed over the brake pedal; in a manual-shift car the left foot should remain on the clutch throughout the maneuver.
3. Reverse turning should be taught at the end of each car move. In other words, when the car is stopped, the wheels are always pointed in the direction of the path to be taken next (but not for left turn).
4. Most maneuvers should be performed initially on wide streets and then proceed to narrow, more heavily traveled streets.
5. Initial position of car in all maneuvers should be stressed as important to successful performance.
6. The student should stop during a maneuver in order to retain control and observe vehicle position.

PARALLEL PARKING. One of the more difficult maneuvers to perform is that of parallel parking. To park successfully the student must (1) know how to control the vehicle, and (2) know an accepted parking procedure. General points that will assist the teacher in presenting this lesson are as follows:

1. If possible, use simulator or classroom mockup to learn parking procedure. Range may be used also to eliminate initial external interference.
2. Use small magnetic traffic board in car to demonstrate procedure.
3. Have student *stop* the vehicle when it is at a 45-degree angle. This serves as his cue to reverse turn and gives student an opportunity to assess vehicle position.
4. Do initial practicing with no other vehicle present on street; or use one vehicle to park behind or in front of; emphasis is on learning the procedure and vehicle control.
5. Choose parking spaces that are somewhat longer than needed during first attempts to park.

6. Have students observe from the curb while another student demonstrates. This helps in gaining understanding of wheel movements and vehicle position.
7. Emphasize that beginning position is very important in parallel parking.
8. Place a strip of tape on the top of the dash area at a 45-degree angle to the axis of the vehicle. When tape is parallel to curb, it is the cue to reverse turn. This might be used to advantage by a smaller person who cannot observe out of rear and side windows.
9. Place a strip of tape vertically at the lower center of the rear window. Have student back, holding the wheel turned sharply right until the car behind appears in the rearview mirror to the left of the tape. This could also be used to advantage by a smaller person.

ANGLE PARKING. Although angle parking is simpler than parallel, there are several problems that could develop. The suggestions that follow should help the teacher in presenting this procedure:

1. Make certain that the vehicle is slowed down to a safe control speed.
2. Have student select parking space considerably ahead of time.
3. Position the car four to five feet from the cars parked along the street.
4. In backing out, have the student go about halfway and stop in order to check traffic. Also, this gives traffic an opportunity to see you.
5. Have left foot poised over brake for necessary sudden stops.

City Driving

There are no specific methods that would adequately explain to a student how to drive in city traffic. However, the following are presented with the thought in mind that the instructor shall use them to advantage when the need arises.

1. Try to create an awareness of common city traffic hazards by showing an appropriate film.
2. Assign the students to make surveys of city traffic.
3. Try to create a relaxed but alert atmosphere when the student is driving.
4. Plan routes where initial traffic confusion is held to a minimum.
5. In rural areas, combine highway and city driving by traveling to a nearby community where a variety of city traffic problems exist.
6. Emphasize the development of proper seeing habits.

Highway Driving

The application of operational and perceptual skills to the open highway is much more complex and demanding than normally admitted by the average driver. Therefore more attention should be given to this all-important aspect of driving in the driver education programs of the nation. The following are suggested as being helpful to the instructor when dealing with this type of driving lesson:

1. Maintain an initial maximum highway speed of 40 to 50 miles per hour.
2. Reemphasize need for keeping line of vision high and eyes moving.
3. Observe other vehicles in relation to the ground (highway surface).
4. Select a highway that has sufficient width in order to help student gain confidence in steering control.
5. Choose highway routes where traffic is smooth and efficient. Try to avoid highways where large volumes of commercial traffic are present.
6. In following other vehicles, teach students to stay well behind the vehicle ahead. The 2–12–adjust method should be learned for car-following purposes.
7. Have students observe other vehicles to check position in lane, speed, and courtesy measures.

PASSING. Passing of another vehicle is one of the most dangerous maneuvers in driving. Care should be exercised in the practicing of this maneuver. Some helpful suggestions follow:

1. Let the students review and study the passing maneuvers by viewing the Ford *Passing* film.
2. Do beginning practice on divided highway to avoid oncoming traffic.
3. If two driver education vehicles are available, let them pass one another on the highway.
4. Perform a "dry run"—that is, have the student perform the maneuver on a highway where there are no vehicles. This allows student to learn the procedure before attempting to apply it.
5. Be sure the student is able to see the car passed in rearview mirror before returning to right lane.
6. Have student sound horn before move is made to left lane. This alerts the driver being passed before your vehicle moves into his blind spot.
7. Always use signals to communicate the fact that you are changing lanes to left—then right.
8. When changing lanes, have the student make a (1) mirror check, (2) visual check, (3) signal, and (4) positive maneuver.

METHODS FOR SIMULATION LESSONS

Teachers of driver and traffic safety education have been using simulator instruction for over two decades in an effort to educate better traffic citizens. All investigations concerned with establishing the effectiveness of simulation systems have resulted in positive encouragement of such programs. For example, a recent study states that "intergroup comparisons on road test scores strongly suggest that simulator instruction over-all transfers positively to actual driving performance."[3]

The methods involved in the successful use of a simulation system are many and varied. A thoughtful instructor does a great deal more than show a programed film. The following are some methods being used by simulation instructors across the country:

1. Turn the film sound off, and let students drive through the film, following the action without the aid of verbal narration.
2. From time to time run film on manual. The teacher may now check only those items singled out as problems to students. This would be done most often in a review lesson.
3. Use film strip or slides to help illustrate specific points that students do not seem to grasp.
4. Use slides of local environment which match simulator scenes.
5. Use a sound film to enhance certain lessons.
6. After simulator lesson go to laboratory vehicle for additional practice. Do this on the same or following day.
7. At points, turn off film and discuss application of procedures or concepts presented.
8. Have student prepare lesson plan of film presentation.
9. From time to time give a short test on knowledge, procedures, or nomenclature.
10. Lead a group discussion on film content.

METHODS FOR MULTIPLE-CAR LESSON

Mass teaching in laboratory instruction involving the use of multiple-car driving ranges has proved to be an effective approach to the preparation of beginning driving students. As mentioned in a previous chapter, there are several advantages realized in the use of such a practice driving program.

All of the methods identified as practical and successful in the dual-control method may also be applied on the driving range. However, there are several additional methods and techniques that need to be identified as unique to instruction given on a driving range.

1. Give each car on the driving range a call number to simplify communicating with each driver.
2. Install adequate communications system in each vehicle. Two-way short-wave radio seems best.
3. Check out each student when new exercise is presented.
4. During initial lessons have all vehicles driven in the same direction.
5. During initial lessons have all cars stop when one car stops.
6. Use check list to assess student performance on each exercise.

[3] Richard Bishop, *Evaluating Simulator Instruction for Accomplishing Driver Education Objectives* (Tallahassee, Fla.: The Florida Institute for Continuing Studies, 1963), p. 17.

7. Move from one area of the range to another in order to observe drivers from different vantage points.
8. Evaluate individual students who seem to be having difficulty.
9. Assign each driver to preplanned exercises each day. This should be based on evaluation of previous accomplishments.
10. When not on the range, use dual-control vehicles. This is to comply with state regulations and for safety.

SPECIAL METHODS

In addition to the methods already identified in the previous sections, there are several unique methods being used by driver educators in an effort to develop competent new drivers. Each of the following may be used in concert with those methods already mentioned in an attempt to enhance teacher effectiveness and student progress.

Skill Test

There are various skill tests that may be used to help students develop vehicle control and sharpen perceptual abilities. Such tests are generally conducted in an isolated parking lot, driving range, or in a low-traffic area. The skill tests most commonly used are as follows:

1. Driving in straight line—forward and backward.
2. Steering in limited space.
3. Stopping from 20 miles per hour.
4. Parking parallel.
5. Determining front and rear limits.
6. Measuring braking distance.
7. Maneuvering straight ahead with left turn in limited space.
8. Driving through barricade course forward and backward.

Left-Foot Braking

Most drivers use the right foot for braking, but some drivers prefer to use the left foot. This seems to be an acceptable practice if the driver feels relaxed and confident in the use of the left foot. Therefore it is suggested that such a person be allowed to continue this parctice. However, if left-foot braking is taught, the person should be instructed to keep the left foot poised over the brake pedal in a ready position at all times. Brakes can be adjusted so that if slight pressure is applied no brake drag occurs nor are brake lights activated. The teacher should be aware of any licensing restrictions before teaching left-foot braking.

376

Commentary Driving

Several years ago the practice of commentary driving emerged from the experience of the London Metropolitan Police Driver School. This is fundamentally a plan in which the student talks or comments about his observations made while behind the wheel.

The teacher tends to assume that what he sees in the traffic scene the students see also. This is not always true. The commentary technique permits the teacher to know what the student actually sees. The driver comments on anything in the traffic environment that might have a bearing on his driving. These would include other drivers, pedestrians, signs, signals, or traffic patterns developing up ahead. If possible, a course should be developed to cover about a 15-to-20-block route. Each situation, sign, anticipated circumstance (an example, presence of pedestrians), and so on, should be assigned a point value. Therefore each student would begin with the maximum number possible. As items are neglected in the student's commentary, points are deducted from the total points possible. A rating scale should be set up in order to evaluate student perfromance as (1) excellent, (2) above average, (3) good, (4) below average, and (5) failure.

The instructor should use this method only after the student has gained a bit of confidence in his driving. It is obvious that commentary driving would do much toward improving the student's powers of observation and attention to the traffic scene.

Strategic Driving

The safe driver operates his vehicle with a well-defined plan and interest to avoid emergency situations in the traffic pattern. This procedure is referred to as *strategic driving*.[4] Basically this approach calls for anticipating and avoiding emergency situations. This is accomplished through the application of the three principles of (1) preparation, (2) anticipation, and (3) emergency.

Preparation refers to the selection of best routes, planned rest pauses, allowance for time interruptions, and the application of a tactical solution to problems. *Anticipation* relates to the actions and expectations of other drivers. The strategic driver anticipates the moves of the other driver by full attention to the driving task. Moreover, every effort is made to communicate with other motorists by use of horn, headlights, brake lights, and proper signals. The third principle, *emergency*, is concerned with the development of safe driving habits to avoid being caught with no place to go in case of an emergency, learning what to do when confronted with an emergency, and practicing on such maneuvers. In this last instance, practice would be accomplished through vicarious experiences. There are several good films dealing with meeting emergency situations.

[4] Theodore Kole and Harold Henderson, "Strategic Driving," *Safety Education* (April 1962), pp. 3-6.

Perception

Many drivers become involved in traffic accidents because of an inability to perceive and interpret input data being received by the eyes. It is possible to train the driver's eyes to "see" better the traffic environment. The following are three methods suggested for this purpose.

FLASH-FILM TECHNIQUE. This is a method that enhances seeing through the showing of a film strip of scenes depicting a variety of traffic situations. Each situation is set up on a before-and-after sequence basis. The student is shown an initial scene, then the screen is blocked out while the following scene is rolled into place. The student is given a predetermined amount of time to view the "what could happen" scene. Usually this is less than a full second. After viewing the scene, the student determines what the proper response to this observed predicament would be. There is a suggested correct response to each film strip frame. The advantages of this method are as follows:[5]

1. It reduces driver mistakes through prior association.
2. It stresses the necessity of 100 per cent attention to the important task of driving.
3. It motivates trainee interest in accident awareness.
4. It helps develop mature attitudes in our younger drivers.
5. It promotes student participation.
6. It is compatible with any teacher's schedule and is low in cost.
7. It trains visual perception and increases visual field.

PERCEPTION OF DRIVING HAZARDS. This method is similar to the preceding one. However, the film strips are not developed on a before-and-after basis. The student sees only what can happen for a specified period of time. Emphasis in this method is placed on the class making a group decision of correct response. This series of film strips was developed by the Center for Safety, New York University, under a research grant from the Shell Oil Company.[6]

FORD SERIES. The Ford Motor Company has developed a series of film strips that assist the beginner driver in the development of visual perception. Basically the film strips are designed to develop specific driving skills but have the added benefit of sharpening the driver's perceptual abilities. These film strips are as follows:[7]

1. *Basic Passing*
2. *Hazard on the Side*
3. *Oncoming Car*
4. *Being Passed*
5. *Urban Passing*

[5] Safety Education Films, Inc., *Safer Driving* (Minneapolis, Minn.: Safety Education Films, Inc., 1956), pp. 10–11.

[6] Center for Safety Education, *Perception of Driving Hazards* (New York: New York University, The Center, 1958).

[7] Ford Motor Company, *The Passing Series* (Dearborn, Mich.: The Company).

Skill Films

It is possible to develop motor skills through the use of films. Although this approach has not been thoroughly explored, Brody demonstrated in a recent study that related driving skills could be taught through the use of specially produced films.[8] The skills taught were (1) starting the engine, (2) moving the car forward and backward, and stopping, (3) performing the X-turn, and (4) parallel parking.

This method has been explored in some schools, and the instructor has available a set of special films or slides that assist in the teaching of fundamental skills. Investigations have revealed that "there is little doubt about the effectiveness of films in teaching perceptual motor skills."[9]

Figure 13-2. Instrumented Vehicle for Use in Practice Driving Lesson (Courtesy Drivex Corporation, Mountain View, Cal.)

Drivometer

Vehicle tracking and speed control are related to driver ability. An instrument has been developed to help train and evaluate drivers.

[8] Leon Brody, "A Study of the Learning of Selected Driving Skills Through Exposure to a Specially Produced Motion Picture Film," *Traffic Safety Research Review*, 5, (June 1961), pp. 25–29.

[9] William H. Allen, *Audio-Visual Communication Research* (Santa Monica, Calif.: System Development Corporation, 1958), p. 11.

The "drivometer" developed by Traffic Safety and Highway Improvement Department, Ford Motor Company, and the University of Michigan gives evidence of being a valuable piece of equipment in a driver education program. The variables recorded by the drivometer are trip time, accelerator reversals, brake applications, speed change, steering wheel reversals, running time, steering reversals per minute, and speed changes per minute. By having such an instrument, it is possible to evaluate day by day the student's ability to coordinate the vehicle controls.[10]

LEARNING ACTIVITIES

1. Develop a teacher aid that would be useful in presenting practice-driving lessons.
2. Develop a check list that could be used by students who are observing another student practice drive.
3. Draw a map of the area close to the school. Develop a two-mile test course where students may be checked on the use of the commentary driving technique.
4. Participate in a panel discussion on the topic "The Use of Driving Range or Simulators in Laboratory Instruction." The teacher will make the specific assignment.
5. Write a term paper on the subject, "Improvement of Perception Through Driver Education Instruction."

SELECTED RESOURCES

Aetna Life & Casualty. *Teacher's Manual—Aetna Drivotrainer System.* Hartford, Conn.: Aetna, 1975.

Allstate Insurance Company. *Teacher Manual for Link-Allstate Driving Simulator System*, Northbrook, Ill.: Allstate, 1974.

Bishop, Richard. *Case Studies of One Car Accidents Involving Young Drivers.* Tallahassee, Fla.: The Florida Institute for Continuing Studies, 1963, p. 41.

____. *Evaluating Simulator Instruction for Accomplishing Driver Education Objectives.* Tallahassee, Fla.: The Florida Institute for Continuing Studies, 1963, p. 17.

Brody, Leon, "A Study of the Learning of Selected Driving Skills Through Exposure to a Specially Produced Motion Picture Film," *Traffic Review,* 5 (June 1961), pp. 25-29.

Ford Motor Company. *The Passing Series.* Dearborn, Mich.: The Company.

Highway Users Federation for Safety and Mobility. *How to Handle Driving Emergencies.* Washington, D.C.: The Federation, 1970.

Kole, Theodore, and Harold Henderson. "Strategic Driving," *Safety Education,* (April 1962), pp. 3-6.

National Research Council. Transportation Research Board. *Driver Performance Studies.* Washington, D.C.: The Board, 1975.

Platt, Fletcher N. *Traffic Safety Research—A Unique Method of Measuring Road, Traffic, Vehicle and Driver Characteristics.* Dearborn, Mich.: Ford Motor Company, 1962, pp. 10-13.

Roberts, H. J. *The Causes, Ecology and Prevention of Traffic Accidents.* Springfield, Ill.: Charles C Thomas, Publishers, 1971.

[10] Fletcher N. Platt, *Traffic Safety Research—A Unique Method of Measuring Road, Traffic, Vehicle and Driver Characteristics* (Dearborn, Mich.: Ford Motor Company, 1962), pp. 10-13.

Chapter 14

Materials and Equipment
for Laboratory Instruction

OBJECTIVE: The student will be able to identify and select appropriate materials and equipment for dual-control, simulation, and multiple-car laboratory instructional programs.

In the conduct of a driver education laboratory program, the teacher must provide an enriched and stimulating program of instruction if the objectives of the program are to be achieved fully. To accomplish this objective the instructor, in a large measure, relies upon suitable instructional materials and appropriate equipment. The proper use and application of these instructional aids determine their motivational value. As the teacher anticipates the purchase of materials and equipment, consideration must be given to the question: What should be the basis for selecting new materials and equipment? In part this question may be answered by giving thoughtful attention to the following guidelines:

1. Be selective, for there is a wide variety of instructional materials from which to choose.
2. Choose materials and equipment that will help meet the learning goals of the course.
3. Consider the creativity and experimentation inherent in teaching when selecting aids to learning.
4. Select materials and equipment with high motivational value.
5. Choose materials and equipment that accomplish something no other learning aid can.
6. Purchase safety equipment (for example, first-aid kit, fire extinguishers, and so on).

The enrichment of learning on the part of the beginner student is one of the objectives of the driver education teacher. This chapter is designed to help the teacher do a better job of selecting materials and equipment that will motivate the student to want to be a good traffic citizen. Moreover, another major purpose of the chapter is to acquaint the instructor with a variety of materials and equipment, and where these may be obtained.

CRITERIA FOR SELECTION

In Chapter 10, a number of guidelines are presented that will assist the teacher in making appropriate selections of classroom materials. Those same criteria will also apply to the selection of materials to be used in the laboratory phase. However, the following criteria will be of particular value in selecting materials and equipment for behind-the-wheel instruction:

1. Does the material follow standards established by national and state policy organizations?
2. Are materials and equipment available from reputable publishers or manufacturers?
3. Does the material or piece of equipment help accomplish some objective that other material or equipment cannot?
4. Are materials up to date with present current philosophy of the traffic safety movement?
5. Will materials and equipment be used enough to justify expenditure of funds?
6. Are materials written by recognized authorities in the traffic safety field?

INSTRUCTIONAL MATERIALS

The teacher of driver education should be familiar with a variety of instructional materials. Because of the great volume of materials available today, the instructor must be selective. Listed in the following sections is a representative group of materials that are appropriate for use in laboratory instruction. Also, sources are listed to advise the teacher relative to the availability of these materials. It is suggested that the teacher develop a personal professional library containing copies of all mentioned publications.

Driving Guides

The driving guides developed in Chapter 12 are a very detailed series of daily lesson plans. Several other guides are available from various sources, including some state departments of education.

The better-known guides are the following:

1. State of Illinois. *Driver Education for Illinois Youth.* Springfield, Ill.: Safety Education Section, Office of Superintendent of Public Instruction, 1972.
2. State of Iowa. *Driver Education for Iowa Schools.* Des Moines, Ia.: Department of Public Instruction, 1971.
3. State of Kentucky. *Driver Education Guide.* Frankfort, Ky.: Department of Education, 1971.
4. State of Louisiana. *Driver and Traffic Safety Education Performance Curriculum.* Baton Rouge, La.: Department of Public Education, 1971.
5. State of Maryland. *Curriculum Guide for Driver and Traffic Safety Education.* Baltimore, Md.: State Department of Education, 1971.
6. The Commonwealth of Massachusetts. *Driver and Traffic Safety Education Curriculum Guide.* Boston, Mass.: Department of Education, 1971.
7. State of Michigan. *Driver Education Programming.* Lansing, Mich.: Department of Education, 1970.
8. State of Minnesota. *Guidelines for Driver Education and Traffic Safety.* St. Paul, Minn.: Department of Education, 1970.
9. State of Wisconsin. *Wisconsin Driver and Traffic Safety Education Guide.* Madison, Wis.: Department of Public Instruction, 1970.
10. State of Wyoming. *Resource Materials for Teaching Driver Education.* Cheyenne, Wyo.: Department of Education, 1972.

Basic References

Instructors of driver education should be familiar with a number of basic references that will help in the planning and teaching of practice driving lessons. Following is a list of textbooks and supplemental references that driver education teachers will find useful in the organizing of a laboratory program. Each of these texts and references can be used also for classroom instruction as discussed in Chapter 10.

TEXTBOOKS. The following textbooks used in high schools across the country contain sections related to behind-the-wheel instruction.

1. American Automobile Association. *Sportsmanlike Driving* (Sixth Edition). New York: McGraw-Hill Book Company, 1974.
2. Bishop, Richard, et al. *Driving: A Task Analysis Approach.* New York: Rand McNally & Company, 1975.
3. Center for Safety Education. *Driver Education and Traffic Safety.* Englewood Cliffs, N.J.: Prentice-Hall, Inc., 1967.
4. Halsey, Maxwell N., et al. *Let's Drive Right.* Glenview, Ill.: Scott, Foresman and Company, 1972.
5. Paulowski, J., et al. *Tomorrow's Drivers.* Chicago: Lyons and Carnahan, 1971.
6. Strasser, Marland K., et al. *Driver Education: Learning to Drive Defensively.* River Forest, Ill.: Laidlaw Brothers, Publishers, 1973.

SUPPLEMENTAL REFERENCES. There are a number of supplemental references that contain valuable information for the teacher to use in doing a better job of organizing and teaching behind-the-wheel lessons. These include the following:

1. Aaron, James E., and Marland K. Strasser. *Driving Task Instruction—Dual-Control, Simulation, and Multiple-Car.* New York: Macmillan Publishing Co., Inc., 1974.

2. American Driver and Traffic Safety Education Association. *Policies and Guidelines for Driver and Traffic Safety Education.* Washington, D. C.: The Association, 1974.

3. American Medical Association. *Alcohol and the Impaired Driver.* Chicago: The Association, 1968.

4. Automotive Safety Foundation. *A Resource Curriculum in Driver and Traffic Safety Education.* Washington, D.C.: The Foundation, 1970.

5 Brody, L., and H. J. Stack. *Highway Safety and Driver Education.* Englewood Cliffs, N.J.: Prentice-Hall, Inc., 1954.

6 Center for Safety Education. *Perception of Driving Hazards.* New York: New York University, The Center, 1958.

7. Finch, John R., and James P. Smith, Jr. *Psychiatric and Legal Aspects of Automobile Fatalities.* Springfield, Ill.: Charles C Thomas, Publisher, 1970.

8. Forbes, T. W. (ed.), *Human Factors in Highway Traffic Safety Research.* New York: John Wiley & Sons, Inc., 1972.

9. McKnight, A. James, and Bert B. Adams. *Driver Education Task Analysis, Volume I: Task Descriptions.* Washington, D.C.: Department of Transportation HS800-367 (November 1970).

10. McKnight, A. James, and Alan G. Hundt. *Driver Education Task Analysis, Volume III: Instructional Objectives.* Washington, D.C.: Department of Transportation PB202-247 (March 1971).

11. National Committee on Uniform Traffic Laws and Ordinances. *Model Traffic Ordinance.* Washington, D.C.: The Committee, 1968.

PERIODICALS. The periodicals identified in Chapter 9 will from time to time contain valuable articles that the teacher should use in the enrichment of his personal background. Moreover, some articles will be suitable for study by the students.

COMPLETE SOURCES

In order to give the teacher complete information as to where various texts, references, and other instructional needs may be obtained, the following sources are listed with complete addresses.

American Optometric Association
7000 Chippewa Street
St. Louis, Missouri 63119

Center for Safety
New York University
New York, New York 10036

Ford Motor Company
The American Road
Dearborn, Michigan 48121

Illinois Office of Education
Safety Education Section
100 N. First Street
Springfield, Illinois 63706

Iowa Department of Public Instruction
Driver and Safety Education Section
Des Moines, Iowa 50319

Kentucky Department of Education
Driver Education Section
Frankfort, Kentucky 40601

Laidlaw Brothers, Publishers
Thatcher and Madison Streets
River Forest, Illinois 60305

Louisiana Department of Education
Safety Education Section
Baton Rouge, Louisiana 70804

Lyons and Carnahan
2500 Prairie Avenue
Chicago, Illinois 60616

Macmillan Publishing Co., Inc.
866 Third Avenue
New York, New York 10022

McGraw-Hill Book Company
330 W. 42nd Street
New York, New York 10022

U.S. Department of Transportation
400 Seventh Street, S.W.
Washington, D.C. 20590

Prentice-Hall, Inc.
Englewood Cliffs, New Jersey 07632

Safety Center
Southern Illinois University
Carbondale, Illinois 62901

EQUIPMENT

For a practice-driving program to be effective, it is necessary for the teacher to have and use the needed equipment. In any laboratory course, whether it is chemistry, physics, or home economics, equipment plays a major role in the presentation of basic ideas and the expression of particular concepts. In the conduct of a driver education laboratory program, learning is enriched and the development of motor skills furthered through the use of appropriate equipment. Moreover, the student is motivated and challenged to do a superior job if he is enrolled in a course in which equipment is available to motivate student interest.

Sufficient funds should be allowed for the purchase of needed equipment when yearly budgets are planned. If budget planning is accomplished on a long-range basis (three to five years), the instructor should be able to acquire necessary equipment without overspending in any one year. Therefore, as suggested earlier, by careful planning and budgeting, a laboratory program will become well equipped over a relatively short period of time.

The following section identifies the equipment considered basic to the conduct of behind-the-wheel instruction. In addition, sources are listed from which the instructor may obtain descriptive materials of equipment desired.

Basic Vehicle Equipment

Every driver education vehicle needs to be outfitted with basic equipment. This equipment is vital in the conduct of the program and in some instances serves to protect the instructor.

PRACTICE-DRIVING VEHICLE. An initial consideration must be the car used for practice-driving purposes. This car should have four doors and be in good mechanical condition. It may be a new or used vehicle. It is suggested that the car have an automatic transmission; however, if more than one car is available, one could be a manual shift. Methods of obtaining practice-driving cars are discussed in Chapter 6.

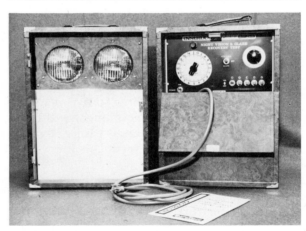

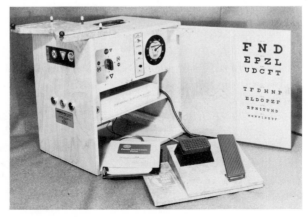

Figure 14-1. Equipment for Laboratory Instruction (Courtesy Bumpa—Tel, Inc.)

Vehicles used in laboratory programs should be well equipped. Certain pieces of equipment have *instructional* value, whereas others are principally used for *safety*. In some states various pieces of equipment are required by law. Instructors should check state guides for this type of information. The basic equipment needed for instruction and safety in laboratory programs are as follows:

1. Dual controls
   a. Brake—bar type, hydraulic, or cable
   b. Clutch (if manual-shift car is used)
   c. Accelerator
   d. Decelerator
2. Seat belts—front and rear, shoulder harness
3. Two side rearview mirrors
4. Two inside rearview mirrors (one for student, one for instructor)
5. Small portable fire extinguishers
6. First aid kit
7. Two cushions—for drivers of small stature
8. Pedal extension—for short drivers
9. Toggle switch
10. Tire-changing equipment
11. Stanchions—for skill exercises
12. Brake reaction detonator
13. Steel tape
14. Stop watch
15. Mechanical-jerk recorder
16. Caution signs for practice area
17. Small portable chalkboard
18. Drivometer
19. Vehicle identification signs

Vehicle Use

The driver education car is a mobile classroom. The teacher should conduct his classes with the same standards that apply to all classes in the school curriculum.

Practice-driving lessons should be taught and supervised in a serious manner. Student conduct should be controlled in order for each lesson to be fully understood and practiced by each student. To eliminate many distractions, student books, coats, and so on, should be placed in the car trunk during the class period.

Vehicle Maintenance

Driver education vehicles should undergo a continuous program of maintenance. Periodic lubrication, oil changes, tire checks, and cleaning should be established on a predetermined schedule. Provisions should be made to house the car, and repairs should be taken care of immediately. A good maintenance program for driver education cars is basic in the interest of safety.

VEHICLE IDENTIFICATION. Each driver education car should be properly identified. The various states have individual requirements for vehicle identification. In some instances the vehicle must be so identified as to have signs visible from both the front and back. In other cases all visible signs must be on the sides of the car or on the top and front. Therefore it is best to contact the appropriate state agency for such information. When courtesy credit identification is allowed, it should be limited to a single line in which the letters do not exceed 1½ inches in height, and in no case are they to be larger than those identifying the school.[1]

Sources of Equipment

There are a number of manufacturers of laboratory equipment. The teacher should be aware of these and have access to descriptive materials on the equipment desired. The following are representative manufacturers of equipment needed for a good laboratory program. The instructor should contact these, requesting materials and pricing information.

Bumpa-Tel, Inc.
P. O. Box 611
Cape Girardeau, Missouri 63701

Education Device Company
Driver Testing and Training Equipment
Tecumseh, Michigan 49286

Instructive Devices, Inc.
147 Armistice Boulevard
Pawtucket, Rhode Island 02860

Intext
Driver Testing Equipment Division
925 Oak Street
Scranton, Pennsylvania 18515

Minnesota Automotive, Inc.
502 Patterson Avenue
Mankato, Minnesota 56001

Scheib Industries, Inc.
305 Hall Street, Box 244
Charlotte, Michigan 48813

Stromberg Hydraulic Brake
and Coupling Company
5453 Northwest Highway
Chicago, Illinois 60630

C. G. Zaun Sales
1340 Winchester Avenue
Glendale, California 91201

SPECIAL EQUIPMENT

The previous section identified numerous pieces of equipment that are basic to the conduct of a quality practice-driving program. In addition, there are several items of a special nature that need to be called to the attention of the driver educator. These are discussed briefly in the following sections.

Simulator

As discussed in Chapter 11, the use of a simulation system to develop operational skills and perceptual process has advanced in

[1] National Commission on Safety Education, *Policies and Practices for Driver and Traffic Safety Education* (Washington, D.C.: National Education Association, 1964), p. 29.

388

recent years to become a standard method for laboratory instruction. The key component piece of equipment in such a system is a simulator. This is an electromechanical device that simulates the interior of a vehicle from the driver's point of view. Figure 14-3 depicts one of the simulators used by schools in the conduct of a simulated practice-driving program. The Aetna Drivotrainer and Link Driving Simulator System are the principal simulators used by schools today. Both systems are available through Doron Precision Systems, Inc., Binghamton, New York.

Driving Range

A driving range can be thought of more as a facility rather than equipment. However, because it is necessary in the development of a multiple-car laboratory program, it is included with the discussion of practice-driving equipment.

The driving range provides all types of driving experiences for the student in an off-the-street protected area. The basic exercises taught are described in Chapter 13, and a layout of a model driving range is shown in Figure 11-3. Since there are no established national construction specifications for multiple-car driving ranges, those instructors interested in the construction of such a facility should contact their respective state department of education for information concerning recommended construction standards. The state supervisor of driver education should have this information available or know where the desired information may be obtained.

Blowout Simulator

By using a blowout simulator, the teacher can give the student experience in responding to tire failure, both front and rear. Although this equipment can be used in a basic dual-control program, it is probably best to incorporate its use into a multiple-car program when a driving range is available.

Equipment for Handicapped

More and more the teacher of driver education is being called upon to cooperate with special education teachers in the development of practice-driving programs for handicapped students. There is an increasing interest on the part of schools to make driving instruction available for handicapped students. The availability of federal funds for equipment suggests an expanded interest by federal agencies in driver education for the handicapped.

Fundamental to the development of such a program is the installation of adaptive equipment for the handicapped. The type of equipment necessary will depend on the type of handicap. Therefore the

Figure 14-2. Typical Vehicles Available to Secondary Schools, Universities, and Colleges for Driver Education Programs (Courtesy Ford Motor Company, Civic and Governmental Affairs)

Figure 14-3. Components of Driving Simulation System (Courtesy Doron Precision Systems, Inc.)

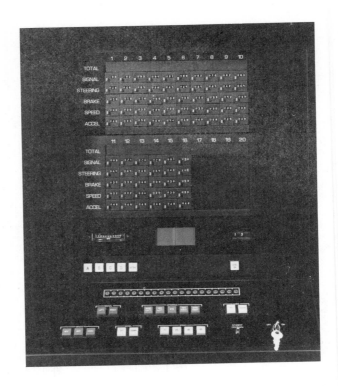

Figure 14-3. *(Continued)*

instructor should know the various types of devices available in order to equip properly the practice-driving vehicle. These devices are hand controls, such as auxiliary accelerator and brakes.

To obtain complete information concerning vehicle equipment for handicapped students, contact the following manufacturers:

FIRMS THAT MANUFACTURE AND/OR DISTRIBUTE CONTROLS FOR HANDICAPPED DRIVERS

Blatnik Precision Controls, Inc.
1523 Cota Avenue
Long Beach, California 90813

Drive-Master Corp.
61 North Mountain Avenue
Montclair, New Jersey

Ferguson Auto Service
1112 North Sheppard Street
Richmond, Virginia 23230

Gresham Driving Aids
P.O. Box 405
Wixom, Michigan 48096

Handicaps, Inc.
4345 South Santa Fe Drive
Englewood, Colorado 80110

Hughes Hand Driving Controls, Inc.
Tevis Bridge Road
Lexington, Missouri 64067

Kroepke Kontrols, Inc.
104 Hawkins Street
Bronx, New York 10464

Manufacturing & Production Services
2932 National Avenue
San Diego, California 92113

Mross Inc.
Star Route, Box 42
Elizabeth, Colorado 80107

Nelson Products
5690-A Sarah Avenue
Sarasota, Florida 33577

Smith's Hand Control
1472 Brookhaven Drive
Southaven, Mississippi 38671

Thompson Hand Control
4333 N.W. 30th Street
Oklahoma City, Oklahoma 73112

Trujillo Industries
5726 W. Washington Boulevard
Los Angeles, California 90016

Wells-Engberg Co.
P.O. Box 6388
Rockford, Illinois 61125

Wright-Way Inc.
P.O. Box 907
Garland, Texas 75040

LEARNING ACTIVITIES

1. Evaluate five of the textbooks used in high school driver education classes. Prepare a report for the instructor on your conclusions.
2. Write 10 state departments of education requesting copies of their state curriculum guide for driver education. Evaluate each and make an oral report to the class, summarizing the merits of each.
3. Write 15 of the sources identified in the chapter from which free or inexpensive materials are available. Request sample copies of specific materials from each source. Summarize each publication on an annotated bibliography card. Keep these materials as the beginning of a resource library.
4. Develop a set of policies governing the use of a driver education vehicle. Make enough copies for each member of the class.

SELECTED RESOURCES

Aaron, James E., and Marland K. Strasser. *Driving Task Instruction—Dual-Control, Simulation, and Multiple-Car.* New York: Macmillan Publishing Co., Inc., 1974.

American Automobile Association. *Practice Driving Guides.* New York: McGraw-Hill Book Company, 1972.

Halsey, Maxwell W. *Skillful Driving.* Garden City, N.Y.: Doubleday & Company, Inc., 1960.

Highway Users Federation for Safety and Mobility. *The Driving Simulator Method.* Washington, D.C.: The Federation (April 1970).

____. *The Multiple-Car Method.* Washington, D.C.: The Federation (March 1972).

Lauer, A. R. *The Psychology of Driving.* Springfield, Ill.: Charles C Thomas, Publisher, 1972.

National Highway Traffic Safety Administration. *Driver Training Simulators, Ranges and Modified Cars.* Springfield, Va.: National Technical Information Service, 1971.

State of Illinois. *Teacher Preparation in Utilizing Driving Simulators.* Springfield, Ill.: Safety Education Section, Office of Education, 1972.

Strasser, Marland K., et al. *Driver Education: Learning to Drive Defensively.* River Forest, Ill: Laidlaw Brothers, Publishers, 1973.

Chapter 15

Methods of Evaluation for Classroom and Laboratory Instruction

OBJECTIVE: The student will be able to demonstrate the ability to develop an evaluation program for dual-control, simulation, and multiple-car instruction.

As an accepted part of American education, driver education is subject to the same evaluative standards, methods, and techniques as other school subjects. Evaluation must be carefully planned in order to assess effectiveness of program planning and teaching. Such a program, to be effective, should allow for adjustments in teaching plans.

Evaluation is the process by which the value or quality of a particular program, idea, or experience is assessed. *Evaluation is, in essence, the process of determining the success or value of either a person's performance or a planned activity. It often includes the degree or level of success or failure.* [1] These procedures may range from subjective judgments to conclusions reached through formal research. All driver education programs should include provision for evaluating the extent to which its objectives are being achieved. It is important that these objectives be clearly stated and consistent with accepted education philosophy and sound administrative practice.

---

[1] Marland K. Strasser et al., *Fundamentals of Safety Education* (New York: Macmillan Co., Inc., 1973), p. 449.

Evaluation Methods

Each teacher of driver and traffic safety education should have an understanding of how to use evaluation procedures and be able to ascertain the scientific worth of test instruments and measurement devices. Instructors should become adept in applying evaluation procedures in order to consume as little teaching time as possible. Tests and other evaluation methods also should be used as instructional devices whenever possible, because many aspects of driver education are adaptable to this practice.

The teacher of driver education should be familiar with evaluation methods as applied to all aspects of the program. Such methods are listed according to three major classifications.

1. Quantitative measurements:
   a. Written tests of general knowledge
   b. Driving skill tests
   c. Tests of attitudes
   d. Hazard recognition tests
2. Qualitative measurements:
   a. Observations of pupil behavior and attitude
   b. Simple ratings by teacher
   c. Check lists, course records, and reports
   d. Student self-appraisals
3. Evaluation by research:
   a. Analysis of driver behavior and reactions
   b. Public opinion polls
   c. Local and state accident trends
   d. Follow-up studies

Evaluation of driver education may be considered in terms of (1) ultimate objectives, including accident prevention; (2) program characteristics and practices; and (3) immediate outcomes or student learnings.[2] The following is a discussion of these three applications of evaluative criteria.

Evaluation of Objectives

The ultimate objectives of a driver education program are (1) preparation for one to live safely in a complex traffic environment, and (2) the development of efficient, responsible, and informed traffic citizens. Therefore "if we want to measure how safe an individual is or, rather, what degree of safe behavior characterizes him, we have to devise test situations that we can describe in some detail so that other

[2] National Commission on Safety Education, *Policies and Practices for Driver and Traffic Safety Education* (Washington, D.C.: National Education Association, 1964), p. 43.

Figure 15-1. Class Participating in Motorcycle Skill Development Drill (Courtesy Safety Education Program, Texas A & M University)

investigators or observers can duplicate them."[3] Methods of evaluating objectives may include scales and written tests of the kinds used in evaluating the program:

1. Opinions of driver education graduates, parents of students or former students, police officials, traffic court judges, and motor vehicle administrators.
2. State department of education annual and special reports plus statistical compilations.
3. Periodic comparative analysis to assess the value of driver and traffic safety education in reducing accidents and moving traffic violations, utilizing:
   a. Permanent school records of student achievement in driver education.
   b. National Safety Council, insurance, industry, or other valid accident data.
   c. Government agency statistics and records on accidents and moving violations.
   d. National Highway Traffic Safety Administration accident data.
   e. Use of public opinion surveys or sampling to assess the support of the public.

In the application of these methods it should be borne in mind that statistical analysis should be based on acceptable scientific procedures to assure their validity and should consider such variables as sex, age, and driving exposure.

[3] National Commission on Safety Education, *Tests and Evaluation Methods Used in Driver and Safety Education* (Washington, D.C.: National Education Association, 1959), p. 6.

Evaluation of Program Characteristics

Driver and traffic safety education programs vary considerably in quality and scope. Therefore if the immediate and ultimate outcomes of a driver education program are to be realised, the program should be based on a sound organization that lends itself to specific evaluative criteria. The fact that a program of driver education tends to meet fundamental evaluative criteria is not a guarantee that the immediate and ultimate objectives will be accomplished. The following is an identification and brief discussion of six standards with which individual programs may be compared.

ORGANIZATION. In the conduct of a driver education program it should be so organized as to do the following:

1. Accommodate all eligible students in a comprehensive classroom and laboratory program.
2. Provide permanent school records on achievement in driver education.
3. Allow time for the conduct of a quality program (preferably a full semester).

INSTRUCTIONAL STAFF. A staff should be provided to accommodate all students desiring to enroll in driver education. In addition to specialized training in driver education, each staff member should meet the same professional teacher education qualifications expected of teachers in other disciplines.

NATURE OF CURRICULUM. The driver education program should provide for satisfactory articulation of classroom instruction with laboratory program. In addition, emphasis should be placed on the importance of personal responsibility, development of attitudes, consideration toward others, respect for traffic law enforcement, and pride in safe and courteous driving.

INSTRUCTIONAL ACTIVITIES. If the program of driver education succeeds, it is dependent in large measure on the planning done by the teacher. Therefore adequate planning and preparation by the teacher should be consdiered as vital to the conduct of a quality program.

PHYSICAL FACILITIES. Adequate classroom and laboratory facilities are essential in the conduct of a driver education program. Such facilities and equipment as necessary should be provided to meet instructional needs in driver and traffic safety education.

METHODS OF EVALUATION. A variety of evaluative techniques and methods should be used in carrying out the driver education program. Several of these are identified later in the chapter.

SELF-EVALUATION. The driver educator should evaluate himself throughout the semester because he works so much without supervision. Teachers should have criteria of which they are constantly aware and self-test themselves. Teaching procedures, lesson planning, clarity of directions, and precision of speech are examples of teacher practices that need self-evaluation.

398

Evaluation of Student Learnings

Immediate outcomes refer to what the student learns throughout the course of his education as a beginner driver. Obviously, learning must reflect competence in the components of the driving task. These components should be derived from a job analysis of the driving task as a whole—that is, the functions from operative skills to social and civic responsibilities of the driver. The task analysis in Chapter 4 lends itself toward serving this purpose. Today, through increasing research evidence and expert opinion of people in behavioral, physical, and biological sciences, it is evident that evaluation of both classroom and laboratory instruction should be directed at assessments of driver capabilities in the following areas.

KNOWLEDGE. A basic knowledge of vehicles, drivers, highways, rules of the road, and safe driving practices (including those involved in emergency situations) is essential to safe and efficient motoring on public highways. Knowledge of this type can be assessed through the following:

1. Standard or teacher-made written test.
2. Visual tests of recognition and understanding of traffic hazards.
3. Instructor observations or ratings in class and in the practice-driving car.

PSYCHOPHYSICAL FUNCTIONS. Evaluation of driver abilities as related to psychophysical performance should be attempted by the teacher. Emphasis should be placed upon assessment of perceptual abilities, speed, and accuracy in decision making, and speed and accuracy of correct responses to decisions. Such determination can be made through use of the following:

1. Appropriate vision-testing equipment.
2. Tachistoscope for improvement of ability to recognize traffic cues.
3. Film strips or slides (can be homemade) in flash presentations.
4. Teacher observations while practice driving.
5. Individual exercises to improve peripheral vision and depth perception.
6. Commentary driving technique.

OPERATIONAL SKILLS. The rating of behind-the-wheel skills is a fundamental evaluation approach utilized by most driver education teachers. Assessment of operational skills may be accomplished through the following:

1. Ratings of student performance while driving (on a street or range), including basic and advanced maneuvers; and specially designed risk-taking exercises.
2. Evaluation of performance in simulators, including fundamental driving skills and maneuvers, plus response to emergency situations.

In each category evaluations may be made by the teacher using (1) available check lists or rating scales, as well as (2) instrumentations now becoming available for purposes of more objective assessment of specific operational skills by the student in the car.

ATTITUDES AND PERSONALITY FACTORS. The importance of attitudes and personality to safe driving has been repeatedly verified through research.[4] Attitudes and personality are related and, therefore, cannot be separated. Both can be changed or modified through educational processes and other measures. It should be understood, however, that this is a difficult process. At the present time evaluation of driver attitudes and personality factors can be accomplished with varying degrees of success through the following:

1. Paper and pencil tests and other kinds that have been validated with some degree of confidence. (A great deal more work is needed in this area.)
2. Systematic observation of driver behavior by qualified teachers, guidance counselor, and school psychologists.

It is desirable for the teacher to use both of these approaches in an effort to appraise attitudes and related personality factors.

SIGNIFICANCE OF EVALUATIVE DETERMINATIONS

Evaluative techniques and methods cover a wide range of measurement potential. Therefore the teacher should be aware of the many ramifications of a good evaluation program. Moreover, the significance of data obtained through evaluation processes should be understood by the teacher.

Evaluation is a function that needs to be employed both during and after a semester. During a course, evaluation will provide an analysis of student progress so that appropriate guidance can be provided and adjustments made in the program and procedure. At the end of a course, evaluation is necessary to determine which students have satisfactorily completed the program and are presumably prepared to be safe drivers. Also, evaluation should be used to determine whether changes may be desirable in a given program and program objectives?

Subsequent, long-range appraisals of driver education must be scientifically designed and carried out under carefully controlled conditions to establish the persisting effects of the course. In other words, how well do driver education graduates tend to perform as traffic citizens over extended periods of time? Is there need for modification of program standards, and perhaps of broad objectives?

Many researchers now recognize that long-range effects of driver education, particularly with reference to accident reduction, defy

[4] U.S. Department of Health, Education, and Welfare, *The Role of Human Factors in Accident Prevention* (Washington, D.C.: The Department, 1960), pp. 33–52.

demonstration because of the countless variables involved, such as exposure to hazards. These effects must and can be assumed by insistence on quality in the organization, administration, and teaching of driver and traffic safety education. The rationality of this approach needs to be effectively conveyed to educational authorities who may be uncertain of the place of driver education in the school curriculum. Also, it must be effectively conveyed to noneducational agencies, such as insurance groups, motor vehicle departments, U.S. Department of Transportation, and legislative bodies, whose assistance is essential for the improvement and expansion of driver education.

In the final analysis, the active support of civic groups and the general public is critically needed. For on this broad base will depend the success of program acceptance by official and nonofficial agencies, as well as by the entire education profession. Needless to say, this support can be secured through the influence of driver education programs of high quality. Only as driver educators evaluate and reevaluate their work can quality programs be assured.

Criteria for Measuring Safe Behavior

In an effort to measure the effectiveness of a driver and traffic safety education program, it is well for the instructor to use some basic guidelines or criteria. Such would allow him to examine the method(s) as to validity, reliability, and usefulness under school conditions. Regardless of whether the measurement would be of behavior, knowledge, or some other factor, one may apply essentially the same criteria. The following criteria are for use by the teacher to determine the evaluation method desired:[5]

1. Is the measure in reality a measure of the degree to which the person used an available procedure of relatively low risk in preference to procedures involving higher risks? In other words, is it a valid measure of safe behavior?
2. Does the method include the specification of the nature of the situation in which the measure was taken?
3. Does the method include the specification of the condition of the individual at the time the measures were taken?
4. Can the measuring conditions be duplicated at another time or by another person? If so, do the repeated measures correlate reasonably highly with the initial measure?
5. Is the measure one that a teacher can use under school conditions?

PROGRAM EVALUATION

There are several methods and techniques to assist the teacher in his effort to evaluate the effectiveness of a driver education program. In some instances the local school system may devise a set of evaluative measures based on national and state recommendations, whereas

[5] National Commission on Safety Education, *Tests and Evaluation Methods Used in Driver and Safety Education*, p. 9.

many other schools may choose to use guidelines available from national organizations or their respective state department of education. If evaluative criteria is not being used, the following are suggested as helpful in program evaluation.

Evaluative Criteria

Published but once every 10 years, the best set of guidelines developed for program evaluation is called *Evaluative Criteria*. Specifically, this is Section 4-5 of the complete volume by the same name. These criteria are used nationally and recognized by most educators as the best overall group of rating materials assembled to assess program and curriculum content. Copies of section 4-5 Driver and Traffic Safety Education (1969) may be obtained from:

> Evaluative Criteria
> National Study of Secondary School Evaluation
> Washington, D.C. 20036

Check list—School Safety Education

Another excellent guideline available for use in program evaluation is *Checklist—School Safety Education*. It evaluates the school's total safety program and has a complete section devoted to driver education. Copies of the check list may be obtained from:

> American Driver and Traffic Safety Education Association
> 1201 Sixteenth Street, N.W.
> Washington, D.C. 20036

Driver Education Status Report

Another accepted technique to help evaluate the driver education program of a school is to compare it with the published report of the *Driver Education Status Report*. By so doing, the teacher and administrator can gain an understanding of how their program rates with others reporting in the program sponsored by the National Safety Council.

The annual report may be requested from:

> National Safety Council
> 444 North Michigan Avenue
> Chicago, Illinois 60611

Classroom Evaluation

A substantial amount of the evaluation done in driver education is accomplished through the classroom phase of the program. In general, instruments used for evaluation purposes are classified as either (1) knowledge, (2) attitude, or (3) skill-measurement devices. The first two are more appropriate for classroom purposes; however, it is possible to assess certain driving skills in the classroom setting.

Brody has stated that "at various stages in driver education it is desirable to take inventory of student progress. This not only indicates the readiness of pupils to advance from one state of learning to the next but also, if properly used, provides an incentive for further learning."[6]

In recent years, research has provided several tests and scales of various kinds that assist the teacher in evaluating student knowledge, values, and attitudes. The following sections identify valid and reliable testing instruments that can be used with confidence by the driver education teacher.

Knowledge

There is an abundance of tests available in the knowledge area. Some tests are standard (scientifically devised for general use), whereas other tests are to be used with a particular text. The following are some of the better-known tests:

1. National Test in Driver Education, Center for Safety, New York University, Washington Square, New York, New York 10036.
2. Knowledge Test for Automobile Drivers, Center for Safety, New York University, Washington Square, New York, New York 10036.
3. Tests designed to accompany text: *Driver Education and Traffic Safety*, Prentice-Hall, Inc., Englewood Cliffs, New Jersey 07632.
4. Tests designed to accompany text: *Let's Drive Right*, Scott, Foresman and Company, Glenview, Illinois 60025.
5. Tests designed to accompany text: *Sportsmanlike Driving*, McGraw-Hill Book Company, New York, New York 10020.
6. Tests designed to accompany text: *Driver Education: Learning to Drive Defensively*, Laidlaw Brothers, Publishers, River Forest, Illinois 60205.

Attitude

Even though the assessment of driver attitudes is important to the determination of fitness to operate a motor vehicle safely and efficiently, it is an area where a great deal of work needs to be undertaken toward the development of valid attitude tests and scales. The first two on the following list are the attitude scales being used most today, and the others identified have been useful to researchers and guidance personnel in working with problem students who in general tend to have poor attitudes toward driving.

[6] Leon Brody and Herbert J. Stack, *Highway Safety and Driver Education* (Englewood Cliffs, N.J.: Prentice-Hall, Inc., 1954), p. 353.

1. Siebrecht Attitude Scale. Center for Safety, New York University, Washington Square, New York, New York 10036.
2. L-C Verbal Response Categories. (Driving Attitude Inventory.) Department of Psychology, Iowa State College, Ames, Iowa 50010.
3. Minnesota Multiphasic Personality Inventory, 304 East 45th Street, New York, New York 10017.
4. California Test of Personality, California Test Bureau, 5916 Hollywood Boulevard, Los Angeles, California 90028.
5. Rogers Test of Personality Adjustment, Association Press, 291 Broadway, New York, New York 10007.

Skill

It is possible to assess certain driving skills in a classroom setting. Apart from fundamental driving skills it is possible to evaluate vision and psychophysical skills. To evaluate driving skills a simulator would be used. With vision and psychophysical skills other classroom equipment would be needed. The following are sources of different types of evaluating equipment.

1. Simulator information available from: Aetna Life Insurance Company, 151 Framington, Hartford, Connecticut 06115.
2. Simulator information available from: Allstate Insurance Company, Allstate Plaza, Northbrook, Illinois 60062.
3. American Automobile Association, 8111 Gatehouse Road, Falls Church, Virginia 22042.
4. Bausch and Lomb Optical Company, Rochester, New York 14600.
5. Heyimum-Bylt, 4945 Edgemere Avenue, Baltimore, Maryland 21233.
6. Keystone View Company, Meadville, Pennsylvania 16335.
7. Porto-Clinic Instruments, Inc., 298 Broadway, New York, New York 10017.
8. Titmus Optical Company, Inc., Petersburg, Virginia 23802.

LABORATORY EVALUATION

The evaluation of practice-driving experiences is necessary to determine student performance and progress. This may be accomplished by utilizing a variety of check lists and road performance tests. Also available are skill test exercises that are helpful in determining a student's ability to control a vehicle. The following tests are among the most frequently used in laboratory program evaluation by driver educators across the nation.

Skill Test

Skill tests are designed to evaluate ability in performing certain driving procedures under controlled conditions. Most tests allow for measurement of fundamental skills—that is, steering, stopping, backing, vehicle control, and so on. The following are two skill tests used extensively today.

Figure 15-2. In-Car Evaluation by Instructor Is Vital for Student Development (Courtesy Marshall University)

1. Trucks and Tractor-Trailer Units, Institute for Public Safety, The Pennsylvania State University, University Park, Pennsylvania 16802.
2. Motor Vehicles, National Junior Chamber of Commerce Teen-age Road-E-O, 21st and Main Street, Tulsa, Oklahoma 74114.

Road Performance Test

Road tests measure the driver's ability to apply fundamental driving skills to a variety of traffic environments. Both operational and perceptual skills may be assessed in road performance tests. The following are road tests available for use in driver education classes.

1. Aaron-Strasser Driver Performance Test—page 267 of this text. The San Dale Press, Bloomington, Illinois 61700.
2. The Abercrombie Driver Test: Rating Scale for Automobile Driver Skills, Center for Safety, New York University, Washington Square, New York, New York 10003.
3. The McGlade Road Test for Use in Driver Licensing, Education, and Employment. Center for Safety, New York University, Washington Square, New York, New York 10002.
4. Road Test—In Traffic for Selecting and Training Truck Drivers. Institute for Public Safety, The Pennsylvania State University, University Park, Pennsylvania 16802.
5. Road Test—In Traffic for Testing, Rating, and Training Passenger Car Drivers. Institute for Public Safety, The Pennsylvania State University, University Park, Pennsylvania 16802.
6. Giving and Scoring Tests. Traffic Institute, Northwestern University, Evanston, Illinois 60204.
7. Driver Education Teacher Performance Inventory. Teacher College, Columbia University, New York, New York 10027.

LEARNING ACTIVITIES

1. Develop a program of evaluation to identify the effectiveness of the organization of driver education courses. Include plans for the continuous evaluation of instruction throughout one semester.
2. Prepare a questionnaire that could be given to graduates of a driver education course to determine course effectiveness.
3. Review three research studies on driver education. Be prepared to report to the class on the nature of the investigations, methods of inquiry, findings, and conclusions.
4. Study the results of the Driver Education Status Report for a recent year. Determine how a classroom and laboratory program could be improved by using the recommendations of the Report.
5. Write a report on the topic, "The Value of Evaluating Driving Education Programs."

SELECTED RESOURCES

Aaron, James E., and Marland K. Strasser. *Driving Task Instruction—Dual-Control, Simulation, and Multiple-Car.* New York: Macmillan Publishing Co., Inc., 1974.

Adams, James Ray. *Behind-the-Wheel Self Analysis in Driver Rehabilitation.* New York: Continental Research Institute, 1971.

Bishop, Richard W. *Evaluating Simulator Instruction for Accomplishing Driver Education Objectives.* Tallahassee, Fla.: The Florida Institute for Continuing University Studies, 1963.

Edwards, Dorothy S., et al. *Evaluation of Laboratory Methods for the Study of Driver Behavior: The Relation Between Simulator and Street Performance.* Silver Spring, Md.: American Institutes for Research, 1969.

Greenshields, Bruce D., and Fletcher N. Platt. *Objective Measurements of Driver Behavior.* New York: Society of Automotive Engineers, Inc., 1964.

Lindauer, Larry B. *A Multivariate Study of Objectively Measured Driver Performance Factors of High School Students.* Unpublished dissertation, Southern Illinois University, 1972.

Platt, Fletcher N., and G. J. Feddersen. *Driver Performance: The Search for Objective Measurements.* Dearborn, Mich.: Ford Motor Company, 1964.

Quensel, Warren P. "An In-Car Evaluation Instrument," *Journal of Traffic Safety Education.* California Driver Education Association, Vol. XXIII, No. 2 (January 1976), pp. 15–16.

Ritzel, Dale O. *The Development of An Evaluation Instrument Relating to Teacher Effectiveness in Driving Simulation.* Unpublished dissertation, Southern Illinois University, 1970.

Road Research Laboratory. *Research on Road Traffic.* London, England: The Laboratory, 1965.

Stack, Herbert J. "A Resume and Evaluation of Research on The Teaching Effectiveness of Simulated Driving Experiences and Conventional Driver Education Methods," *Traffic Safety Research Review.* Vol. 3, No. 4 (December 1959).

Strasser, Marland K., et al. *Fundamentals of Safety Education.* New York: Macmillan Publishing Co., Inc., 1973.

EXTENDING DRIVER AND TRAFFIC EDUCATION

The final section of the text is concerned with the extending of driver and traffic safety education. The important areas of public relations, adult education, research, The Highway Safety Act and the future of driver education are presented.

Included in Part IV are the following chapters:

Chapter 16

Public Relations for Driver and Traffic Safety Education

OBJECTIVE: The student will be able to identify, select, and apply appropriate techniques to the development of a sound public relations program for driver education.

There is no subject area in the secondary school curriculum that has made more rapid progress than driver education in terms of program expansion to meet the needs of such a great percentage of the student population. This rapid growth is substantially because driver education provides an educational experience that is essential to successful living in the United States today. Also, this instruction is universally desired by both students and parents alike. Virtually every study that has been made shows that both student and parent groups recommend that the schools provide a complete program for driver education to be made available to every student approaching legal driving age.

The driver education student learns techniques and develops behavior that will lead to his personal safety on the highways, will contribute to his pleasure and economy in driving, and will help him to become a more useful citizen in a society that has grown almost wholly dependent on the automobile for its social and economic survival. However, if driver education is to continue to grow and meet the needs of all students, the nature, scope, and objectives of the program must be better understood by all segments of society. This must include the educators who are responsible for the total educational program of the student. It must include the citizens of every community who support and finance the program and the agencies who sponsor and support driver education. Also, it must include the legislators who make provision for the financial support that makes possible a complete program of driver education for all students. Every driver education teacher has a personal responsibility for informing these groups of the full meaning of driver education and to create a favorable opinion in their minds with regard to the values of this educational program for the youth of the nation. Smith stated, ". . . Despite all the talk, I often think that many teachers still don't fully realize the importance of public support or how to go about building it."[1]

School public relations was defined by Bortner as "a process which seeks to foster understanding and friendly *working* relations between schools and their communities."[2] This chapter will be devoted to a consideration of the many facets of public relations responsibilities of driver educators in achieving these friendly working relationships with the community. It will also be concerned with the manner in which public relations in driver education must be approached if we are to have an informed public who will provide the support necessary to insure continued growth and improvement of the program. The following Principles of School Public Relations are listed here to serve as guidelines for public relations activities in driver education:[3]

    A. School Public Relations Must Be Honest in Intent and Execution.
    B. School Public Relations Must Be Intrinsic
    C. School Public Relations Must Be Continuous
    D. School Public Relations Must Be Positive in Approach
    E. School Public Relations Must Be Comprehensive
    F. School Public Relations Should Be Sensitive to Its Publics
    G. The Ideas Communicated Must Be Simple

CREATING A FAVORABLE PUBLIC IMAGE

A basic objective of most public relations work today is to create a favorable public image for the product, service, or candidate for which the program is designed. This must also be true of public relations activities in the interest of driver education. We must create a favorable public image with regard to the need and values of driver education instruction for the youth of the nation. The public image of driver education must be that of an academically sound program that meets a real educational need of every student. How can this be achieved? What means can be used to create this favorable public image for driver education? What are the responsibilities of the driver educator for creating this favorable public image?

[1] Lawton K. Smith, "How You Can Build Public Support for Driver Education," *Safety Education* (April 1964), p. 25.

[2] Doyle M. Bortner, *Public Relations for Teachers* (New York: Simmons-Bordman Publishing Corporation, 1959), p. 3.

[3] American Association of School Administrators, *Public Relations for America's Schools—Twenty-Eighth Yearbook* (Washington, The Association, 1950), pp. 16–33.

410

A Quality Program

The first prerequisite to the creation of a favorable public image for driver education is the development of a quality program. If anything short of quality instruction is sold to the community as a "good driver education program" the results might well indicate that driver education does not achieve its stated objectives of developing sound, socially responsible attitudes and a high degree of driving skills on the part of the student. "To a far greater extent than is true with other school offerings, driver and traffic safety education is in the public eye. Citizens see student groups and the instructor daily in the practice driving car. Of vital importance, therefore, is the quality of the program as seen by the public and as experienced by those who will enroll in it."[4]

Quality instruction means that the program must have a well-developed course of study designed to meet program objectives and not merely an expedient means of completing the minimum standards in either classroom or laboratory instruction. The best in both text and supplementary materials should be provided the students. The necessary teaching aids and equipment must be made available for instructional purposes. Instruction in driver education must be scheduled in the same manner as other classes. The objective of scheduling must be effectiveness of instruction and not merely reaching a large number of students for a minimum expenditure of funds in a minimum period of time. And, finally, the driver education class must be conducted by an enthusiastic, interested, and well-prepared teacher who understands the need for well-trained traffic citizens. Unless these conditions are met, we will not have a quality product for which to solicit public support.

An Effective Teacher

There is no course in the curriculum that can meet its objectives without an effective instructor in charge. This is particularly true in driver and traffic safety education. The classroom instruction provides a large measure of attitude development and behavioral change that requires an informed, inspired, and motivated teacher. The laboratory experience requires effective teaching knowledge and skills that also demand a very high degree of patience and judgment on the part of the teacher.

To teach a course in driver education that will create a favorable public image requires a dedicated and well-informed person. The driver education teacher must set a good example for his students and present a good example to the community. The teacher whose driving habits set a poor example to his students loses their respect, and they feel that he is teaching them to "do as I say, not as I do."

[4] American Driver and Traffic Safety Education Association, *Policies and Guidelines for Driver and Traffic Safety Education* (Washington, D.C.: The Association, 1974), p. 28.

411

This destroys the favorable image of driver education in the eyes of the students. A teacher whose driving habits represent a poor example to the community is the poorest possible example of public relations. This fact is well expressed in the infrequent but still quite damaging newspaper headlines that announce the citing of a driver education teacher for a traffic violation. It makes no difference that the facts are frequently inaccurate and that perhaps the driver is not actually a driver education teacher. The headlines relating to improper use of a driver education car create an improper image. It becomes axiomatic that an effective teacher who sets a good example for both the students and the community becomes an essential element of good public relations for driver education.

Getting Active Participation

A key factor in obtaining active support for any program is the involvement of all interested agencies and parties in the planning and execution of the program, whatever it might be. This is particularly true of driver education because its objectives are of such vital importance to so many segments of the community. The driver educator must be sensitive to all of the publics involved. The development of a sound curriculum and the actual instruction are primarily the responsibility of the instructor. However, it is desirable to involve interested parties of private, public, quasi-public, and public support agencies in the framing of broad objectives of the program and the execution of the process of obtaining substantial public support.

The assistance of all school personnel from students through administration and the parents should be solicited to determine actual instructional needs and to assure that the driver education program becomes an integral part of the total educational experience of every student. At the same time it is desirable to bring representatives of the P-TA, service clubs, safety council, and all other interested community groups and agencies into the planning of the support phase of the program. If community organizations and private agencies with an interest in traffic safety are to function successfully in the development of support for the expansion and improvement of driver education, they must be informed with regard to program objectives and content so that they will have a complete understanding of the program for which they seek support. There is no better way to provide this background of understanding than by including them in program planning. It then becomes the responsibility of the driver education teacher to bring these people together and provide them an opportunity to learn the nature and scope of the driver education program and to permit them to lend their suggestions as to how they can operate most effectively to support this activity.

Providing Recognition

It has been said many times that safety can be achieved if we do not care who receives the credit. This has been well recognized by

412

safety professionals for many years. It becomes their responsibility to do a substantial portion of the work essential to the development of accident prevention programs, but they can not achieve safety by their work alone. It is only through the full cooperation of many segments of the community that the desired conditions of safety will be achieved. To obtain this community cooperation it is necessary to provide means of recognition for those persons and organizations who willingly give of their time, energies, and monies to provide program support.

Recognition for participation in support of driver education activities can take many forms. It may be a certificate presented to an automobile dealer who has loaned cars to the school district for the laboratory phase of the program. It may be mention in a news story of an organization that has provided necessary support for a particular activity. It may be a letter of appreciation to a guest speaker who has made a significant contribution to the instructional program in the classroom. These are all aspects of good community relations. However, it must be remembered that these examples represent only a few of the hundreds of good public relations activities carried on by driver educators. These types of recognition give cooperating groups a feeling that driver education is "their program." Then they will have a proprietary interest in its excellence and success and will work willingly toward these goals. Driver educators must remember that one of the most important aspects of public relations for driver education in the community is the development of a broad base of participation of all interested segments of the community in the planning and development of support for the program, followed by proper recognition for their contribution.

Professional Organizations

Professional organizations in driver education have an important responsibility for creating a favorable public opinion for driver education in the secondary schools. In Chapter 5 the nature and scope of professional organization were discussed in detail. However, it is well to specify their role in public relations at this time.

Local, state, and national driver education associations have been organized throughout the nation to bring together those teachers who are working in driver education for the primary purpose of providing opportunities for professional growth. Their programs and activities represent the best thinking of leading driver educators in America today. It is through these organizations that improvement in instructional procedures and strengthening of program objectives must come. Also, they must provide leadership in the formulation of desirable legislative programs for the improvement of quality in the instructional program and the standards of qualification for teachers in the field. Also, these organizations provide unique opportunities for good public relations with all elements of the community. They should invite representatives of community agencies to participate in the activities of their organizations both as speakers and as observers. Through the conduct of their association activities they are educating these people to the objectives of driver education. Far too many of the associations meet only with their own members. They should invite teachers from other subject areas, counselors, administrators, P-TA members, public officials, members of sustaining organizations, and other community agencies to meet with them at their regular meetings. The leadership personnel of professional driver education associations have the responsibility of making the program of their association an important phase of the broader program of creating a favorable public opinion of driver education.

ESTABLISHING A PUBLIC RELATIONS CONTACT

There are many ways in which the driver education instructor or the safety supervisor can establish a public relations contact with the numerous groups who have an interest in driver education. It would be impossible to list all of the techniques of obtaining public support that have been used in working with these diverse groups. However, in the following pages, some proven techniques of developing a favorable public image for the program will be described as indicative of the approach that must be made. In actual practice, the number of ways that community relations for driver education can be used will be limited only by the ingenuity of the individual driver educator.

For the purpose of this discussion, the areas of public relations contacts will be divided into three important areas as follows: within the school, within the community, and with cooperating agencies and resource persons.

Within the School

It is quite evident that the opposition to driver education in the secondary schools has come from within the schools.[5] This means that driver education supporters have done their poorest job of public relations with their own colleagues and other persons closely related to the school itself. They have failed to inform these people of the objectives of driver education and to explain its significance in the educational experience of young people. They have also failed to impress them with the academic significance of driver education and that a properly taught course can be a real challenge to the students. It is essential that driver education teachers inform all persons closely associated with secondary school education concerning the true nature of driver education.

Community relations contacts within the school should include students, teachers, adult driver education classes, administrators, and board members, parents of driver education students, and Parent-Teacher Associations.

[5] Los Angeles City School Districts, Evaluation and Research Section, *Research Report No. 229, An Evaluation of Some Aspects of the Driver Training Program in Los Angeles City High Schools* (Los Angeles: The School Districts, 1961), pp. 19–43.

414

STUDENTS. The greatest potential long-range source of strong public support for driver education are the more than 3 million students who complete driver education in the public schools each year.[6] If they receive a well-organized and properly presented instructional program that they feel has made a real contribution to their total educational experience, they will be future supporters of the program. If they receive inadequate and uninspired instruction that merely qualifies them for an insurance reduction or a driver license at an earlier age, they will become an important segment of the opposition to the program.

Because of the importance of the automobile in their future lives, the students have the right to expect the driver education class to be a meaningful experience. Because of the close personal contact with the instructor in the laboratory phase of the class, they form definite patterns of thinking about the value of the program. An inspired and interested teacher who will help them develop the technical skills to become an efficient driver and provide the inspiration to develop desirable patterns of socially acceptable use of the automobile can impress upon them the importance of driver education. Students are, however, extremely sensitive to the uninterested and uninformed classroom teacher who "shows movies" rather than preparing a meaningful lesson. They are also repulsed by the disinterested laboratory teacher who is obviously teaching after school or on Saturday merely to augment his regular salary and has little capacity or interest in developing excellence in driving performance. The driver education teacher has a unique opportunity to develop a favorable public image of the driver education program among students by his own interest and example and by providing a challenging and worthwhile program of instruction.

TEACHERS. Classroom teachers, particularly of the traditional academic subject areas, have been among the most persistent opponents of driver education in the secondary schools. There are a variety of reasons for this. Many of them have been assigned, against their will, to provide either classroom instruction or laboratory instruction as a matter of scheduling or other administrative convenience when they had little or no training or interest in the subject area. The classes have often been scheduled in such a way that driver education instruction has interfered with the achievement of the objectives of the program of their own primary interest. Sometimes they are required to take instructional time from their own classes to teach driver education. In many cases these teachers have not understood the purposes and objectives of driver education and have felt that it is an educational frill that has been forced on the schools. They feel that it is really a responsibility that should be assumed by the home or other community agencies. Many of these teachers have also observed poor instruction by full-time driver education teachers in some schools. These factors explain, at least in part, why numerous

[6] National Highway Traffic Safety Administration. *Statewide Highway Safety Program Assessment—A National Estimate of Performance.* (Washington, D.C.: The Administration, July 1975), p. 21.

studies have shown that the greatest opposition to driver education comes from within the teaching fraternity.

The driver education teacher has many opportunities to inform other members of the faculty of the importance of driver education. He must reflect his dedication to his field and present an instructional program that has the respect of the students in the school. He must use every opportunity to inform other faculty members of the true nature of the driver education program and to demonstrate by his behavior that the driver education teacher is a highly qualified and professional educator who is a credit to the teaching profession as a whole. Above all, he must take every opportunity to point out to other faculty members that driver education is not a threat to other areas of instruction, from the standpoint of time in the curriculum or of budget, that it will not interfere with the student's opportunity to develop academic excellence in other areas of his educational experience. Because of the opposition to driver education that has been expressed from the faculty groups in some areas, it is of utmost importance that driver educators do a superior job of public relations with this group. "You can't expect support from a faculty and administration that only dimly understand the nature and value of the course you're teaching."[7]

ADULT CLASSES. Adult classes in driver education conducted by public schools provide a unique opportunity to gain support for the high school driver education program. For most of these people, this instruction will provide the only direct contact that they have had with the schools for many years. They are strongly motivated to their task of learning to drive, or they would not be enrolled in the class. Any success that they have in learning to drive and obtaining their driver license will be identified with their contact with the schools.

A pleasant, well-prepared teacher who offers a well-organized program of driver education to adult classes can be one of the most successful public relations persons for the program. However, a terse, short-spoken, poorly prepared teacher who merely rides with the adult can be the worst of public relations persons. The high-quality instruction in adult driver education classes conducted by the secondary schools has been one of the most important factors in creating a favorable public image for high school driver education and in gaining strong community support for the program.

ADMINISTRATION. In communities where the school administrator and school board feel that driver and traffic safety education has educational merit, they usually find a way to include this instruction in the school curriculum. However, if the administrator and board members feel that driver education is an educational frill that encroaches upon the student's pursuit for an academic background, they find many reasons why they do not have the time or money to provide these classes. It is, then, very important that these persons are kept informed of the merits of high school driver education and advised of the best and most efficient means of including this instruction in the regular school program. This can be done by directing to

[7]Smith, op. cit., p. 27.

their attention current literature in the field, studies showing the values of the program, the academic basis for driver education, insurance economies of driver education instruction, and the strong parent and citizen support for the program. When classes are conducted the driver education teachers and safety supervisors should make well-prepared annual reports of progress and future needs of the program to both the superintendent and the board. Be ever mindful of the fact that driver education should be revealed always in light of its proper place in the total educational program of the school.

PARENTS. The greatest support for driver education comes from the parents of students who are eligible for this instruction.[8] This overwhelming support has been revealed in numerous studies. It is often heard that parents refuse to permit their youngsters to drive until they have completed instruction in driver education in the high schools. In many cases even strong opponents of driver education in general have demanded that their own youngsters receive this instruction in schools. This vital interest on the part of parents should form a prime target for improved effort of the driver educator to gain local support for their programs.

Too often the support of parents is assumed by the teachers, and little or no contact is made with them even though many legitimate and worthwhile opportunities for contact exist. A school open house or a parent's night provides an occasion to exhibit testing devices, simulators, and other materials and devices used in the instructional program. The parents of new students in driver education classes can be brought together in a meeting in which the teacher will explain to them the nature and objectives of the instruction and what it will do for their youngsters. This is particularly true if the school is using simulators or a range program that will most likely be totally unfamiliar to the parent.

Written communications to the parent are also important. At the beginning of the program a letter should be sent to the student's home outlining the program and its objectives and explaining to the parents the liability and insurance implications involved. Many parents expect the driver education program to develop expert drivers in the brief period of time allotted to this instruction. Because of this fact the teacher should send a letter to the parent upon the student's completion of instruction, advising the parent of the strengths and weaknesses of the student in the various aspects of driving.[9] Also, he should encourage the parent to permit the student to gain further experience in driving under his direction and to check him particularly on the points where the student has shown weaknesses in his instructional programs. These direct contacts with the parents provide a good opportunity for teachers to develop a favorable impression of the driver education course.

[8] Los Angeles City School Districts, Evaluation and Research Section, op. cit., p. 28.

[9] State Department of Education, *A Guide—Driver Education in Florida Secondary Schools, Bulletin 6* (Tallahassee, Fla.: The Department, 1963), pp. 94–95.

417

PARENT-TEACHER ASSOCIATIONS. Parent-teacher associations on the local, state, and national levels have provided strong continued support for high school driver education. The strengthening of driver education is a vital part of their national objectives, as indicated by this suggestion from their Action Program. "Support legislation and needed measures for traffic safety, such as driver education for youth."[10] The work of these groups should be recognized and their continued support should be sought.

The driver education teacher should be an active member of his local parent-teacher organization and attend all of the meetings. Many times teachers have presented interesting programs to parent-teacher groups, explaining the course and its objectives to them. It is particularly desirable to have students participate in these programs, because it enables the parents and other teachers as well to observe the interest and accomplishments of the students. It is also important to invite representatives of the P-TA to participate in professional activities of the driver education teachers. They have a great deal to contribute to the development of professional organizations, such as state and local driver education associations, and they are favorably impressed by the dedication and competence of the driver education teachers as they meet for the purpose of their own professional growth.

Within the Community

Informed community agencies and organizations have been virtually unanimous in support of driver education in the high schools. Thus the total community becomes the greatest source of support for the program. It can not be assumed, however, that all community agencies and organizations are properly informed with regard to the nature and scope of the high school driver education program. It is a responsibility of driver educators to become acquainted with community leaders and to work continuously to inform these groups about the driver education program and to advise them in any possible way. If the public relations objectives of creating a favorable public image are to be realized, this work must be done in a cooperative and positive manner and never in such a way as to invoke suspicion or unfavorable reactions from the groups with which driver educators work.

MEDIA AGENCIES. Newspapers, radio, television, and magazines have devoted a great deal of time and space to driver education. Most of this information has been developed toward the creation of a favorable public image for the program, but particularly the periodicals have directed much information in opposition. The supporters of driver education are largely responsible for the fact that greater use is not made of the media resources.

Radio and television stations make available a great amount of public service time, and the newspapers and periodicals will print

[10] National Congress of Parents and Teachers, *New Adventures in PTA Leadership and Responsibility—Action Program* (Chicago: The Congress, 1972), p. 12.

meaningful information. However, it must be remembered that all media groups are interested in materials of general interest to their viewing, listening, and reading publics. Such material should be prepared with great care so that it will provide sound information and interest all the public. Driver education teachers have many opportunities to provide programs for local radio and television stations and to obtain local stories for newspapers that will inform the public of the program. They should develop ideas of types of presentations that might be effective and discuss them with media representatives. Student participation in radio and television programs is particularly effective. Items of interest in local driver education programs are always welcome as news stories in local newspapers. National periodicals and house publications of various business organizations are possible sources of public information, but they are usually written by persons with national experience in the program because of nationwide readership. This is a field that needs greater attention by leaders in the safety field to attract greater attention and support of the program.

CIVIC, SERVICE, AND RELIGIOUS GROUPS. These groups have generally been supporters of driver education in high schools. Driver educators must work more closely with them by gaining total community support for the program. These groups exist in every community, and all of them meet regularly and are interested in obtaining a programs that will be of interest to their members. One thing that most of them have in common is their interest in youth. Many of them have specific youth activities that they sponsor on a regular basis.

Many such organizations would welcome a program to be conducted by the driver education teacher or by members of the driver education classes. Contact presidents or program chairmen of these organizations, and explain what you are doing in driver education and see if it would be of interest to their membership. When such a program is developed be sure that it is carefully planned and that it will provide both an interesting and informative meeting. Always provide such a group an opportunity to ask questions as a part of the program, because they are extremely interested. Be sure to determine the exact length of time that you will have, and plan your program to meet the time allocation. Most of these organizations are composed of busy persons who plan a definite period for the meeting and then want to leave to tend to other matters. Presenting a program to such a group that goes beyond the allotted time is poor public relations and will not create the favorable public image that you desire.

WOMEN'S ORGANIZATIONS. The Federation of Women's Clubs, National Women's Conference of Highway Safety Leaders, the Business and Professional Women's Clubs, and other women's groups have given a great deal of support to driver education, particularly in legislative matters. They have been active also in other areas of traffic safety, including effective seat-belt campaigns and their well-known program of "Go to Court as a Visitor, Not a Violator."

Because the support of women's organizations is so essential to the continued growth of high school driver education, the teacher in this area has a responsibility to inform these people of the nature and scope of the program, the problems involved, and accomplishments that are being realized within the specific community. They should be encouraged to participate in special meetings dealing with driver education and should be informed at the local level of legislation that is proposed or introduced into the state legislature and how it will affect the high school program. It is only when the women's organizations are well informed that they will be able to lend their support to driver education effectively.

TEEN-AGE CONFERENCES. It is a curious fact that adults have long criticized the driving habits of teen-age drivers, yet in so many instances refused to provide driver education classes in high schools to improve teen-age driving, especially when the teenagers have asked for it repeatedly. Virtually every teen-age traffic safety conference recommends that a complete program of driver education instruction be provided to the student as he approaches the legal driving age. This desire of teen-agers for proper instruction has been a strong factor in support of the program in many schools. If potential young drivers resented or did not want the instruction, it is certain that they would express themselves, and in the face of such opposition driver education would most likely soon be removed from the curriculum. At the present time there are few subjects that would be taken as an elective by such a great percentage of the students as driver education.

The first teen-age conference of record was held in Yolo County, California, in 1945.[11] The first statewide teen-age conference was held in Colorado in 1954. Since that time there have been hundreds of such conferences held throughout the country on state, national, and local levels. Although these conferences are largely student-directed and most participants are students, it still provides adults an opportunity to provide excellent leadership in placing the importance of traffic safety in general and the high school driver education program in particular before students. This continued support of the teenagers for driver education is one of the most desirable types of support we have, and every driver education instructor should work with them in any way he can.

THE DRIVER EDUCATION CAR. The driver education car is a portable classroom that moves continually through the community. The general public has an opportunity to observe the manner in which the teacher and students conduct themselves and the manner in which instruction is carried on.

The teacher should be continually aware of his responsibility to create a favorable image for driver education by the professional manner in which he conducts his class in the laboratory situation. Unfortunately this is not always done. Some poor public relations practices that have been reported occurring in driver education cars include: (1) stopping to treat the students at a doughnut shop, (2) parking on a back street for both the students and instructor to take a smoke break, (3) a seat belt hanging under the door on the teacher's

---

[11] Marland K. Strasser, "New Emphasis on Old Technique," *Safety Education* (December 1945), pp. 4–5.

side, (4) the car parked in front of a local tavern, and (5) students out of order in the back seat. Such practices create a very unfavorable opinion of driver education in the minds of persons in the community. However, if the laboratory car is used in a professional manner, with instruction being carried on as in any other school classroom, this can provide one of the best public relations media for the driver education program in the community.

Driver education cars should be used for instructional purposes only. When these cars are used for other purposes, the general public will be unfavorably impressed with the purposes and objectives of driver education. If such cars must be used for other purposes, all identification with the driver education program should be removed.

COMMUNITY FUNCTIONS. There are a large number of community fairs, exhibits parades, and similar functions conducted in all parts of the country. These activities provide an excellent opportunity for informing the public about the driver education program of local schools. Some of the activities that have been conducted in conjunction with these events have included the following:

1. A driver education float in a community parade to encourage local school officials to include instruction in the school.
2. Exhibits displaying driver testing devices and distributing literature. Students operate the testing devices and test the general public.
3. Display of trailers with driver simulators to acquaint members of the community with the nature of the program in operation at the local school.
4. Students and/or teachers located in the booth of some exhibiting agency for the purpose of distributing literature and answering questions on driver education.
5. Student participation in community vehicle safety check programs.

Of course, there are many more types of activities that have been conducted successfully. If the driver education teacher is interested in the promoting of driver education, he should be alert to these many opportunities to bring his story to the community on occasions when large groups are gathered together.

LEGISLATORS. With the increase in the number of states providing financial reimbursement for driver education and the legislation requiring driver education for youths to obtain a driver license at an earlier age, the matter of legislation has become increasingly important to persons interested in driver education. This involves a different type of community relations in working with legislators. Legislators are experienced in the many ways various organizations attempt to promote programs related to their specific interests. However, they are most interested in factual information that will help them to understand the issues, and they are vitally interested in what their constituents are thinking with regard to the issues.

On the state level the driver education teacher can be most effective working with citizen organizations interested in the promotion of driver education legislation. They can act as consultants and provide

421

valuable information to these people. On the local level they can perform a similar function with media agencies and other organizations, but they can also inform their legislators what they feel about the program. Many driver education teachers are personally acquainted with members of the legislature. If so, they should see them personally and explain the issue involved and ask their support. However, do not threaten legislators when presenting an issue. A legislator always appreciates receiving a letter thanking him for his interest when he has supported a measure that you favor.

Cooperating Agencies and Resource Persons

The driver education teacher works cooperatively with many agencies and organizations representing local, state, and national groups. Such groups have long been strong supporters of driver education and have made significant contributions to the program in many ways. They have spent millions of dollars and provided countless man-hours of service time in every phase of the program, from its early promotion to supplying materials and equipment or lecture services in the classroom.

Agencies and individuals who assist in the program should be given every recognition possible for the contributions that they make to the local classes. Every possible type of cooperation and courtesy should be extended to them by the teachers and administrators. When their services or materials are utilized, appropriate recognition should be given, and all films and other materials should be returned promptly in good condition so that they can be used by other persons. In some instances films and cars have been returned in poor and unusable conditions. It is difficult to see how friends of driver education can continue to support schools that follow such practices. These are examples of the very poorest type of public relations for the driver education program and should always be avoided.

A good public relations gesture is to write, or have your school administrator write, to the superior of the person who has worked with your program and express appreciation for the assistance and cooperation provided. This is a small gesture but it is a most effective type of good public relations.

The following paragraphs describe some of the specific public relations aspects of working with some of the most frequently encountered groups of cooperating agencies.

THE AUTOMOBILE INDUSTRY. The major automobile manufacturers and their dealers have contributed materially to the advancement of driver education. They have produced visual aids of many types, developed special equipment, and provided cars for laboratory instruction without cost to the schools. During the 1974-75 school year they provided, on a loan basis, 42,000 cars valued at about 183 million dollars.[12] From a public relations point of view it is

---

[12] Highway Users Federation for Safety and Mobility. *Highway Users Federation Reporter.* (Washington, D.C.: The Federation, December 1975), p. 4.

important that appropriate recognition be given the industry contribution to the program. Cars on loan from dealers should be used only in the driver education program, and they should be returned to the dealers in the very best of condition. Unfortunately, many cars have been so poorly maintained that the dealers have discontinued the distribution to a number of schools. It is recommended that the school arrange with the dealer an agreement for returning the cars so that the condition of the car will meet approval of the dealer. It is also desirable for the school to prepare a special certificate to be presented to the dealer in recognition of his cooperation.

THE INSURANCE INDUSTRY. The insurance industry was one of the early promoters and has been a continued supporter of driver education. Insurance firms have prepared many materials for use in driver education classes, including textbooks, pamphlets, films, and others. They also provide guest speakers for driver education classes throughout the country and have cooperated with educators in the preparation of insurance manuals for use in driver education classes. It is sound public relations to provide their guest speakers with specific topics, time, and place of guest presentations that they make to driver education classes. When they appear, the teacher should see that they receive an appropriate letter of appreciation for the contribution that they have made.

AUTOMOBILE CLUBS. Automobile clubs have done a substantial amount of promotional work in the driver education field. Over the years they have prepared teachers, developed materials, served as guest lecturers in classes, aided in the distribution of cars, and cooperated in program promotion in many ways. It is fitting that local schools make appropriate recognition of the cooperation that they make to their programs.

SAFETY COUNCILS. Obtaining public support for safety activities is a primary function of both the National Safety Council and local safety councils. Particularly local chapters of the Council have provided important community leadership in the promotion of driver education in numerous communities. It is desirable for teachers and administrators to work closely with safety council personnel in planning program expansion and improvement. Appropriate recognition should be given to the contribution that they make to the program.

PUBLIC OFFICIALS. Public officials whose responsibilities relate to traffic safety have been most helpful in the promotion and support of the driver education movement. Police agencies who make enforcement contacts with young drivers were among the first to recognize the need for this program. The courts and the driver license personnel have worked closely with teachers in the improvement of driver education instruction. Driver education students visit local courts and police offices to obtain information relating to enforcement aspects of the program. These students should be advised by their instructors with regard to proper conduct while on these visits, and follow-up letters to the officials should express your appreciation of their cooperation in helping make your instruction more meaningful to students.

The driver educator should work cooperatively with these groups and never unjustly or ill-advisedly direct criticism toward them if he expects their continued support and cooperation. A classic example of poor public relations with licensing officials was the teacher who drove his students over the route that the examiners followed in their tests. When one of the students taking the license examination was directed to make a left turn he informed the examiner, "You are supposed to turn right here." This almost resulted in legislation preventing driver education cars from traveling at any time in the areas where driver license tests were being given. This action understandably disturbed the examiners and constitutes an aggravated example of poor public relations. The manner in which most teachers work cooperatively with courts, police, and licensing agencies is a firm indication of how the support of public officials can be obtained by following sound public relations practices.

GUEST SPEAKERS. Many private citizens and public officials with specific interest in various phases of traffic control act as guest speakers in driver education classes. It is particularly important from a public relations point of view that these people make their optimum contribution to the class and that they leave the driver education classroom with a favorable image of the program.

It is desirable to meet with a guest speaker in advance of his presentation to acquaint him with the exact purpose of his presentation and outline as closely as possible the nature of the presentation you would like him to make. To ask an insurance man to talk on "Teen-age Drivers" is such a vague assignment that it leaves him in a difficult position to know what to say. If he knows that he is to deal with the various phases of automobile insurance protection as they relate to teen-age drivers, he is in a much better position to make a useful contribution to the class. These are busy men who are taking their time to be of assistance to you. Let them know just exactly what time they are to appear, where the classroom is located, how many students will be involved, how much time they will have, how much time should be devoted to questions by students, and other pertinent information that will be helpful to them. These facts should be confirmed by letter several days prior to the speaker's appearance in order to prevent any misunderstandings. Always show them the courtesy of sending a letter from either the teacher, the administrator, or both, expressing the appreciation of the school for the contribution that they have made to the class.

MEDICAL ASSOCIATIONS. The American Medical Association and its many local organizations have shown increasing interest in medical aspects of automobile accidents in recent years. These associations have an influential position in the community. They also have a common interest with the objectives of the driver education classes. It is desirable that the driver education instructor work closely with this group wherever possible. A good example of a cooperative project involving the medical association is the seat-belt campaign in which they actively participated in the early 1960s.

424

LEARNING ACTIVITIES

1. Set up guidelines to be used for the driver education public relations program in a secondary school.
2. Describe five different ways in which recognition could be given to community agencies for their support of driver education.
3. Prepare a student participation program to be presented before a local service club.
4. Describe, in detail, how you would proceed in obtaining the support of the local safety council in cooperating in a seat-belt campaign sponsored by the driver education class.
5. Write a feature story or an editorial on driver education to submit to the local newspaper.
6. Write a letter of appreciation to a guest speaker who has appeared before your driver education class.
7. Conduct a survey in your community to determine how well local citizens are informed on the subject of high school driver education.

SELECTED RESOURCES

American Driver and Traffic Safety Education Association. *Policies and Guidelines for Driver and Traffic Safety Education.* Washington, D.C.: The Association, 1974.

Bortner, Doyle M. *Public Relations for Teachers.* New York: Simmons-Bordman Publishing Corporation, 1959.

Dapper, Gloria. *Public Relations for Educators.* New York: Macmillan Publishing Company, Inc., 1964.

Los Angeles City School Districts, Evaluation and Research Section. *Research Report No. 229, An Evaluation of Some Aspect of the Driver Training Program in Los Angeles City High Schools.* Los Angeles: The School Districts, 1961.

National Congress of Parents and Teachers. *New Adventures in PTA Leadership and Responsibility—Action Program.* Chicago: The Congress, 1962.

National Highway Traffic Safety Administration. *Guide for Teacher Preparation in Driver Education: Secondary School Edition.* Washington, D.C.: The Administration (July 1974).

National Safety Council. *Driver Education Status Report.* Chicago: The Council, 1974.

Smith, Lawton K. "How You Can Build Public Support for Driver Education." *Safety Education* (April 1964), pp. 25–29.

State Departments of Education. *Driver Education Bulletins.*

Strasser, Marland K. et al. *Fundamentals of Safety Education.* New York: Macmillan Publishing Co., Inc., 1973.

Chapter 17

The Education of Adult Drivers

OBJECTIVE: The student will be able to identify various types of adult programs and determine appropriate guidelines for the organization of each.

With the continual changing in traffic laws within the various states, the ever-changing types of highway and traffic engineering developments, and the increasing complexity of traffic patterns, there is a continuous need for education and reeducation programs to meet the needs of many groups of adult drivers. Some adults are learning to drive for the first time, some are driving as a vocation, some have not adjusted to changing traffic conditions, and others have become accident repeaters or chronic traffic law violators. All of these groups need to obtain knowledge of traffic laws and safe driving practices, acquire proper attitudes of driver responsibility, and develop adequate driving skills to become successful drivers. Stack said, "Studies have shown that many adults are incredibly uninformed regarding good driving practices and the rules of the road. And research with so-called accident-repeaters—who are responsible for a disproportionately large number of accidents—discloses not only a lack of knowledge concerning good driving, but also serious weaknesses in the attitudes that are so vital to safety on the road."[1] The problems of adult drivers represent a challenge to all driver educators.

As the nation approaches the time when there will be 130 million licensed drivers, greater attention must be given to the various educational needs of the adult driving population. This need will continue

[1] The Center for Safety Education, *Driver Education for Adults* (New York: The Center, n.d.), p. 1.

to grow even if driver education becomes universal in the secondary schools of the nation. It is now an increasing concern to police officials, driver license administrators, commercial fleet operators, and other agencies interested in traffic safety. Educators must determine their responsibility for adult education and develop programs necessary to meet those responsibilities.

This chapter will consider the driver education needs for all adults including those young adults who have not received an adequate program of driver education in the secondary schools. The adult driver education program will be divided into the following phases:

1. A brief history of adult driver education.
2. Adult driver education in secondary schools.
3. Special types of adult driver education programs.
4. Educating commercial drivers.

THE EVOLUTION OF DRIVER EDUCATION FOR ADULTS

There were no formal programs of education for drivers in the early days of the automobile. The automobile was a relatively simple mechanism; there was little traffic congestion as it is known today, and the driver had to have some mechanical skill because breakdowns were frequent and repair facilities were few. Most drivers acquired what skill they possessed in a trial-and-error fashion, driving on infrequently used byways, or received meager instructions in the basic mechanical operations of the vehicle from usually unqualified friends. In order to sell cars, automobile salesmen sometimes gave meager instruction in basic operations to purchasers of their product. When mass-production techniques placed automobiles economically within the range of a large segment of the population, the inadequacies of these simple means of developing driving proficiency became evident.

As states gradually began to establish the driver license as a means of determining basic competency to drive successfully, rather than as a mere revenue measure, there was a demand for instruction that would enable the applicant to pass the driving test. Private driving schools and classes sponsored by public service organizations were established to provide this training. It was considered, however, the responsibility of the individual to obtain the driving proficiency required to pass the licensing examination.

As automobiles increased in numbers and traffic casualties began to mount, the social aspect of the problem came into focus. Both public and private agencies developed a concern for improving the quality of the driving public. Many automobile clubs, YMCA and YWCA organizations, and other service-oriented groups sponsored some type of educational programs for drivers. During the depression years of the early 1930s, some federal projects of the Work Projects Administration (WPA) were established to provide programs of education and reeducation of drivers. This program, of course, was abandoned with the termination of the WPA. Official state agencies

427

concerned with traffic safety also sponsored educational programs for drivers. During this period, the commercial driving school industry emerged. Courts set up classes to reeducate accident repeaters and chronic violators. Commercial fleet owners recognized the need for programs for their drivers to reduce the economic toll of accidents. During World War II, the armed forces became aware of the safe driving inadequacies of men inducted into the service. All of these factors, coupled with a continually mounting list of traffic casualties, clearly defined the need for organized programs of education for adult drivers. They also established the basis for the promotion of high school driver education as a means of putting better-qualified drivers on the road.

ADULT DRIVER EDUCATION
IN THE SECONDARY SCHOOLS

The public schools have over the years assumed an increasing responsibility for the education of adults and out-of-school youth. Public funds have been provided to support these programs, their staff and facilities have been made available for the conduct of adult education programs, and their administrators have assumed a responsibility for the direction of adult education. The schools have developed well-rounded adult programs not limited to one area, such as vocational, remedial, or academic subjects. The public school responsibility for adult education has been well accepted. The statement *Adult Education in the Public Schools* was jointly released in 1961 by the following national organizations: the American Association of School Administrators, the Council of Chief State School Officers, the National Association of Public School Adult Educators, and the National Congress of Parents and Teachers. In part, this statement said:[2]

> Founding our position on the truth that a society is only as sound and fine as its members, we believe that public school adult education is a logical extension of the community's educational responsibility. With wise direction, it can make a significant contribution toward sustaining and raising the quality of citizenship in this nation. This, we think, can best be done by the public schools as they provide intelligently for the functional educational needs of adults on the job, in the home, as citizens, and as they cooperatively work with community organizations in offering sound opportunities for adults to cultivate their mental, moral, and spiritual talents as individuals. This, we believe, is a public responsibility. It is also a significant and vital opportunity for the public schools of America to step up to the challenges of today's world.

The application of this position to the need for public schools to provide quality instruction in driver education for adults is recognized by driver educators. A statement relating to this position was adopted

[2] National Association of Public School Adult Educators, *Adult Education in the Public Schools* (Washington, D.C.: National Education Association, 1961), p. 8.

428

by the American Driver and Traffic Safety Education Association in June 1963. In part, this statement of the Association read:[3]

> Since every adult is a potential driver, vitally concerned with the implications of safe driving for his or her life, limb, and well-being, inclusion of driver education in the adult education curriculum is essential.
>
> Through years of experience and research, 30 hours of classroom study plus 6 hours of practice driving instruction, taught by fully qualified teachers, have been established as minimum requirements for an effective high school course in driver education. Such a course is a powerful factor in the reduction of the highway accident toll.

The schools have met the challenge of educating adult drivers in a number of ways. Many have established the recommended program for teaching new drivers, whereas others have found it necessary to reduce the classroom time. Continuation schools have provided minimum standard courses for out-of-school youth. Public schools have also offered, through adult education programs, driver improvement classes, refresher classes for licensed drivers, special classes for members of the armed services, and special emphasis on traffic laws in English-language classes for a variety of ethnic groups.

Adult Driver Education Classes

Adult education classes are usually conducted on a much less formally structured basis than a regular school program. A large portion of the classes are terminal in nature, with the student interested only in the immediate value received by him in the particular class and not in graduation credit or a future college career. However, many adult programs do lead to a high-school diploma. In most cases the student in an adult driver education class is looking toward the immediate objective of obtaining a license to drive.

Although the problems of establishing an adult driver education class are the same as in high school classes, they are frequently approached differently to meet the somewhat different objectives. In adult classes where the same standards are maintained as those in high school classes these differences are usually very minor. This section will discuss the following aspects of adult driver education classes: organization, curriculum, scheduling, teacher selection, student selection, reimbursement, and summary of the general program.

ORGANIZATION. The organization of adult classes provides essentially the same problems as in high school classes. However, this will be determined to a degree by the type of program offered. These classes should have an appropriate classroom, adequate textbooks, instructional materials, testing devices and other visual teaching aids,

[3] American Driver and Traffic Safety Education Association, *Driver Education for Adults and Out-of-School Youth.* (Washington, D.C.: The Association, 1964) (Mimeographed), p. 1.

a dual-control car, and a qualified teacher. The facilities of the high school program are usually made available to adult classes. Schools with simulators or driving ranges usually make these available to adult students. The school must make sure that they have appropriate insurance coverage and that the student has an instruction permit before he is allowed to begin lessons in the car. Appropriate records and reports should be made for adult classes, just as is done for high school classes. When possible, it is desirable to follow up the students to determine if they obtain their licenses and become successful drivers. This is an important factor in evaluating the effectiveness of adult driver education instruction.

CURRICULUM. It is desirable to follow the same curriculum in adult classes as in the high school program. However, for a number of reasons, this is often difficult to do. The basic difference is usually in the scope of the classroom instruction, which varies from none at all to classes meeting the recommended minimum standards of time allocation. The latter cases are the exception. "Because the average adult is pressed for time and anxious to learn quickly, a 20-hour intensive course in adult driver education has been developed which eliminates some of the less important items included in the longer courses."[4] Many courses do not even meet the intensive 20-hour standards. Because a 30-hour course is recognized as a basic minimum, it is obvious that most adult classes place a much lesser emphasis on the important phases of attitude development and knowledge and greater emphasis on the manipulative skills. This is one phase of adult driver education that needs serious evaluation by driver educators.

SCHEDULING. The scheduling of adult classes usually differs considerably from high school classes. The classroom work is frequently given in two- or three-hour blocks and only once or twice a week. The usual semester program is not always followed. A typical class may be scheduled in 10- or 12-week blocks. Laboratory work may be scheduled also for longer blocks of time. This provides more driving time, and the students are able to complete the course more quickly.

TEACHER SELECTION. The high school driver education teacher is frequently assigned to adult driver education classes. However, because adult classes do not always have the same credential requirements, it is instruction on a limited type of credential. Although this is done, it is not recommended. Although the high school teacher is usually best qualified, it is not in the interest of the most effective instruction to have a teacher in a full daytime laboratory program devote too many hours per week to behind-the-wheel instruction for adults. Some programs are so extensive that they employ an adult driver education teacher on a full-time basis. It is desirable for the adult program teacher to meet the same certification standards as those required in the high school classes.

STUDENT SELECTION. Students for adult classes are usually enrolled on a first-come, first-served basis. When an excessive number

---

[4] The Center for Safety Education, op. cit., p. 5

register, a waiting list is established for future classes. Most enrollees are more mature persons, usually women, who have never learned to drive but now find that it is necessary to do so. However, a number of students who were unable to take driver education in high school classes frequently enroll for the adult program. Some of the older adults have driven previously or have some driving skills and are essentially interested in refresher training or completion of their training so that they can pass a driver license examination. This difference in student composition of the adult education class requires some adjustment to differing instructional needs on the part of students.

FINANCING. The manner in which adult driver education classes are reimbursed varies with the schools and depends to a considerable degree on the manner in which adult education classes in general are financed in the various states. Sometimes they are solely a community responsibility, whereas in some cases there is state reimbursement on an attendance basis. Generally speaking, the classroom program is financed in the same manner as other adult education classes. Because of the extra costs involved in small-group instruction in the laboratory phase of the program, there is frequently a laboratory fee charged to the student. These fees vary greatly from school to school, depending on school policy and the financial condition of the adult education program. Classes are sometimes financed by a combination of a tuition fee and tax monies from the regular adult school budget. The amount of instructional time in both phases of the program is usually influenced by the amount of fees charged and the financial structure of the adult education program.

IN SUMMARY. There are over 50,000 persons who receive some driver education instruction in adult programs in the public schools each year. This represents a substantial contribution to traffic safety in the nation. There is need for continued evaluation of adult education responsibilities in this area to determine more accurately the place of public schools in educating adults in traffic safety.

It is interesting to note the position of adult driver education in gaining support for the high school program. Frequently, parents in adult classes have become strong supporters of high school classes. When they see, from personal experience, the values to be derived from quality instruction in driver education, the parents have made strong demands on schools that a similar program be made available to their youngsters in school as they approach legal driving age.

Continuation High Schools

In many large districts there are continuation high schools of different types that provide a part-time educational program for students who have dropped out of full-time high school classes to obtain employment or for other reasons. In many instances, these students will have need for knowledge of safe driving as a part of their job responsibilities. It is logical that such school programs should include driver education as a part of their curriculum. These classes frequently are

431

conducted on the same basis as driver education classes in the regular school program. This assures the same quality program, meeting the standards of time, quality of instruction, and certification of teachers as found in driver education classes in the high school.

Reeducation of Adult Drivers

Many adult drivers who have driven more or less successfully for a period of years have developed poor driving habits or have failed to keep up to date with changes in traffic laws and changing traffic conditions. Adult education programs have sponsored a number of classes for reeducation of adult drivers. These have included driving clinics, short refresher classes of six to eight hours instruction, and courses of study relating to rules of the road, particularly designed for senior citizens. The National Safety Council's Defense Driving Course is used in many such classes. Some adults desire only instruction in such skills as parking, expressway driving, or learning to drive standard transmission cars. This represents a potential field of adult traffic education in public schools that warrants further study and consideration.

English-Language Classes for Foreign-Born

With the increased concentration of traffic and greater numbers of high-speed highways and expressways, the ability to read quickly and comprehend the meaning of traffic signals and directional signs becomes more significant in the safe flow of traffic. At least one state, California, has recognized this factor by requiring a reading knowledge in English of common signs and markings as a requirement for licensing. To assist in making this program more effective, the Adult Education Bureau of the State Department of Education organized a workshop, including representatives of the Department of Motor Vehicles, driver education teachers, and teachers in adult classes of English for foreign-born persons who were attempting to obtain United States citizenship. This group developed instructional materials that could be used to assist these persons in meeting the driver license requirements. This is an excellent example of the diversity of adult traffic safety education possibilities in public school adult education programs.

Truck Driver Training

The training of truck drivers is a relatively untapped area of adult education service to the traffic safety movement that has great possibilities, particularly in metropolitan areas, where there are large numbers of drivers available that could profit from this experience. Such a program has been in successful operation in the adult education program of several school systems for a number of years. In some

432

instances area vocational schools have developed programs of this nature. The demand for this program came from industry. Safety educators and representatives of industry cooperatively developed a curriculum for the course. The instruction is given primarily by qualified commercial fleet supervisors, and the heavy equipment necessary to conduct the program is provided by industry. The classes, which are held on Saturdays, are conducted as a regular part of the adult education program.

Traffic Court Schools and Driver Improvement Classes

The adult education programs have conducted some type of traffic court schools for many years and in some cases have more recently instituted driver improvement classes. These are essentially the same types of program with similar objectives, but they show some differences in approach and in the selection of personnel. Both programs are based on the philosophy that it is better to educate the motorist in an effort to have him improve his driving behavior and skills or to send him to a therapy session than it is to punish him with a fine, imprisonment, or suspension or revocation of his license.[5]

Traffic court schools have been in operation since the 1930s. The courts usually have referred to these schools persons with one or more accidents or violations. In many instances, they have been teen-age drivers who could profit from additional knowledge about laws and driving practices as well as emphasis on proper driving attitudes. Many classes have enrolled volunteers who were not traffic violators. The traffic-court school idea is a sound concept. Usually, it involves substituting an 8- to 12-hour course of instruction for a fine. The attempt is made to correct the traffic violator by locating his disabilities and providing appropriate training. However, many schools have held classes of fewer or more hours than those suggested. Driver education teachers, police officers, driver improvement analysts, and driver license examiners have all acted as instructors in these courses.

Great emphasis has been placed during the past few years on what is called *driver improvement*. These programs are conducted by personnel of the driver licensing agency and consist primarily of calling in accident repeaters and chronic violators for an individual interview with a driver improvement analyst. The driver improvement classes enroll persons who are accumulating a bad traffic record but have not yet reached the point total for a personal interview. They enroll a larger percentage of persons beyond 21 years of age than most traffic court schools. If, in larger groups, a significant number of these people can be made safe drivers and not require a personal interview, it can create greater highway safety and reduce the cost of the remedial program of driver improvement. Studies are being conducted to

[5] National Highway Traffic Safety Administration. *Statewide Highway Safety Program Assessment—A National Estimate of Performance.* Washington, D.C.: The Administration, (July 1975), pp. 105–106.

433

determine ways of making these classes more effective in the broad program of traffic accident prevention. This could become an important traffic safety education function of public school adult education programs or university continuing education efforts.

The Armed Forces

The U.S. Navy, Coast Guard, and Air Force have programs of driver education for their personnel. In these programs some high schools provide, on a contract basis, instruction for all new personnel. In other instances that service or station has its own instructors to conduct such programs. This program of driver education usually meets the standards of time, curriculum, and teacher certification for high school driver education classes as established by the state department of education of the state in which the course is being conducted. Special attention is given to the particular driving conditions under which the service-related driver will be required to operate.

SPECIAL TYPES OF ADULT DRIVER EDUCATION

The problem of educating adult drivers is much broader than only those functions conducted through the adult education departments of the public schools. It is a concern of a number of both public and private agencies which have programs and projects that relate either directly or indirectly to the education of the adult driver. This section will be concerned with special types of adult driver education programs and activities that are not a function of either the adult education programs of the public schools or the education of professional drivers. The following areas of adult education will be discussed: programs for senior citizens, commercial driving schools, school bus driver instruction, driver education in the armed forces, driver improvement, traffic violator schools, and public information.

Senior Citizen Programs

In view of the increased number of older drivers, many states and agencies are developing driver education programs for senior citizens. These persons are usually 65 years of age and over. Programs for this population are usually designed to assist older adults in passing license reexaminations, improving skills, and updating knowledge of traffic safety and traffic laws. The states of Illinois and Michigan along with several other states have established such programs.

434

Commercial Driving Schools

There are about 2,222 commercial driving schools in the United States giving instruction to more than 1 million drivers each year.[6] Their instruction is given primarily to mature adults, but they also teach many young adults who were unable to take a complete course of driver education in high school. This establishes the commercial driving school industry as a major factor in the education of adult drivers and an important part of the total traffic safety effort.

The commercial driving school industry has confronted many problems. Largely because of lack of provision for regulation from appropriate state agencies, there have been many commercial schools that were not operated in the public interest. It has been said that many of the commercial schools are doing a thoroughly adequate instructional job, turning out drivers who are well trained and who have satisfactory driving records; however, there are many schools whose standards are low, whose instruction is poor, and whose chief aim seems to be to get the applicant through the license examination as quickly as possible. The better schools in the industry have recognized this problem and in several states have organized driving school associations. Some of their primary projects have been to urge legislation providing for regulation of commercial driving schools by an appropriate state agency. A number of states now have such laws. They have worked to raise standards for instructors, although they are still not generally as high as for high school driver education. They also conduct conferences and workshops for the professional growth of their teachers. These efforts have led to improvement of the general quality of instruction in the industry.

Instruction in commercial driving schools is essentially in behind-the-wheel driving. The average student paying for instruction wants to feel that he is making direct progress toward his goal of obtaining a driver license. This means that primary emphasis is on operational skills and that little opportunity is afforded for the important factor of building strong positive attitudes that classroom instruction affords. Commercial schools realize this problem and have encouraged classroom instruction for their students, but it has been very limited in actual practice.

School Bus Drivers

There are about 340,000 school buses transporting nearly 21.5 million students to and from school daily in the nation. Their safety record is so good that it has been said that the safest place to be in the United States is in a school bus. The reason for this is that a balanced program of safety for school bus operation has been established. One of the most important factors in this program has been

[6] National Safety Council, *Driver Education Status Report.* (Chicago: The Council, 1974), p. 35.

the training of school bus drivers. The U.S. Department of Transportation has enacted *National Highway Safety Program Standard No.* 17, *Pupil Transportation*, which includes standards on the training of school bus drivers.[7] With this federal standard, the training programs for school bus drivers should be of an improved quality and should be maintained at a quality level. The training of school bus drivers, therefore, constitutes a major program in the education of adult drivers.

The manner in which education for school bus drivers is carried out is a state responsibility, and procedures differ greatly from state to state. It is customary for the states to establish standards and then permit the local districts to provide their own instruction. In practice, this will vary from an informal approach, such as a supervisor riding with a new driver, to some well-developed program of instruction. State departments have taken positive leadership in this field in some states. In Michigan, the colleges have training programs for school bus drivers that are conducted in the field for local districts. In New Mexico, the State Department of Education conducts training in local districts during the year and holds an annual workshop containing a variety of classes, including basic and advanced driver training, auto mechanics, first aid, adolescent psychology, and other subjects. In Illinois, the Office of Education conducts training programs for supervisors and drivers. Official state departments in many other states conduct statewide or regional workshops for the instruction of school bus drivers in various aspects of school bus safety. Such programs are being designed to meet the federal standard mentioned here.

Armed Forces

Automobile accidents constitute a major source of death and injury to personnel in all branches of the service. They also result in a substantial amount of damage to government property. As a result, several branches of the service have inaugurated driver education programs conducted by their own personnel on a number of different bases. These programs usually include classroom and actual driving instruction. A number of these programs include instruction using multimedia programs and driving simulation. In addition to the basic driver education program, most of the services anticipate a remedial program for accident repeaters and chronic traffic violators. The program of the armed services no doubt constitutes a major element of education of adult drivers.

Driver Improvement

During the past few years, motor vehicle administrators have been emphasizing the use of driver-licensing procedures as a means

---

[7] U.S. Department of Transportation, *Standard No. 17, Pupil Transportation.* (Washington, D.C.: The Department), 1972.

of improving the driving practices of problem drivers. "To improve the attitudes and driving performances of drivers who, because of traffic violations and/or accident involvement, are known to constitute a hazard on the highways; and to instill in those drivers the will to better their driving practices."[8] Although it is performed by motor vehicle administrative agencies and differs from the usual concept of education in a classroom situation, the driver improvement function is a form of education of adult drivers.

The procedures of driver improvement involve the writing of advisory letters informing the driver of his traffic record, a review examination to determine if a physical disability or lack of knowledge or skill is the basis of his problem, and finally, an interview to learn more about him and determine what action may be taken to improve his driving or to place him on probation. Many of the states have established, through law or administrative order, a so-called point system that is used as a basis for calling the driver for an interview. Points are assigned for various traffic violations, and when the driver has accumulated a specified number of points, he is called for an interview with a driver improvement analyst. It is an expensive procedure to provide a driver with a personal interview as a means of improving his driving behavior, but it is considered an important measure for increasing safety on the highways.

Traffic Violator Schools

Traffic violator schools are essentially the same as traffic court schools and frequently follow a similar curriculum. The distinction is made here to indicate that this type of school is conducted by agencies other than the public school adult education departments, such as police departments or directly or indirectly by the courts. These classes have been called by a number of names, such as juvenile violator schools, traffic safety schools, police traffic schools, jaywalking schools, traffic violators schools, and teen-age traffic schools. The curriculum in such programs has varied from a lecture plus an assigned essay on traffic safety to a well-organized course of instruction. Some classes are restricted to pedestrian violators. These classes and those given through adult education departments have contributed to traffic safety. Judge Finesilver of Denver, Colorado, has stated, "Traffic schools, driver-improvement schools, and so-called violators schools conducted under the direct or indirect auspices of traffic courts were created to fill the general and pressing need in our community for a more thorough and effective driver education. These schools serve a purpose in educating and re-educating our motorists."[9]

[8] American Association of Motor Vehicle Administrators, *Guide to Driver Improvement.* (Washington, D.C.: The Association, 1965), p. 3.

[9] Sherman G. Finesilver, *An Analytical Report on Driver Improvement Schools with Recommendation for Improving Traffic Safety* (Denver: City and County of Denver, 1958) (Mimeographed), p. 5.

Public Information

A great deal of adult traffic safety education is achieved through the process of public information. "For the most part, adults are beyond the reach of formal education. Therefore, we must rely largely upon informal means of group—or mass—methods of education."[10] Many agencies, both public and private, conduct public information functions designed largely to provide adult education for drivers. These would include police agencies, motor vehicle departments, safety councils, automobile clubs, and many others. In addition to broad use of communications media for traffic safety education, these groups conduct conferences, workshops, and clinics designed for public education in traffic safety. They also provide speakers and resource persons for many types of civic and service groups.

Figure 17-1. Professional Drivers Receiving Training Through Use of Multimedia System (Courtesy Greyhound Lines, Inc.)

EDUCATING THE PROFESSIONAL DRIVER

There are over 8 million professional drivers in the United States, and another large group who, although they are employed essentially for technical, mechanical, or sales skills, must drive an automobile in the performance of their jobs. Commercial fleet owners, who operate expensive equipment carrying either costly merchandise cargoes or

[10] Marland K. Strasser, et al. Fundamentals of Safety Education (New York: Macmillan Publishing Co., Inc., 1973), p. 388.

passengers, have found that it is imperative to have an effective program of driver selection, education, and supervision if they are to conduct their businesses profitably. As a result, most major fleet operators have a well-developed educational program for their drivers that includes an introductory or vestibule training period for new employees, a continuous education program for in-service drivers, and as much supervision as the nature of the operation permits. This driver education program is usually conducted by a training specialist or a safety supervisor. These programs have been effective in reducing costly accidents for industry. Brody stated: "Since 1934 there has been a 63 per cent decrease in motor truck accidents per 100,000 vehicle miles driven. The sharpest decline has occurred since 1947. It is more than coincidence that during this same period, commercial fleet managements have been developing and extending their programs of selection, training, and good management."[11] In this section, attention will be given to the following: instructing the new driver, continuous education of the driver, and college programs for driver training.

Instructing the New Driver

The first step in the development of a program of instruction of the new driver is the development of a job analysis. When the specific requirements of the job are determined, the new employee can be trained to meet those requirements successfully. The duration of the instruction period and the type of instruction can be determined by the demands of the job and the qualifications of the new employee. In addition to education in the specific responsibilities of the driving task, it is desirable to give the new employee an orientation to company policies and practices so that he will understand his relationship to the overall operation.

Continuous Education

After the new employee is trained to perform his driving tasks, most fleet operations conduct a program of continuous education. This educational process will take many forms. The driver must be supervised and checked periodically to determine if he has developed bad driving practices that will require further training. If he is assigned to new or different types of equipment, he must be trained in the skills required to perform the new operations. Considerable attention is given to reeducation of problem drivers who have been involved in accidents or in other ways are not carrying out their responsibilities properly. If the driver cannot be reeducated to perform his job properly, he may be dismissed or transferred to other work. Management cannot afford to continue the employment of accident-repeater drivers.

[11] Leon Brody, "About the Commercial Vehicle Driver," *Safety Education Digest* (Spring 1954), p. 11.

Many fleets conduct types of educational programs other than driver instruction. These include periodic safety meetings, contests, incentive programs, the distribution of safety literature, and other types of educational activities. Many fleets participate in the National Safety Council Safe Driver Award program, which involves pins signifying the years of safe driving for the individual driver and group citations to the winning fleets in competition with similar types of operations.

College Programs

Colleges and universities throughout the nation have participated, usually through extension or continuous education divisions, in the education of commercial fleet personnel. They have also conducted research projects that have benefited commercial driving groups and prepared safety materials for their use.

Through the program of the National Committee on Motor Vehicle Fleet Supervisor Training, there are more than 50 institutions of higher education that conduct classes for commercial fleet operators. These are usually one-week intensive courses for supervisory personnel, but other courses, sometimes only two or three days in length, are taught for maintenance supervisors or other specialized personnel. Teaching personnel for these courses are usually experienced fleet supervisors and staff of the Institute of Public Safety at Pennsylvania State University, the base from which the program is operated.

Several colleges have offered other types of driver instruction for professional driving operations. North Carolina State conducts a program designed primarily for drivers and "driver-trainers." The colleges in Michigan and some other states have participated in school bus driver training programs. However, this has never become a major program in the colleges and universities.

LEARNING ACTIVITIES

1. Visit the adult education department of a public school district giving adult driver education. Evaluate the program in both classroom and laboratory instruction.
2. Visit a traffic court school not conducted by the public school. Evaluate the program on the basis of (a) curriculum, (b) physical environment and materials of instruction, (c) instruction, and (d) teacher qualification.
3. Prepare a curriculum for a six-hour adult driver education class for new drivers and a curriculum for a six-hour class for a traffic violator school. Tell how they differ. Why?
4. Visit a commercial driving school. Report to the class on the ways in which they differ from a high school program.
5. Attend a safety meeting of commercial drivers. Prepare a written report telling how effective it was from an educational point of view.

440

SELECTED RESOURCES

Aaron, James E. "Adult Driver Education," *Safety Education Digest* (1957), pp. 24–26.

American Association of Motor Vehicle Administrators. *Driver License Administrator's Guide to Driver Improvement.* Washington, D.C.: The Association, 1965.

American Driver and Traffic Safety Education Association. *Driver Education for Adults and Out-of-School Youth.* Washington, D.C.: The Association, 1964. (Mimeographed)

American Medical Association. *Physician's Guide for Determining Driver Limitation.* Chicago: The Association, 1973.

Brody, Leon. "About the Commercial Vehicle Driver," *Safety Education Digest* (Spring 1954), pp. 5–15.

Center for Safety Education. *Driver Education for Adults.* New York: New York University. The Center for Safety Education.

Harno, R.M., and R.C. Peck. *The Effectiveness of A Uniform Traffic School Curriculum for Negligent Drivers.* Sacramento, Calif.: State Department of Motor Vehicles, June 1971.

Marsh, W.C. *Modifying Negligent Driving Behavior—Evaluation of Selected Driver Improvement Techniques.* Sacramento, Calif.: State Department of Motor Vehicles (March 1971).

Miller, Harry L. *Teaching and Learning in Adult Education.* New York: Macmillan Publishing Co., Inc.,1964.

National Association of Public School Adult Educators. *Adult Education in the Public Schools.* Washington, D.C.: National Education Association, 1961.

Scott, B.Y., and H.M. Greenberg. *Effect of Group Sessions in Changing Driver Attitudes.* Albany, N.Y.: State Department of Motor Vehicles, 1965.

Strasser, Marland K., et al. *Fundamentals of Safety Education.* New York: Macmillan Publishing Co., Inc., 1973.

Chapter **18**

The Highway Safety Act

OBJECTIVE: The student will be able to identify those events that were the forerunners of the Highway Safety Act and gain knowledge of the Highway Safety Program Standards and their application to a state's highway safety program.

Safety on the streets and highways of the nation is one of the most important unsolved problems of our times. Any phenomenon that has taken the lives of more than 2 million of our citizens and creates an economic loss of approximately $21 billion annually must be so recognized. It is unbelievable that the American nation, so saturated with proven organizational and managerial abilities, should fail for so long to recognize the need for the application of sound business principles to the practical problems of safe highway transportation.

The Highway Safety Act of 1966 represents such an approach. This program emerged in response to the need for a uniform national program with legislation to support the National Highway Safety Program Standards established by the U.S. Department of Transportation. It represents a thought-out, balanced approach to a major national social problem. An understanding of its implications is a responsibility of every thoughtful citizen. A knowledge of its many facets and their ramifications is essential to any driver educator who purports to teach the youth of this nation to become responsible and knowledgeable traffic citizens and safer drivers. The first sections of this chapter present an historical development of those activities that preceded the enactment of the Highway Safety Act of 1966.

Growth into Chaos

From the introduction of automobiles on the market around the turn of the twentieth century to the period of the post-World War I era of prosperity in the early 1920s, the number of automobiles in use in the United States increased very rapidly. The number of registered motor vehicles rose from 4,192 in 1900 to 130 million in 1975.[1] Early growth in automobile manufacture was a steady but somewhat gradual process because of cumbersome and almost deliberate methods of production. However, with the application of mass-production techniques to the manufacture of motor vehicles, they were reduced in price to the point where a much larger number of persons could afford them. More efficient cars resulting from improved methods of engineering and design made it practicable and desirable for nearly every family to own one. The disorganized, helter-skelter rush of citizens, businessmen, and public officials to meet the growing demand for more automobiles and to provide adequate control of their use could not be wholly unexpected.

The problems created by the evolution of this new mode of transportation were many and complex. Laws and ordinances related to transportation were written with the horse and buggy in mind. New laws were added to meet the need for local and eventually state controls as the range of vehicle travel increased with improved manufacturing procedures. Strange-appearing laws, such as those requiring the driver to phone ahead to local officials if he were driving into town, or requiring a man on foot carrying a lantern to proceed the vehicle at night, were enacted. Some of them though seldom used are still in effect in a few communities.

Sheriff's deputies and local police, untrained in highway traffic problems, were charged with new enforcement responsibilities. Courts, designed to meet entirely different needs, faced a rising number of cases originating out of motor vehicle use. Streets and roadways constructed to carry relatively light loads in slow moving horse-drawn vehicles were now accommodating heavy trucks and high-speed automobiles. Traffic engineering was as yet unheard of, so relatively little consideration was given to the great traffic congestion ahead.

Early licensing of drivers and registration of vehicles were considered to be revenue measures conducted by tax-collecting agencies in the counties or states rather than safety measures regulated by motor vehicle administrators. Education of new drivers through a specific program of instruction, or traffic safety education through programs of public information were virtually unheard-of phenomena. Citizens were not even aware of the dimension of the traffic problems that existed, let alone being organized to support efforts toward their control. Problems of research and proper medical care of traffic injury victims were not specifically directed to special traffic conditions. When the national fatality rate rose to over 20,000 per year

---

[1] Motor Vehicle Manufacturers Association, *Automobile Facts and Figures* (Detroit: The Association, 1975), p. 24.

443

in the mid-1920s,[2] the stage was appropriately set for public-spirited citizens, business leaders, and governmental officials to assess the need for an organized and systematic approach to the solution of this increasingly serious, badly neglected highway crash problem.

The Balanced Program Concept

By the 1920s many organizations and individuals had shown a growing interest and concern in the traffic accident problem. This process actually began with the organization of the National Safety Council in 1913, although the Council's primary emphasis at that time was industrial safety. The schools were beginning to provide traffic safety instruction. States and local communities were organizing safety councils to help cope with the hazards of traffic conditions.

The increasing seriousness of the highway accident problem was recognized by the federal government. In 1924 Herbert Hoover, then Secretary of Commerce, convened the National Conference on Street and Highway Safety. This represented the first nationwide effort to bring leaders in the field of traffic safety together to study the many implications involved. Some of the elements of the traffic safety problem considered at this conference included "statistics, traffic control, construction and engineering, city planning and zoning, insurance, education, and motor vehicle and public relations."[3]

The National Conference on Street and Highway Safety brought forth a new concept of the means of control of traffic accidents, one that is essentially the basic approach contained in the Highway Safety Act. That was the "balanced program" concept. This concept recognizes that there are many elements of the traffic safety problem and that each of them must be given full attention if traffic crashes are to be brought to the irreducible minimum. There is no easy way to achieve traffic safety. There is no single formula to do the job. The achievement of highway safety requires a constant, dilligent, patient, systematic, costly, broad-scale, and long-range application of all proven controls of all phases of the traffic problem.

A position of leadership in the promotion of the balanced program concept was taken by the Automotive Safety Foundation, which was founded in 1937. Under its direction the Standard Highway Safety Program for states was inaugurated in 1937. By 1939 this balanced approach to highway safety had been endorsed by more than 50 national agencies. This was converted into a Wartime Traffic Program in 1943 to help conserve the human and economic resources of the nation that were being directed toward the war effort. The balanced program concept emerging from the conference in 1924 was becoming a practicing reality at the time of the convening of the President's Conference in 1946, shortly after the close of World War II.

[2] National Safety Council, *Accident Facts* (Chicago: The Council, 1975), p. 58.

[3] The President's Committee for Traffic Safety, *Proceedings: Western Regional Conference for Women's National Organizations on Efficient Highway Transportation and Reduction of Traffic Accidents* (Washington, D.C.: The Committee, 1964), p. 1.

The Uniform Vehicle Code

The confusion and driving hazards resulting from the many conflicting, and sometimes contradictory, rules of the road as well as other regulations regarding vehicle use suggested the positive need for measures that would lead to greater harmony in traffic laws between the states and municipalities. The result was the development and recommendation for adoption by all jurisdictions, in the interest of safe and efficient highway transportation, of the Uniform Vehicle Code for state laws and the Model Traffic Ordinance for municipalities. These documents, which are merely recommended guides for cities and states, were first produced in 1925–25 (Uniform Vehicle Code) and 1927–28 (Model Traffic Ordinance) by a committee of the National Conference on Street and Highway Safety in cooperation with the National Conference of Commissioners on Uniform State laws. The Uniform Vehicle Code and the Model Traffic Ordinance have been reviewed and revised periodically over the years to keep their recommendations up to date as a result of changing conditions of highway transportation.

The responsibility for uniformity in traffic laws is now a function of the National Committee on Uniform Traffic Laws and Ordinances. The Committee is composed of 100 members, representing public officials charged with responsibility for highway safety at local, state, and national levels and representatives of private organizations and business interests who have a concern for this problem. The Committee has a small staff under the direction of an Executive Director, with offices in Washington, D.C. In addition to its work with the Committee in revisions of these documents, the staff follows the activities in state legislatures throughout the nation as they pertain to legislation relating to the many provisions of the Uniform Vehicle Code.

The Uniform Vehicle Code and the Model Traffic Ordinance contain suggested and recommended laws and ordinances proposed for voluntary enactment by state and local governments. Comparison studies of the Uniform Code with state laws have been completed in most states. However, because the rate of progress toward absolute uniformity had been slow, there were numerous proposals for a Federal Traffic Code to be enacted by Congress. This was generally considered to be a drastic remedy that might well prove to be less desirable in the long-range view than voluntary compliance by state and local jurisdictions, even though it might be a considerably slower process.

The original Uniform Vehicle Code was written in five separate acts, relating to different areas of motor vehicle use.

Act I. Uniform Motor Vehicle Administration, Registration, Certificate of Title and Antitheft Act.
Act II. Uniform Motor Vehicle Operators' and Chauffeurs' License Act.
Act III. Uniform Motor Vehicle Civil Liability Act.

Act IV. Uniform Motor Vehicle Safety Responsibility Act.
Act V. Uniform Act Regulating Traffic on Highways.

The model Traffic Ordinance is consistent with the state laws recommended in the Uniform Vehicle Code. In addition, it makes numerous provisions for matters of specific concern to the municipalities. The Model Ordinance contains recommended sections for inclusion in local ordinances concerning the control of motor vehicles, pedestrians, and bicycles. It also recommends procedures for accident reporting and making arrests. In its administrative sections the Model Ordinance recommends the establishment of a traffic division within the police department, the office of city engineer, a traffic commission, and a traffic violations bureau under the jurisdiction of the court.

THE PRESIDENT'S HIGHWAY SAFETY CONFERENCE—1946

Immediately following the cessation of hostilities of World War II there was a dramatic increase in traffic casualties. Traffic death rates had been greatly reduced during the war years, primarily as a result of a reduction in driving during gasoline rationing and a stoppage of production in civilian automobiles during that period. With cars and gasoline again readily available, travel increased greatly, and the accident rates did too. This brought a general concern for highway safety that ultimately resulted in the calling of a national conference on highway safety problems by President Truman.

The President's Highway Safety Conference, composed of about 2,000 public officials and interested citizens, was held in Washington, D.C., in May 1946. There were delegates from each of the then 48 states, including eight state governors. Observers from 45 foreign countries also attended. In preconference planning sessions, technical experts in various areas of the highway safety field prepared study materials and recommendations, following the balanced program concept in the following areas:

1. Laws and Ordinances.
2. Accident Records.
3. Education.
4. Enforcement.
5. Engineering
6. Public Information.
7. Motor Vehicle Administration.
8. Organized Public Support.

These recommendations were approved by the conference delegates and developed into the first Action Program for Highway Safety. "This stands as the master plan for a balanced and comprehensive traffic program applicable in whole or in part by all governmental jurisdictions and by organizations of private citizens. It brings the best of the time-tested methods for preventing traffic accidents."[4]

[4] Norman Damon, "The Action Program for Highway Safety," *The Annals of the American Academy of Political and Social Science* (November 1958), p. 122.

Of this Action Program President Truman told the conference delegates: "We will attain the objectives of this Conference—that of saving lives and the terrific drain on the economic resources of America—only if the principles established here are carried back to every community where Americans live and work—where every man, woman, and child is either a pedestrian or a motorist or both. Effective State and local application of the program developed by this Conference will reduce traffic accidents."[5]

The recommendations of the President's Conference in 1946 have formed the basic plan for comprehensive traffic safety programing since that date.

THE WHITE HOUSE CONFERENCE
ON TRAFFIC SAFETY—1954

By 1954 the principles of the Action Program were well accepted nationally by traffic safety specialists. An assessment of progress over the eight-year period revealed the soundness of the Action Program. However, it was not being applied rapidly enough or on a broad enough basis to have the greatest potential effect in reducing traffic accidents. On the recommendations of a Business Advisory group, President Eisenhower called the White House Conference on Traffic Safety in Washington, D.C., in 1954. Emphasis at this conference was concentrated on building citizen support for traffic safety activities included in the Action Program. For this purpose delegates chosen to attend the conference were substantially representatives of citizen organizations rather than safety specialists. The following groups were invited: media agencies, business and industry, labor, women's organizations, farm organizations, and civic and religious organizations.

Although the White House Conference of 1954 was attended by a broad representation of citizen groups, there was still a need to bring the Action Program closer to the people. As a result there were regional meetings of the White House Conference held in four sections of the nation in 1956 and again in 1958. A direct result of these meetings was the development of several state wide traffic safety citizen support organizations that have proven to be an effective force in obtaining increased legislative and administrative implementation of many aspects of the Action Program on the state level.

THE PRESIDENT'S COMMITTEE FOR TRAFFIC SAFETY

One of the most encouraging developments of the 1954 Conference was the announcement of the creation of the President's Committee

[5] The President's Highway Safety Conference, *Action Program* (Washington, D.C.: The Conference, 1946), p. ii.

for Traffic Safety. This Committee consisted of 18 members who were outstanding citizen leaders throughout the nation, in addition to four members of the President's cabinet who served as ex officio members. From its creation in 1954 until its phasing out in 1966, the President's Committee provided consistent leadership as a coordinating force to gain broad acceptance and effective implementation of all phases of the Action Program.

The Program of the Committee was carried out by a small staff in Washington, D.C., under the direction of an Executive Director. Among its other activities, the President's Committee for Traffic Safety sponsored numerous regional conferences emphasizing the citizen support functions related to the various phases of the Action Program. The Committee established in 1955 an Advisory Council of national organizations, associations of public officials, and federal agencies which advised and assisted in the development and execution of Committee activities.

THE ACTION PROGRAM

The Action Program for Highway Safety provided a blueprint for action in the development of a balanced program of traffic safety activities. Public officials on the state and local levels could take inventory of their own efforts in traffic safety in relation to the recommendations of the Action Program and establish a list of priority needs, those things that required primary attention at the moment, to strengthen their own programs. This gave citizen groups a definite list of "Official Needs," established on a priority basis, toward which they could direct their own activities. This assured the greatest attention being given to real needs rather than a disorganized pattern of activities of confusing and frequently unrelated or conflicting efforts toward traffic safety.

THE HIGHWAY SAFETY ACT OF 1966

As presented in the first part of this chapter, the states have passed legislation, committees have been formed, and various programs developed in the interest of highway safety. Because of the lack of a national uniform traffic safety program and a mounting crash problem, the federal government was persuaded to embark upon the formulation of a highway safety program that would establish standards against which to measure a state's performance in the implementation of the Highway Safety Program Standards.

The U.S. Congress passed and the President signed the National Highway Safety Act of 1966 which has been termed "historic legislation," as far as highway safety is concerned. The implementatation of this national legislation was given to the newly created U.S. Department of Transportation. Subsequent legislation established these functions administratively in the National Highway Traffic Safety Administration (NHTSA). In addition, 3.5 of the 18 highway safety standards were assigned to the Federal Highway Administration (FHWA) as the responsible agency.

National Highway Safety Program Standards

Section 402 of The Highway Safety Act is as follows:

(a) Each State shall have a highway safety program approved by the Secretary, designed to reduce traffic accidents and deaths, injuries, and property damage resulting therefrom. Such programs shall be in accordance with uniform standards promulgated by the Secretary. Such uniform standards shall be expressed in terms of performance criteria. Such uniform standards shall be promulgated by the Secretary so as to improve driver performance (including, but not limited to, driver education, driver testing to determine proficiency to operate motor vehicles, driver examinations (both physical and mental) and driver licensing) and to improve pedestrian performance. In addition such uniform standards shall include, but not be limited to, provisions for an effective record system of accidents (including injuries and deaths resulting therefrom), accident investigations to determine the probable causes of accidents, injuries, and deaths, vehicle registration, operation, and inspection, highway design and maintenance (including lighting, markings, and surface treatment), traffic control, vehicle codes and laws, surveillance of traffic for detection and correction of high or potentially high accident locations, and emergency services. Such standards as are applicable to State highway safety programs shall, to the extent determined appropriate by the Secretary, be applicable to federally administered areas where a Federal department or agency controls the highway or supervises traffic operations. The Secretary shall be authorized to amend or waive standards on a temporary basis for the purpose of evaluating new or different highway safety programs instituted on an experimental, pilot, or demonstration basis by one or more States, where the Secretary finds that the public interest would be served by such amendment or waiver.

(b) (1) The Secretary shall not approve any State highway safety program under this section which does not—

(A) provide that the Governor of the State shall be responsible for the administration of the program.

(B) authorize political subdivisions of such State to carry out local highway safety programs within their jurisdictions as a part of the State highway safety program if such local highway safety programs are approved by the Governor and are in accordance with the uniform standards of the Secretary promulgated under this section.

(C) provide that at least 40 per centum of all Federal funds apportioned under this section to such State for any fiscal year will be expended by the political subdivisions of such State in carrying out local highway safety programs authorized in accordance with subparagraph (B) of this paragraph.

(D) provide that the aggregate expenditure of funds of the State and political subdivisions thereof, exclusive of Federal funds, for highway safety programs will be maintained at a level which does

449

not fall below the average level of such expenditures for its last two full fiscal years preceding the date of enactment of this section.

(E) provide for comprehensive driver training programs, including (1) the initiation of a State program for driver education in the school systems or for a significant expansion and improvement of such a program already in existence, to be administered by appropriate school officials under the supervision of the Governor as set forth in subparagraph (A) of this paragraph; (2) the training of qualified school instructors and their certification; (3) appropriate regulation of other driver training schools, including licensing of the schools and certification of their instructors, (4) adult driver training programs, and programs for the retraining of selected drivers; and (5) adequate research, development and procurement of practice driving facilities, simulators, and other similar teaching aids for both school and other driver training use.

After the establishment of the National Highway Safety Bureau—now National Highway Traffic Safety Administration—the staff began to develop a series of program standards based upon the interpretation of Section 402. Ultimately 18 standards were developed. They are:

1. Periodic Motor Vehicle Inspection.
2. Motor Vehicle Registration.
3. Motorcycle Safety.
4. Driver Education.
5. Driver Licensing.
6. Codes and Laws.
7. Traffic Courts.
8. Alcohol in Relation to Highway Safety.
9. Identification and Surveillance of Accident Locations.
10. Traffic Records.
11. Emergency Medical Services.
12. Highway Design, Construction, and Maintenance.
13. Traffic Control Devices.
14. Pedestrian Safety.
15. Police Traffic Services.
16. Debris Hazard Control and Cleanup.
17. Pupil Transportation.
18. Accident Investigation and Reporting.

The main points of these standards are as follows:

The Federal Standards

1.
PERIODIC MOTOR VEHICLE INSPECTION

Vehicles with faulty equipment contribute to traffic crashes so each state shall have a program for periodic inspection of vehicles.

2.
MOTOR VEHICLE REGISTRATION

Each state shall have a motor vehicle registration program which will provide rapid identification of the vehicle and its owner for accident research, safety program development, and enforcement purposes.

3.
MOTORCYCLE SAFETY

Only persons physically and mentally qualified shall be licensed to operate a motorcycle and both driver and passenger shall use protective safety equipment.

4.
DRIVER EDUCATION

A driver education program shall be available for all youths of licensing age. Adult driver training and commercial driving schools must be licensed and instructors certified.

5.
DRIVER LICENSING

A driver licensing program must be established to insure only persons physically and mentally qualified are licensed. The program must not unjustly restrict or deny the privilege to drive.

6.
CODES AND LAWS

Uniformity of traffic codes and laws throughout the state and with other states shall be implemented.

7.
TRAFFIC COURTS

All traffic courts shall complement and support local and statewide traffic safety objectives.

8.
ALCOHOL IN RELATION TO HIGHWAY SAFETY

A program to achieve a reduction in those traffic crashes arising in whole or in part from persons driving under the influence of alcohol is mandatory.

9.
IDENTIFICATION AND SURVEILLANCE OF ACCIDENT LOCATIONS

A program for identifying locations having high crash rates or losses, as well as potentially high hazard sites, shall be developed and maintained.

10.
TRAFFIC RECORDS

Information regarding drivers, vehicles, crashes, and highways shall be uniform for purposes of analysis and correlation.

11.
EMERGENCY
MEDICAL SERVICES

A program shall be established to assure that persons involved in highway crashes shall receive prompt emergency medical care by trained and qualified personnel.

12.
HIGHWAY DESIGN,
CONSTRUCTION,
AND MAINTENANCE

A program of highway design, construction, and maintenance to improve highway safety shall be implemented.

13.
TRAFFIC
ENGINEERING SERVICES

The use of traffic control devices (signs, markings, signals, etc.) and other traffic engineering measures to reduce traffic crashes will be in accordance with the national standards.

14.
PEDESTRIAN
SAFEY

A program which includes pedestrian education, night crosswalk lighting, alcohol involvement records, and application of traffic engineering practices, will be part of the ongoing effort to promote pedestrian safety.

15.
POLICE
TRAFFIC SERVICES

There shall be a program to insure the provision of efficient and effective police services to prevent traffic crashes, aid the injured, maintain safe and orderly movement of traffic, provide for recruit training, practice selective enforcement and establish procedures defining primary operational authority.

16.
DEBRIS HAZARD
CONTROL
AND CLEANUP

Rapid, orderly, and safe removal from the roadway of wreckage, spillage, and debris from crashes to reduce the likelihood of secondary crashes is mandatory.

17.
PUPIL
TRANSPORTATION

Continuous improvement is needed in school bus equipment and maintenance; selection, training, and supervision of drivers and maintenance personnel; and administration of safe pupil transportation.

18.
ACCIDENT INVESTIGATION
AND REPORTING

A uniform, comprehensive accident investigation program is needed to gather traffic accident information and enter it into the traffic records system for planning, evaluating, and furthering highway safety program goals.

452

Funding Principles

Section 402 contains provisions for the funding of highway safety program standard implementation. In addition, Section 403 has provision for the funding of NHTSA research activities. The basis for such funding is as follows:

Congress appropriates monies to the U.S. Department of Transportation for support of highway safety activities. Within the budget, approved funds are identified by category as to how the funds are to be spent. Funds for 402 activity are usually to support state and community programs. Such funds are then allocated to the states, based upon a formula of state population and highway mileage. Use of the funds by the state requires that 60 per cent be spent on state projects and 40 per cent be spent on local projects. Each state typically has its own management approach to the utilization of highway safety monies. However, regardless of the approach used, all funds are to be spent based upon the state's Comprehensive Highway Safety Program Plan approved by the Secretary of Transportation. This a four-year projection of priority activities. Also, the funds are to be spent in accordance with the state's Annual Work Plan which is a year-by-year plan of program activities and spending priorities.

Funds allocated by Congress for Section 403 projects are basically for research. Such monies are used by NHTSA for in-house research, for contract research, or in support of special state emphasis programs.

Governor's Highway Safety Representative

Although the Highway Safety Act requires that the governor be responsible for the implementation of the Highway Safety Program Standards, the governor may name a person and/or agency to represent him. In all states, a Governor's Highway Safety Representative has been named and is responsible for the administration of Highway Safety Act program activities.

Since driver education is one of the standards eligible for funding under the Highway Safety Act, driver education supervisors and teachers should establish a contact with the Governor's Highway Safety Representative Office to determine the extent of participation by local school districts.

The National Highway Safety Advisory Committee

The National Highway Safety Advisory Committee was created by the National Highway Safety Act of 1966. The Committee "shall advise, consult with, and make recommendations to the Secretary (of Transportation) on matters relating to the activities and functions of the Department (of Transportation) in the field of highway safety."[6]

[6]Public Law 89-564, 89th Congress, S.3052, Highway Safety, September 9, 1966, p. 4.

453

The Act specifically calls for the Committee to review and publicize its comments on new or revised Highway Safety Program Standards and to recommend specific research projects. The 35 members of the Committee represent state and local governments, public and private interests concerned with highway safety, research scientists, and others who are expert in the field. The diverse and independent membership of this Committee, appointed by the President, provides a unique medium through which issues, concepts, philosophies, policies, and program directions can be examined in public debate and discussion. The Committee provides affected and concerned groups with a means of communicating with those responsible for administering highway safety programs in the Department of Transportation.

THE HOPE FOR THE FUTURE

All projections of the extent of highway transportation in the future indicate that there will be a continuation of the present dramatic rate of growth in registered vehicles, licensed drivers, and vehicle miles traveled. This will mean a continuous rapid growth of exposure to traffic hazards. As the density of vehicles on the highways continues to become greater, the degree of the hazards to safe driving will become magnified. It seems only logical to conclude that all available knowledge will be applied constantly to every phase of highway safety as a means of control of the needless destruction of lives and property.

The Highway Safety Act of 1966 has been effective. The mileage death rate has been reduced to 3.45 fatalities per 100 million vehicle-miles of travel. Application of the principles of the Highway Safety Program Standards during the past decade unquestionably played an important part in this reduction. It appears impossible to conceive that something less than a balanced program of traffic safety activities would be tolerated for the future. Public officials are increasingly aware of its accident-prevention potential, and organized citizen groups are giving increasing support to this approach to the solution of highway safety problems. Can traffic accidents be reduced by one half or two thirds by application of known techniques of accident prevention? The answer is not now known. However, we can safely conclude that this provides the best-known approach to the reduction of traffic accidents to the irreducible minimum.

LEARNING ACTIVITIES

1. Write a paper on the subject, "The Highway Safety Act of 1966."
2. Prepare a talk to be given before your class explaining the organization and function of the Governor's Highway Safety Representative in your state.
3. Write a paper on "The Approach to the Use of 402 Funds" as applied to your state.
4. Write the National Highway Traffic Safety Administration, 400 7th Street, S.W., Washington, D.C., and request a copy of its recent annual report. Review the report and make a brief presentation to your class.

SELECTED RESOURCES

Baldwin, David. "Dimensions of the Traffic Problem," *The Annals of the American Academy of Political and Social Science* (November 1958), pp. 9–14.

Damon, Norman. "The Action Program for Highway Safety," *The Annals of the American Academy of Political and Social Science* (November 1958), pp. 15–26.

Morony, Louis R. "The Law Must Hurry to Catch Up," *The Annals of the American Academy of Political and Social Science* (November 1958), pp. 34–41.

National Highway Traffic Safety Administration. *Statewide Highway Safety Program Assessment—A National Estimate of Performance.* Washington, D.C.: The Administration (July 1975).

The Eno Foundation for Highway Traffic Control. *Traffic Safety A National Problem.* Saugatuck, Conn.: The Foundation, 1967.

The President's Committee for Traffic Safety. *Education: A Section of the Action Program for Highway Safety.* Washington, D.C.: The Committee, 1962.

U.S. Department of Transportation. *National Highway Safety Advisory Committee Annual Report, 1974.* Washington, D.C.: The Department (September 1975).

U.S. Department of Transportation. *National Motor Vehicle Safety Advisory Council Annual Report, 1974.* Washington, D.C.: The Department (September 1975).

Chapter 19

Research Review and Needs

OBJECTIVE: The student will be able to learn of early research studies, kinds of research, and research study design features and to apply such learnings to the selection of research needs and future studies.

Historically one of the final recommendations of many meetings, conferences, or informal discussions of driver educators is that there is a need for more research. This is unquestionably a sound conclusion. It has been stated, "The quality and progress of driver and traffic safety education rest in part on the returns from continuing research activities."[1] McGlade said:[2]

> Traffic accident prevention is coming of age as a scientific endeavor, with all the conflicts and vicissitudes the process of maturation entails. Its level of sophistication is not yet equal to the complexity of the traffic problem, but the gap is closing. The traffic problem can be in a large measure resolved if the continuing refinement of prevention efforts overtakes the rate of increase in complexity of the problem itself.
>
> It appears that we are approaching the point of diminishing returns with respect to empirical observations of traffic problems as the basis of instituting changes in traffic safety programming.
>
> Now, more than ever, we must depend on research. There is considerable danger if we do not—the danger that opinion, rather than

[1] American Driver and Traffic Safety Education Association, *Policies and Guidelines for Driver Education* (Washington, D.C.: The Association, 1974), p. 29.

[2] Frank McGlade, "Traffic Accident Research: Review and Prognosis," *Traffic Quarterly* (October 1958), p. 559.

scientifically derived facts, will become the sole basis for change. Change based on hunches unsupported by scientific evidence can work irreparable damage in lives lost and time and money wasted.

It often goes unmentioned that there is also a pressing need for a much greater degree of application of existing research findings to many phases of the instructional program of driver and traffic safety education for the purpose of improvement and enrichment of instruction. This need was pointed out in the social sciences by Selltiz as follows: "But it is not only the student who needs to know about research methods. The positions for which social science students are likely to be preparing themselves—teaching, administration in government or business, community consultation, social work—increasingly call for the ability to evaluate and to use research results: to judge whether a study has been carried out in such a way that one can have reasonable confidence in its findings and whether its findings are applicable to the specific situation at hand."[3] This statement is equally true for the driver education student.

Not only do we need a greater body of factual data in the direct and related fields of driver education, but we must make a much greater use of existing data to provide more purposeful instruction. It becomes necessary, then, for the driver educator to learn how to locate, evaluate and apply research findings to his own instructional program. To achieve these objectives will require a basic knowledge of research methodology and techniques and an acquaintance with research findings and research needs of the field.

It will be the purpose of this chapter to provide the driver educator with an understanding of some of the fundamental elements of research activities and overview of driver and safety education research. The following areas will be explored: (1) What is research? (2) Driver and Traffic Safety Research. (3) Who should conduct research? (4) Conducting a research project, validity and reliability, action research, the application of research findings, sources of assistance, and needed research.

WHAT IS RESEARCH?

Before discussing the subject of research and research needs in driver and traffic safety education, it is well to determine what we mean by the term *research*. *Webster's New World Dictionary of the American Language* defines *research as "careful systematic, patient study and investigation in some field of knowledge, undertaken to establish facts or principles."* This definition will be the one used in the development of this chapter.

---

[3] Claire Selltiz et al., *Research Methods in Social Relations* (New York: Holt, Rinehart and Winston, Publishers, 1959), p. 6.

RESEARCH IN DRIVER
AND TRAFFIC SAFETY EDUCATION

There is an increasing realization by students of the subject that the problem of traffic safety cannot be solved through the use of any single panacea. There are many aspects of control, and they must all be applied in the fullest measure and in proper relation one to another if we are to reduce accidents appreciably. These facts emphasize the interdisciplinary approach that must be followed in achieving safety on our highways. Research in traffic safety must follow this pattern if it is to serve the need for providing safer highway transportation. The past few years have seen much greater research activities in all phases of traffic accident control. Also, there have been studies conducted following a team approach which brings together doctors, psychologists, traffic safety researchers, and persons representing other aspects of the problem being investigated so as to study together the total problem as it relates to all disciplines involved. To achieve competence in his field, the driver educator must become familiar with research in these many fields as it relates to the program of driver and traffic safety education.

Research in driver and traffic safety has increased in quality during the 40-year period of the evolution of driver education. The development of research in this field, will be discussed in these three phases: early studies, current studies, and related traffic safety research.

Early Studies

As driver education began to expand rapidly within the framework of the secondary school program, there were many persons concerned with the effectiveness of this instruction as a means of reducing traffic accidents and convictions for moving violations among young drivers. Although no other part of the school curriculum is forced to justify its existence on a cost basis, there was a feeling by many persons that this was a means of justifying instruction in driver education. The result was a series of studies in the late 1940s and early 1950s comparing the accident and violation experience of young drivers with and without driver education instruction. These studies were conducted by departments of motor vehicles, departments of education, local school districts, and by some private agencies interested in the promotion of driver education.

The general conclusion of the evaluation studies of driver education was that students with instruction had fewer crashes, had less severe accidents, and had fewer convictions for moving violations. Although the findings varied somewhat in their exact results, they suggested grounds for the common claim that "trained drivers had only one half as many accidents as untrained drivers."

There were many difficult-to-control variables that caused trained researchers to question the validity of these studies as a group although they did not question the value of driver education as such. Because of the newness of the program, there was considerable

458

variation in the content of the course and the qualifications of the teachers providing the instruction. The method of selecting students to take driver education did not alwyas provide for a random sampling of that age group. In many cases, the size of the sampling was inadequate. In most of the studies there was no control over the important factor of exposure to driving hazards by the groups studied. These factors caused some persons to question the validity of most of the studies conducted during this period and indicated that proper conclusions concerning the value of driver education should be based upon existing evidence. A number of these early studies are reviewed in the following evaluation studies of driver education: *Driver Education in High Schools* by Edward Lane-Reticker and *A Critical Analysis of Driver Education Research*, prepared by the NEA Research Division.

In addition to studies of evaluation, there were also studies relating to other phases of the driver education program. Research indicated that there was little correlation between such physical characteristics as strength of grip, hand steadiness, reaction time, and some characteristics of vision and accident-free driving. This was contrary to commonly held beliefs at the time. The Siebrecht Attitude Scale for the measurement of driver attitudes was developed. This placed greater emphasis on the teaching of positive attitudes in driver education classes. Research was conducted also relating to handicapped drivers and other factors of importance to the field of driver education.

Figure 19-1. Continued Research on Motorcycle Instructional Methods Through the Use of a Motorcycle Simulator (Courtesy Scheib Industries, Inc.)

Current Studies

Since 1960 there have been studies conducted in Connecticut, Illinois, New York, and in Lansing, Michigan, comparing driving success of the trained and untrained young drivers. These studies have been considerably more extensive than previous studies of this nature, particulary in the size of the samples. The Illinois study involved a group of over 500,000 young drivers based on a five-year study of driving performance. As with the earlier studies mentioned previously, the conclusions of these studies indicate a substantially better record of both accident involvement and convictions for moving violations on the part of the trained as compared with the untrained drivers. They suggest the belief that driver education improves the driving performance of young drivers is well founded.

A promising factor of more recent research in the field of driver and traffic safety education is the emphasis on matters pertaining to improved administration and instruction in the program. Further, the development of a driver education task analysis has established reliable criteria against which to evaluate the effectiveness of a driver education curriculum and instruction.[4] The introduction of the use of simulation in the laboratory phase of driver education has led to several studies indicating the value of simulation in the development of quality instruction. The multiple-car range plan has been studied also. Additional studies have related to improved techniques of teaching sound driver attitudes, evaluating teacher performance in dual-control car instruction, and other phases of driver and traffic safety education. A recent study by the National Highway Traffic Safety Administration has determined that driver education is at least 15 per cent cost effective. Such data should continue to lend support to the worth of driver education programs.[5] This emphasis on research will, if continued, lead to a much greater effectiveness of driver education. Research is an important aspect of control of highway accidents.

Related Traffic Safety Research

Research in traffic safety in fields related to driver education has progressed more rapidly than in driver education itself. This includes the fields of driver licensing, driver improvement, highway, traffic, and automotive engineering, driver attitudes and behavior, the use of accident records, medical aspects of driving, and many other phases of the highway safety program. Examples of such research are the studies conducted at Michigan State University, Southern Illinois

[4] A. James McKnight, and Bert B. Adams, *Driver Education Task Analysis, Volume II: Task Analysis Methods* (Washington, D.C.: Department of Transportation, PB197-688 (HumRRO Report IR D1-70-1), (November 1970).

[5] National Highway Traffic Safety Administration, *The Driver Education Evaluation Program (DEEP) Study.* (Washington, D.C.: The Administration, July 1975).

University, and the University of North Carolina. As a result of studies completed at these and other universities, new directions have been established and specific programs redirected. The National Highway Traffic Safety Administration has contracted for any number of studies that have been valuable in validating many areas of concern.

A review of other studies in traffic safety will not be made here, because they are too numerous to mention. However, it should be pointed out that the driver educator must survey current traffic safety research literature continuously to bring the latest information to his driver education students. There are numerous professional journals in education, psychology, medicine, engineering, and other related areas of traffic safety that report the findings of important research studies in this field. *Journal of Safety Research*, published by the National Safety Council, and *The Highway Literature Review*, published by the National Highway Traffic Safety Administration, are the best sources of current research relating to traffic safety. There are also theses and dissertations being written at colleges and universities throughout the nation that relate to various aspects of the driver and traffic safety education program.

WHO SHOULD CONDUCT RESEARCH?

Research is a very complex and exacting undertaking requiring a high degree of specialized training and experience in the discipline in which the research is being conducted and in the methodology of research. Goldstein stated: "Successful research has two basic requirements: substantive knowledge of the subject under study and skill in the pertinent techniques of investigation. Both are necessary, and neither assures the presence of the other. For research in accident prevention, one must know the world of accidents and the appropriate world of research methodology."[6]

The person qualified to conduct purposeful research in driver and traffic safety education must have a background of training and experience in both traffic accident prevention and in research methodology. The limited opportunity at the university level for obtaining a substantive knowledge in the area of traffic accident prevention has limited the number of prospective persons qualified to conduct research in this field. For this reason, much of the available research has been conducted by persons trained in other disciplines who have devoted particular attention to the field of accident prevention. The growth of research programs in traffic accident prevention at the university level will provide a greater number of qualified persons to conduct the needed research.

There are, however, types of useful investigations relating to various aspects of driver and traffic safety education that can be undertaken by high school teachers, college and university instructors, and

[6] Leon G. Goldstein, "Accident Prevention Research—What It Takes, Who Can Do It," *Public Health Reports* (July 1963), p. 565.

departments of education or departments of motor vehicles personnel. We need further study as well as improved techniques of instruction. We need more specific knowledge with regard to types of preparation necessary for successful teaching of driver education. Additional information relating to program costs, improved administrative practices and procedures, and evaluation of effectiveness of the instructional program are types of investigation that can continue to be conducted by institutions and agencies interested in the growth and improvement of driver and traffic safety education.

CONDUCTING A RESEARCH PROJECT

It will be helpful in preparing to conduct research or in reviewing research reports to review briefly the steps in conducting a research project. Because of the brief treatment of this subject at this point, it will be helpful for the student to refer to the selected references at the end of the chapter to review in greater depth the various aspects of conducting research. This section will include a brief outline of the following aspects of conducting the research project: The project outline, classifications of research, research methods, and conclusions and recommendations.

The Project Outline

In research, as in any other constructive activity, there must be some basic plan of action if the outcomes are to be desirable. There have been numerous terms used to describe this activity including *brief, working outline, plan of action,* and others. However, the form of these working plans are very similar regardless of the name given to them. McGrath, Jelinek, and Wochner point out that for most research projects the following subdivisions of the working plan are considered important:[7]

1. Statement of the problem.
2. Definition of the problem.
3. Evaluation of the problem.
4. Bibliography.
5. Briefs of related research studies.
6. Procedures, methods, and techniques.
7. Instruments to be used.
8. Tentative outline of the study.

[7] G. D. McGrath, James J. Jelinek, and Raymond E. Wochner, *Education Research Methods (New York: The Ronald Press Company, 1963), p. 128.*

462

CLASSIFICATION OF RESEARCH

Research has been classified into different types or categories of scientific investigation. These classifications require the application of different tools of investigation and result in obtaining different types of facts or principles that will prove useful to the driver educator. Although the nomenclature for these classifications sometimes differs, they can generally be thought of as *historical, descriptive*, and *experimental*.

Historical

The solution of present problems can often be achieved through a knowledge and understanding of how those problems were approached in the past. Thus historical research can make a contribution to the solutions of problems facing driver educators today if past practices are carefully analyzed in terms of present or future action. For example, an historical study of the organization of professional driver education teacher associations may reveal that an important factor in developing a strong state association of driver educators is the creation of local chapters. These chapters can serve as a focal point of membership promotion for the parent body.

Although historical research data is gathered from both primary and secondary sources dealing with past experience, it requires the same systematic type of investigation as other classes of research. "Historical research is the application of the scientific method of inquiry to historical problems. It demands standards of careful methodology and spirit comparable to those which characterize other types of research. Historical research involves identification and limitation of the problem; formulation of the hypothesis; collection, organization, verification, validation, and analysis of data; testing the hypothesis; and writing of the historical account. All of these steps lead to new understanding of the past and its relevance to the present and future."[8]

Descriptive

A second classification of research involves arriving at significant conclusions drawn from comparisons, contrasts, or relationships of one kind or another based on conditions that exist at present. This type of research is referred to as descriptive or normative survey research. "Descriptive research describes and interprets *what is*. It is concerned with conditions or relationships that exist; practices that prevail; beliefs, points of view, or attitudes that are held; processes that are going on; effects that are being felt; or trends that are developing."[9]

[8] John W. Best, *Research in Education* (Englewood Cliffs, N.J.: Prentice-Hall, Inc., 1959), p. 86.

[9] Ibid, p. 102.

Descriptive research includes surveys, case studies, community studies, comparative studies, activity analysis, and trend studies, all of which are used frequently in many aspects of safety education. Questionnaires circulated to determine the number of schools providing a particular type of driver education course or to determine safety supervision practices in various school systems, and rating scales for experts to evaluate certain practices or procedures in driver education instruction, are examples of descriptive or normative research.

Experimental

A third classification, and one that is probably most popular in education today, is experimental research. Best says: "Experimental research is the description and analysis of what will be, or what will occur, under carefully controlled conditions. It is the classical methodology of the science laboratory, and is probably the most difficult and exacting of all methods of research."[10] Experimental research dealing with various aspects of teaching both classroom and laboratory driver education will have an important influence upon the effectiveness of the program in the future. Even though the teacher does not usually conduct such research, he must interpret research findings in terms of improved instruction. "Certainly it seems desirable for the classroom teacher to have a knowledge of the fundamentals of experimental methods and of illustrative investigations, but not to attempt formal experimental studies without the counsel of an appropriate expert in statistics and experimental design."[11]

Experimental research involves the use of controlled conditions and an analysis of the resultant data based upon probability. The experimenter places controls on a group, lets only one item vary, and then analyzes the way in which the uncontrolled condition varied. For example, a school system may wish to discover which of two methods, classroom presentation or television presentation, will produce the best results. A single group of students is divided into two equal-sized groups either randomly or on the basis of matched pairs. All the factors of instruction, such as time and content, are the same, with type of presentation being the only variable. If all other factors are held constant, differences between the two groups must be because of chance or difference in type of presentation. Statistical treatment of the data will describe the extent of the possibility that chance rather than the different type of presentation may have caused the difference in results.

[10] Ibid., p. 125.

[11] Carter V. Good, *Introduction to Educational Research* (New York: Appleton-Century-Crofts, 1959), pp. 375–76.

METHODS OF RESEARCH

The methods used in solving a scholarly problem are of utmost importance. Obviously, if wrong techniques are used a correct solution can hardly be reached. The techniques used in investigating a research problem will depend upon the nature of the problem itself.

Research methods include these principal steps: first, locating and collecting the data necessary to serve as a basis for any solution; second, analyzing and classifying these data in a logical manner; and third, interpreting these data so as to arrive at a preliminary hypothesis that can be tested and shown to be either correct or incorrect.

Documentary research is widely used in all fields of investigation. This is principally a method of testing a hypothesis by locating and analyzing data from documents and records of many kinds. The experimental method of research is one in which controlled conditions are established for testing a hypothesis. Sometimes this requires special equipment or a laboratory. Another method used in traffic safety research is the survey. This is a process for learning pertinent information about an existing situation. The interview and the questionnaire are the principal manners of gathering data in the survey method.

CONCLUSIONS AND RECOMMENDATIONS

The conclusions and recommendations chapter of a research project looks backward and also forward by considering applications, recommendations, and needed research. This chapter is of particular value in that it presents information regarding the problem investigated, conclusions, limitations, applications, and recommendations. In a sense, this chapter stands apart from the remainder of the investigation. This is because conclusions and recommendations are not normally a part of any research study and thus are reported as added information.

VALIDITY AND RELIABILITY

The driver educator interested in either conducting research or making use of research findings must give consideration to the factors of validity and reliability. These qualities are as important in research as they are in the selection or construction of tests.

"*Validity* is the characteristic of a study or program of evaluation to accomplish what it originally planned. An attitude scale is valid only if it correctly evaluates the attitudes of people being tested. Research findings are valid when they accurately and correctly show the results originally sought."[12] For example, a research design planned to discover the "extent to which driver education reduces traffic accidents" is valid only if the relationship discovered is a

---

[12] Marland K. Strasser, et al., *Fundamentals of Safety Education* (New York: Macmillan Publishing Co., Inc., 1973), p. 472.

correct one. The study may show the extent that driver education reduces traffic accidents. However, this study would be *invalid* if future research showed that the driver education students drive fewer miles per year on the average than persons who do not take driver education. This would show that the difference between the groups was possibly the result of exposure rather than education.

Reliability refers primarily to dependability of evidence that can be verified by subsequent studies. "When research findings are described as reliable, repetition of the study would result in similar results. Similarly, a reliable test is one in which scores would be nearly identical if the test were repeated for the same group—providing additional learning had not taken place."[13]

ACTION RESEARCH

Many driver education teachers and supervisors are continually conducting studies and experiments that are designed to improve their curriculum offerings. This process of conducting research activities as a participant rather than an observer is frequently referred to as *Action Research*. "Action research is based on the assumption that the involvement of teachers in a scientific study of an on-the-job problem is a promising approach to inservice education."[14]

Although the primary purpose of action research is the improvement of the curriculum, it is also a means of providing professional growth. Action research provides for improvement of instruction through a strengthening of curricular offerings and through improving the quality of instruction.

THE APPLICATION OF RESEARCH FINDINGS

Research in highway safety will not result in a desirable reduction of traffic accidents unless broad application is made of the findings reported. The studies conducted demonstrating the value of seat belts in reducing fatalities and the severity of injuries in automobile accidents will not be effective until seat belts are in universal use. Nor will research evidence related to improvement of instruction in driver education reduce accidents until driver educators incorporate such findings in their curriculum.

The practical application to the teaching situation of knowledge made available through research becomes a direct responsibility of the driver education teacher. Brody states: ". . . The art of scientific investigation needs to be regarded as an intrinsic part of the everyday teaching process. That is to say, teachers must really get to know their students; they must learn to interpret not only student accidents but

[13] Ibid., p. 472.

[14] Abraham Shumsky, *The Action Research Way of Learning* (New York: Columbia University Press, 1958), p. 3.

also their near-accidents and critical behaviors; and they must be able to design their instruction efforts accordingly."[15]

If the teacher is to improve instruction through the application of research findings, he must have a basic knowledge of research. He must be familiar with primary sources that report such research findings and how to find reports of other basic and related studies. The teacher must also have a knowledge of research procedures that will enable him to study and interpret accurately the findings and conclusions of the research report. Finally, he must be competent to incorporate effectively the research findings into his instructional program in a meaningful way. To achieve these competencies necessary for effective instruction in driver and traffic safety education, the teacher must have training in the fundamentals of research. Although many driver education teachers may never conduct significant research studies themselves, they will all make application of research findings in their instructional programs if such programs are to be most effective in contributing to the prevention of traffic accidents.

SOURCES OF ASSISTANCE

There are numerous sources of assistance for persons interested in conducting studies relating to various aspects of driver education. Such sources include school research and development centers, colleges and universities, and state agencies interested in traffic safety education.

There are numerous studies being conducted by local school districts relating to improvement of instruction in all areas of the school curriculum. This has been less true in driver and traffic safety education than in other instructional areas. Interested driver educators should explore the possibility of conducting studies in driver education with the cooperation and assistance of school research and development personnel.

With the increased number of institutions of higher education offering advanced degrees in driver and traffic safety education, there are broader opportunities for interested and qualified teachers to conduct research at both the master's and doctoral level. Such studies could investigate problems of both administration and instruction in driver education.

With the expanded use of data processing systems in many state departments of motor vehicles, there is more information relating to young drivers than has been available in the past. This provides a source of data that can be used to determine the effectiveness of driver education instruction, characteristics of teen-age traffic violators, and causes of accidents involving young drivers.

[15] Leon Brody, "Research and the Future of Traffic Safety," *ADTSEA News and Views* (June 1964), p. 24.

467

Figure 19-2. Research Activity with the Use of a Blowout Simulator (Courtesy Scheib Industries, Inc.)

NEEDED RESEARCH

There is a continuous interest in research being conducted in the area of traffic safety. The increase in available funds, both public and private, during the past few years has stimulated research efforts in all phases of the program. The passage of the Highway Safety Act of 1966 has made available millions of dollars for research activity. However, there is still a very small amount of sponsored research conducted in highway safety as compared with other important social problems when the annual toll of lives taken in traffic accidents is considered. Because the amount of research is comparatively limited, it is desirable to determine the kinds of research that will be most helpful in strengthening driver and traffic safety education as a means of traffic accident prevention.

There are several areas of research needs in driver education. These are outlined as follows:[16]

Curriculum

Determination of the extent to which current instructional materials incorporate existing research findings on collision occurrence, perceptual motor skills, and problem-solving approaches.

[16] American Driver and Traffic Safety Education Association, op. cit., p. 30.

468

Development and dissemination of guidelines to teachers for curriculum improvement and program evaluation.

Development of effective traffic safety education for such special groups as problem drivers and operators of special vehicles.

Identification of the critical risk situations which the young driver is likely to encounter while driving, and development of effective educational treatments for decision making in such situations.

Determination of cost-effectiveness of instructional elements and materials.

Teacher Qualifications

Development of procedures for preparing and certificating teachers on the basis of exhibited competencies.

Methods

Assessment of skill development in vehicular guidance and control through use of off-street multiple-car driving ranges, simulators, and planned exercises.

Development and evaluation of effective techniques for modifying driver attitudes and related behaviors.

Special Problems

Development of follow-up instruction to reinforce learnings from the initial driver education course.

Development of methods for preparing students to cope successfully with driving emergencies.

Development of measures to determine rate of knowledge and skill loss in the absence of practice.

Determination of the lag time between driver education and licensing of students.

Stimulating Research Activity

In order to stimulate research activity, lines of communication should be clearly established between teachers and university staffs and traffic safety officials and between educators of research specialists.

Assuming that teachers, administrators, university safety center staffs, and research scientists communicate effectively, all will benefit from such an alliance. Interrelated contacts should be established at local, state, and national levels. Communications seems to be the key to the success of research in the future.

LEARNING ACTIVITIES

1. Prepare an outline for a research project in an area related to traffic safety.

2. Review a research study in traffic, and report on it to the class. What classification of research was it? What research methods were used? Were the conclusions valid? Explain why in each case.
3. Design and conduct an action research study that could be carried out as an assignment in high school driver education class.
4. Review a research report in traffic safety. Prepare a paper explaining how the findings could be used to enrich the instructional program in a high school driver education class.

SELECTED RESOURCES

Association for the Aid of Crippled Children. *Accident Research: Methods and Approaches.* New York: The Association, 1964.

_____. *Behavioral Approaches to Accident Research.* New York: The Association, 1961.

Chapanis, Alphonse. *Research Techniques in Human Engineering.* Baltimore: The Johns Hopkins University Press, 1959.

Dunbar, Flanders, and Leon Brody. *Basic Aspects and Applications of the Psychology of Safety.* New York: The Center for Safety Education, New York University, 1959.

Forbes, T. W. *Human Factors in Highway Traffic Safety Research.* New York: John Wiley & Sons, Inc., 1972.

Fox, Bernard H., and James H. Fox. *Alcohol and Traffic Accidents.* Washington, D.C.: U.S. Public Health Service, 1963.

Hayes, Robert B., et al. *Immediate Standardized Learning Reinforcement to a Complex Mental-Motor Skill (Driver Training) Using Electronically Coordinated Motion Pictures.* Harrisburg, Pa.: Department of Public Instruction.

Lane-Reticker, Edward. *Driver Education in High Schools.* Chapel Hill, N.C.: University of North Carolina, 1953.

National Commission on Safety Education. *A Critical Analysis of Driver Education Research.* Washington, D.C.: National Education Association, 1957.

_____. *Research Needs in Traffic Safety Education.* Washington, D.C.: National Education Association, 1956.

National Research Council. Transportation Research Board. *Driver Performance Studies (530).* Washington, D.C.: The Board, 1975.

National Safety Council. *Journal of Safety Research.* Chicago: The Council, published quarterly.

Stratemeyer, Clara G. *Accident Research for Better Safety Teaching.* Washington, D.C.: National Education Association, 1964.

Suchman, Edward A., and Alfred L. Scherzer. *Current Research in Childhood Accidents.* New York: Association for the Aid of Crippled Children, 1960.

Travers, Robert M. W. *An Introduction to Educational Research*, 2nd ed. New York: Macmillan Publishing Co., Inc., 1964.

Chapter 20

A Look Toward the Future

OBJECTIVE: The student will be able to identify those trends in driver education and gain an insight as to the role of driver education during the decade of 1977–1987.

It seems appropriate that a textbook in a subject area so dynamic and rapidly changing as driver and traffic safety education should close with some speculation about the future. Speculation is usually filled with optimism, but at the same time is liable to error. How will the dramatic changes of the next decade influence the use of the automobile as both a social and economic force in society? How immobile will the stolid public apathy remain to the great social and economic waste of human and natural resources of the nation as the death toll from traffic accidents rises beyond the 50,000-a-year mark? These questions will be answered only with the passage of time. But there are predictions that can be made at present with a reasonable degree of certainty. Such predictions would include the following: (1) By 1985 there will be more than 150 million registered motor vehicles operated by more than 150 million licensed drivers. (2) There will be well over 1.2 trillion miles of travel per year. (3) Unless there is a reversal of the mileage death rate, the annual traffic fatality toll will escalate.

It would appear that there should be an ever-increasing public demand for higher standards of driver performance and a decreasing tolerance for a socially irresponsible manner of vehicle operation by drivers. If so, a more complete program of continuous education for all drivers would appear to be inevitable. This would call for an

471

increase in quantity and an improvement in quality of high school driver education as well as a greater application of the educational process to all phases of control of adult drivers. A prognosis of driver and traffic safety education for the decade ahead may be written in terms of trends and developments of the decade just past.

NEW CONCEPTS EMERGE

It would appear that by 1985 there will emerge some new concepts with regard to the control of traffic accidents that may well have application to education. What they will be are only matters of conjecture at this time. However, there are bases upon which to predict what two of these concepts may be. First, a form of driver education may be established, at least in some states, as a prerequisite to driver licensing. Second, the concept of driver education may be broadened to include not only high school driver education but all phases of education of drivers as well.

Prelicensing Driver Education

In 1955 the legislature of the State of Michigan enacted a law establishing the minimum driving age at 18. However, if the applicant had successfully completed a course of driver education, he would be eligible for a license at 16. This legislation, of course, had the effect of increasing the number of high school students receiving this instruction. Since that time, several other states have passed laws that permit the issuance of driver licenses at an earlier age to persons having had high school driver education, and still other states are now considering it. By 1985, this practice will probably be followed in other states, with the result that more students will be enrolled in the program. At this writing, 25 states have laws requiring driver education as a prerequisite to licensing.[1]

There has been some discussion with regard to the need for an organized program of driver education instruction as a prerequisite to the licensing of all new drivers regardless of age. With the proven value of driver education as a factor in traffic accident reduction, this would appear to be a desirable condition of licensing and would provide a measure of protection to the applicant as well as other users of the highways. Such a requirement would increase enrollments in adult public school driver education classes and commercial driving schools as well. During the next decade we could well see, at least in some states, requiring evidence of having successfully completed an approved program of driver education as a condition of obtaining a driver license regardless of age.

---

[1] National Safety Council, *Driver Education Status Report.* (Chicago: The Council, 1974), p. 17.

472

The Education of Drivers

The term *driver education* has come to have specific connotation of high school driver education as defined in *Policies and Guidelines for Driver and Traffic Safety Education*, published by the American Driver and Traffic Safety Education Association. However, the expression *driver education* may apply equally well to certain programs of postlicensing education or driver improvement because organized instruction or application of educational principles is involved. This has led to much confusion in trying to differentiate between prelicensing education and the more or less continuous process of re-education of licensed drivers, particularly those who have become involved in repeated accidents or are chronic traffic law violators. The term *the education of drivers* may become a broader expression, including both prelicensing driver education and postlicensing education of a refresher or remedial nature.

HIGH SCHOOL DRIVER EDUCATION

Although the dramatic explosion in program growth from 1946 to 1955 was somewhat decelerated, the period from 1955 to 1975 has been one of a continuous increase in quantity and improvement in quality of high school driver education.[2] The unquestioned need for high quality of new drivers in the next decade and the strong organized support for driver education would indicate the continuance of this trend. There will be many factors responsible for this growth and improvement in the high school program. They will include additional research findings, better organization and supervision of instruction, improved materials and equipment to conduct quality programs, higher standards of teacher certification, and greater professional dedication of teaching personnel. Some states are now requiring certification for simulator and range instructors. It is conceivable that national conferences on driver education will be held during this decade, which will further upgrade the standards of instruction and teacher qualifications.

Scope of the Program

In the 1974–75 school year, 89 per cent of the public high school students in the nation, or some 3.2 million of the eligible students,[3] were enrolled in at least a minimum program in both classroom and laboratory instruction. With the forces of legislation relating driver education to licensing age, provisions for state reimbursement for instruction, and strong public support, these percentages should increase

[2] National Highway Traffic Safety Administration, *Statewide Highway Safety Program Assessment—A National Estimate of Performance.* (Washington, D.C.: The Administration, July 1975), pp. 89–98.

[3] Ibid., p. 21.

by 1985. Progress should be made toward achieving the Highway Safety Act recommendation that "the ultimate goal should be that every beginning driver be given the opportunity to complete an approved course in driver education."[4]

A Quality Program

As the rapid expansion of driver education in the secondary schools has moved steadily ahead since the close of World War II, there has been a growing concern among leading driver educators that there has not been an equally rapid progress in improvement of the quality of instruction. This has been a result of many inadequacies related to the newness of the discipline. These would include lack of general acceptance on the part of many educators, which results in secondary consideration in program organization and scheduling, evolving instructional standards, limited instructional materials, and teaching certification standards. The encouraging improvement in these conditions since 1955 would justify the conclusion that the quality of the driver education program would improve materially in the decade ahead.

A Place in General Education

Driver education is rapidly becoming an accepted part of the desirable general education experiences of all secondary school youth. It is a subject area that relates directly and immediately to the daily experiences of every student. As instructional standards and teacher certification requirements are raised to the level of other accepted disciplines, driver education will gain full acceptance as a part of general education. It will assume, as it already has done in many school districts, a regular place in the school curriculum, with its own well-qualified professional staff. This is in direct contrast to its frequent position as a noncredit, extracurricular program taught by an inadequately prepared, disinterested, part-time teacher when it was introduced into most schools in the early 1940s.

State Financial Support

Thirty-three states have made provision for special state reimbursement for the total program of driver education, usually for the laboratory phase only, since the first such law was enacted in Delaware in 1947.[5] The interest shown in this movement by other state legislatures, particularly in view of the movement toward establishing high school driver education as a condition of licensing, would lead to the assumption that this trend will continue to gather momentum during the next ten years.

[4] National Highway Traffic Safety Administration, *Highway Safety Program Manual, Vol. 4, Driver Education.* (Washington, D.C.: The Administration, 1969).

[5] National Safety Council, op. cit., p. 32.

Supervision

The primary purpose of supervision is the improvement of instruction. Supervision has been defined as "all efforts of designated school officials directed toward providing leadership to teachers and other educational workers in the improvement of instruction; involves the stimulation of professional growth and development of teachers, the selection and revision of educational objectives, materials of instruction, and methods of teaching, and evaluation of instruction."[6] The steady growth in supervision in driver education during the past ten years has been an important factor in program growth and improvement in the quality of instruction.

All states now have department of education supervisory personnel assigned full-time to driver education. They act as consultants, prepare materials, conduct professional workshops for teachers, and work with community groups interested in the program. Such state supervision frequently accompanies provision for state financial assistance for driver education. Many school districts also now employ either full- or part-time supervisors in this area.

A most important development during the past decade has been the designation, by many secondary schools, of department heads in driver education. This places authority and responsibility for improvement of instruction in the hands of an interested and qualified person who can devote a greater effort to insuring the achievement of the stated objectives of the program. This trend toward more specific supervisory responsibility for driver education at all levels will continue with the positive results of improved quality in instruction.

Equipment

Obtaining dual-control automobiles has been an important, but rarely unsurmountable, administrative problem since production of private passenger cars began after the close of World War II. Major manufacturers made available, on a loan basis, cars for the program. Many schools have purchased their own equipment or obtained it on a lease or rental basis. However, the major portion of the laboratory cars are furnished through local automobile dealers, who in return receive a rebate from the manufacturers for cars used in high school driver education classes. The automobile industry on this basis now supplies each year over 42,000 cars for use in public schools. It is estimated that by 1985, if laboratory instruction is made available to all eligible students by that time, there will be a need for approximately 50,000 cars. The industry appears willing to supply the needs of the schools conducting classes even to this extent so that instruction should not be denied students because laboratory cars are not available. There are now 2,300 schools using driving simulation systems, and some 788 multiple-car facilities in use. A large majority of

[6] Carter V. Good (ed.), *Directory of Education* (New York: McGraw-Hill Book Company, 1973), p. 574.

475

these have been financed through the use of the Highway Safety Act funds.

The rapid development in teaching systems will make more effective teaching in the classroom possible. New improvements and refinements in simulators will contribute to improvement of instruction in the laboratory phase of the program.

Materials

One of the basic necessities for conducting a successful instructional program is the availability of both textbooks and supplementary materials. Since 1965 there have been some new textbooks for high school driver education in addition to those texts that had been used previously. This provides a broad selection of texts for driver education teachers that compares favorably with the selection of textbooks in other areas.

There has been, for many years, a wide variety of supplementary materials, in both pamphlet and audio-visual form, for uses in driver education classes. The trend appears to be toward greater numbers of such materials prepared specifically for use in driver education classes made readily available by agencies interested in the education of young drivers. Examples of these types of materials are the charts, filmstrips, and tests on automobile insurance multimedia systems. It would appear that a greater selection of high-quality materials in both textbooks and supplementary materials will be available in the years ahead.

Teacher Qualifications

A major problem of program growth has always been an inadequate supply of properly prepared teachers to meet the needs of the driver education program. Many teachers assigned to these classes had either no formal preparation in the subject area or only a single basic course in driver education. During the past decade the trend has been a continual increase in requirements for certification of driver education teachers. A number of states now require a teaching minor in the subject area or its equivalent. This trend has made it possible for colleges and universities to employ full-time safety and driver education instructors and establish programs that provide an adequate background for the teacher candidate to become knowledgeable in his field. Many advanced degrees are being awarded to candidates specializing in driver education. This trend, stimulated by The Highway Safety Act of 1966, is firmly established, and it appears certain that new teachers entering the field in the next 10 years will be substantially better prepared than their predecessors.

476

Classroom Instruction

Classroom instruction is the basic core of a successful driver education program. It is in the classroom that the student must acquire the positive attitude of a socially responsible user of the automobile on the highway. He must also learn the many elements essential to becoming a properly prepared traffic citizen. Among other things this includes a knowledge of rules of the road, safe driving practices, driver limitation and characteristics, and natural forces, as well as insurance and other economic factors involved. Also, he must have some knowledge of the need for adequate controls of traffic problems, such as education, engineering, enforcement, and driver licensing if he is to be a good traffic citizen.

The 30-hour minimum established by various conferences on high school driver education does not provide adequate time to conduct a class that would include all of these areas. This fact has been recognized by driver educators for many years. A large number of classes now provide from 45 class periods to a full semester for classroom instruction. The recommendations of ADTSEA are for a full-semester course (90 hours) to achieve the objectives of the program.[7]

During the next decade there will probably be a gradual increase in the time allocation provided for the classroom phase of driver education. The use of closed circuit television, now used in a few schools, and other teaching devices and systems will receive further consideration in driver education classroom instruction.

Laboratory Instruction

The laboratory phase of driver education, which remained little changed for a period of many years, has undergone considerable change during the past decade. Research has been conducted in the area of evaluation of teacher performance that will result in the improvement of quality of instruction. There has been additional consideration to the problem of pupil evaluation that will be helpful as well. Teacher preparation institutions are providing more adequate instruction in the laboratory phase of the program, and most new teachers now teach at least one nondriver to drive as a part of their regular preparation program. Many colleges and universities provide practice teaching experience in laboratory instruction. This trend, which will continue in the next decade, will improve the quality of instruction in the high school program.

Driver simulators were used on an experimental basis in laboratory driver education in the late 1940s. However, they did not approach the broad use enjoyed today until about 1960. The early experimental use established the facts that, when properly used, simulators would improve the quality of instruction and appreciably reduce the

[7] American Driver and Traffic Safety Education Association, *Policies and Guidelines for Driver and Traffic Safety Education* (Washington, D.C.: The Association, 1974), p. 15.

unit cost per pupil completing the course. The introduction of a second simulator into general use in 1963 stimulated interest in this technique of instruction and brought many new and superior developments in driver simulation. The wide-screen color films, with improved filming and instructional techniques, have greatly improved this method of teaching. The wide use of simulator units housed in portable trailers that can be moved from school to school has made the program much more flexible. A lease, rather than purchase arrangement for obtaining equipment, has made the use of simulators much more feasilbe than before in many districts. This trend of expanded use of driver simulation in high schools will continue; however, the pace will be slower because of the lack of funding for such equipment. Another possibility in the decade ahead could be the emergence of a more sophisticated simulation system.

Figure 20-1. Multiple-Car Facilities Will Be Used More Extensively in the Future (Courtesy Scheib Industries, Inc.)

A multiple-car program was introduced in Chicago, Detroit, and several other Michigan cities in the early 1940s. Although it was used with success in these places, the multiple-car plan did not spread with any degree of rapidity until the last few years. This system is now

478

used widely in Maryland, Michigan, Illinois, and Tennessee. The program gives promise of further development in the years ahead. As the offering of evasive/emergency driver education expands, multiple-car facilities will be needed. During the next decade there will be considerable experimentation with a program of laboratory instruction that will combine the use of driving simulators, the multiple-car plan, and dual-control cars.

Figure 20-2. Motorcycle Instruction Will Expand Extensively in the Next Decade (Courtesy Safety Education Program, Texas A & M University)

With the significant increase in the number of motorcycles in use, the secondary schools and universities will be asked to develop training programs for new riders and teachers. The inclusion of motorcycle rider instruction as an extension of current laboratory programs will no doubt become a reality in the decade ahead. (See Appendix for course outline.)

Driver Education in Nonpublic High Schools

Driver education has progressed much more slowly in the nonpublic high schools than in public high schools. This is due primarily to the two factors of finances and educational philosophy. Undoubtedly more nonpublic schools would participate in the program if funds were available or if they participated in programs of reimbursement from state funds as provided for public schools in many states. However, the nonpublic schools tend to conduct the more traditional academic type of curriculum that does not lend itself so readily to a degree of flexibility that is helpful in scheduling driver education classes. There are few indications at the present time that a noticeable pattern of growth can be anticipated in these schools in the immediate future.

479

Support for Driver Education

The rapid growth in high school driver education is largely due to the strong support that has been given to the program by both public officials and citizen groups. During the past decade, high school driver education has been challenged as being too costly and a "frill" subject having no place in the academic program of the secondary schools. A number of school districts have considered discontinuing the class, but in most instances the course has been continued because of strong public demand. Studies in Los Angeles[8] and other sections of the country have revealed an overwhelming public support of the continuance and expansion of driver education. The public feels that, regardless of the cost involved, driver education is a responsibility of public schools. It is interesting to note that the group that expresses the greatest opposition to driver education instruction comprises the teachers of other subjects.

Over the years, numerous conferences on high school driver education have been attended by hundreds of delegates from all states, with representatives of women's organizations, civic and service groups, and interested segments of business and industry in attendance. The indicated support of these groups at these and other conferences on traffic safety would suggest that public support for driver education in the decade ahead would be greater and more articulate than at any time in the past. With such a strong base of public support, the continued growth and improvement of the program would appear to be inevitable.

Professional Organization

Since the organization of the first driver education association in Iowa in 1947, there have been similar groups formed in 47 other states. The American Driver and Traffic Safety Education Association was organized in 1957, giving the movement a national professional organization. In 1960 this Association became a department of the National Education Association, but in 1975 its status changed and it became an independent organization located in Washington, D.C. These groups have been involved in a period of facing the many problems of organization and development to be found in all new areas. However, most of them are now firmly established and performing many services for their members and the profession. The period from 1977 to 1987 should witness a substantial degree of maturity developing with these professional organizations that will contribute materially to the improvement in the quality of the instructional program in driver education.

[8] Los Angeles City School Districts, Evaluation and Research Section, *Research Report No. 229, An Evaluation of Some Aspects of the Driver Training Program in Los Angeles City High Schools* (Los Angeles: The School Districts, 1961), pp. 19-43.

480

Research

Research in all areas of traffic safety has been greatly accelerated in the past few years. Studies have been conducted by motor vehicle departments and other state agencies, the federal government, universities, and private agencies. These studies have investigated problems of engineering, relating to both cars and highways, and driver performance as revealed in motor vehicle department records. There have also been studies relating to driver behavior and attitudes. Many additional studies related specifically to education have investigated the status of teacher preparation, supervision, and other aspects of the program, as well as evaluation studies of program effectiveness in terms of accident reduction among teen-age drivers. It is hoped that future studies will be directed toward the problems of providing more effective instruction in various aspects of the program. With a greater interest than ever before in traffic safety research and greater amounts of research funds, public and private sector, available for qualified projects, it would appear that greater amounts of needed research will be conducted in the near future.

EDUCATING ADULT DRIVERS

The trend has been toward a concept of continuous education for all drivers as a means of control of traffic accidents. This educational program can be divided into the following classifications of education for adult drivers: prelicensing adult driver education and postlicensing adult driver education.

Prelicensing Adult Driver Education

Prelicensing driver education instruction for adults and out-of-school youth has been conducted by both private and public agencies for many years Although there have been classes, particularly in adult education departments of public schools, that have provided a minimum program of classroom instruction, it is essentially a laboratory program. For a number of years commercial driving schools have been teaching more than 1 million drivers a year, and the public schools have taught in excess of 50,000 annually. This trend should continue as in the past unless there is legislation requiring evidence of driver education instruction as a condition of licensing of all drivers regardless of age. Such legislation would increase immediately the number of adults taught by both public and private agencies.

Postlicensing Adult Driver Education

Postlicensing education of adult drivers has received greater attention during the past decade than ever before. This activity has been

481

concentrated in agencies responsible for motor vehicle administration essentially through driver improvement programs. There is sufficient evidence that these programs have provided effective means of problem-driver rehabilitation. They will undoubtedly be expanded. Traffic court schools and various types of adult high school classes have also operated in the area of driver reeducation and rehabilitation. Most such programs have been essentially classroom instruction. If it is determined that a lack of driving skills is a basic cause of accident involvement for problem drivers, it is possible that a program of remedial laboratory instruction could be conducted by both public and private agencies.

PROFESSIONAL DRIVERS

Professional drivers will probably continue to receive greater attention from the standpoint of preservice and continuous education than any other group for two reasons: First, there is a direct dollar relationship to the performance of professional drivers and the success of the operation of their employer. Second, they are usually under a more or less direct supervisory control and are readily available for examination, review, and necessary remedial action. Professional drivers can be broadly classified as those employed for driving responsibilities by commercial organizations and the armed services.

Commercial Drivers

The emphasis on careful selection, placement, and education of drivers in commercial operations, begun in the early 1940s, has continued and become even more intensified during the past 10 years. During this period there has been an increase in research to determine more completely the physical and emotional qualities as well as the educational needs of commercial drivers in order that they might improve their already excellent driving record. The economic implications of the safety record of commercial drivers will become more significant as competition becomes even greater within the industry. It can, therefore, be assumed that a continuous program of education and research for commercial drivers will be evident during the decade ahead.

Armed Services

It has been evident to the various branches of the armed services since the experience of World War II that it is necessary for them to provide special education for service personnel to operate successfully the mechanized equipment so essential in modern military operations. The problems of death and injury in off-duty accidents of

482

personnel who have completed expensive programs of military training have become a matter of great concern to most branches of the service during the past few years. The result has been the establishment of special driver education programs by most of the services within recent years. These programs have included traffic safety lectures, workshops, and formal programs of driver education. Many programs with well-developed courses of study for both the classroom and laboratory phases of driver education have been inaugurated. A number of military installations have obtained driver simulators and multimedia systems to be used in both introductory educational programs and remedial programs for accident-involved drivers. The recently developed program of the Coast Guard has provided, on a pilot basis, a complete program of driver education for all new personnel. The next 10 years may well see all branches of the services providing driver education classes for all new inductees.

OPPORTUNITIES FOR QUALIFIED PERSONNEL

As suggested in this chapter, it is likely that the trend toward providing a broader program of education of all drivers, regardless of age, will continue. Perhaps some type of education will become a prerequisite for licensing. Professional drivers will continue to receive organized programs of driver instruction. In addition, it is probable that greater emphasis will be placed on reeducation of all types of problem drivers. Standards of instruction in all of these programs will continue to be increased, and the requirements for certifying instructional personnel will be raised to insure the quality of instruction.

An increase in emphasis on the education of all drivers will expand the need for trained personnel to meet both instructional and supervisory demands. The driver educator of the next decade will be a dedicated, fulltime teacher who has a more thorough academic preparation for his specific responsibilities than in the past. There should be many opportunities for well-qualified driver educators in the following areas:

1. Driver and traffic safety classes in high school.
2. Adult high school driver education classes.
3. Remedial and driver improvement classes in adult high school programs.
4. Supervision of driver and traffic safety at local and state levels.
5. Consultant or part-time driver education specialists with commercial fleet operations.
6. Full-time supervisory positions in commercial fleet operations.
7. Driver education and supervision in the armed forces.
8. Research in all areas of driver and traffic safety education.
9. Employment as driver and traffic safety specialists with both public and private agencies interested in highway safety.

LEARNING ACTIVITIES

1. Describe for the class the concept "The Education of Drivers" as discussed in the text. Explain how the elements of this concept are related to the program in your state.
2. Make a projection showing the number of students in your state that will reach legal driving age for each of the next 10 years. Predict how many of them will receive a complete program of driver education.
3. Conduct a debate in class on the subject, "Resolved That Formal Instruction in Driver Education Should Be a Prerequisite for All New Driver Licenses."
4. Write a paper telling how professional organizations in driver education can shape the future in this subject field.

SELECTED RESOURCES

Aaron, James E., and Marland K. Strasser. *Driving Task Instruction—Dual-Control, Simulation and Multiple-Car.* New York: Macmillan Publishing Co., Inc., 1974.

American Driver and Traffic Safety Education Association. *Policies and Guidelines for Motorcycle Safety Education: On-Street Riders.* Washington, D.C.: The Association, 1974.

Automotive Safety Foundation. *A Resource Curriculum in Driver and Traffic Safety Education.* Washington, D.C.: The Foundation, 1970.

Gagne, Robert M. *The Conditions of Learning.* New York: Holt, Rinehart and Winston Publishers, 1970.

Kenel, Francis C. "A Driver Education Curriculum for the 70's," *Journal of Traffic Safety Education.* California Driver Education Association (January 1972), Vol. XIX, No. 2, pp. 18–20.

McKnight, A. James, and Bert B. Adams. *Driver Education Task Analysis, Volume II: Task Analysis Methods.* Washington, D.C.: Department of Transportation, PB197–688 (HumRRO Interim Report IR-D1-70-1), November 1970.

McKnight, A. James, and Alan G. Hundt. *Driver Education Task Analysis, Volume III: Instructional Objectives.* Washington, D.C.: Department of Transportation, PB202–247 (HumRRO Technical Report 71-9), March 1971.

Motorcycle Safety Foundation. *Motorcycle Rider Course.* Linthicum, Md.: The Foundation, 1976.

National Highway Traffic Safety Administration. *The Driver Education Evaluation Program (DEEP) Study.* Washington, D.C.: The Administration (July 1975.

National Safety Council, Traffic Education and Traffic Committee. *Internship Programs in Highway Safety.* Chicago: The Committee, 1976.

Rashevski, Nicolas. "Man-Machine Interaction in Automobile Driving," *Traffic Safety Research Review.* Chicago: National Safety Council (December 1965), pp. 101–107.

State of Illinois. *Driver Education for Illinois Youth.* Springfield, Ill.: Safety Education Section, Office of the Superintendent of Public Instruction, 1972.

Appendix

COURSE OUTLINE IN DRIVING SIMULATION

The teacher of simulation shall have had the minimum preparation of at least one semester hour college credit (course), or its equivalent, on the methodology of simulation teaching in driver education, approved by the Office of Education. This minimum preparation shall be designed so as to provide experiences, knowledge, and understandings of the following nature:

I. Introduction to Simulation
   A. Simulation is a growing trend in education and is similar to programed learning used in education at present.
   B. Simulation strengthens the bond between knowing and doing.
   C. Simulation recognizes values of multisensory experiences as being generally superior to singular sensory experiences.
II. Objectives.
   A. Objectives of teacher preparation in driving simulation:
      1. To introduce teachers or prospective teachers to driving simulation.
      2. To appreciate the benefits and limitations of driving simulation.
      3. To learn methods of instruction in driving simulation.
      4. To understand the proper use of simulation equipment and how to maintain it adequately.
      5. To provide experiences in driving simulation instruction.

B. Objectives of driving simulation:
1. To introduce students to driving in a nonthreatening environment.
2. To provide students with a greater variety of driving experience.
3. To provide students with experiences for recognizing driving hazards and dispensing with them appropriately in a programed sequence.
4. To provide students practice, in complete safety, in driving under special conditions, emergencies, night driving, and so on.

III. Methods of Instruction.
A. Lesson programing.
B. Film usage:
1. Orientation to learning objectives of film.
2. Presentation techniques.
3. Evaluation of learning.
C. Nonfilm drills (dry-run) with verbal cues.
D. Utilization of reference materials.
E. Use of additional teaching aids; for example, film strips.
F. Scheduling of students.
G. Variations in methods as prescribed by behind-the-wheel experiences (whether integrated with simulation or subsequent to simulation).

IV. Equipment
A. Films and film care.
B. Film projector usage and maintenance.
C. Instructor station benefits and limitations.
D. Simulators options:
1. Classroom installation.
2. Trailer installation—single and expandable arrangement.
3. Purchase plans.
4. Rental plans.
E. Additional teaching aids:
1. Film strips.
2. Slides.
3. Flashlight pointer.
4. Magnetic Boards.
5. Traffic tables.
6. Other aids.

V. Evaluation.
A. Film-cued student response score sheet or error indicator.
B. Student self-error identification.
C. Teacher-observed error identification.
D. Teacher observation of student responses—skill and attitude.
E. Paper and pencil tests of discussion; of film experiences; of film strip, slides; and other experiences.

VI. Teaching Practice
A. Programing simulator experiences of themselves and with/for behind-the-wheel experiences.

486

B. Operation and simple maintenance of equipment.
C. Experience in effecting the transfer of learning from simulator to on-the-street vehicle.
D. Primary responsibility for several simulator class sessions.

COURSE OUTLINE IN MULTIPLE-CAR DRIVING RANGE PLAN

The teacher of the multiple-car driving range shall have had the minimum preparation of at least one semester hour college credit (course), or its equivalent, on the methodology of multiple-car driving range teaching in driver education, approved by the Office of Education. This minimum preparation shall be designed so as to provide experiences, knowledge, and understandings of the following nature:

I. Objectives of a Multiple-Car Driving Range Plan
   A. Develops basic operational skills.
   B. Develops perceptual skills.
   C. Provides repetition without interference.
   D. Provides for individual differences.
   E. Provides more actual driving experience.
   F. Provides low risk to students and instructor.
   G. Builds self-confidence.
   H. Fosters individual responsibility and decision making.
   I. Provides instructor greater opportunity to observe behavior.
   J. Provides instructor greater opportunity to work with individual student problems which may or may not be directly related to driving skills.
II. Advantages and Disadvantages of the Range Plan
   A. Advantages:
      1. Low-risk driving experience.
      s. Good teacher-pupil ratio.
      3. Reduced cost.
      4. Control of learning situation.
      5. Use of area for dual purpose.
      6. Additional driving experience.
      7. Development of self-reliance.
   B. Disadvantages:
      1. Limited experience:
         a. Low rates of speed.
         b. Traffic predictability.
      2. Initial cost:
         a. Availability of land.
         b. Procurement and maintenance of autos.
      3. Setting up and dismantling.
      4. Snow removal.
      5. Exposure of instructor to weather.
III. Administrative Considerations
   A. Land acquisition.

B. Construction:
   1. Materials: gravel, concrete, asphalt.
   2. Drainage.
C. Single or dual purposes.
D. Vehicles:
   1. Purchase—loan—lease—rental.
   2. Storage, maintenance, and gasing.
   3. Movement to and from range.
E. Insurance for teachers, students, and vehicles.
F. Responsibilities and teacher load.
G. Setting up and dismantling range.
H. Accident reports.
I. Security:
   1. Vandalism.
   2. Attractive nuisance.

IV. Necessary Equipment
A. Communication systems.
B. Paint: uniform standards.
C. Signs: uniform standards—mountings of concrete, wood, socket.
D. Curbing: permanent, portable
E. Traffic cones and flags.
F. Storage facilities for equipment.
G. Emergencies: gasoline, battery jumper cables, battery charger.
H. Instructor shelter.
I. Instructor clothing.
   1. Rainwear.
   2. Winterwear.
J. Instructor transportation on range.

V. Layout and Design of driving Range
A. Physical size:
   1. Minimum of 400′ × 200′ if Range and BTW (Behind-The-Wheel instruction) program only; smaller if simulation is involved.
   2. Area laid out for efficient control.
B. Design:
   1. Parking: diagonal, perpendicular, parallel.
   2. Garage.
   3. Dead-end street.
   4. Hill (5 per cent grade if feasible).
   5. Four-way intersection.
   6. Figure eight and "X."
   7. One-way street(s).
   8. Curve.
   9. Passing straightaway—400′, if possible.
  10. 15′–25′ turn radii.
  11. Skid pan area.
  12. Off-road recovery area.
  13. Traffic mix situations.

14. Lane width: $10'-12'$.
15. Special turn lanes and prohibited turns.

VI. Safety Considerations
  A. Fenced area.
  B. Printed range rules and procedures.
  C. Established speed limits, following distances, turn regulations, and so on.
  D. Parking areas offset one lane.
  E. Student observers in car: back seat, mixed/same sex.
  F. Daily orientation.
  G. Teacher present at all times.
  H. For teacher to help students, communication system must be clear.
  I. Discipline measures.

VII. Curricular Aspects
  A. Methods:
    1. Integrate safe practices throughout program.
    2. Lesson plans:
      a. Orient students to facility and individual lessons:
        (1) Picture, slide, or transparency of range in class.
        (2) Picture, slide, or transparency of new exercise in class.
      b. Allow sufficient leeway for individual differences:
        (1) Remedial.
        (2) Acceleration.
  B. Procedure for teaching:
    1. One teacher for 4–12 cars.
    2. Demonstration of new exercise.
    3. Review of previous exercise.
    4. Group drill.
    5. Teacher at new exercise "station" to assist students.
    6. Communication depends upon succinct terminology.
    7. Student assistants.
    8. Operating under adverse conditions.
    9. Articulation with BTW instructor.
  C. Scheduling:
    1. Basic factors:
      a. Two hours of range gives one hour of BTW equivalency.
      b. Desired Range/BTW ratio.
      c. Minimum BTW in ANY program is 120 minutes.
      d. Number of teachers.
      e. Number of cars.
      f. Periods per day and teacher load.
      g. Minutes per period.
      h. Days per school year.
      i. Student availability.
  D. Evaluation:
    1. Skills.
    2. Awareness of potential conflict points.
    3. Observed behavior.

4. Paper and pencil tests.
5. Student self-evaluation.
6. Observer evaluation.
7. BTW evaluation

TYPICAL CLASSROOM AND LABORATORY SCHEDULES

SCHEDULE A

For full-time teaching load. 36 to 60 students, depending on periods available. Continue alternating groups *for semester.*

Period	1st Week M | T | W | T | F					2nd Week M | T | W | T | F					3rd Week M | T | W | T | F					4th Week M | T | W | T | F				
I	Classroom instruction 5 periods per week for one semester.																			
II	Orientation projects.					1	2	3	1	2	3	1	2	3	1	2	3	1	2	3
III						4	5	6	4	5	6	4	5	6	4	5	6	4	5	6
IV	Securing permits, etc.					7	8	9	7	8	9	7	8	9	7	8	9	7	8	9
V						10	11	12	10	11	12	10	11	12	10	11	12	10	11	12
VI	Additional periods for practice driving, as needed.																			

1st week, preliminary work for practice driving. Numbers indicate driving groups of 3 to 4 students each.

SCHEDULE B

Comprehensive Plan—Three-Week Block of Time

36 students in class
4 periods per day

Periods	M	T	W	T	F	M	T	W	T	F	M	T	W	T	F
1 2	1	2	3	1	2	3	1	2	3	1	2	3	1	2	3
3 4	c	c	c	c	c	c	c	c	c	c	c	c	c	c	c
5 6	4	5	6	4	5	6	4	5	6	4	5	6	4	5	6
7	7	8	9	7	8	9	7	8	9	7	8	9	7	8	9

90 days of classroom instruction.
30 days in car (groups of 4).
7½ hours of driving per student.

This plan illustrates a schedule for instructing 120 students per year using a 6-period day (60 students each semester). Each student receives 30 hours of classroom instruction and 6 hours driving instruction. Each semester is divided into nine 10-day blocks. Of these, 3 blocks (spaced throughout the semester) are devoted to classroom instruction and 6 blocks are devoted to practice driving. Ten students are assigned per period. For practice-driving instruction the students are divided into 3 groups, with the extra student rotating among the groups.

One Semester

Periods	10 Days 1 Time Span	10 Days 2 Time Span	10 Days 3 Time Span	10 Days 4 Time Span	10 Days 5 Time Span	10 Days 6 Time Span	10 Days 7 Time Span	10 Days 8 Time Span	10 Days 9 Time Span
1	Class 10 students	Group A B C	Group A B C	Group A B C	Class 10 students	Group A B C	Group A B C	Group A B C	Class 10 students
2	Class 10 students	Group A B C	Group A B C	Group A B C	Class 10 students	Group A B C	Group A B C	Group A B C	Class 10 students
3	Class 10 students	Group A B C	Group A B C	Group A B C	Class 10 students	Group A B C	Group A B C	Group A B C	Class 10 students
4	Class 10 students	Group A B C	Group A B C	Group A B C	Class 10 students	Group A B C	Group A B C	Group A B C	Class 10 students
5	Class 10 students	Group A B C	Group A B C	Group A B C	Class 10 students	Group A B C	Group A B C	Group A B C	Class 10 students
6	Class 10 students	Group A B C	Group A B C	Group A B C	Class 10 students	Group A B C	Group A B C	Group A B C	Class 10 students

SCHEDULE D

Using this schedule 150 students can receive 36 hours of classroom instruction and 6 hours of practice-driving instruction. The 150 students are divided into 5 sections of 30 students, each section completing the course during consecutive 36-day periods. Each section is scheduled for classroom instruction, one period per day, and practice-driving instruction for 18 days in groups of 3. This plan would require two periods per day devoted to driver education for an 18-day period.

1st Period	36 Days — Class, 1st Section — 30 Students		36 Days — Class, 2nd Section — 30 Students		36 Days — Class, 3rd Section — 30 Students		36 Days — Class, 4th Section — 30 Students		36 Days — Class, 5th Section — 30 Students	
	18 Days	18 Days	18 Days	18 Days	18 Days	18 Days	18 Days	18 Days	18 Days	18 Days
2nd Period	Group 1-A 3 students	Group 1-B 3 students	Group 1-A 3 students	Group 1-B 3 students	Group 1-A 3 students	Group 1-B 3 students	Group 1-A 3 students	Group 1-B 3 students	Group 1-A 3 students	Group 1-B 3 students
3rd Period	Group 2-A 3 students	Group 2-B 3 students	Group 2-A 3 students	Group 2-B 3 students	Group 2-A 3 students	Group 2-B 3 students	Group 2-A 3 students	Group 2-B 3 students	Group 2-A 3 students	Group 2-B 3 students
4th Period	Group 3-A 3 students	Group 3-B 3 students	Group 3-A 3 students	Group 3-B 3 students	Group 3-A 3 students	Group 3-B 3 students	Group 3-A 3 students	Group 3-B 3 students	Group 3-A 3 students	Group 3-B 3 students
5th Period	Group 4-A 3 students	Group 4-B 3 students	Group 4-A 3 students	Group 4-B 3 students	Group 4-A 3 students	Group 4-B 3 students	Group 4-A 3 students	Group 4-B 3 students	Group 4-A 3 students	Group 4-B 3 students
6th Period	Group 5-A 3 students	Group 5-B 3 students	Group 5-A 3 students	Group 5-B 3 students	Group 5-A 3 students	Group 5-B 3 students	Group 5-A 3 students	Group 5-B 3 students	Group 5-A 3 students	Group 5-B 3 students

SCHEDULE E

Each group I, II, III of 27 students is assigned, as shown in the foregoing schedule, to either the driver education classroom or the simulator and the in-car phases. These groups of 27 are divided into 9 sections of three students each and are designated A, B, C, D, E, F, G, H, and I and are rotated between the simulator and the dual-control cars according to this schedule:

	M	T	W	T	F	M	T	W	T	F	M	T	W	T	F	M	T	W	T	F	M	T	W	T	F	M	T	W	T	F	M	T	W
Simulator Classroom	A	E	I	D	H	C	G	B	F	A	E	I	D	H	C	G	B	F	A	E	I	D	H	C	G	B	F	A	E	I	D	H	C
	B	F	A	E	I	D	H	C	G	B	F	A	E	I	D	H	C	G	B	F	A	E	I	D	H	C	G	B	F	A	E	I	D
	C	G	B	F	A	E	I	D	H	C	G	B	F	A	E	I	D	H	C	G	B	F	A	E	I	D	H	C	G	B	F	A	E
	D	H	C	G	B	F	A	E	I	D	H	C	G	B	F	A	E	I	D	H	C	G	B	F	A	E	I	D	H	C	G	B	F
	E	I	D	H	C	G	B	F	A	E	I	D	H	C	G	B	F	A	E	I	D	H	C	G	B	F	A	E	I	D	H	C	G
Dual-Control Cars 1	F	A	E	I	D	H	C	G	B	F	A	E	I	D	H	C	G	B	F	A	E	I	D	H	C	G	B	F	A	E	I	D	H
2	G	B	F	A	E	I	D	H	C	G	B	F	A	E	I	D	H	C	G	B	F	A	E	I	D	H	C	G	B	F	A	E	I
3	H	C	G	B	F	A	E	I	D	H	C	G	B	F	A	E	I	D	H	C	G	B	F	A	E	I	D	H	C	G	B	F	A
4	I	D	H	C	G	B	F	A	E	I	D	H	C	G	B	F	A	E	I	D	H	C	G	B	F	A	E	I	D	H	C	G	B

SCHEDULE F

Classroom Phase

Classes per day	First Semester	
	40 days	40 days
2	32 students each period	32 students each period

Simulation Phase
(8 simulation cars in this case)

Classes per day	First Semester					
	4 days	18 days	18 days	18 days	18 days	4 days
4	0	8 students each period	8 students each period	8 students each period	8 students each period	0

In-Car Phase
(1 dual-control car—4 students per car)

Classes per day	First Semester					
	6 days	18 days	18 days	18 days	18 days	2 days
8	0	4 students each period	4 students each period	4 students each period	4 students each period	0

SCHEDULE G

The course runs for one full semester. There are 30 students per class, and they meet one hour each day for the 18 weeks.

$$18 \times 5 = 90\text{-hour course}$$

Each student spends:

> 45 hours in classroom instruction
> 18 hours in simulator
> 18 hours observation of simulator
> 3 hours in car
> <u>6</u> hours observation in the car
> 90 hours

494

There are six periods per day:

$$6 \times 30 = 180 \text{ students per semester}$$
$$\underline{2 \text{ semesters}}$$
$$360 \text{ students per year}$$

There are (1) two instructors per hour, (2) one dual-control car, and (3) one 15-unit simulator installation.

All behind-the-wheel time comes out of class hours.

SCHEDULE H
Typical Multiple-Car Driving Range Schedule

Cars	Lgth. Course	Periods of Inst.			Students Enrolled*	
		Cl.	Pd.	Total	Semester	Year
12	9	18	27	45	120	240
	6	12	18	30	180	360
10	9	18	27	45	100	200
	6	12	18	30	150	300

*Instructor handling 60 students each 6 weeks.

MOTORCYCLE RIDER COURSE

Instruction in learning how to operate a motorcycle should follow an acceptable pattern for the development of rider skills. The outline below is based on the Motorcycle Safety Foundation's research and development efforts. For information concerning the Motorcycle Rider Course materials the reader should contact the Motorcycle Safety Foundation, 6755 Elkridge Landing Road, Linthicum, Maryland 21090.

Unit 1: Introduction to Motorcycling
  What you will be doing in this course.
  Activities in this unit.
  How the course works.
  What the course covers.
  Why the course is offered.
  How your performance will be evaluated.
  How motorcycles differ from other vehicles.
  What laws every rider must know.
  Unit 1 self test.
Unit 2: Motorcycle Controls
  What you will be doing.
  Why you need to learn these things.
  Controls and devices.
  Unit 2 self test.
Unit 3: Riding the Motorcycle
  What you will be doing.
  Why you need to follow these routines.
  Using protective gear properly.

Index

498

500